GW00992492

Battle for the Castle

Battle for the Castle

The Myth of Czechoslovakia in Europe, 1914–1948

Andrea Orzoff

OXFORD
UNIVERSITY PRESS
2009

OXFORD
UNIVERSITY PRESS

Oxford University Press, Inc., publishes works that further
Oxford University's objective of excellence
in research, scholarship, and education.

Oxford New York
Auckland Cape Town Dar es Salaam Hong Kong Karachi
Kuala Lumpur Madrid Melbourne Mexico City Nairobi
New Delhi Shanghai Taipei Toronto

With offices in
Argentina Austria Brazil Chile Czech Republic France Greece
Guatemala Hungary Italy Japan Poland Portugal Singapore
South Korea Switzerland Thailand Turkey Ukraine Vietnam

Published by Oxford University Press, Inc.
198 Madison Avenue, New York, New York 10016
www.oup.com

Library of Congress Cataloging-in-Publication Data

Orzoff, Andrea.
Battle for the castle : the myth of Czechoslovakia in Europe, 1914–1948 / Andrea Orzoff.
p. cm.
Includes bibliographical references and index.
ISBN 978-0-19-536781-2
1. Propaganda—Czechoslovakia. 2. Political culture—Czechoslovakia. 3. Czechoslovakia—Relations.
4. Masaryk, T. G. (Tomáš Garrigue), 1850–1937. 5. Beneš, Edvard, 1884–1948. I. Title.
JN2222.Z13P856 2009
943.703'2–dc22 2008038396

Parts of the work appeared in slightly different form in the following articles:

Andrea Orzoff, "Prague P.E.N. and Cultural Nationalism, 1924–1938,"
Nationalities Papers 29/2 (2001): 243–265.
By permission of Taylor & Francis. http://www.informaworld.com.

Andrea Orzoff, "'The Literary Organ of Politics': Tomáš Masaryk and Political Journalism,
1925–1929," *Slavic Review* 63, no. 2 (Summer 2004): 275–300.
By permission of the American Association for the Advancement of Slavic Studies.

Andrea Orzoff, "The Empire without Qualities: Austro-Hungarian Newspapers
and the Outbreak of War in 1914," in *A Call to Arms: Propaganda, Public Opinion,
and Newspapers in the Great War*, ed. Troy R. E. Paddock © 2004 by Troy R. E. Paddock.
Reproduced with permission of Greenwood Publishing Group, Inc., Westport, CT.

Andrea Orzoff, "The Husbandman: Tomáš Masaryk's Leader Cult in Interwar
Czechoslovakia," *Austria History Yearbook* 39 (2008).
By permission of *Austria History Yearbook* and the Center for Austrian Studies.

1 3 5 7 9 8 6 4 2
Printed in the United States of America
on acid-free paper

Para Iñigo, Samuel, y Mateo, de mi corazón.
Gracias a la vida, que me ha dado tanto . . .

History is mere history. Myths are what matter: they determine the type of history a country is bound to create and repeat.

—Jorge Luis Borges

A myth is at the same time imperfectible and unquestionable; time or knowledge will not make it better or worse.

—Roland Barthes

. . . the French fuss so much about the nation because it is a living problem, became one when they set the nation up as an ideal, remained one because they found they could not realize the ideal. . . . When one gets down to facts, things become awkward.

—Eugen Weber

Acknowledgments

This book has been a long time in coming, and I am glad to be able to thank all who helped it along the way. Many institutions and organizations have graciously supported my writing and research: my thanks to the American Council of Learned Societies, the Deutscher Akademischer Austauschdienst, the International Research and Exchanges Board, the National Endowment for the Humanities, New Mexico State University, and Stanford University. Passages in this book were adapted from articles appearing in the *Austrian History Yearbook, Nationalities Papers,* the *Slavic Review,* and in Troy Paddock, ed., *A Call to Arms: Propaganda, Public Opinion, and Newspapers in the Great War.* I thank these journals, the University of Minnesota's Center for Austrian Studies, Taylor and Francis, and Praeger Press for permission to use this material. I also thank the two anonymous readers for Oxford for their thoughtful comments, and my remarkable editor, Susan Ferber, who patiently guided the manuscript and its author. I presented parts of this book at Columbia University's Harriman Institute, Rutgers University's Center for European Studies, the Yale University History Department's Slavic and East European Reading Group, and at several yearly conventions of the American

Association for the Advancement of Slavic Studies. I am grateful to audience members for excellent questions.

My personal thanks begin with mentors and teachers. Peter Hayes and Barbara Newman of Northwestern University modeled for me the best of academic life: rigorous inquiry joined to perspective and humor. At Stanford and beyond, Norman Naimark has been a *Doktorvater* in the truest sense, providing challenging questions, unstinting encouragement, and sane counsel. I also learned much from Stanford historians Keith Baker, Nancy Shields Kollmann, Carolyn Lougee, Paul Robinson, and James J. Sheehan. Nancy Meriwether Wingfield's generous support, critique, and wry wit have been invaluable. I hope Dena Goodman of the University of Michigan and Brett Gary of New York University will see the influence of their own scholarship in these pages; I am also grateful for their cameraderie and advice. In Prague, Dagmara Hájková, the late Jan Havránek, Robert Kváček, the late Vladimír Macura, Jiří Opelík, Ivan Šedivý, and Zbyněk Zeman are and were unfailingly kind. Vladimír's untimely death was a great loss to the international scholarly community. I hope he would have liked this book; certainly his criticisms would have sharpened it.

I relied on helpful archivists and librarians in Prague and the United States, including Eva Javorská of the Archiv Kancelář Prezidenta Republiky; Dagmara Hájková and Jan Bílek of the Masaryk Institute; Vlasta Měšťanková of the former Státní Ústřední Archiv; Molly Molloy of the Stanford University Libraries; June Ferris at the University of Chicago; Angela Cannon in the Slavic Research Center at the University of Illinois; and archivists at the National Archives in College Park, Maryland, and the Harry Ransom Center in Austin, Texas, who helped ensure that my brief visits were productive. The indefatigable Information Delivery Services staff of the New Mexico State University library made writing this book in Las Cruces far easier than anticipated, as did Lawrence Creider.

Other scholars and friends delivered me from error and made the writing of this book more enjoyable. Warm thanks to the Stanford *zadruga* and to East and Central Europeanists across the country and the Atlantic: Brad Abrams, Hugh Agnew, Chad Bryant, Peter Bugge (who was kind enough to read several chapters in draft form), Holly Case, Katya and Michael David-Fox, Melissa Feinberg, Stuart Finkel, Ben Frommer, Paul Hanebrink, Milan Hauner, Owen Johnson, Pieter Judson, T. Mills Kelly, Laurie Koloski, Igor Lukes, Caitlin Murdock, Patrick Patterson, Lynn Patyk, Marci Shore, James Ward, and Martina Winkler. My topnotch colleagues in New Mexico State's History Department have read chapters and provided encouragement, as have Elizabeth Schirmer, Mark Cioc, Margaret Jacobs, and John Nieto-Phillips. Andrew Michta, at the 1997 Woodrow Wilson International

Center's Junior Scholars Seminar for East-Central Europe, asked me the question that sparked this book. Participants in Jindřich Toman's Czech Workshop at the University of Michigan encouraged me when my faith in this project had ebbed. Benno Ennker of the University of Tübingen and Heidi Hein-Kircher of Marburg's Herder-Institut offered timely insight and intellectual provocation.

My two wonderful adopted Czech families—Zuzana Vanišová and Martin and Ondřej Vaniš in Prague, and Bohuš, Zdena, David, and Marketa Havel/lová in Brno and Belgium—have haunted *antikvariaty* on my behalf, helped with exotic declensions, taken me skiing in the Jeseníky and vineyard-hopping in southern Moravia, played me the music of the Bohemian Renaissance, and taught me to make *ovocné knedliky.* Prague (and Dobřichovice, and Vienna) would not be the same without Andreas Beckmann and Lena Knilli, Kathleen Hayes, Anna "Naninka" Vaničková, and Jonathan Terra, as well as paní Slávka Peroutková.

The love of my family and friends forms the bedrock on which my intellectual life rests. I cannot really express sufficient thanks—here or anywhere—to my mother and father, Melinda and Kenneth Orzoff; my sisters, Michelle Lazar and Eileen Orzoff, and their families; and the rest of my extended family in Chicago, Portland, and Lima. I am also grateful to the many dear friends who have patiently asked after this book for years: there are more than I have room to mention here, but especially Wendy Shapiro, Rohanna Doylida, Melissa Rosenblum, Robin Shwetzer, Colin Denby Swanson, Susannah Skyer Gupta, Jamie Bronstein, Stu Finkel, Lynn Patyk, and our beloved Las Cruces "playgroup," who have become our New Mexico family. Wynne Broms occupies a special place.

Last but never least, I thank my husband Iñigo García-Bryce. His support and critique strengthened this book; his robustly absurd sense of humor and generous spirit enlivened my life outside it. He is a daily blessing to me, as are my sons Samuel and Mateo. They have all lovingly waited out my need to spend so much time with this book, which is dedicated to them.

Contents

Battle for the Castle

INTRODUCTION

The Golden Republic

The truth will prevail.

—Jan Hus, fifteenth-century Bohemian religious reformer

It was my belief that the truth would prevail, but I did not expect it to prevail unaided.

—Edvard Beneš, Czechoslovak foreign minister and president

Vinohradská třída is a long, busy thoroughfare connecting Prague's leafy eastern suburbs to its bustling historical center. The street rings with tram bells and car horns; Czechs, not tourists, fill the sidewalks. Grime coats fanciful fin de siècle wedding-cake apartment buildings and stern socialist realist hulks. Near the corner of Budečská ulice, quite close to Prague's first Western-style luxury shopping mall, sits a four-story office building. At street level, its façade is unremarkable concrete. From across the street, though, the passerby can see an elegant mansard roof, the sweeping lines of interwar Prague modernist style, and between the second and third floors, in large letters, the word ORBIS. The passerby might assume the reference to the globe has something to do with the building's current tenant, an agency promoting travel to the Czech Republic.

In fact, Orbis existed in another world and another time. Between the First and Second World Wars, the building on Vinohradská was home to the publishing house of the First Czechoslovak Republic's Ministry of Foreign Affairs, dominated by President Tomáš Garrigue Masaryk and longtime foreign minister (later President) Edvard Beneš. Those who founded Orbis, staffed its offices and newspapers, wrote its books, and consulted with its leaders understood their everyday task to be nothing less than the survival of their state. Their work was intended to persuade the world—especially the West—of the moral and strategic necessity of Czechoslovakia's continued existence, and to heighten Western commitment to the young republic. To support this idea, the writers and editors of Orbis borrowed liberally from the society around them: events, personalities, relationships, statistics, places. And myths. In large part, Orbis was a propaganda agency, producing and selling myth to defend the Czechoslovak state.

Although recent historical writing on interwar Czechoslovakia has taught us much about political practice in that highly idealized democracy, we still know relatively little about the centrality of myth creation, leader cults, public relations, propaganda, and the mass media to First Republic political culture. The relationship between Czechoslovak democracy and mythmaking was profound, not just because rhetoric about democracy constituted a crucial element of Czechoslovak political mythology. Czechoslovak political myth, and the propaganda that disseminated that myth, had wide-ranging international implications. Many observers, Czech and otherwise, understood Czechoslovakia to be the linchpin of the Versailles order: if Czechoslovakia fell, so too would fall Europe's increasingly rickety postwar peace. Thus even the most picayune domestic squabbles in this small country could potentially echo across the entire continent, and the success or failure of its propaganda efforts might have much wider repercussions.

Czechoslovak propaganda drew on a long history of European persuasion, ranging from the election appeals on the walls of Pompeii to the Catholic Church's seventeenth-century Sacred Congregation de Propaganda Fide, intended to combat the Reformation. French revolutionary propaganda after 1792 spread the inflammatory ideas of Diderot and Voltaire throughout the continent; when the revolution's foes demonized its ideology as well as its armies, propaganda began to acquire its scurrilous reputation.[1] During the nineteenth century, propaganda and cultural relations were one of many venues in which Europe's states vied for supremacy. Napoleon pioneered the leader cult, founding his own newspapers to celebrate military campaigns and commissioning medals, coins, and paintings presenting the emperor in noble Roman dress.[2] The long-standing French preoccupation with French literacy and loyalty in its colonies abroad led to the creation of the Alliance française, while Wilhelmine Germany built schools and ran cultural programs for Germans outside the Reich.[3]

The First World War is often credited with the creation of modern propaganda. Belligerents on both sides intensified their use of word and image—including, for the first time, film—to persuade the home front to hold on, the military to fight on, neutral states to join in, and enemy civilians and soldiers to give up.[4] At the war's outset, the British cable ship *Telconia* cut direct subterranean cables linking Germany and the United States. Meanwhile, the Foreign Office created a secret war propaganda office. Once the carefully crafted news items came over the British-controlled wires, editors at American papers chose what they thought would most interest their readers, unaware of any censorship. The British also tried to convince prominent Americans to advocate entering the war. Unofficial British sources echoed similar ideas: theater, radio, cinema, museum exhibitions, schoolbooks, and children's literature, among other venues, espoused themes comparable to those emerging from Wellington House.[5] (German propaganda in the United States emerged from private German-American friendship societies or "bunds": the suspicious consistency of sources and message, followed by the German invasion of neutral Belgium, rendered the German message less plausible.)[6]

From within the multinational Austro-Hungarian, Russian, and Ottoman empires, East-Central European peoples waged their own propaganda battles, often at cross-purposes.[7] Great Power propaganda was directed at armies and populations; East-Central European propaganda and cultural diplomacy focused wholly on West European and American elites, and to a lesser extent on ethnic "colonies" abroad, such as American Czechs and Slovaks. Czechs, Serbs, Romanians, Greeks, Poles, and Croats and Slovenes calling themselves Yugoslavs, among others, traveled widely in the United States, rallying the support of émigré groups, promising them and their ethnic kin prominent roles in the states they hoped to create at war's end.[8] Representatives of the Austrian nationalities crowded the hallways of diplomatic offices in Washington, Paris, and London; gradually developed friendships with influential government figures and journalists; and hosted elegant dinners, where they regaled Great Power literati and political leaders with stories of glorious national pasts and dedication to the ideals of the democratic West. The great Polish pianist Paderewski's 1916 concert and speech at the White House moved President Wilson profoundly, even, according to Paderewski's supporters, influencing Wilson's inclusion of Poland in the Fourteen Points.[9]

They also participated in symbolic assemblies hoping to persuade the West that they would be good citizens of the postwar international community. They had help from unexpected sources, such as George Creel's Committee of Public Information, the American counterpart to Wellington House, which organized a meeting of the Oppressed Nationalities of Central Europe in September 1918 at Carnegie Hall. The event's motto was "The Will of the People of Austria-Hungary." University professor Masaryk, self-appointed spokesman for an independent Czechoslovakia, and Paderewski, speaking on the Poles' behalf, made fulsome declarations of their mutual admiration; they read a resolution thanking the United States and its allies for their support and reaffirming the importance of creating "a united and independent democratic Poland" as well as freeing the Habsburg subject peoples from the burdensome yoke of Austria-Hungary. These speeches were greeted with enthusiastic applause. Creel helped Masaryk to bring the group's resolution to President Wilson, who responded with support for Austria's dissolution. The "oppressed peoples" then decided to form an organization, the Mid-European Democratic Union, which embarked on its own propaganda crusade during the final weeks of the war.[10]

At the Paris peace talks, this kind of unofficial diplomacy or personal propaganda was widespread. Charles Seymour, Yale University history professor and consultant with the American delegation, wrote to his wife during the winter of 1918–1919, "I am beginning my work as social laborer again . . . dinner with [Romanian leader Ion] Bratianu tomorrow, lunch with Italian liberals on Saturday, dinner with the Serbs in the evening, and dinner with Czechoslovaks—Kramarz [sic] and Beneš—on Monday." During this same period, the Polish delegation hosted a luncheon for the Americans that lasted until dusk; the Americans were treated to a long line of experts extolling Poland's virtues and defending the territorial claims it had presented to the conference. Queen Marie of Romania was among the most notorious East European personalities at the conference, who came to Paris to aid Romania's cause (and, most likely, to shop). She was certain her flirtatious importuning of the conference leaders would strengthen Romania's position: "I had pleaded, explained . . . I had given my country a living face."[11]

The attendees of the Paris peace talks left firmly convinced of the significance of propaganda, for good or ill. Certainly Czechoslovak and Polish political control of their states on the ground during the last months of 1918 and much of 1919 helped establish the case for independent statehood and to set state boundaries; certainly Piłsudski's Polish Legions, the Czechoslovak Legions, and their respective victories over the Bolsheviks in eastern Poland and Siberia helped the Great Powers realize the potential strength of these new would-be allies. But the Great Powers' decisions to support East-Central European independence had already been made by then.[12] Historian Zbyněk Zeman's comment about the Czechs can stand for other East-Central European peoples as well:

> Instead of manning barricades and settling their accounts with the authorities on the home ground, . . . they gradually penetrated the editorial offices of newspapers, the chanceries of the Allied foreign ministries, and the higher reaches of the Allied leadership. . . . It was an enterprise in which publicity and propaganda, as well as personal contacts and the persuasiveness of the revolutionaries, initially played

> a more important role than the actual military clout of the Czechoslovak leaders on the Allied side. H.A.L. Fisher, the historian and politician, remarked that "... Czechoslovakia is the child of propaganda."[13]

After the cataclysmic upheaval of the Great War, which ended three empires, brought Bolshevism to power in Russia, and threatened Bolshevik-style revolutions across much of the rest of the continent, Europe's concern with propaganda endured into the interwar period. Propaganda constituted part of Europe's attempt to create a new interwar order. Propaganda's integral relationship to nationalism allowed cultural elites to transcribe symbolic or moral values into political discourse; propaganda was a means of recontextualizing shared experience, reestablishing the boundaries of the national community, and renovating public concepts of good, evil, redemption, and sacrifice in the face of seeming threat. The French, for example, continued their outreach to Francophones abroad in the face of perceived German competition. A French foreign ministry official explained this approach in nationalistic terms: only French culture could be "this treasure of new ideas, of liberal aspirations, and of refined traditions ... [foreign elites are] desirous also of acquiring that elegance of expression and that flower of humanism which our literature, our art and our science represent."[14] Weimar Germany, in turn, in 1920 created a Directorate for Germanism Abroad, aimed at maintaining the national sentiment of thousands of ethnic Germans living outside the newly reduced German borders.[15] Foreign minister Gustav Stresemann, in 1925, asked the Reichstag for more money for the *Auslandsdeutschen*, claiming that they were "engaged in a battle for the preservation of their nationality."[16] The Soviet Union poured energy into propaganda, mobilizing agitprop at home to win over a reluctant population, while also enthusiastically creating various Friends of the Soviet Union societies (in some twenty countries by 1927) and carefully fostering cultural and intellectual contact between Soviet and foreign intellectuals, among other attempts at cultural diplomacy and propaganda.[17]

Ironically, the British—the Great War's propaganda experts—were so embarrassed by postwar revelations of their wartime information control and exaggeration that their cultural diplomacy arm, the British Council, was not established until 1934.[18] Postwar British and American cultural elites railed against propaganda, finding it omnipresent and uniquely dangerous to good governance. The Great War had brought about a sea change in propagandistic techniques, and in the cooptation of the mass media and cultural industries by state governments. Strict control of information and censorship, doctored photographs and carefully crafted films, and the involvement of mass-circulation newspapers all seemed to represent a qualitative change from previous attempts to win hearts and minds. Lord Ponsonby's inquiry into wartime atrocity propaganda, which found little or no evidence to verify any of the horrific stories emerging from the war, reinforced the increasing dread in the popular mind about the putative power of propaganda: "The injection of the poison of hatred into men's minds by means of falsehood is a greater evil in wartime than the actual loss of life. The defilement of the human soul is worse than the destruction of the human body." Similarly, the U.S. Senate initiated hearings to investigate the American entry into the First World War, publicizing the British wartime propaganda campaign—to general shock—and concluding that the United States had been inveigled into the war effort.[19]

In contrast, the vulnerable states of postimperial East-Central Europe viewed propaganda as a necessary, fundamental tool of statesmanship, and a crucial conduit to the Great Powers. Their foreign ministries devoted entire divisions to propaganda. Each state—and often leaders of national minorities within states—used cultural diplomacy and recruited prominent allies abroad to espouse its virtues. By the mid-1920s, each Habsburg successor state paid journalists or newspapers in London, Paris, and Geneva to write positive articles or promote desired policies. Friendly authors and academics were subsidized; admiring works of history were kept in print; concerts of music by national composers were given; sophisticated dinners and social occasions were carefully arranged, both in Great Power and East-Central European capitals. The propagandistic stakes were high; the very existence of these states seemed predicated on it. Although the Great Power leaders had brought the postwar states into being, many inhabitants of Great Britain and France only dimly understood where these states were and who inhabited them, much less why it was worthwhile to support them. It would thus be important for all East-Central European peoples to try to educate the West about themselves, to make an impression on electorates as well as leadership, and if possible to exert wide-ranging cultural influence. At the same time, they would need to teach themselves about the West, about Europe more generally, and about participation in the democratic process.

The Czechs—specifically, the leaders of their wartime émigré nationalist movement and postwar state, Tomáš Garrigue Masaryk and Edvard Beneš—can stand as exemplars. Even before the First World War ended, Masaryk and Beneš had decided that international and domestic propaganda would have to be intense complementary efforts for the postwar Czechoslovak state. The world, particularly the Great Powers, had to be taught about this new parliamentary democracy at Europe's heart. At home, the need for a form of enlightened political instruction seemed just as pressing. Neither Masaryk nor Beneš trusted the abilities of most "Czechoslovaks" to adjust to the new post-Versailles Europe, nor did they trust Czech political parties or parliamentary leaders to teach them. Thus Masaryk and Beneš created what historians and contemporaries dubbed the *Hrad* (Castle), named after Prague Castle, where Masaryk resided when in Prague. An informal but extremely powerful nexus of institutions and allies, the Castle would help Masaryk and Beneš affect the political process from outside the halls of Parliament. Its members included a coterie of literary intellectuals, who led the country's propaganda effort along with Masaryk and Beneš, and who also viewed propaganda as a beneficial, elite-driven, civic education. These intellectuals, along with Masaryk and Beneš, helped craft the national myth later to become enshrined in—or confused with—the history of the First Republic.

East-Central European interwar campaigns of cultural diplomacy rested on a discourse of Europe and Europeanness. Each state cited its adherence to European cultural norms as proof of its moral worthiness, and thus its defense by the Great Powers. Of course, each state defined Europeanness differently, according to its unique mix of historical circumstance and preferred practices. The "Czechoslovaks" had succeeded in persuading the American and French leadership, and some British diplomats, of their European qualities—their rationalism, tolerance, efficiency, and adherence to democratic norms—by the time the Paris peace talks began in 1919:

> Everyone in Paris knew how Beneš and Masaryk had devoted their lives to freeing their people from the Austrian Empire. . . . Almost everyone in Paris liked and admired the Czechs and their leaders. The Poles were dashing and brave, but quite unreasonable; the Rumanians charming and clever, but sadly devious; the Yugoslavs, well, rather Balkan. The Czechs were refreshingly Western. . . . Beneš and Masaryk were unfailingly cooperative, reasonable and persuasive as they stressed the Czechs' deep-seated democratic traditions and their aversion to militarism, oligarchy, high finance, indeed all that the old Germany and Austria-Hungary had stood for.[20]

But conservative and revanchist states could also mine the discourse of Europe. The Hungarians, for example, insisted that the new Czechoslovakia was as awkward a political conglomeration as its neologism of a name, and tried to remind West European audiences of Hungarian worthiness, based on centuries of acting as Europe's Christian bastion against the invading infidel Turks.[21] They and other revisionist states argued that Wilson and the Paris peacemakers had dismembered the ancient Habsburg monarchy, unseating one of Europe's oldest dynasties, and created instead weak, artificial, Balkanized states, which by implication did not deserve Western support.[22]

One of the most important weapons in the interwar European propaganda war was the adoption of West European habits of sociability. It became clear to the East-Central Europeans relatively early on that luxurious hospitality (with a tacit political agenda) was more than a nicety of etiquette. This kind of sociability played an urgent part in interwar East-Central European cultural diplomacy, particularly in winning over conservative sectors of Great Power opinion. East-Central European elites participated wholeheartedly in international organizations based on sociability, such as the International P.E.N. Club, a literary association affiliated with the League of Nations. East-Central European P.E.N. chapters were generally sponsored, and their expenses paid, by their country's Ministry of Foreign Affairs, which also tended to view P.E.N. involvement as a means of garnering prestige for their state. These states also built their own Western-style elegant gentlemen's clubs for the purpose of winning over visiting foreigners.

But the foreigners—particularly the British—were difficult to woo. Their resistance came from long habit: Western attitudes toward the Slavs placed them at best between East and West, decidedly not *of* the West. Internal European prejudices, described by one historian as "nesting orientalisms," dismissed the eastern part of the continent as barbaric, as opposed to the West's putative "cleanliness, order, self-control, strength of character, sense of law, justice, efficient administration" and presumed ethnic and linguistic homogeneity.[23] Popular British culture continued to traffic in stereotypes after the Great War, as in Agatha Christie's 1925 *The Secret of Chimneys*, which presented an imaginary Balkan state, Herzoslovakia. Its inhabitants were a "most uncivilized people. A race of brigands. . . . [National h]obby, assassinating kings and having revolutions."[24] Christie located her "uncivilized," unstable state in the Balkans, but its name linked this "race of brigands" unmistakably to Czechoslovakia. The First Republic's putative Westernness was undone by this connection to Hercegovina, tinderbox of the First World War, putative source of assassins and terrorists.

This kind of cultural imagery had a political counterpart. The powers at the Paris Peace Conference, most importantly the British, already distrusted many of the East-Central Europeans—including the Czechs—in 1919, and their suspicion grew over the interwar years.[25] Meanwhile, after the U.S. Senate refused to ratify the Versailles treaty with Germany in 1919, American isolationists repeatedly reminded the public of European deviousness, especially via propaganda, and the danger of involvement in European affairs.[26] Thus the task of Czechoslovak—and Yugoslav and Polish—propagandists was Sisyphean. The Czechs did not neglect defenses beyond propagandistic appeals. Beneš worked hard to create and maintain the Little Entente, a mutual defense pact among Czechoslovakia, Yugoslavia, and Romania, with talk of also involving the Poles.[27] By the late 1930s, the Czechoslovak border with Austria and Germany was highly fortified, and the country's military was generally considered one of the strongest in the region. Still, the Castle leaders were under no misconceptions about their ability to withstand a concerted German attack alone. The West had brought them into being: surely it would want to keep alive the states it had created. Propaganda's chances of success were uncertain at best, yet the idea of abandoning the West, Czechoslovakia's patron and defender, was unthinkable. Masaryk and Beneš were not persuaded by the increasingly negative connotations attributed to propaganda; it was too crucial a tool of statecraft to abandon.

The Czechoslovak National Myth

At the heart of Czechoslovakia's propaganda effort lay the "Czechoslovak" modern national myth, crafted by many, but disseminated above all by Masaryk, Beneš, and the Castle. It is, in fact, a Czech myth, as many observers then and now have noted.[28] The story goes like this: under Habsburg rule, the innately democratic, peace-loving, tolerant Czechs were viciously repressed by bellicose, authoritarian, reactionary Austrians, under whose regime the Czech language and national consciousness almost died out. Czech identity was rescued by a heroic, devoted group of intellectuals, dubbed the Awakeners, who brought the dormant nation back to life by recrafting literary Czech, retelling Czech history, and making political claims on behalf of a "Czech nation." Jan Hus, the one-eyed Hussite general Jan Žižka, the Union of the Czech Brethren, the Battle of White Mountain: these fifteenth- and sixteenth-century historical figures and events were emotionally resonant signs within a coherent narrative of moral rectitude, victimization by aggressive Germans (or the Catholic Church, embodied in the Habsburgs), and persistent attachment to presumed Czech national values, particularly that lodestar, the Czech language.

After 1918, the myth continued, Czechoslovakia made itself an island of democratic values, rationalism, and fair mindedness amid a Europe falling quickly into the thrall of authoritarianism and fascism. The Czechs, now the leading nationality within the multiethnic Czechoslovak state, continued to be depicted as a tolerant, prosperous, cosmopolitan people at the heart of Europe, embodying Europe's proudest ideals, the quintessential liberal inhabitants of an ideal civic sphere. They were also innately centrist, moderate, pragmatic realists—a "myth of mythlessness," of being too rational a people to need such fables.[29] The mythic Czechoslovakia extended effortless tolerance to its many nationalities and religions: Czechs, Slovaks, Germans, Hungarians, Ruthenes (Ukrainians), Poles, Jews, Catholics, Protestants, and Uniates were unproblematically absorbed into the new state and transformed into "Czechoslovaks." (Although this book does not entirely reproduce that supposition, it does reflect the preponderance of Czechs among those who created the Castle myth, and the relative absence of other Czechoslovak state peoples within the myth.) The myth of the Czechoslovak state accompanied a presidential leader cult for Tomáš Masaryk, a dignified septuagenarian with a neat white mustache and an international reputation. Masaryk's personal myth cast him as a benevolent, disinterested father of the people, a moral example and philosopher-king, far from the hurly-burly of political deal making. A similar, far less successful myth was crafted for Foreign Minister (later President) Edvard Beneš, highlighting his diplomatic talent and the esteem in which he was held in Western capitals.

The Castle leaders did not construct and dictate a unitary narrative, used faithfully by all Castle supporters. Rather, the process was haphazard and creative. Different mythic elements appealed to, and were emphasized by, different groups of Castle allies. Non-Castle figures adopted the myth's terms for their own purposes. Beyond this internal multivalence, the Castle myth has always had external critics, from the interwar era to the present day. Historians and journalists have pointed out Masaryk's flaws as well as his virtues. They have also noted the state's weaknesses and the characteristics it shared with the rest of interwar Europe, including an aging, static political elite, an ambivalence toward democratic legal structure and practice, and a political culture as prone to corruption and secrecy as that of any other European state. In their many attempts to deny the Castle legitimacy, right-wing politicians (most prominently Karel Kramář and Jiří Stříbrný) contested Masaryk's and Beneš's claim to have been the most important figures in founding Czechoslovakia, and their continued leadership of the state. The twin challenges of Communism and right-wing authoritarianism threatened democracy in Czechoslovakia as elsewhere; Czechoslovakia's multiethnic character translated in fact to Czech predominance over Slovaks, Germans, Ruthenians, and Hungarians. There were strong elements of continuity between the democratic First Republic (1918–1938) and the authoritarian Second Republic (1938–1939) as well as the Czech collaboration with Nazi occupiers.[30] However, the myth's influence remains strong. If, as anthropologist Benedict Anderson has written, the nation requires a "narrative of 'identity,'" the identity of the modern-day Czech Republic and its predecessor are above all constituted by references to this noble, democratic mythic narrative.[31]

The myth's lasting influence and tremendous emotive, if not explanatory, power came from its final element: the intermingling of the myth with European realpolitik. After 1938, the myth shifted to depict Czechs (now less frequently "Czechoslovaks") as victims—of geography, the perfidy of the West, and internal fifth columns. The first betrayal, at Munich in 1938, was by Czechoslovakia's Western allies and creators France and Great Britain, who essentially handed the country to the Nazis. In this portrayal, the First Republic's Slovaks, Hungarians, and Germans—the last group understood, mythically, as aliens since time immemorial—celebrated its demise. The second betrayal followed in 1948 at the hands of the Soviet Union, now portrayed as another barbarian aggressor, and a handful of ruthless, Stalinized Czechoslovak Communists and fellow travelers.[32] Czechoslovakia then disappeared behind the Iron Curtain, forgotten by the West, save when Czechoslovak attempts to reform Communism failed in 1968 and Soviet-bloc tanks rolled into Prague.

For some observers, the myth seemed close enough to fact to be mistaken for it. Émigré author Milan Kundera adapted it for Cold War readers in his much-reprinted essay "The Tragedy of Central Europe," which argued that the world had forgotten the essential Europeanness of those countries trapped behind the Iron Curtain. Kundera's particular twist made the Czechs part of a nostalgic, Catholic, romanticized Central Europe rather than the Soviet Eastern Europe.[33] This reading anachronistically and simply identified the interwar era with Westernness. Kundera ignored the First Republic's anti-German (whether Habsburg, Reich, or Sudeten) tendencies, as well as Castle concern about a Habsburg restoration. Meanwhile, Western-language academic historiography and political analysis, much of it written by Czech émigrés or their students, reiterated and elaborated themes from this set of myths. The myth was recast for a scholarly context as Czechoslovak exceptionalism, which taught that the Czechs were more urbane and worldly, and less prone to religious superstition, than the rest of Eastern Europe; they embraced Western models, economically, culturally, and politically; and, perhaps as important, they were the victims of capricious fortune, granted on the one hand wise leaders such as Masaryk and Beneš, and on the other the West's shameful neglect.

After the Velvet Revolution and the fall of the Soviet Empire, the myth was reinvigorated by a new philosopher-president. Václav Havel attempted to secure the West's support for Czechoslovakia in part by reminding the world of the Czechs' democratic heritage and twinning his image with Masaryk's. When the Czechs entered NATO, U.S. Secretary of State Madeleine Albright—herself of Czech heritage, the daughter of a historian who had worked with Beneš—invoked the myth, saying of Masaryk, "He inspired an entire generation of Czechoslovaks by his life, his beliefs and his works. There was a time people thought he should be president of the world, as it was known in the '30s. He was the philosopher president."[34] And before the United States attacked Iraq in 2003, Defense Secretary Donald Rumsfeld described the energetic, democratic, courageous, freedom-loving "New Europe"—the new NATO members of East-Central Europe, including the Czechs—as opposed to the jaded, blind Old Europe—France and Germany, resolutely opposed to the war. This language and symbolic division of Europe directly recalls the First World War, echoing that of Slavophile historian Robert Seton-Watson, though Rumsfeld's use invoked a different set of allies and enemies.[35]

This book attempts to historicize the myth, the circumstances of its creation and elaboration, and its many uses at home and abroad. Masaryk and Beneš drew on earlier strains of romantic and triumphalist historiography to craft this mythic narrative, initially for Great War exile propaganda. They and their Castle colleagues then adapted and wielded the myth for propagandistic use within the competitive context of interwar European international relations, where propaganda was one among many means of drawing closer to the European Great Power states. At home, Masaryk and Beneš employed tactics similar to those they used abroad—relying on their relationships with the mass media and cultural elites—to further their political goals. At home, too, they used the mythic narrative to claim moral high ground and legitimate their own power. Both domestically and internationally, the mythic narrative provided the content, propaganda the means of dissemination.

Coming to Terms

Classical Athenian philosophers and rhetoricians differentiated between *mythos* and *logos*, discursive strategies for presenting the fabulous, poetic, or absurd as opposed to the factual and reasonable.[36] I hope to avoid too much entanglement in that long-standing dichotomy. My use of the term "myth" to describe the Czechoslovak national narrative is not intended to be pejorative, although at points in this book I do note the work of the myth in obscuring certain political actions or tendencies.. Rather, the term "myth" helps highlight the essentialist, fabulistic narrative underscoring political and academic discourse on the "natively democratic" Czechs and Czechoslovakia since 1918, and orients discussion of the narrative's genealogy and later adaptations.

All states emplot and employ myths as a means of imbuing the national past and future with order and intelligibility. Some of the most powerful European national myths emerged during the nineteenth century, such as the French claim to represent Europe itself, to be the bearers of *civilisation* and Enlightenment, and the Polish self-presentation as the "Christ of Nations," emphasizing the *antemurale* myth so common in Central and Eastern Europe, where "martyred nations" claim to have bled for Europe.[37] Myths can provide a sense of origins, permanent values, authority, and moral wisdom. Their truth or falsehood is relatively insignificant.[38] I use "myth" and "mythology" to denote a worldview based on identifiably ideological narratives or images claiming to be universally valid, yet only accepted as true by certain audiences at certain times. The mythic story, the teller, the audience, and the circumstances of the telling can vary considerably: although the main mythic narrative usually remains recognizable, its elements can be rearranged. However it is presented, effective myth is both historical and predictive: it interprets the group's glorious past, using it as a guide or an essential pattern for the future. Leader cults, frequently associated with political myths, are similarly complex.[39]

Many important interpreters of myth, such as Georges Sorel and Ernst Cassirer, have emphasized its irrational or mystical nature, relating this quality to its ability to motivate its believers, but believers are often able to analyze elements of myths quite rationally, accepting some while rejecting others.[40] This book emphasizes myth as a relatively orderly system of symbols, possessing its own internal logic, transformed into narrative.[41] My focus is on the use of myth, its political and cultural function in legitimating power, the "moral universe of meaning" it invokes, its definition of peoplehood, and its evolution and (surprisingly long) life.[42]

The term propaganda, like myth, is frequently used as a disparaging epithet. Yet to understand it that way in this case would be singularly anachronistic. In the eyes of the Castle leaders and many observers, propaganda had materially contributed to Austria's downfall and had brought about the Czech national "revolution."[43] Rather than seeing propaganda as a danger to independent civic thought, Masaryk and Beneš viewed it as a useful form of civic education and an essential tool of statecraft. They boasted of their wartime propaganda skill in their memoirs, carefully planned the new state's propaganda organizations, and kept them under their personal control, trusting only their closest intimates. Masaryk and Beneš understood propaganda to be a crucial means of communicating with the masses and besting their political foes; cultural diplomacy was a parallel effort to reach elites abroad.

The propaganda efforts analyzed in *Battle for the Castle* illustrate some larger questions in European history and the history of nationalism. The struggles over myth discussed here provide a detailed depiction of the gradual, complex, and conflictive process of nation building and mythmaking. Interwar Czechoslovakia makes clear both the importance and the limitation of state power in shaping and influencing nationalist discourses. Outside the Castle, other leaders and groups drew on, recombined, and reinvented local nationalist traditions. The Agrarian Party's slogan "Venkov jedna rodina" (the countryside is one family), as well as the Czech Fascists' "Nic než národ" (nothing [other] than the nation), were voiced by authoritative political leaders and articulated by intellectuals and writers who lent legitimacy to their ideas. It is important to note the simultaneous invention of multiple traditions, and to look at the processes by which some myths are enshrined while others, at least temporarily, disappear.

Czechoslovakia and the other post-Habsburg states of East-Central Europe shared the central dilemma presented in this book: their interwar nation building was dual, simultaneously domestic and international. East-Central European governments had to knit together new polities, often fractious and multiethnic, while also effectively presenting abroad the image of a unified, successful nation. Most of them, like Czechoslovakia, failed in this task. The complaints of minority nationalities did not escape the West's attention but, more important, as Hitler's power grew, Great Power elite opinion increasingly retreated to the kind of cynical realism represented by appeasement. The West's overwhelming concern was the maintenance of empire abroad and the avoidance of war. *Battle for the Castle* illustrates both the domestic and international sides of the Czechoslovak attempt to craft a unified nation.

East-Central European nation-building efforts abroad rested on futile, competitive discourses of Europe. But such arguments have rarely worked: East-Central Europe, including Czechoslovakia, has long been defined as other than the West.[44] This book makes clear that after 1918, the successor states of the nineteenth-century empires continued to constitute an Eastern Europe. The term connoted a complex admixture of attitudes toward the Great Power states: a combination of dependence on them, defensiveness toward them, fear of absorption by them, and attempts to portray their own states as similar to them. Interwar Western Europe became both the guarantor of security and the arbiter of cultural and political progressiveness for the rest of the continent. East-Central European interwar propaganda and Great Power reception demonstrate that an Eastern Europe of *mentalités* existed decades before a physical Iron Curtain.[45] But this book joins a "new diplomatic history" in focusing on the contributions of the mass media, public opinion, and individual citizen initiative to international affairs.[46]

My decision to focus on the Castle, the mass media, and popular culture, rather than on votes and arguments on the floor of Parliament, stems from the consensus among political historians of the First Republic that Parliament's significance was relatively limited. Many scholars have argued that the heart of political conflicts in interwar Czechoslovakia lay in the battles between the Castle and the Pětka (the Five), the unofficial coalition of the most important Czech political party leaders.[47] The Pětka's control of parliamentary issues, aimed at ensuring passage of important legislation and protecting each party's control over particular ministries or resources, meant that real wrangling among parties or nationalities until the late 1930s was rare, suppressed, or ignored. In other words, any study of First Republic politics focused on party and parliamentary affairs misses much of the picture.

Instead, this study highlights the centrality of the press and propaganda—indeed, the world of middlebrow literary culture more generally—to interwar Czech and European politics. The leaders of the Pětka and the Castle argued vociferously in the pages of their partisan journals, as well as in their correspondence and via personal intermediaries. Journalists, authors, intellectuals, and editors had direct political impact. They helped craft cults of personality; they helped to iterate and adapt national myths. This book takes for granted a close relationship between Czech intellectuals, Czech political leaders (themselves intellectuals), and the symbols and discursive elements of Czech nationalism. It posits that of all groups in interwar Czechoslovakia, the Castle's intellectuals became the most intimately affiliated with the "propagation of the national idea," as Max Weber put it.[48]

Any study of intellectuals must deal with definitions. Like cultural anthropologist Katherine Verdery and sociologist Zygmunt Bauman, I understand intellectuals functionally: they are professionals dealing with ideas, who establish their role in society and their relationship to power mainly through conflict, expressed in written form. They gain recognition by framing the discourses society uses to understand itself and the cultural values underscoring the national community. But there are always competing discourses and values. In Czechoslovakia, the nation served as what Verdery calls a master symbol, a locus of ideological contention that lent added significance to public conflict when wielded by intellectuals and political leaders.[49]

Finally, all historians of Czechoslovakia have to contend with questions of national nomenclature. The Castle understood its task as defending and trying to promote an attachment to Czechoslovakia, denoting a Czech-led state merely tolerant of the state's other ethnic groups. Hence this book's conscious usage of the term "nation" to refer to the Czech nationality within the Czechoslovak nation-state. The term "state" refers either to Czechoslovakia as a political entity or to its government and administration. A last, related point: I use "Czech" to describe speakers of the Czech language and adherents of or themes within the Czech nationalist movement. "Czechoslovak" refers to the First Czechoslovak Republic's government, to the state more generally, and to the myth Masaryk and Beneš crafted. Less frequently, I use "Czechoslovak" to refer to citizens of the state; in that sense the term refers more to rhetoric than to reality, as one of this book's observations is that the state, its leaders, and its myth failed to create a truly "Czechoslovak" civic identity.

Battles and the Castle

The chapters of this book treat different aspects of the modern Czechoslovak myth's creation and use. Chapter 1 describes the highly nationalized Czech political and intellectual culture of the late nineteenth century, in which Masaryk, and to a lesser extent Beneš, came of age, and which constituted an important element in the modern Czechoslovak myth. "Nationally aware" Czechs celebrated the Czech language and cultural heritage, contrasting them with the supposedly Habsburg and German vices of aggression, repression, and dogmatism. They were inspired by the romantic nationalism of historian František Palacký, whose multivolume *History of the Czech Nation in Bohemia and Moravia* reinterpreted the Czech medieval past as a charged interaction between Slavs and Germans, a matrix for modern Czech nationalism. Palacký's themes were later simplified and popularized by other nationalist historians and authors, who translated them into Czech national consciousness. Masaryk claimed to reject Palacký's ideas even while relying on them, trying to link the fifteenth-century Hussites to early twentieth-century progressive liberalism, ethnic tolerance, and an ecumenical Christian spirituality. His attempt to practice a morally influential "unpolitical" politics within the Austrian imperial parliament, or Reichsrat, was inspired by those ideas as well.

Masaryk's and Beneš's work abroad during the First World War, also described in chapter 1, presented their version of the Czech past, present, and future to a Great Power audience, via propaganda, cultural diplomacy, and the British, French, and American mass media. Their wartime experiences, and their steady faith in the truth of Czech (now equated with Czechoslovak) nationalism, led the two men to develop a vision of postwar politics that remained remarkably consistent through the interwar era: admiration for Western values, reliance on the Great Powers of Western Europe, and intent to shape the First Czechoslovak Republic in their image. Achieving these goals would require substantial remaking of Czech political life, which Masaryk and Beneš viewed as provincial, uninformed, and prone to wrong-headed political notions that might alienate the state from its Great Power guarantors. Their vision became the Castle's agenda, at home and abroad.

Chapter 2 details the Castle's means of gathering and disseminating information, raising funds, and exerting influence, involving many government institutions as well as personal friendships. One of the most important elements of the Castle apparatus was the propaganda section of Beneš's foreign ministry, which was actively involved with European intellectual and literary culture. Through propaganda, the Castle funded journalists, writers, and academics; it published and distributed their books, translating them into all the major languages, via Orbis, the Foreign Ministry's semiprivate publishing house, or Čin, the publishing house owned by a Czechoslovak Legionnaire organization loyal to the Castle. The Castle paid the expenses of the Czech chapter of the International P.E.N. Club, which Beneš and the writer-members viewed and used as a propagandistic forum. The Third Section sponsored trips abroad for authors, artists, and musicians, and built the *Společenský klub* (Social Club), a luxurious gentleman's club in the heart of downtown Prague, for entertaining visiting foreigners and socializing with Castle allies and intelligentsia.

Throughout the interwar period, the Castle faced many political challenges. At home, as chapter 3 explains, the Castle fought to dominate national politics and to frame Czech nationalism; parliamentary leaders and factions fought back. Of its enemies, the Castle viewed the radical Right as the most dangerous. As opposed to the Castle's Western-leaning cosmopolitanism, the Right espoused Czech chauvinism, combined with aggressive anti-German sentiment and glorification of the Czechoslovak Legionnaires (Czechoslovak World War I veterans) and the mythic Slavic forebears of the Czech nation. In letters, in meetings, and in highly public legal causes célèbres, the Castle and the Right vied not just for political but also for mythic advantage. One of the most important arenas for mythical combat was the press. Masaryk and Beneš involved themselves deeply in the affairs of the mass media, founding and abandoning various newspapers and journals, and developing relationships with prominent journalists to propagate their ideas. The Castle also worked to encourage the development of Masaryk's personality cult; it published pamphlets of his writings, books of photographs showing Masaryk sitting ramrod-straight on horseback or cuddling his grandchildren, and worshipful biographies in almost every European language. The Castle's work at home was devoted to winning support from influential figures and sectors of the electorate, and limiting the power of groups and people the Castle deemed harmful.

Chapter 4 presents Czechoslovakia's problematic international position, which became more precarious as the 1930s wore on. German and Hungarian propagandists had made inroads into the sympathies of the British elite, who had long found the Treaty of Versailles distasteful and who mistrusted Edvard Beneš. The growing distance between the British and French governments weakened the Czechoslovak position vis-à-vis the Nazi threat. The Castle relied on its diplomatic corps but also remained highly involved with the foreign press, fighting to persuade the Great Power media—and through them, Great Power electorates and leaders—of Czechoslovakia's strategic and moral importance. The myth abroad relied on Masaryk, using him to represent the Czechoslovak state. In contrast to the domestic variant, which involved delegitimizing political figures the Castle saw as dangerous, the myth abroad claimed the country's backing of the Castle and its values as a fait accompli, portraying Czechoslovakia as an idyllic, tolerant, multiethnic state, a Switzerland of the East. But other successor states—and discontented Czechoslovak nationalities—wove their own mythic propaganda narratives, in which Czechoslovakia was weak, hypocritical, and repressive. The Castle's "struggle for world sympathy" did not take place in a vacuum.[50] Both within and outside interwar Czechoslovakia, the Castle's version of modern Czech nationalism was challenged by competing myth-narratives.

Chapter 5 explains the Castle myth's tragedies and victories. During the Republic's last three rocky years, the Castle's Europeanized adaptation of Czech nationalism was given greater credence by several books written by Castle intellectuals, including *Conversations with Masaryk* by Karel Čapek and Ferdinand Peroutka's multivolume history of the Republic's early years, *Building the State*. Both were written with the Castle's strong support and echo, whether strongly or subtly, the Castle mythic narrative. But it was the Nazis who made these texts presciently elegiac, elevating would-be myth to apparent fact. By December 1938, Čapek was dead, Beneš was in exile in London, and the Nazis had annexed the Sudetenland and would soon occupy Prague. Beneš's second wartime exile reiterated the themes his interwar propaganda campaign had developed: that Czechs were natural democrats and pacifists, that Czechoslovakia had been more devoted to European ideals than Europe itself, and that it now needed Europe's aid and a second liberation. But, significantly modifying the interwar myth, Beneš balanced these themes with the political necessity of coming to terms with the Soviet Union. Czech and Slovak intellectuals, between 1945 and 1948, criticized Masaryk's republic and the Castle myth even while retaining elements of them both—most powerfully, maintaining public reverence for Masaryk and adapting his interwar leader cult to the post-1945 era. Every political faction, including the Communists, claimed Masaryk as its own.

After the 1948 Communist takeover, the idea of a democratic Czechoslovakia was relegated to the realm of the mythic. By then many Czechoslovaks had already turned away from the Castle myth and its creators. The postwar Czechoslovak Communists were the largest party in Czech history, and drew a substantial plurality of votes in the 1946 elections. But for opponents of the regime and émigrés, many of them former Castle staffers, the power of an idealized Czechoslovak democracy only gained strength in response to the horror of the Communist coup. The epilogue notes the continuing dominance of the Castle myth in the English-language academic writings of émigrés, expatriates, and allies, defending and mourning the Castle's golden republic. The Castle's final mythographic triumph came about nostalgically, through the literary work of exile and underground historians, journalists, politicians, and the Westerners they taught or influenced.

All successful myths incorporate elements of generally recognized truth, and the Castle myth is no exception.[51] The interwar Czechoslovak Republic was, by the 1930s, the lone Habsburg successor state to retain democratic norms and practices. Its minority nationalities, religious believers, and political groupings enjoyed greater tolerance than they would have elsewhere in the region. Czechoslovakia was, as the myth claimed, closer economically to the wealthy West than many of its neighbors, thanks to the Austrian Empire's nineteenth-century industrialization of the Bohemian lands and to the stringent deflationary policies of the Czechoslovak leadership after 1918. Masaryk and Beneš were devoted to democracy, as they understood that term, and rejected violent revolutionary change. They also believed in the principles of collective security and peaceful coexistence, which constituted the underpinnings of the postwar peace and Czechoslovakia's existence.

But the mythologized national narrative obscures important facts about interwar Czechoslovakia. Masaryk and Beneš harbored real doubts about parliamentary democracy even as they fought to defend it. At times they even contemplated leading executive coups d'etat to control an unruly Parliament, or denying the vote to troublesome groups within the electorate, such as soldiers or women. Some of their behind-the-scenes meddling in the affairs of the press or individual politicians' careers was questionable in a democratic context. Moreover, other groups within Czech politics, especially the Pětka and its successors, rebuked or ignored the wishes of the voters and refused to cede power to the next generation. Czechoslovak rule has been described as a gerontocracy, in which most of the leading politicians came of age under Austria and kept tight control over their parliamentarians.[52] In short, Czechoslovakia had more in common with its neighbors than the myth implies, such as Pitsudski's Poland, Horthyite Hungary, and even late Weimar Germany's "authoritarian democracy," increasingly dependent on an authoritarian chancellor to maneuver around a hamstrung and divided Parliament. Study of the real Czechoslovak democracy can teach us far more about the functioning of interwar democracies and European politics than can the idealized golden republic, the romance of the mythic notwithstanding.

The myth (and closed archives during the Communist era) also obscured, for a long time, the actual political engagement of Tomáš Garrigue Masaryk, whose complex vision and equally ambiguous politics lay at the core of First Republic political culture. Rather than the figurehead president suggested by the myth and its texts, archival documents and newer historiography portray Masaryk as an active, canny politician. He was more than willing to use connections, the bully pulpit of the presidency, his substantial charisma, and his personal finances to back his allies and block his opponents. He never went so far as to establish martial law or ban oppositional political parties, even those he considered dangerous. Nevertheless, Masaryk was no philosopher-king. He never quite relinquished the particularist, hierarchical political framework he had learned under imperial Austria. A political pugilist, he sometimes lacked the grace and wisdom to know when to abandon the fight.

Masaryk is often quoted as saying he hoped for fifty years of peace, so that the Czechoslovak Republic could firmly establish itself. In the end, the Republic only got twenty, which have been termed "decades of crisis."[53] That despairing epithet is borne out by a competitive, tense atmosphere, both domestically and internationally. The intellectuals discussed here did battle on behalf of the Castle, its ideas, and its leaders, defending not just their political agenda but their larger vision for Czechoslovakia and for Europe. This book tells this story but also conveys the interrelated story of a much wider conflict, which in the end swept up the young Czechoslovak state. To paraphrase former British Foreign Secretary Anthony Eden, while good policy can be ruined by bad propaganda, good propaganda cannot correct for bad policy; the propagandists of Orbis proved helpless against European realpolitik.[54]

The Castle lost its battle. But, just as clearly, it won the mythic war. Its symbols and narrative, rooted in and extending those of the nineteenth century, restructured Czech national self-understanding. The myth's shifts and reinterpretations set out what it meant to be Czechoslovak, and briefly established an illusion of community, at least for (some) Czechs and Slovaks, if not for Czechoslovakia's other inhabitants. Castle mythic politics set the terms, during and after the interwar years, for discussing the legitimate use of power. The Castle's propaganda apparatus, and its connections to prominent writers and academics, helped spread the myth throughout Czechoslovakia and Europe, and then to the United States, where it lingered in political and academic discourse for generations, shaping American understanding of the Czechs, East-Central Europe, and Europe more generally. Setting out the historical evolution of this powerful mythology that has underpinned Czech nationalism during the twentieth century and beyond can help us continue to better understand, and to move beyond, the myth.

1

Myth and Wartime

In autumn 1915, the young academic and journalist Edvard Beneš fled Prague on a forged passport. He was trying to evade the Austrian authorities, who knew he had been one of a group of Czechs plotting against the empire from the moment the Great War broke out in autumn 1914. Beneš made it to Switzerland and from there to Paris. Along with his mentor, the academic sociologist and public gadfly Tomáš Garrigue Masaryk, and the dashing Slovak astronomer and pilot Milan Rastislav Štefánik, Beneš spent the rest of the war agitating for the establishment of an independent Czechoslovakia. Their work succeeded beyond their wildest imagining. On November 4, 1918, in a car flying the Czechoslovak state colors, Beneš was driven to the Paris peace talks as foreign minister of the new Czechoslovak state.[1]

This story—of a few inconsequential professors successfully petitioning the Great Powers, amassing an army, and persuading the world's leaders to guarantee the existence of a new state—is also the story of the creation of that state's myth, and its propagation via propaganda. Masaryk, Beneš, and Štefánik devoted an enormous amount of energy and resources to propaganda and cultural diplomacy, within and outside governmental circles. They established the equivalent of a propaganda ministry and press agency in several Great Power capitals. They also dedicated considerable time to cultivating contacts in political circles, academe, and the highest levels of society, not to mention Czech and Slovak colonies abroad.

The story they told, on the pages of journal articles, in private salons, in lecture halls, emphasized what became a familiar set of themes. The Czechs, so the story went, were as Western in their values and in their political inclinations as the Westerners themselves: they were Enlightenment rationalists yearning to be free of Austrian repression. They ought to be joined with their fellow Slavs, the Slovaks, to lead an East European state that was dedicated to tolerance, egalitarianism, and human rights, and was capable of joining with the West. Not coincidentally, this same state, with Western support, might help withstand German aggression and contain Bolshevik social radicalism. The myth did not linger too long on the Germans in Bohemia and Moravia, or Hungarians in Slovakia. Nor did it pause to consider too deeply how Czechoslovakia might actually defend itself against a rearmed Germany or what it might mean for the West to have binding international commitments in Central and Eastern Europe.

Although Masaryk and Beneš were working in a novel scenario, their ideas displayed marked continuity with the past, drawing heavily on romantic nineteenth-century interpretations of Czech history. Since 1820, the political imaginary developed in Bohemia and Moravia had involved radical, even utopian attempts to reconfigure Austrian political culture to suit Czech nationalist goals and hopes.[2] This chapter aims to contextualize Masaryk, Beneš, and Czech nationalism against the backdrop of the nineteenth century. Czech nationalist ideological traditions and the Czech political infrastructure, including political parties and their partisan press, were established during this period. This era's events and leaders also provided the vocabulary for modern Czech nationalist discourse. Masaryk and Beneš selected some parts of the nineteenth-century tradition and minimized others in creating and representing abroad what became the "Czechoslovak" nation. Moreover, they and other politicians continued to shift and reinvent the terms of Czech and Czechoslovak mythology, during and after the war, using nineteenth-century nationalist themes.

The chapter's second goal is to explain how Masaryk's and Beneš's work abroad during the war shifted the terms, and some of the content, of Czech nationalism for the rest of the century. Before 1914, Masaryk and Beneš were academics, Masaryk famed mainly as a public intellectual and the leader of a tiny party in the Reichsrat (Austria's imperial parliament); Beneš, a sociologist and freelance journalist, was almost completely unknown. They were of minuscule political importance compared with the leaders of the well-established Czech party system, who declined to follow them into exile. Not until 1917 were they certain that domestic political leaders supported their work abroad. Their vision of a Western-leaning Czechoslovak republic competed with firmly rooted notions of a re-created Czech kingdom, most likely with a Romanov on the throne, situated within a Russian-led greater Slavic empire.

The war shifted the terms of this conversation. Certain nationalist themes or emphases suddenly became more plausible, others less significant or even, briefly, ridiculous. For example, the Bolshevik Revolution put paid to the fantasy of a European Slavic federation ruled by Romanovs. Also, wartime activity would legitimate, or discredit, postwar leadership. In Czechoslovakia as elsewhere in Europe, the ideas and experiences of the First World War influenced political and cultural elites and their actions for the next twenty years. In particular, the outcome of the war granted credence to Masaryk and Beneš's unconventional interpretation of Czech nationalism—to their modernization of the Czech nationalist myth. Their triumphant wartime experience became an important card to play within the political shuffling and dealing of the First Czechoslovak Republic. But it did not constitute an automatic trumping of other Czech politicians, either philosophically or in terms of direct power. The claims that Czech national values meant automatic adherence to the ideals and politics of the Western Great Powers, or that Masaryk and Beneš deserved credit as the founders of the new state, aroused considerable dissent in 1918 and afterward.

Bookish Radicals

Unlike Beneš, Tomáš Masaryk already possessed authority and a considerable reputation by 1914. But almost no one would have predicted that his influence would ever transcend the printed page. As a professor at Prague's Charles University, his students—many of whom would later take leading positions in Czech letters, art, and, to a lesser extent, in politics—found his persona and ideas mesmerizing. Masaryk's reinvention of the Czech national past, as well as his vaguely progressive, morality-laden discussion of democracy, would both become central to Czech political culture in the twentieth century.[3]

Masaryk was born in 1850 near Hodonín on the Moravian-Slovak border. His father, once a serf, served as a coachman, bailiff, and farmer on a large estate. His mother was a former cook who had served in grand households; it was she who inspired young Tomáš to pursue his studies. The family moved often from estate to estate in southeastern Moravia, and Tomáš's education—his route out of the static social hierarchy of the empire's provinces—was often interrupted for lack of money.[4] Like most Czechs and Slovaks of that time, Masaryk experienced his life through different languages: he spoke Slovak with his father, German and "Moravian" with his mother, and was educated in German.[5]

Masaryk was strikingly confident and determined from an early age. He studied philosophy in Vienna, where he then taught until moving to the Czech university in Prague in 1882.[6] Masaryk's command of English led to his being one of relatively few Austrian academics to emphasize the British philosophical tradition, particularly David Hume's Enlightenment skepticism. He also became politically active, addressing the working classes, feminists, and young intellectuals in his articles and public lectures.

Masaryk came of age in the complex aftermath of the failed liberal revolution of 1848. Bohemia and Moravia's relatively late and intense process of economic and political modernization, beginning in the 1860s, saw a massive influx of formerly agrarian Czech speakers into urban areas seeking industrial work. By 1913, Bohemia and Moravia contained fully one-half of Austria-Hungary's industry. As Czech-speaking peasants became city dwellers, previously German-speaking municipalities became Czech—first demographically, and soon culturally, or "nationally." Even in the countryside, Bohemians and Moravians found themselves and their lives transformed by late-nineteenth-century nationalist modernization. Their everyday experiences increasingly took place in Czech: schooling, newspapers and books, banks, bureaucracy, and local and imperial politics. In the 1860s, relatively few Bohemian high schools taught Czech; by 1890, twice as many taught in Czech as in German. And the Czech language was increasingly conflated with Czech national identity and desire for political autonomy. Naming streets and creating public monuments meant nationalist conflict.[7]

The most important interpreter of Czech national identity during this period—and the dominant figure of nineteenth-century Czech cultural life—was historian and politician František Palacký. His work influenced all Czech intellectuals of the era, including Masaryk; his subject, the medieval Czech past, became one of the most powerful sources of Czech nationalist symbolism. Born in Moravia and German-speaking for most of his life, Palacký was educated in Pressburg (now Bratislava, Slovakia's capital) and moved to Prague in 1823.[8] He drew on documents in ten languages, gathered from seventy different European archives, to write a five-volume history of the Czech nation in Bohemia and Moravia during the Middle Ages. This monumental achievement earned him the title Father of the Nation.[9] The gratitude of the putatively unified Czech nation is easy to understand, given Palacký's depiction of the Czechs. In his writings, they were "unusually progressive, enlightened, devoted to productive and useful work: not aggressive but heroic ... greatly responsible for the progress of humanity, but suffering cruelly through the disfavor of fate."[10] One historian has summarized Palacký's portrait of the Czechs as "Slavic liberalism."[11]

Palacký argued that the thirteenth-century immigration by Germans into Bohemia destroyed the "Slavic democracy" that had originally taken root there, and brought with it West European feudalism, leading to serfdom. His heroes were the proto-Reformation preacher and activist Jan Hus and his followers, known as the Hussites. Hus rejected corruption within the Catholic Church, such as the sale of indulgences; he insisted on each individual's equality in the eyes of God and advocated that both clergy and laity be granted communion "in two kinds" (both wine and wafer). He was mainly supported by Czech speakers; Bohemian Germans tended to support the Vatican and its ally, the Holy Roman Emperor. The Hussites were in essence trying to modernize Europe and were sacrificed for it, Palacký stated.[12] Hus was burned at the stake at the Council of Constance in 1415, but Czech resistance to the Vatican continued until the seventeenth century, when—according to Palacký—Czech Protestantism was defeated at the Battle of Bilá hora (White Mountain) in 1620, the first engagement of the Thirty Years' War, and Bohemia and Moravia were subsumed into the Habsburg Empire.

In Palacký's recounting, the Hussites fought not just for religious freedom but to defend Czech national identity against the Germans, whose origins were a "nation of predators (*Räubervölker*)."[13] The Czech Hussites were freedom-loving, democratic, tolerant, egalitarian, morally righteous, and pacifistic until unjustly attacked. These were the qualities permanently bred into the Czechs by their national history, Palacký implied.[14] The medieval Catholic Church and its Central European representative, the emperor of the repressive Holy Roman Empire, who lured Hus to an unfair trial and a martyr's death, denied the Czechs rightful independence and glory.[15] Palacký's remembered Czech kingdom was the center of a vast Central European empire; his Prague was the shining imperial capital of Charles IV.[16] Surely this greatness was waiting to be recaptured.

Later Czech patriots simplified Palacký's writings, juxtaposing Czechs, representive of all that was virtuous and civilized, against Germans, characterized by barbarism and brute force. Elements of this binary moral opposition can be found in Palacký's work, but on the whole he rejected this interpretation, often stating that the Czechs would not be as developed without their involvement in a German-speaking, westward-leaning empire. Palacký's Czechs are a bridge between Germandom and Slavdom, between East and West.[17] But these nuances escaped many patriotic readers, who interpreted the rest of Czech history in a nationalist light. The forces who lost at Bilá hora were mainly German-speaking officers, commanding a mercenary army, yet the "emotive martyrology" of romantic Czech nationalist historiography portrayed these forces as both heroic and Czech. The Bohemians who fled after Bilá hora, in fact at least half German speakers, were rewritten as Czechs; their flight became the reason why the Czechs lacked a native aristocracy. The succeeding two centuries of Habsburg rule were described as the *doba temna*, or Age of Darkness.[18]

Nationalist intellectuals translated the glorious Czech past from Palacký's five volumes of dense scholarship into Czech popular consciousness. Perhaps the most important venue was the body of historical novels by Alois Jirásek, "the Czech Walter Scott," serialized in newspapers and magazines between 1887 and 1914. Accessible to all classes, these novels focused on the Hussite past and the lives of the early Awakeners, the nineteenth-century literary patriots who reclaimed Czech.[19] Likewise, various nationally minded Czechs claimed to have discovered thirteenth-century Czech manuscripts of poems, legends, and prophecies, including the *Piseň pod Vyšehradem* (*Song beneath Vyšehrad*, "found" in 1816), the *Rukopis královédvorský* (*Queen's Court* manuscript, 1817), the *Rukopis zelenohorský* (*Green Mountain* manuscript, 1818), and the *Libušino proroctví* (*Libuše's Prophecy*, 1849).[20] The main idea conveyed in each was "that the Czechs were running their own state while the Germans were still rootling about for acorns," and that the Germans were the Czechs' ancient enemy.[21] Czech literary elites received the manuscripts enthusiastically; they remained significant for popular understanding of Czech national history throughout the century. Even Palacký defended them.[22]

Masaryk first stepped onto the public stage to rebut these false nationalist manuscripts. Amid a storm of catcalls and accusations of treason to the nation, Masaryk lent his journal *Athenaeum* to editorialists who debunked the texts.[23] Then, in 1899, Masaryk defended a Jewish vagrant, Leopold Hilsner, against a charge of blood libel. In both these unpopular causes célèbres, Masaryk sought to separate the Czech national cause from fabrications and "medieval" bigotry—in effect, to save the nation from itself.[24] Meanwhile, in 1891, he was elected to the Reichsrat for the Young Czech Party, along with the two other politicized intellectuals with whom he had founded the Realist group and the journal *Čas* (*Time*): academic economist Josef Kaizl and lawyer Karel Kramář, who would lead the Young Czechs after 1900.[25] Substantial disagreements with the party, Kramář, and Kaizl led Masaryk to resign his mandate in 1893. He returned to the Reichsrat in 1907 as the sole representative of a tiny, intellectual-dominated party, the Progressives (Realists). In forming the Progressives, Masaryk intended to be a "leaven and ferment, like the British Fabians"—a constructive but consistent critic. His Czech parliamentary colleagues frequently referred to him as an enfant terrible, influential but "isolated from the mainstream of Czech politics."[26]

Between his Reichsrat stints, from 1893 to 1898, Masaryk published influential books, often containing academic lectures or journalistic polemics from his journal *Naše doba* (*Our Age*).[27] These works ranged from reactions to contemporary issues and contemplation of the meaning of Czech history to analyses of Karl Marx and nineteenth-century journalist and Czech Awakener Karel Havlíček Borovský. But throughout his writings, Masaryk returned to the two central intellectual and political problems of his day. First, he analyzed the limitations of Central European liberalism, and forecast the future of democratic praxis in Bohemia and Moravia. Second, Masaryk pondered the historical meaning and rightful future of the Czech nation, recasting Palacký's ideas and those of other Czech Awakeners within a specifically European vision.

European liberalism had once insisted on the individual's inviolate and universal natural rights, protecting that individual against a tyrannical state. Liberalism had widened the ranks of potential political actors, in some cases allowing all educated property owners to cast a vote or serve in office. Austrian liberalism exploded into belated political prominence in the revolutions of spring 1848; although the revolutions were defeated, liberalism made its impact felt. In the 1860s, liberals began reshaping Austrian social and political institutions. They imposed a constitution on a reluctant emperor in 1867 and developed a system of secular public education. But Austrian liberalism, like the Austro-German nationalist movements it influenced, paired emancipatory promise with a rigid hierarchy. Some individuals were understood to be active and independent, while others were deemed passive and dependent, incapable of rational political engagement. While liberalism's agenda continued to dominate Habsburg politics, the liberals themselves were removed from power by 1879. Both the Old and Young Czechs, initially left-liberal parties, echoed German liberals by moving to the center, and even to the right. By 1890 the Young Czechs represented social and economic conservatism.[28] Austrian German liberalism was similarly marked by its practice, particularly in Bohemia and Moravia, of defending German privilege and authoritarianism against Czech nationalist calls for increased democracy and self-rule.[29]

Masaryk clearly understood that Austrian liberalism's internal contradictions led to a denial of Czech sovereignty. He associated with the Austrian German liberal leader Ernst von Plener the idea "that the freedom of individuals, and the autonomy and equality of national groups, had to be sacrificed in favor of the modern centralized state, and safeguarded by those in already privileged positions, namely Austrian Germans." All the same, Masaryk's work and life bear traces both of European liberal ideals and Austrian liberal practice. Liberal tenets, such as the importance of critical reason in the public sphere and the "natural" or universal rights pertaining to every human being, underscored Masaryk's intellectual work. Yet he claimed to reject liberalism utterly, and his late-nineteenth-century writings caricatured it. Masaryk accused liberalism of promoting hyperrational individualism, exploitation, and competition at the expense of cooperation and collectives, particularly the nation. (In contrast, Masaryk praised the Czech nation as an ideal collective, both politically and ethically; for example, he claimed that out of a sense of shared commitment to the national project, wealthy Czechs would naturally help the poor.)[30] He retained a resistance to formal liberalism throughout his life. Even in 1925, Masaryk's personal secretary recalled him saying, "Liberalism and the bourgeoisie have failed everywhere. In England, Lloyd George. Here, Kramář."[31]

Realism, the movement Masaryk sponsored along with Kramář and Kaizl, stemmed from his dissatisfaction with the current Austro-German political and intellectual context, including liberalism. Influenced by Comte and Hume, Masaryk took a positivist view of politics. He believed that political conflicts arose from inadequate knowledge; scientific inquiry would necessarily grant the world greater insight into people's circumstances, and improved information would lead naturally to greater social justice. Thus politics, correctly practiced, was a practical extension of sociology, which (as Masaryk understood it) hoped to unify all academic disciplines into a single logical system. Czech intellectual and scholarly life had to improve, the better to enlighten Czech leaders and thinkers, so that Czech politics could find an appropriate path for the Czech nation. Czech Realism was vaguely reformist, lacking a well-articulated political and social program, unlike its contemporary, Polish Realism, which called concretely for improved civic education—in part via the press, "the only national institution"—as one means of helping the Polish nation deepen its intellectual and spiritual development to survive under foreign imperial repression.[32]

The most central idea in Masaryk's political glossary was democracy, about which he wrote and spoke all his life. Yet he used the term imprecisely, referring to an idealized state and society, rather to legal or formal characteristics such as universal suffrage and free elections. Masarykian democracy is less a political structure than a worldview, almost religious in scope.[33] In fact, at the end of his life, Masaryk noted that "my goal was religious and moral: politics was just an instrument."[34] For example, Masaryk viewed Hussitism—that matrix of eternal Czech values—as primarily religious, and only secondarily national: "*If religion is religion*, i.e., a singular and independent spiritual and cultural power, then it is not possible to derive it from another power, neither from *nationality*, nor from *economics*, *nor from anything at all other than religion.*"[35] Masaryk believed that democracy's rule of law and egalitarian ethos allowed human beings to progress to a state in which they were more moral, more fully human, and would approach their brethren with tolerance, empathy, reasonableness, and self-restraint. (Similarly, he reduced the essence of Marxism to a variant on the biblical commandment to love one's neighbor; he condemned its doctrine of class warfare for setting man against man.)[36] Masaryk's vision of democracy did not exclude hierarchies or differences among people, but neither of these facts justified exploitation.[37] Governance, and the citizens governed, had to be fair-minded and humane: democracy would make them both so.

An example of his complex, inexact thought on democracy can be found in one of his most frequently quoted sayings, the sweeping comment in his 1925 wartime memoir *Světová revoluce* (*World Revolution*): "Jesus, not Caesar: that is the meaning of our history and democracy."[38] Masaryk explained that democracy evolved from theocracy, since state absolutism had replaced religious absolutism, and democracy emerged in reaction to state absolutism. In that sense, Masaryk wrote, democracy represented the culmination of the separation of church and state, and appropriately so. Modern democrats, Masaryk concluded, would take as their task "realizing Jesus' religion and ethics, his pure and unblemished religion of humanity (*lidskosti*)"—but without interference from the state. Modern religion ought to inform democratic civic life, rather than being an instrument of political domination wielded by the state.[39] Masaryk's ideal Czech democracy was also normatively tolerant:

> In Austria there was no freedom of conscience; in our democratic republic true freedom of conscience, tolerance, and a recognition of the good and the better must be not just codified but also practiced . . . in all areas of public life. It is a national necessity, a demand made by our historical development: Palacký's philosophy of our history, which valued the Czech Brethren as its highest point; pure Christianity, that is, Jesus' teachings and his commandment of love, is the will [and testament] of the father of our nation as well as of our history—democracy is a political form of humanness (*lidskosti*). Out of Habsburg theocracy we will develop tolerance in democracy.[40]

An equally problematic Masarykian term was *humanita*, usually translated as humanity or humanism. In his 1894 treatise *The Czech Question*, Masaryk joined other nineteenth-century Czech nationalist writers in linking the Czech present to heroic fifteenth-century Bohemia, and arguing that Czechs were most fully "human" when they were nationally aware.

Humanita provided the foundation of national identity: each nation constituted a representative form of its members' *humanita*.[41] *Humanita* was also the basis of Masarykian democracy, since his democratic vision required citizens to recognize the basic *humanita* of their fellows and treat them accordingly.[42] Since *humanita* was at the heart of civic relations and Czech history, Masaryk argued, Czechs had to face what he termed "the social question"—the inequities produced by modern industrialized society—and work to eradicate social injustice.[43] Masaryk linked *humanita* to the writings and actions of Jan Hus; seventeenth-century exile bishop and intellectual Jan Amos Komenský (Comenius) and the Czech Brethren, a pacifist wing of the Hussite movement; and the nineteenth-century philologists Josef Dobrovský and Ján Kollár.

In occasional descents from the lofty heights, Masaryk wrote about democratic practice. But his communitarian vision of democratic Czech ideals did not square with his relatively elitist, paternalistic approach to democratic politics, clearly influenced by Austrian liberalism. Although he frequently described democracy as a discussion between elected officials and voters, via the press and the voting booth, clearly one voice was to dominate. The people were easily deceived, he believed. Though their will ought to determine general political orientation, trained elites should work out specific policy.[44] His schema left little room for grassroots organization or agitation; politics should be orderly, directed by professionals who would make dispassionate decisions for the common good. To bridge the distance between the elites and the masses, Masaryk advocated educating the electorate.[45] This insistence on civic education as crucial to democratic praxis provides helpful context for Masaryk's later views on propaganda and the mass media.

Masaryk amended Palacký's thoughts on Czech history and national identity, proposing a different national hero. Palacký, Jirásek, and other nationalists had venerated the Czech-speaking peasantry for preserving Czech folk traditions and the Czech language while assimilated, cosmopolitan city folk took up German under Habsburg pressure.[46] Masaryk contended that the Czech nation's true fulfillment would come from embracing the liberal ideals inherent in its *humanita*, rather those of the peasant village. Like Palacký, Masaryk elided the fifteenth and nineteenth centuries, seeking eternal Czech values; but Masaryk rejected some of Palacký's tenets, finding his ideas exaggerated, quietistic, and too focused on the glories of the Czech past.[47] Masaryk argued that modern Czechs should read the crusading journalist Karel Havlíček Borovský, whom he described as appropriately progressive, democratic, and focused on the Czech nation's future possibilities within Europe. Havlíček Borovský, editor of *Národní noviny* (*National News*), had harnessed the power of the press to advance the causes of national autonomy and liberal politics. His witty feuilletons frequently criticized Russian imperial politics and British rule in Ireland; both his Czech readers and the imperial government understood that Havlíček's real target was Austrian autocracy. In 1851 the government confined him in the Tyrol, where he became seriously ill and died soon after his release, one of the first martyrs for the Czech national cause. Havlíček had been an early supporter of extending the franchise to every man within the empire. He encouraged Czech nationalist activism and advocated the separation of church and state. For Masaryk, Palacký and Havlíček represented different stages of a national evolution. Palacký awakened the Czechs: Havlíček taught them of their potential as an enlightened European nation.[48] Like Havlíček, Masaryk attempted to link the values of Hussite nationalism to progressive liberalism, ethnic tolerance, and (Masaryk's own contribution) a secularized Christian spirituality.

Other Czech intellectuals disputed Masaryk's vision of the Czech national past and future, especially his search for suprahistorical moral principles. Historian Josef Pekař and other members of the historical "school" led by Charles University historian Jaroslav Goll argued publicly with Masaryk for decades. Pekař defended Austria's contribution to Czech development; he dismissed Masaryk's "mystical ideology" and his spurious connection between the Czech Reformation and the Enlightenment-influenced Awakeners.[49] Economist and former Reichsrat colleague Josef Kaizl resisted Masaryk's claims to link the *humanita* of the medieval Czech Brethren with that of the later Czech Enlightenment and its liberal anticlericalism. Kaizl saw Masaryk's position as fundamentally religious and antiliberal, even unenlightened.[50] Antonin Hajn, leader of the prewar Progressive Movement, disagreed with the implication, clear throughout Masaryk's work, that politics were less important than individual or collective spiritual orientation.[51] Even Masaryk's admirers would make similar comments throughout the interwar period; in the late 1930s, this would become one of many critiques of the First Republic and its president.

Masaryk was an influential figure on the eve of the First World War, however intricate and ambivalent his ideas. Nothing even remotely similar could be said of his student and protégé, Edvard Beneš. From Kožlany u Rakovník, a small town in western Bohemia, Beneš was the youngest of ten children in a family of humble means. In 1904, he entered the Czech side of Prague's Charles University to study philosophy. He became one of many young intellectuals writing for Masaryk's Realist publication, *Čas*, and also for the Social Democratic *Právo Lidu*. But Beneš distinguished himself by the dispatches he sent home from his studies at the Sorbonne, the University of Dijon (where he earned a law degree), and in London. Beneš's years abroad helped form his ideas about European geopolitics, which in turn were of tremendous importance for the country he helped bring into being.[52]

Beneš returned home enamored with the "rational and organized" West, where, with the help of his brother Vojta, he had written various meticulous academic analyses. He noted the internal divisions in French and British society, but believed that these complexities would heal.[53] Beneš was especially infatuated with Paris, which he saw as "almost miraculously . . . a magnificent synthesis of modern civilization."[54] Perhaps surprisingly for a man later considered a dispassionate, mechanical technocrat, Beneš also fell in love with, and studied, the French revolutionary tradition: "extremist movements, revolutionary syndicalism, French Socialism, anti-militarism, and anarchism, the French and Russian revolutions with all their offshoots." His time in Germany, by contrast, filled him with dread. Beneš described the German mindset as "herdlike" and chauvinistic. Europe east of the Rhine seemed to him "intuitivist and mystical," a "welter of nationalities" prone to "empty mechanical doctrinairism . . . blind and fanatical pursuit of an idée fixe."[55] These prejudices—the French and British as somehow both civilized and passionately revolutionary (only in the name of the right cause, of course), the Germans as a faceless, countless army of Prussians, and the rest of Europe as a disorganized, excessively nationalized, overzealous mess in need of correction and a proper model for future development—would linger in Beneš's postwar politics.

Masaryk had read and liked Beneš's journalistic dispatches from France and Germany. When Beneš returned, the two men met, and Masaryk offered to help him obtain a university post. Beneš joined Masaryk's Realist (Progressive) Party and wrote for *Čas* as well as the Social Democratic *Právo Lidu*. But he found Masaryk's politics occasionally overly romantic, emphasizing in contrast his own dispassionate rationalism: "to suppress passions and sentiments, to master them by means of the intellect and to preserve a political calm and balance. . . . I always consciously practised politics in a scientific spirit."[56] Despite his occasional disagreements with his mentor, the rest of Beneš's life would be marked by his dedication to Masaryk, and his daring, ingenious approach to Czech nationalist goals abroad.

Whether scientific or not, Czechs were "practicing politics" extensively by 1914. Czech politics within Austria had diversified considerably from its origins as a single, capacious nationalist movement. By the 1880s a range of mass-based Czech parties existed, differentiated by class and ideology; these same parties would dominate the interwar Czechoslovak parliament as well. Aside from the weakening of the Social Democrats due to the Communist

made it abundantly clear that little effective work would be done there. Masaryk prepared to work abroad, corresponding with Henry Wickham Steed, former London *Times* correspondent in Vienna. Beneš pledged four thousand crowns to help him and provided intelligence from a Czech employee of the Viennese Ministry of the Interior.[79] Masaryk spent part of September and October 1914 in the Netherlands, hoping to contact Sorbonne Professor Ernest Denis, who had written favorably about the Czechs. While there, he talked with Wickham Steed and Seton-Watson, one of the Czechs' most important defenders.[80] British educated opinion, on the eve of the war, considered the Czechs "a highly organized, highly educated, keen, hardworking democracy" and a bulwark against German aggression. This was ready soil on which Masaryk and Beneš might build.[81]

In his talks with Seton-Watson, then working for the British Secret Service, Masaryk demonstrated a capacity for bold political gamesmanship.[82] He disingenuously portrayed himself as the Czech parties' representative, in effect assuming the role of a head of state. Those parties, he claimed, unanimously supported Czech independence. "To attain independence is the . . . aim of all Bohemia . . . there are only some few individual adherents of Austria. No politician of any repute is among them." Masaryk postulated the existence of an independent postwar Czech kingdom, ruled by a member of one of the West European dynastic families or even the Serbian king (though, he admitted, most Czechs were Russophiles and would welcome a Romanov monarch). Masaryk's postwar state would include the Slovaks—he claimed simply that "the Slovaks are Bohemians"—and all Germans on Czech soil, arguing that it would be impossible to separate out German-speaking border districts: "Bohemia is a quite unique example of a mixed country; in no country are two nationalities so intermixed and interwoven."[83]

In Prague between these visits, Masaryk rallied a group of *Čas* journalists to work secretly with him against the Habsburgs: Beneš, Jan Herben, Přemysl Šámal, Cyril Dušek, and a few others.[84] The Austrian police were watching, and arrested some of Masaryk's allies—who had begun to call themselves the *Maffie* (Mafia)—as early as November 1914. The remaining *Maffie* members managed to share ideas and information, to communicate with Vienna, and to fund Masaryk's work and travel with the help of Charles Crane, a Czechophile American industrialist, as well as various Czech societies in the United States.[85] Masaryk later recalled, "Beneš financed the beginning of our revolution . . . we were hard up for money all through the war; I don't think there was ever such a cheap revolution in the world before."[86]

In mid-December 1914, when Masaryk left Austria for his wartime exile, he named the young, untested Beneš his second-in-command. Descriptions of Beneš as a glorified secretary, "efficient, hard-working, discreet and completely loyal," understate his courage and organizational talent.[87] While Masaryk established connections in Geneva, Beneš directed *Maffie* activity in Prague, creating alliances with erstwhile adversaries like Karel Kramář. Beneš traveled to Germany to buy newspapers and magazines banned in Austria-Hungary, smuggling them brazenly back across the border to cite in the pages of *Čas*.[88] Author and journalist Karel Čapek recalled with astonishment Beneš's fearlessness; almost as soon as they met, Čapek remembered, Beneš asked whether Čapek would consider routing his next trip abroad through Switzerland and smuggle *Maffie* messages. "Give some thought to how you would hide them," Beneš nonchalantly told him. "You know that you could hang for it."[89] In a spring 1915 public lecture, as Austrian repression worsened, Beneš openly called for revolution. Austria-Hungary's end would bring Central European despotism to a close, he claimed, but would open the door to social revolution; the Czechs had to be prepared to choose the right path.[90]

Most Czech politicians disagreed, rebuffing *Maffie* attempts to enlist their help. Masaryk's policy seemed to them a foolhardy gamble; Masaryk's and Beneš's high-minded notion of politics as moral guidance for the nation, much less their planning for independence after the war, was a "fantastic scheme."[91] Kramář was willing to collaborate against the Habsburgs, but preferred to do it at home, waiting for the tsarist liberators. By the spring of 1915, Kramář and Rašín had joined a newly reconstituted *Maffie*, as did other party leaders. Still, the Austrian secret police maintained their vigilance. Kramář was arrested in May 1915, and Rašín was arrested that July.[92]

Masaryk now changed strategy and asked Beneš to join him abroad.[93] He had realized that Western leaders and electorates knew little and cared less about the Czechs. Masaryk would have to work and organize publicly, and explain the need for an independent Czech state. He could not do it alone.[94] In August 1915, Beneš escaped from Prague to Paris. He, Masaryk, and Slovak Milan Rastislav Štefánik created the Czech Committee Abroad, which in February 1916 became the Czechoslovak National Council, essentially a government in exile and propaganda apparatus. Masaryk spent the war in London, the United States, and Russia; Beneš remained in Paris, where he began making connections to Parisian intellectual and political life. The French minister of war was Beneš's former professor, Eisenmann; Beneš soon developed a reputation as a respected source of information about Austria-Hungary, drawing on Czechs in Switzerland and the Viennese and Budapest newspapers provided him by the ministry itself. Beneš also presented the Czech case before the committee for foreign affairs in the French Senate. He wrote for and arranged propaganda campaigns in French publications; he socialized with French journalists, particularly editor Gauvain of the *Journal des Débats*; and he lectured on Czechoslovakia and the other "oppressed nations of Austria-Hungary" at the Sorbonne.[95] Masaryk came often to Paris and met with prominent politicians and journalists in an effort to counteract the strong Austrophile and Hungarophile tendencies he believed prevalent in France.[96] He also spent time in Geneva and Amsterdam, where he tried to persuade prominent politicians that a free and independent Central Europe could help contain future German aggression. Liberating the Habsburg nations, he argued, would be another way to satisfy the Entente's stated war aim of defending democracy and freedom.[97]

Masaryk did the same in London, where his tireless activity established him as the face of the Czech resistance abroad. Since May 1915, when he had delivered to George Clerk in the British Foreign Office a memorandum on an independent Bohemia's place in a "new Europe," he had developed ties to pro-Slavic British diplomats.[98] Seton-Watson and Wickham Steed helped secure him a professorship at King's College, London; he also lectured at Cambridge, Oxford, and in London clubs.[99] He wrote for the Sunday *Times, The Nation, Spectator, The Weekly Dispatch, Everyman*, and Seton-Watson's *The New Europe*. He visited academics, journalists, and consular officials in Edinburgh and London, and attended Saturday salons at the home of Wickham Steed, by then political editor of the *Times* and fast ally of the Czechoslovak cause.[100] He also established a Czech Press Bureau on Piccadilly Circus, with the help of émigré Czechs in London. The slogan "Kingdom of Bohemia" was displayed prominently in the windows along with war maps and maps of Berlin's "plan" to dominate Central and southeastern Europe on its way to Baghdad. The office sold Czech needlework, *La Nation Tchèque* and *The New Europe*, and many other propaganda pamphlets.[101] Wickham Steed helped them coordinate their press office's efforts with Crewe House, the British propaganda organization led by Lord Northcliffe.[102] The Czech resistance effort abroad would create similar organizations in Rome, Geneva, Kiev (after the Russian Revolution), and the United States during 1917.[103] The exiles also succeeded in sponsoring commemorations of Jan Hus's martyrdom in most of England's churches.[104]

Masaryk and Beneš did not act alone. Particularly in France, they relied on the dashing Slovak émigré Štefánik, an astronomer, meteorologist, and officer in the French air force.[105] Štefánik, with his personal charm and impressive connections throughout government and society's highest circles, would be the third of Czechoslovakia's Founding Fathers. More politically conservative than Masaryk and Beneš, Štefánik nonetheless shared their vision for postwar Europe.[106] Other, less helpful collaborators did not, such as Agrarian Josef Dürich, sent abroad by Karel Kramář to ensure that Masaryk's pro-Western viewpoint did not dominate the discussion of an independent postwar Bohemia, which Kramář envisioned as part of a Russian-ruled "great Slav Empire." Dürich negotiated separately with the French and the Russians through 1916, then faded into insignificance once the tsarist government fell. Dürich irritated Masaryk, who wrote snidely in his memoirs that "the ambitions of the sundry bibulous aspirants to the future Russian Satrapy of Bohemia gave a little trouble."[107]

Masaryk and Beneš coordinated their activities closely through incessant correspondence. Their tone was relatively formal, always using the formal *vy* rather than the more intimate *ty*. Beneš addressed Masaryk as "Dear Professor and Valued Friend," while Masaryk initially used the same standard address ("Valued Friend" or "Dear Friend" [*Milý příteli*]), soon abbreviating it to "DF (*Mpř*)." But the content was forthright and intimate. The two moved from language to language, communicating in Czech, English, and French. They strategized together how to handle Dürich and other challenges, warned one another about alarming articles in the Prague press, and expressed concern about one another's health as well as that of Štefánik. They worried together about their family members in Austria; Beneš was especially concerned about his wife's imprisonment in late 1916. Masaryk was the strategist, often calming or reassuring Beneš after setbacks and sending instructions: Beneš provided crucial information and connections, acting as administrator and organizer.[108]

The Czechoslovak exiles also coordinated their efforts with other "oppressed nations": the Poles, "Yugoslavs," and Serbs.[109] Geopolitical logic forced the Czechs to assist the other Austrian Slavs. The Czechs would only gain autonomy if Austria-Hungary were substantially defeated—if the Entente refused a separate peace with the Dual Monarchy and supported Austria-Hungary's non-German-speaking peoples. Here the diplomatic dominoes became complicated. The Entente had promised Italy much of the Adriatic under the terms of the 1915 Treaty of London, territory also claimed by the Croats, Slovenes, and Serbs agitating for the creation of a new "Yugoslav" state. If Italy, supported by the Entente, contested the Yugoslav claim, Czech requests for Austro-Hungarian territory would also be denied. Untangling the Italian-Yugoslav knot was one of Beneš's central concerns.[110]

But there were other reasons for Czechoslovak-Yugoslav allegiance. Czech nationalists had developed cultural ties with the South Slavs under Austria-Hungary, which had treated both peoples as equally suspect. Croat nationalists, such as Stjepan Radić, studied in Prague during the 1880s and fell under Masaryk's spell. They brought home his belief in basing national struggle on everyday "small acts (*drobná práce*)," particularly education and agitation among the lower classes. His influence was such that one historian refers to the Croats as "political Masarykists."[111] As early as his first conversations with Seton-Watson in autumn 1914, Masaryk had suggested that the postwar Czechoslovak and Yugoslav states cooperate, indeed that they be territorially connected, with land taken from Hungary.[112] Once war broke out, they shared Great Power promoters—in Paris, among others, Professor Ernest Denis, editor Gauvain of the *Journal des Debats*, and Minister of War Eisenmann, and Steed and Seton-Watson in London—and were discussed by the same journals, specifically Seton-Watson's *New Europe* and Denis's *La Nation Tchèque*, begun in May 1915, coedited by Czech journalist Lev Sychrava and funded by Czech émigrés in the United States.[113] Sir George Clerk recalled meeting both Czechs and South Slavs in London as the war began: "We grew familiar with mysterious gentlemen in varying types of frock coats . . . who were then able to develop the claims of unknown and uncouth . . . nationalities which had, unbeknown to British statesmen, been groaning for centuries under Habsburg oppression. Croats, Slovenes, . . . Jugoslavs, . . . Czechoslovak professors . . ."[114] The Czechoslovak National Council's first public manifesto in November 1915 declared "deep sympathy with our brothers the Serbs and the Russians, and with the Poles."[115]

But the Czechs' Yugoslav brothers were divided. The Serbs, represented by Serbian Prime Minister Nikola Pašić, understood South Slav unification as Serbian expansion, or at the least, unification of all Serbs, including those in Habsburg South Slav lands. The second group—Croats and Slovenes, led by Frano Supilo and Ante Trumbić, collectively known as the Yugoslav Committee (Jugoslavenski odbor, or JO)—wanted to create an entirely new state to preserve the autonomy for each South Slav people.[116] The Czechs recognized, but preferred to minimize, these internal tensions. Beneš later recalled almost daily contact with the Yugoslav delegation in Paris during the war, and claimed to work easily with both Yugoslav groupings.[117] Serb legation heads in Paris, London, Rome, Russia, and the United States facilitated the movement of Czech POWs to France in 1917; Alexander, the Serbian heir apparent, was in regular contact with Masaryk.[118]

Czech-Polish relations were cooler. Polish Legion leader Józef Piłsudski distrusted the Russians and supported the Habsburgs; Poles knew firsthand the reality of Romanov rule in East-Central Europe. A weakened, federalized Austria-Hungary might grant them some protection from Germany and Russia, and Emperor Karl might grant the Poles more territory.[119] Later, the Poles divided into two camps: Roman Dmówski leading a pro-Entente, anti-German Polish National Committee in Paris, and Piłsudski leading the Polish Legion's seizure of power in Warsaw and protecting Poland against a hungry Bolshevik Russia. This further complicated cooperation, although at one point Dmówski did propose a Czech-Polish federation.[120] In the last year of the war, when the Poles agreed on the impossibility of a separate peace with Austria-Hungary, the Polish and Czech émigrés in Paris were able to better coordinate their work.[121]

For all the exiles, propaganda and cultural diplomacy were of crucial importance. Connections mattered—to academics, politicians, journalists, and elegant society hostesses alike, in Paris, London, Geneva, and Washington. Rather than trying to persuade the public, the Czechs set out to cultivate elite opinion. Their lone attempt to reach the public was their London office, established in 1916 on Piccadilly Circus, its windows covered with pro-Czechoslovak writings and maps to attract the gaze of passersby. Mostly, their goal was for their allies to espouse their cause, rather than having to indelicately do it themselves. Masaryk advised that the Czechs ought to "influence by ideas and arguments and remain personally in the background."[122] For example, Štefánik crafted "confidential memoranda," supposedly solely and specifically for members of the uppermost echelons of French society, who were given the document in an atmosphere of high secrecy. Beneš recalled that most recipients of the memoranda were thrilled to propagate the information they contained.[123] They had frequent personal meetings with high-ranking leaders and cultural figures in the West—and in the East, where until the Bolshevik Revolution Masaryk relied on the assistance of Pavel Miliukov, a fellow historian, a leader of the Constitutional Democratic Party, and Russian foreign minister under the short-lived Provisional Government.[124]

Outside the halls of government and the salons of high society, Beneš and Masaryk relied on universities. They believed that scholars could be useful to them, "despite knowing that politicians viewed them with suspicion."[125] In addition to his other university lectures, Masaryk gave the inaugural address at the School of Slavonic Studies at King's College on October 19, 1915, titled "The Problem of Small Nations in the European Crisis," which he later remembered as his "first [large-scale] political success."[126] He also spoke at the University of Paris's Institute of Slav Studies on "The Slavs among the Nations," where he was introduced, unsurprisingly, by Ernest Denis; the audience, described as "select," granted him "vigorous applause."[127] Over the course of the war, Beneš spoke repeatedly at the Societé de Sociologie, where he addressed Leon Bourgeois and Emile Durkheim, as well as the Comité National des Etudes; in 1917, he also spoke at public lectures organized by French scholars to explain the Russian Revolution to the Parisian public.[128] The Czechoslovaks also believed firmly in the propagandistic value of high culture, taking the Poles as their example: Masaryk lamented the Czechs' lack of a Paderewski or Henryk Sienkiewicz, whose historical novel *Quo Vadis* Masaryk credited with attracting sympathy for the Polish cause.[129]

Another element of Czechoslovak wartime propaganda was the publication of, and contribution to, newspapers and journals in Western languages. One of the most important of these was Seton-Watson's *The New Europe*, published in London between 1916 and 1922. Masaryk was a regular contributor on a wide range of topics but always returned to one central theme: the absolutist, reactionary, and dangerous proclivities of the House of Habsburg. The Austrian dynasty would never be trustworthy, he implied, no matter how urgent its entreaties for a separate peace: "[The Austrian Kaiser] Francis Joseph is a warning example of the perils of monarchism—of the gross immorality of unrestricted absolutism masquerading under modern constitutional and parliamentary forms in order to hide its own nakedness."[130] Unlike the secular states of Western Europe, Austria would never extricate itself from its antiquated political Catholicism: "Catholicism in Austria, having crushed the Reformation, especially in Bohemia, is spiritually inert and stagnant, relying completely on the police state of Vienna.... In Austria clericalism means the misuse of religion for political ends."[131] Masaryk likened the Austrian domination of Central Europe to German desires to dominate the Near East: the liberation of a Czechoslovak state could be the key to limiting German power.[132]

In Paris, Denis's *La Nation Tchèque* remained extremely important throughout the war, although the Czechs began publishing their own periodicals, such as *Le Monde Slave*, a scholarly journal.[133] Beneš himself wrote for *Journal des Débats, Le Temps, Paris Midi*, and *La Victoire*, trying to ensure that the Czechoslovak cause would be raised in the Parisian press at least twice each week.[134] Russian and American newspapers were also part of the plan. The newspaper *Čechoslovák* began publishing independently in Petrograd in June 1915; by July 1917 it was regarded as the Czechoslovak National Council's voice in Russia.[135] In the United States, Czech and Slovak émigrés established a Slav Press Bureau in May 1918, which Beneš credited with distributing bulletins to five hundred papers across the country. Beneš also wrote for American Czech newspapers.[136]

Masaryk's and Beneš's wartime memoirs obscure the arduous creative and organizational effort which brought the Czechoslovak national myth into being and propagated it on two continents. Rather, they characterize Czech wartime propaganda as self-evidently factual, *quod erat demonstrandum*. Their work, they recalled, involved merely bringing those facts to light. "Several of our propaganda publications... were models of what propaganda should be, for they provided a graphic statement of our case, and at the same time were accurate as to the facts," Beneš wrote.[137] Masaryk, too, emphasized that Czech propaganda was exemplary in its honesty: "not to distort facts or make boasts; not to make empty promises... to let facts speak for themselves, and use them as evidence; so-and-so is in your interest, and therefore your duty. . . . To lie and exaggerate is the worst propaganda of all."[138] Illumination of these "facts," without pollution or obfuscation from other sources (such as German or Hungarian propaganda) would inevitably produce support for the Czech cause.

The last prong of the National Council's strategy was coordination with Czech politicians in Prague and Vienna. But until the spring of 1917, this proved difficult. The Habsburg authorities pressured the Czechs, while the war's outcome seemed none too clear; leading politicians at home were either uncertain or imprisoned. Meanwhile, throughout the war efforts were made via unofficial channels to craft a separate peace between the Allies and Austria-Hungary, worrying the Czech leaders. If the Czech domestic leaders were to disavow the National Council and its work abroad, the Allies might find Austria-Hungary a more plausible partner in the postwar peace process.[139] The possibilities of Czechoslovak independence would disappear. The exiles' fears seemed to be borne out in January 1917, when, under pressure from Austrian Foreign Minister Count Ottokar Czernin and led by Social Democrat Bohumír Šmerál, the League of Czech Deputies in the Austro-Hungarian Reichsrat publicly declared their loyalty to the empire.[140]

Spring 1917 heralded real change. The Americans entered the war in April; the following January, President Wilson would demand the "autonomous" development of Austria-Hungary's peoples. But the Russian Revolution had a far more profound effect on the Czechs than the American entry into the war. When the house of Romanov fell, so too did the possibility of uniting European Slavic lands under a Romanov prince.[141] Moreover, the rhetoric of national self-determination and democracy propagated by both Soviet Russia and America at this point fueled the imaginations of Czech politicians. For the first time, mainstream Czech political thought began to consider seriously an independent Czech or Czechoslovak state. A group of leading Czech intellectuals published a manifesto urging the deputies to speak openly on behalf of the Czech nation.[142] The inexperienced Austrian Emperor Karl, upon his accession, announced a general amnesty of all political prisoners; released at this time were many Czech nationalists jailed during the war for treason, including Karel Kramář and poet Viktor Dyk. Karl summoned the Reichsrat for the first time since 1914. The possibility of a return to constitutional rule was rumored.

Meanwhile, Masaryk and Beneš sent an urgent message to Prague before the Reichsrat convened on May 30. They pled with the Czech deputies to refuse to vote for a war budget or troop levy, to demand freedom of speech in the Czech and Slovak lands and the release of all Czech and Slovak political prisoners, and to demand states' rights, or autonomy for the Czech and Slovak lands. "We realized the difficult situation of our leading politicians at home," recalled Beneš, "and we did not expect them to achieve impossibilities. All that we wanted was that they should not lose ground."[143] Nor did they. On May 30, from the floor of the Reichsrat, the Czech deputies demanded states' rights, discussed the concept of national self-determination, and asserted the desire for a democratic Czech state allied with Slovakia, although they did allow the possibility of that state being a constituent part of a new, federated Austria-Hungary. The Yugoslavs, Poles, and Ukrainians made similar statements.[144] On April 1, Austrian Foreign Minister Count Czernin publicly assailed those "Masaryks" among the Czechs who, by opposing the imperial administration, were prolonging the war—thus reassuring the Allies that the Czechs were firmly on their side. The aftermath of the ensuing Sixtus Affair, which bound Austria even more tightly to Germany, persuaded the Allies that a separate peace with Austria was impossible.[145] Throughout 1917, Czech politicians at home openly repudiated the imperial administration's calls for unity.

The pace of events quickened in 1918. As Germany and Austria-Hungary concluded a peace with revolutionary Russia on March 3, Czech deputies were among those who insisted that the non-Russian nations dominated by the former tsarist empire participate as equals in the peace negotiations—which, of course, would imply that political representatives of the non-German nations of Austria-Hungary ought also to take part. Czech deputies also refused to help revise the Austro-Hungarian imperial constitution, insisting that they were waiting for the postwar peace conference.[146] Various Czech political parties and spokesmen publicly began discussing Czechoslovak independence. In July 1918, thirty politicians, led by Karel Kramář and Agrarian leader Antonín Švehla, formed a Czechoslovak National Committee in which all Czech political parties were represented.[147]

But propaganda, alliance with other nationalities, and support from politicians at home would not commit the Allies to destroying Austria-Hungary. Masaryk recalled that in the early years of the war, the Yugoslavs had a greater reputation by far than the Czechs, thanks in part to "Serbia's heroic battle."[148] Without an army, Masaryk wrote to Beneš in early 1915, the Czechs would "obtain nothing from anybody."[149] The best hope for a potential Czechoslovak Army was the Czechs and Slovaks living in Russia, who in 1914 had volunteered to serve in the tsarist army as a means of demonstrating loyalty; but the tsarist government used them mainly for intelligence.[150] In 1916 Josef Dürich had tried to bring them to France, along with Czech POWs in Russia, as part of a Russian military unit—thus subjecting Czech independence to Russian control of Eastern Europe, and supporting the Czech Neo-Slavists opposed to Masaryk and Beneš. The Russian Revolution foiled Dürich's plans, and helped Masaryk and Beneš realize that the moment had come to extract the core of their army—now grown to include many thousands of Czech POWs and Czechs at work in the Russian armaments industry. Masaryk went to Russia in May 1917 and stayed for nearly a year, literally dodging bullets as the Bolsheviks fought for control of Moscow, negotiating with Russian authorities and forming connections with the Czech soldiers, now calling themselves the Czechoslovak Legions.[151]

Almost 45,000 Czechoslovak troops were stationed near Kiev while power in Russia fell first to the Provisional Government and then to the Bolsheviks. The Czechoslovaks were directly in the path of the German advance, through the territory they would soon claim in the Treaty of Brest-Litovsk, but the Legions were undersupplied and could not hope to prevail. The Czechoslovak troops might also have been arrested or commandeered by the Bolsheviks to be used as industrial forced laborers or for fighting the Whites (anti-Bolsheviks).[152] The Legions had to be moved out of German and Bolshevik hands as soon as possible. After months of negotiation, Masaryk and the Bolshevik authorities agreed that the Czechoslovak troops would be regarded as the military force of a neutral power and allowed to leave Russian soil as soon as possible.[153] The Bolsheviks worried that the Legions might join the Whites or the Japanese Army. Trotsky demanded that the Czechoslovaks remain in Russia and form the core of the reconstituted Russian Army; the British, doubtful that the Czechs could make it back to Europe, proposed that they ought to occupy Siberia or ally themselves with the White general Semyonov.

Masaryk's initial hunch turned out to be correct: the Great Powers were increasingly intrigued by the Legions in Siberia, and the good they might do for the Entente's war effort. Czechoslovak Legions had also made their presence felt in March 1918 in Italy; the Allies used them in espionage and in some of the nastiest scrapes on the western front.[154] That June, during the last German offense on the western front, Clemenceau told Beneš, "I want all your soldiers in France." Beneš answered, "You can count on me. I will go with you all the way."[155] France recognized the Czechoslovak right to independence on June 29, the British on August 8, and the Americans on September 2.[156] The Czechoslovak National Council needed to devote real energy to protecting its army.

But extracting the Legions from Russia was difficult, beginning with the logistical problem of moving them across Eurasia to Vladivostok, Tokyo, the United States, and then to Europe. Some Legionnaire leaders developed relationships with White leaders; others encountered fighting forces and engaged with them. By the end of April, Czechoslovak troops were divided into three groups widely distributed across Siberia; 70,000 Czechoslovak Legionnaires, along with Japanese troops, controlled the entire Siberian railway from early September to early October 1918.[157] British Foreign Minister Arthur Balfour noted approvingly that the Czechs "had formed the only element in Russia which had shown itself able to cope with the Bolshevik chaos."[158] The Legions' Siberian escapade had also made an impression on the Americans; when Wilson, under Allied pressure, sent American troops to Siberia, the reason he gave was to protect the Legions. American popular opinion until then had found "the tangled national problems of Central Europe . . . quite strange," Masaryk recalled, but when the Legions attracted American admiration, "we held victory in our hands."[159] Beneš believed "our Siberian army was our strongest political factor . . . during the Peace Conference, I made use of its retention in Siberia to win our peace terms." At war's end, Czech and Slovak volunteers from France, Italy, the United States, and Canada, and roughly 10,000 Czechoslovak troops from the Soviet Union, were fighting in the western and eastern theaters as well as Siberia.[160]

The Dual Monarchy's armies won their last battle in autumn 1917 at Caporetto, but for naught. In the Viennese Reichsrat as well as the empire's provinces, national self-determination and independence were on everyone's lips, from Poles and Ukrainians to South Slavs—and Czechs.[161] The Americans only reluctantly abandoned the possibility of resuscitating Austria-Hungary; the British, who had long viewed Austria-Hungary as "Europe's watchdog in the East," clung to hope until spring 1918, after the failure of the Smuts-Mensdorff negotiations.[162] Nonetheless, public rhetoric was dismissive. British spokesmen disdained Austrian diplomats' continued efforts to conclude a separate peace as "pathetic proposals," Emperor Karl's last-minute offer to federalize the empire as "Austria's Death Repentance."[163] Woodrow Wilson called Austria-Hungary "an old building whose sides had been held together by props."[164]

The Czechs, like the other Habsburg peoples, contributed to this impression by establishing a de facto Czechoslovak state before the postwar peace talks convened. "A *fait accompli* carried through without noise or struggle," Beneš wrote, "and the domination of the situation are now decisive." Leading Prague politicians—former Young Czech, now States'-Rights Democrat (soon to be National Democrat) Karel Kramář, Realist Přemysl Šámal, Social Democrat Gustav Habrman, and head of the Živnostenská (Tradesman's) Bank Jaroslav Preiss—were allowed to travel to Geneva in late October 1918 to confer with Masaryk and Beneš. The empire's economic situation was dire and the lure of Bolshevism in Vienna and Budapest was strong; the threat of political radicalism, hunger riots, and, perhaps, occupation by German troops remained. To maintain order and Czech political control, the Praguers had drawn up detailed plans for the transition from monarchy to independent republic. All agreed quickly that Masaryk would be president of the new state, Kramář prime minister, and that Beneš and Štefánik should remain in their positions as minister of foreign affairs and of war, respectively.

They also agreed that the Germans in Bohemia and Moravia should be granted at least one cabinet position, albeit without portfolio—that is, they were loath to allow German control over any aspect of governance. While this meeting was being held, on October 28, Austria-Hungary's capitulation was announced in Prague, and Alois Rašín, Antonín Švehla, Jiří Stříbrný, and František Soukup of the Czech National Committee demanded that authority in Bohemia, Moravia, and Slovakia be ceded to them.[165] The Slovaks, kept under tight political control by the Magyars until spring 1918, had formed a Slovak National Council, which on October 30 demanded the right of self-determination and noted, "The Slovak nation is a part of the Czechoslovak nation, united in language and in the history of its culture."[166] Masaryk and Beneš's revolution had succeeded: the road to an independent Czechoslovakia had been cleared.

The Czechoslovaks were the lone Austrian nationality to approach their independent statehood harmoniously. The Poles were internally divided between the Polish Committee in Paris and the Warsaw government; the Zagreb National Committee and the Serbian government in Belgrade could not reach a decision on the nature of the Yugoslav state. But the Praguers cooperated exultantly with Masaryk and Beneš. On November 14 in Prague, the "revolutionary" or provisional Czechoslovak National Assembly met, each party's number of seats based on its showing in the 1911 election. The assembly lauded the work of the National Council, began deliberations to write a new constitution, and established law and order; prime minister Kramář welcomed the Slovaks and expressed hope that the Germans would sit beside their Czech and Slovak colleagues.[167] In Paris, Beneš and Masaryk fought at each turn for the preservation of Czechoslovakia's "historic" frontiers in Bohemia and Moravia, but for the establishment of ethnic frontiers in Slovakia; Sub-Carpathian Ruthenia became part of the postwar republic after discussions between Masaryk and the American Ruthenian leader Gregory Zatkovič. The American negotiators objected, but the Czech arguments prevailed.[168] Meanwhile, Masaryk returned home as president, stopping in London, Paris, and Padua, and visiting Czechoslovak troops along the way. Masaryk was concerned, Beneš later recalled, and very serious rather than triumphant: "we have reached the top," he said several times, "but it is easier to reach the top than to stay there."[169]

Facing a New World

By war's end, the dream of an independent Czechoslovak republic had become one of Europe's many realized dreams. The Allies, particularly the French, had smiled on the country's creation; East-Central Europe had been remade in those allies' idealized collective image, trumpeting the ideals of democracy, transparency, cooperation, and peace, and their triumph over absolutism. Masaryk and Beneš saw the Great War as the culmination of the global battle between theocratic absolutism and humanistic democracy, paralleling Czech struggles for independence. As Beneš wrote, the war's "meaning was identical with that of our national revolution which accompanied it.... We were successful in our struggle because we adjusted our movement to the scope of world events. We rightly joined our struggle with the struggle of universal democracy."[170] Yet the war had marked their thought in other ways. Their understanding of national identity, international politics, and the meaning of the First World War for Europe attempted to bridge past and present, linking themes from the nineteenth century's nationalist legacy to their own belief in progressive liberalism and in the universalist, Wilsonian political and ideological aftermath of the war. For Masaryk and Beneš, the Czech—now Czechoslovak—national moral character aligned itself naturally with the West European Great Power states, understood simplistically as representing an antidote to Austria and as a set of civilized ideals and practices. They hoped Czechoslovaks would abandon prideful Czech national provincialism and short-sighted, savage internecine attacks, which might hinder Czechoslovakia's relationship with the wider world.

The war, as understood by Masaryk and Beneš, reminded the Czech nation of its profound connections to the so-called "Western" intellectual legacy—"from the beginnings of our development in Europe we have been politically and culturally linked not just to Germany but also to France, Italy, and England"—and especially to the universal ideals preached first by Jan Hus, later by scholar and educator Jan Amos Comenius, and then by the nineteenth-century nationalists.[171] They had fought against Vienna and Rome to defend freedom of conscience against repression, much the same way the Entente fought against the Central Powers. As Beneš wrote, "Our own national traditions, our age-long contest for freedom of opinions, our democratic ideals as expressed in our reformation and national revival, and our political struggle during the nineteenth century, predestined us for the Allied camp from the very beginning."[172] Masaryk's and Beneš's postwar writings reinterpreted Czech nationalism's genealogy, linking Czech farmers and merchants to Voltaire and the Abbé Sieyes. Czech nationalism, like all nationalisms, wrote Beneš, ought to be based on the "humanitarian philosophy of the French Revolution, which proclaimed the rights of man and the citizen." Serving the nation, therefore, meant serving all of humanity, as Beneš wrote after the war: "For him who believes in the ideals of humanity, every step, every act, every sentiment is a service to humanity, to the nation, and to the progress of his own individuality at the same time."[173] A Western-leaning, high-minded, educated, tolerant, cosmopolitan, even multiethnic (for Štefánik was a Slovak, and Masaryk had been raised speaking Slovak and German) variant of Czechness had triumphed.

Yet these conclusions were contradicted by other lessons taught by the war. One was the notion that language determines ethnicity (or belonging to a nation) and worldview. While residents of Central Europe might speak more than one language out of convenience, only one could be their true mother tongue. Prior to 1848, this belief had been far from widespread: in the Bohemian and Moravian crownlands, identity had been rooted in a call for Bohemian states' rights, "corporative and socioeconomic" affiliations as peasants, artisans, nobles, or burghers, and a supranational loyalty to the Habsburg dynasty or empire even while differing with its concrete policies (in Czech, *rakušactví*).[174] After 1848, this pluralistic, fluid sense of local, regional, and imperial belonging slowly disappeared, in part due to increasing popular pressure as well as the Habsburgs' occasional decisions to recognize national affiliation—denoted by language—as a subcitizenship. By the end of the First World War, all was national: "There is no such thing as a common human culture: there are only national cultures."[175] Another tenet of nineteenth-century nationalism validated by the war: Czechs were Slavs, culturally (and perhaps morally) distinct from, and potentially opposed to, Germans. The lure of an idealized Slavdom, while not realized in postwar Russian domination of the Czech lands, would not disappear from Czech political culture, despite Masaryk's admonition that "our politics must be above all Czech . . . thus they will be genuinely global and thus also Slav."[176]

Another important wartime lesson was the significance of Great Power support. Czechoslovakia and its leaders had been brave, industrious, and lucky, but without the Great Powers, their efforts would have been in vain. "[W]e ourselves would never have won our liberty by our own strength and labour. It was a joint achievement [with the Allies]. Every Czechoslovak is under an obligation always to bear this in mind," Beneš admonished.[177] The Czechoslovak Legions had played a crucial role in earning the Czechs recognition by the Great Powers; Masaryk's attachment to the Legions would soon become a central element in legitimating his postwar exercise of power. Yet, strangely, Masaryk and Beneš's myth did not rest overlong on emphasizing the Legions' valor or significance. The Hussites featured more prominently in Masaryk's postwar memoirs than did the Legions. He once noted that he had won the affection of the Legions "mainly, I think, because I was severe with them. . . . I noticed a great deal in common between soldiers and children."[178] This dual approach to the Legionnaires and to military might in general—paternalistic, dependent, and dismissive by turns—would remain consistent throughout the interwar period.

Tomáš Garrigue Masaryk's postwar anointing as the country's democratic savior was related to both these developments. A personality cult of Masaryk was deliberately crafted and encouraged from the moment Masaryk returned to Czech soil in December 1918. This strategy was in part pragmatic: even Karel Kramář, no friend of Masaryk, told Beneš in November 1918 that the country needed Masaryk to return quickly, to calm the spark of Bolshevism within the Czech Social Democrats and to unite Czech politics behind some larger ideal: "The need in Prague . . . was for a deus ex machina."[179] But the country's first president needed to be internationally known. The vision of Masaryk as great European and great Czech, lifting the country beyond the difficulties of postwar rebuilding, would be deliberately continued throughout the interwar period, and would constitute a central element of the new country's national self-understanding.

Nor was it just Czechoslovakia that would need to be rebuilt. Beneš's dedication to the League of Nations and its underlying postulate of collective security represented an equally radical commitment to its larger task: to ask Europe's peoples to look beyond their own parochial concerns and work actively for the common good, now understood to reach beyond national borders. In effect, this amounted to a gradual political and moral re-creation not just of Czechoslovakia, but of Europe itself. Masaryk described this task before the war was half over:

> The Allies have proclaimed as their aim the reconstruction and regeneration of Europe, and it is evidence that this cannot be attained merely by re-shaping the map. Europe's whole mentality must be changed. Her regeneration must be as much moral and spiritual as political. . . . Its foremost demand is true equality—alike in the inward and the outward sphere—an equality which extends to every citizen and every nation.[180]

This radicalism, attributed to politicians counted among the most rational and moderate in interwar Europe, is less surprising than it might seem. Their ethos matched their era. Masaryk and Beneš had helped destroy Europe's great, ancient empires; they had guided the Great Powers in remaking the map of Europe; their own national, democratic "revolution" had roughly coincided with the Bolshevik Revolution, a shocking and fearful political experiment, not to mention Bela Kun's short-lived socialist revolution in neighboring Hungary. Their wartime memoirs reflect this sense of upheaval: Masaryk titled his recollections *Světová revoluce* (*World Revolution*). Moreover, they believed that their own metamorphosis from autocracy to democracy reflected a larger trend of global development. The upheaval of the Great War and the new, egalitarian international regime it had created would inspire all countries to move toward greater equality and freedom. "It appeared that the most solid internal safeguard of Czechoslovakia's continued existence was the formation of a new supranational civil society."[181] Of course, timing and luck had much to do with their triumph. The World War proved a crucible for the formation of new states and state myths all over the world, but some states were more fortunate than others. Czech political goals coincided, at least somewhat, with the visions and compromises of the planners at Versailles, as opposed to unsuccessful Japanese, Chinese, Irish, and Indian arguments for home rule or autonomy, much less a League of Nations covenant clause requiring members to eschew racial discrimination.[182]

The political remaking of the world had occurred violently, with astonishing speed. The ideal "supranational civil society" would take much longer to create and would be shaped by words, not arms. Masaryk and Beneš had devoted years to arduous, spectacularly successful propaganda work. Propaganda would remain as worthy—and as difficult—in the fragile new Czechoslovakia. In Paris in 1919, even before returning to Czechoslovakia from their wartime service abroad, Masaryk and Beneš drew up plans for a governmental office addressing propaganda, to remain under their direct control. The office would inform the world about the new state and ensure the Czechoslovak point of view was well represented in the newspapers and academic circles of Great Power states, just as Masaryk and Beneš had during the war. Also, the office would distribute propaganda for use abroad: educational materials, newspaper and magazine articles, and diplomatic briefs on issues pertinent to Czechoslovak interests. Finally, it would remedy the new government's lack of foreign experience and linguistic competence by maintaining an archive and press service, which would gather, sort, and report on foreign affairs to various domestic agencies and organizations, educating the Czech press about the world. The press agency was to be ostensibly independent or private, but would be controlled by and dependent on the Ministry of Foreign Affairs, under Beneš's purview.[183] The propaganda office was also to track the Czechoslovak media's coverage of foreign affairs. Its chief would create regular reports on domestic issues for the foreign minister, as well as embassies, consulates, and foreign press offices about the republic's internal situation.

Masaryk and Beneš's concerns with propaganda, information, and the press were central to their postwar vision. The world and Czechoslovakia had to learn about one another: Masaryk and Beneš were the ones to teach them. Other Czech political leaders saw the world through ideological blinders, and were far from the groundswell of revolutionary history that had carried Masaryk, Beneš, and Czechoslovakia to freedom and success. Information was important, but it had to be the right information, provided by the right sources. Clearly, Masaryk and Beneš's predominantly oppositional relationship to the Czech parliamentary leadership was left unchanged by the war. The reluctance of most of those leaders to aid the resistance effort abroad for the first few years of the war, their clinging to hopes of placing the Romanovs on the Czech throne, and their willingness to declare their loyalty to the Habsburgs in 1917 were not easily forgotten. Masaryk and Beneš had been on the right side of history; the country's new parliament and its leadership would need to be taught or to arrive at those same conclusions.[184]

Concretely, this meant that Masaryk and Beneš would insist on the president's ability to work unhindered for the greater good as he understood it, and for Beneš to remain foreign minister in perpetuity, regardless of party affiliation or the electoral fortunes of that party. Masaryk's conception of power and authority during the war was shaped by the era's two most influential leaders: Woodrow Wilson's high-minded international morality and Vladimir Lenin's bloody, revolutionary Bolshevism. Neither of these models emphasized democratic civic engagement; they focused on the centrality of one visionary leader. Emanuel Rádl, a historian, philosopher, and one of Masaryk's most observant critics, noted in 1928: "It is the characteristic feature of humanitarian democracy in Masaryk's interpretation that it speaks from the point of view of a statesman who possesses sovereign power and limits it out of his sympathy for other men. Thus it does not see democracy as defective when the authority of the state... apparatus has practically no limitations."[185]

All in all, Masaryk and Beneš's wartime triumph left them certain that their cosmopolitan, enlightened interpretation of Czech history and nationalism had always been right, that the prophetic moral rectitude and intransigence manifested by Jan Hus and the Czech Brethren had touched them as well, and that the Great Powers had borne out the correctness of their vision. They hoped to create a Czechoslovakia capable of uniting behind a pro-European democratic framework and taking its place beside its brother nations, supported by its Great Power patrons. The war had remade the world; now, Masaryk and Beneš dared assume that the postwar order would remake its citizens, helping further that naturally progressive political development which seemed to be asserting itself all over the Continent. The two Czech leaders would aid these tendencies via propaganda, which would teach Czechoslovaks about their proper place in the world and the meaning of their national history, and which would teach the world about the importance of Czechoslovakia as a cornerstone of a peaceful, democratic Central Europe.

Thus Masaryk and Beneš had complementary tasks ahead. Civic education, via propaganda and the mass media, was urgently needed. Czechs had to be taught how to be democratic citizens, and about the new Europe in which they found themselves; Europeans had to be taught about Czechoslovakia, its history and its potential. Propaganda work abroad had to be balanced and matched with propaganda work at home, and they would need to control both message and venue. These priorities implied a larger need. Masaryk and Beneš's wartime work might be rendered useless if Czech voters and parliamentary leaders failed to understand that national politics now had international stakes. To counter the established parties, with decades of organization and considerable resources, not least among them their party newspapers, Masaryk and Beneš would need their own system of loyal institutions, colleagues, and resources. Without these, they might be limited to figureheads, unable to affect domestic politics in a meaningful way. For all these reasons, even as the war ended, Masaryk and Beneš began to create the basic structure of the powerful, informal political organization they would control throughout the postwar years: the Castle.

2

The Castle

[I]t is genuinely possible to serve politics, actively and practically, while not serving a single party.
—*Karel Čapek*

I try to supervise everything.
—*Tomáš Garrigue Masaryk*

The myth of the First Czechoslovak Republic rested on an unspoken understanding that Czechoslovakia, alone in East-Central Europe, was a true democracy, whose leaders were devoted to democratic ideals and practice. Most of Czechoslovakia's neighbors were authoritarian regimes by the mid-1920s, making this judgment seem plausible. But no system of government is pure. Czechoslovak democracy contained the usual messiness and imperfection, swept as far as possible out of sight. Playing its role in that democratic impurity was the Castle, Masaryk and Beneš's powerful, informal political organization. By 1922, the Castle was one of two extraconstitutional power centers to dominate Czechoslovak political culture until the end of the First Republic; the other was the equally unofficial group of parliamentary bosses, the Pětka (the Five), frequently opposed to the Castle. Masaryk used his personal charisma and influence, together with Castle organizations, to evade the constitutional limitations on his presidential power. This chapter is the first of two to turn to the role the Castle played in the nitty-gritty of Czechoslovak domestic politics. Focusing on challenges to the Castle and its responses allows us to assess "mythic politics"—the Castle's battle over political symbolism as a proxy realm of contestation over actual political power.

In the 1890 Program of the Realist Party, Masaryk and his cofounders had resolved to work for the "moral, intellectual and material elevation (of the nation)," and in particular, its "inner strengthening."[1] As president of the interwar republic, Masaryk remained faithful to this same vision, shaping a public persona as the nation's educator and model of enlightenment. The Castle was to provide Czechoslovakia's source of political guidance and clarity, helping its citizens navigate a new, more complex era. Masaryk and Beneš were deeply concerned very early on about Czechoslovaks' ability to *odrakouštět se*—to de-Austrianize themselves. This term indicated the process of becoming independent citizens, by which Czechs and Slovaks would end their centuries-long habits of civic passivity or hostility developed under Austria-Hungary.[2] However, in Masaryk's and Beneš's view, this transition from subjecthood to electorate would need to take place under the watchful guidance of an enlightened political elite, whose ideas would help the citizens of the new state to orient themselves in a changed Europe.

Struggles between the Castle and Parliament marked the interwar period. Nominally, the preponderance of power within the interwar republic was allocated to Parliament, the young country's only directly elected institution. This emphasis on the legislative emerged naturally from the overwhelming support for "universal, direct, and secret suffrage" as opposed to the limited voting rights and parliamentary domination by the emperor under Austria; the postwar tide of revolutionary democracy based on councils also emphasized the importance of the collective. In the first, provisional constitution, the Czechoslovak president was a figurehead, easily controlled by the National Assembly and even the cabinet. His veto could be overridden. A cabinet minister had to sign onto any executive act by the president.[3] But Castle allies ensured that the 1920 revised constitution granted Masaryk greater power, despite the desires of party leaders to turn him and his office into little more than a symbol.[4] Both Masaryk and Beneš felt forcefully that in contrast to the British model of democracy, with an ornamental head of state, Czechoslovakia would need an active president.[5] The Castle position was defended by various of the constitution's framers, including journalist and parliamentarian Jan Herben and attorneys Václav Bouček and Přemysl Šámal, both former Realists and *Maffie* members.[6]

Historian Jiří Kunc has noted that this battle, so often depicted as either a personal dispute between Masaryk and the party leaders or a conflict between the domestic and foreign resistance against the Habsburg monarchy, was neither of those things. Rather, it was a clash over the nature of Czechoslovak politics and government, a skirmish common to many democracies: would the parties dominate, or would the executive?[7] From the 1870s on, the largest Czech parties had resisted and mistrusted executive power, jealously guarding their territory and privileges. For his part, Masaryk had long disliked what he saw as the parties' excessive bureaucratism and internecine warfare. Even when Czechoslovakia's parliament managed to remain stable and orderly, Masaryk and Beneš tended to doubt its wisdom and its leaders' dedication to the ideals of democracy and Versailles.

Like Karel Havlíček Borovský, writes historian H. Gordon Skilling, "Masaryk continued to believe that parliamentary politics was not the only kind of political work, and was often not the most effective... [way to] raise the political level of the people."[8] Masaryk's own party, the Realists, had been founded with the explicit hope of providing moral leadership and intellectual clarity to Habsburg politics.[9] The Castle justified its interwar political dominance with similar claims. Masaryk's sense that a strong presidency could be more responsive to the people's will, more truly democratic than the parties' control of Parliament, led him to establish his own office, and later the Castle, as a political force against Parliament.[10] The Castle became a symbolic bully pulpit, a means for the executive branch of the government to contest or subvert Parliament without revising the constitution or moving toward overt authoritarianism.

Masaryk repeatedly won his battles with Parliament, both as the constitution was being revised and throughout the interwar period. No party leader commanded authority sufficient to counter the president; the First Republic has been termed a "presidential democracy."[11] Masaryk could appoint and dismiss ministers, even the prime minister. He could dissolve Parliament. He could appoint large groups of civil servants. In short, the First Republic's constitutional checks and balances were few, and were relatively easily subverted by the executive branch. The First Republic's much-vaunted adherence to democracy was in fact quite limited, far more oligarchical than democratic; perhaps the most appropriate descriptive term would be Walter Lippmann's "managed democracy."[12] Masaryk was one of the First Republic's primary managers, thanks to the Castle's personnel, its connections, and the institutions and funding it controlled. And, continuing his earlier political habits, he still saw himself as nonpartisan, or perhaps a better term would be suprapartisan, deriving his political ideals from philosophical and moral imperatives rather than party ideology. The Castle also saw itself as suprapartisan, identifying itself unproblematically with the good of the republic as a whole.

Czechoslovak parliamentarians and political journalists began discussing publicly the Castle's existence as a rival political institution, practically a party without a mass base, as early as 1920.[13] Originally, the term referred to people assisted by the president as well as his supporters. The Castle encompassed the presidential chancellery, Beneš's Ministry of Foreign

Affairs, and departments in other ministries, such as the Ministry of the Interior. Masaryk and Beneš also drew on discretionary funds awarded them by Parliament, as well as their own personal wealth, and their long friendships with many influential figures, among them powerful bankers, parliamentary leaders, and cabinet ministers, whom they could trust to defend the Castle's perspective or goals. The Castle's political methods also included publishing articles in loyal newspapers, written by faithful journalists or placed by Castle-friendly editors.[14] This is not to say that the Castle always operated as a unified bloc. Within the Castle, there were wings to the left and right; frequently individuals and institutions worked at what seemed like cross-purposes, or remained ignorant of related initiatives.[15] Nonetheless, as a whole the Castle comprised an extraordinarily powerful nexus of information gathering, fund-raising, and direct political influence.

Abstractly, the Castle can be understood to represent various ideologies and policies. First, the Castle stood for the political ideas and intentions—especially in the realm of foreign policy—articulated by Masaryk and Beneš. In this way, defense of the Castle also implied defense of the country's orientation toward Western Europe against politicians who would weaken or realign Czechoslovakia's attachments to its Western guarantors. The most prominent of these was Karel Kramář, who refused to abandon the idea of a Slavic federation under the Russian throne. In 1919, he argued that the Czechoslovak Legions in Siberia ought to be brought back to their country not via Vladivostok but via Moscow, where they could aid the Russian White forces in fighting the Bolsheviks. The Poles were fighting the Bolsheviks, Kramář insisted; once the anti-Bolshevik Russian forces were "liberated," without Czechoslovak help, they would not be quick to forget who had deserted them in their hour of need.[16] Kramář and his National Democratic Party quickly moved rightward, retaining some neo-Slav dreams and a large measure of Czech chauvinism, leavened with deep suspicion of the new president and foreign minister. Weakening Kramář, his party, and the Right generally became a linchpin of Masaryk and Beneš's plans to lead Czechoslovakia down the path toward the West instead of the Slavic East, as well as toward the values Masaryk and Beneš believed the West represented: reason, democracy, tolerance, enlightenment, civilization—and, of course, security.

More specifically, the Castle dedicated itself to the new Europe constructed by the postwar peace treaties—a logical association given that Czechoslovakia herself had been constructed by those treaties—and a resistance to any effort to change the postwar order. The Castle was particularly concerned about an *Anschluss* between Germany and Austria, which would leave Czechoslovakia ringed on three sides by states opposed to Versailles.

Beneš's diplomatic efforts centered on concluding bilateral agreements with other European states as well as embedding Czechoslovakia firmly in European and global organizations such as the Little Entente, the diplomatic alliance Beneš crafted to unite Czechoslovakia, Yugoslavia, and Romania, and the League of Nations. Domestically, Castle affiliation meant invoking Masaryk's and Beneš's position as founders and liberators of the new state, against the claims of the Czech politicians who had remained in Czechoslovakia during the war. Those politicians led Parliament and the parties. Within Parliament, Castle policy tended to support the center-Left and work to deny legitimacy to conservatives, especially those who failed to chastise—or who joined—the radical right: Czech fascists, and to a lesser extent Slovak and German autonomists. Since the Castle claimed to embody not just the Czechoslovak state but also a democratic ideal, Castle defenders portrayed any opposition to the Castle, Masaryk, or Beneš as an assault on democracy and stability, a betrayal of the country and nation, and a step toward fascism and dictatorship.

Both the Castle and the battles it waged over ideology, policy, politicians, and history resist simplistic summary. As historian Antonín Klímek has written, the Castle was simultaneously an ideological stance, an "atmosphere," a shifting set of institutions and characters, and domestic and international political agendas, all with Masaryk and Beneš at their center.[17] This chapter presents the origins and structure of Castle institutions, with the goal of explaining the different components of the Castle machine, and how they all worked together to articulate and propagate Castle ideology and policy. This activity almost always involved conflict: members of the Castle often disagreed, and parliamentarians never granted the Castle a completely open road. Its efforts and obstacles in establishing a functional political organization help us understand Masaryk and Beneš's approach to mythmaking, their limitations, and their opponents—who had their own myths to craft, grudges to nurse, and allies to tend.

The Political Playing Field

The history of the Castle requires revisiting the tumultuous early years of the First Czechoslovak Republic. Like the rest of the continent, Czechoslovakia experienced postwar political turmoil and economic hardship. By war's end, Austria-Hungary had been stripped of food, fuel, and consumer goods: prices for basic foodstuffs and daily necessities had skyrocketed.[18] The new Czechoslovak republic lacked a functioning transportation network and a well-integrated agricultural and industrial market system; it kept most of Austria-Hungary's industry but lost the empire's traditional markets.[19] At first, Czechoslovakia retained the inflated Austrian crown even as Vienna and Budapest desperately printed more bills. A drastic 1919 deflationary currency reform stabilized the state, at great cost to the middle and lower classes.[20] The American Relief Administration sent 6 million dollars' worth of food and clothing to the charity Československá dítě peče (Czechoslovak Child Relief), chaired by Masaryk's daughter Alice Masaryková, which ran more than 2,000 soup kitchens through 1920, feeding 500,000 children daily, particularly in urban areas.[21] Meanwhile, Czechoslovak troops responded to socialist and nationalist uprisings in Slovakia, Subcarpathian Ruthenia, and the former duchy of Těšín.[22]

Although Czechoslovakia avoided revolutions and coups d'état, its political structure contained undemocratic elements from the outset. The "revolutionary" provisional assembly conveniently elided issues of minority representation; only 40 out of 256 seats were granted to the Slovaks, and none at all to the Germans, Hungarians, Poles, or Ruthenians. Many of the Slovak seats were filled by "nonpartisan" Czechs, such as Alice Masaryková.[23] The provisional assembly then passed important legislation, from the constitution to the Language Law, meaning that Czechoslovakia's minorities were not consulted on the establishment of the state. In fact, all of Czechoslovakia's peoples were de facto denied input on this process; Czechoslovakia was the only country in interwar Eastern Europe to eliminate a referendum on the country's constitution after its drafting.[24] Minority relations remained tense, despite the relatively generous guarantees made to Czechoslovakia's national minorities in the 1920 constitution. Czech-German riots were common in cities and provinces during the republic's first few years.[25] Often rioting was directed against the country's Jews as well, as in November 1920, when rioters broke into the Jewish Town Hall in the center of Prague, ruining furnishings and paintings and destroying documents.[26] Still, the constitution was consistent with others in Europe: it established a bicameral parliament, which would elect the president; suffrage and civil rights were equally guaranteed all citizens, and minority protections followed international precedent established in the Treaty of Saint-Germain.[27]

The political shift to the left following the Great War wrought two substantial changes in Czech parliamentary politics. The first affected the Social Democrats, the country's largest postwar party. In 1920–1921, the party's large, vocal, and discontented left wing seceded to form the Czechoslovak Communist Party. The Social Democrats in time recovered from this blow, although they never regained their early postwar levels of voter support. The conservative National Democrats were also devastated. Previously the States'-Rights Nationally Democratic Party [*sic*], the National Democrats were the last incarnation of the powerful Young Czech coalition party that had long dominated nineteenth-century Czech politics. Even before the republic, the Young Czechs' economic and social conservatism had cost them voters; the Agrarians outstripped them by the 1880s, and the Social Democrats by 1918. Still, after 1918, many veterans of the nineteenth-century Czech national movement hoped the National Democrats might unite various factions under one political roof and create a center-Right party. The National Democrats began the interwar period strongly, occupying 46 of the 256 seats in the first National Assembly and chairing the financial and industrial ministries. Party leader Kramář served as the country's first prime minister and traveled to Paris to participate in the Paris Peace Conference. But in the 1919 elections, the National Democrats garnered only 9.6 percent of the vote, the smallest number of any of the main Czech parties. Masaryk tried to delay Kramář from stepping down, and insisted on keeping the other National Democratic ministers in the government.[28] Kramář, who had distrusted Masaryk since the 1880s, suspected the president had a hand in his misfortune. Their personal antipathy increased as the National Democrats' electoral returns diminished: although the party retained influence among Czechoslovakia's financial and industrial elite, it also moved hard to the right, worrying the Castle and adding to its distrust of Parliament.[29]

Earlier historical depictions of Parliament as the center of Czechoslovak politics have been replaced with a more cynical view of parliamentary goings-on.[30] Voting was compulsory and voters chose among parties, not among individual politicians: they could not alter the party candidate lists. Elections seemed—and to an extent, were—unimportant.[31] In fact, even rank-and-file members of Parliament had trouble materially influencing their parties' development after a 1919 dispute within the Social Democratic Party. Two Social Democrats tried to form a splinter party while retaining their seats; the party leadership argued successfully that the party should retain the seats and distribute them to other Social Democrats. This set a precedent: parliamentary mandates belonged to the party, not the individual politician. Parliamentary leaders insisted on absolute discipline. A politician voting his conscience rather than the party line became a pariah. At best, he would be scolded and threatened, at worst replaced.[32] Internal dissenters tended to join or form rival parties, with the exception of the Agrarians, after 1921 the country's largest interwar party; the Agrarians managed to retain their left and right wings and maintain a limited degree of internal pluralism.

The leaders' ironclad control over their parties was mirrored in their hold on Parliament, thanks to the formation of the Pětka. This regular, unofficial, highly secretive meeting of political party bosses determined Parliament's course and was a formidable factor in Czech political culture. The leaders of the five largest Czech political parties began meeting informally in 1920 at the suggestion of Agrarian leader Antonín Švehla, to limit the impact of the chaos within the Social Democrats, and the related general strike on Parliament.[33] Perceptions of early parliamentary anarchy were widespread: in 1921, "German deputies amused themselves by throwing stinkbombs in the Parliament, and . . . the Czech and Slovak parties found it easier to quarrel than to agree on constructive policies."[34] When President Masaryk fell ill that year, the need for the Pětka became all the more clear. Historians have concluded that the republic's early upheavals and its relatively insignificant experience with parliamentary democracy made the Pětka both a necessary stabilizing force and a source of oligarchical, unconstitutional power, transforming both parliament and government into a rubber stamp for Pětka decisions.[35] Also, the Pětka's insistence on pragmatic problem solving lessened its ability to contend with the state's pressing long-term problems, such as full integration of Czechoslovakia's minorities and ensuring even-handed industrial or economic development of the state's different regions.[36]

Initially, Masaryk approved of the Pětka; he also considered parliamentary debate "raw" and approved of disciplined expert leadership to bring about compromise.[37] He also trusted its members, especially the National Democrat Alois Rašín, Švehla, and the National Socialist deputy chairman Jiří Stříbrný. But the president had clearly envisioned the Pětka's role to be limited, merely to coordinate parliamentary activity; moreover, he believed that Parliament itself would for the most part follow the Castle's wishes and direction. This proved naive. When the Pětka contested the president's authority, Masaryk countered by opposing the Pětka.

Masaryk was equally concerned with parliamentary disorder during this period and considered establishing a directorate of himself, Beneš, and the members of the National Committee to lead a brief dictatorship in 1919. Such a governing structure would allow for the resolution of "many burning questions."[38] Many years later, in conversation with Karel Čapek, Masaryk claimed that dictatorship could be more truly populist than parliamentary rule. "When the war ended, I thought: we will have a republic, but at the beginning [it would have] dictatorial tendencies. . . . I [was] not worried [about it]. . . . Dictatorship interrupts Parliament, but makes possible the rule of the people; therefore it makes democracy possible."[39] In fact, suspicion of Parliament was common in the First Republic, a hangover from Czech mistrust of the Austrian Reichsrat and Diets.[40] Even longtime Prime Minister Švehla preferred to prepare legislative agendas in the relative ease and seclusion of the Pětka. Švehla appears to have attended only about one-third of the parliamentary sessions occurring under his watch as prime minister.[41]

The Castle and the Pětka distrusted one another. Each accused the other of undemocratic tendencies, and both were right. In 1925, Masaryk characterized the party leaders this way: "The parliaments are not yet representatives of the nation, the people, the masses, but of parties and basically of cliques, of influential and strong—I don't say: leading!—individuals."[42] As a counterpoise to a Parliament obsessed with dividing the spoils of power according to party affiliation and maintaining utmost control over their fiefdoms, the Castle leaders proposed beneficent rule by an enlightened, "permanently revolutionary" elite bent on transforming both government and population according to its vision.[43] In 1925, the Austrian ambassador sent back a report to Vienna that read, "Masaryk is . . . no friend of the present governing system; more and more he views the governing Pětka as an unsuitable instrument of state-machinery."[44]

One contentious issue between the Castle and the Pětka was the presidential appointment of cabinets of civil servants. When parliamentary coalitions were weak, or when they broke down completely, Masaryk's usual response was to create a "technicians' cabinet" or "cabinet of experts," of nonpartisan academics. This form of governance reached back to Czech politics under Austria.[45] Several times during the early 1920s Masaryk appointed such cabinets, usually under the leadership of Jan Černý, the minister-president of Moravia. The Pětka resisted expert cabinets not for any lack of competence but for their reliance on the president and Beneš, who was frequently the only experienced politician within them.[46] The Pětka allowed them only reluctantly, hoping first to find parliamentary solutions, which grated on Masaryk.

Another sticking point was the foreign minister himself. Beneš was one of the Pětka's most purposeful opponents during his brief tenure as prime minister from 1921 to 1922; the Pětka leaders returned the open opposition, nearly paralyzing the government. Unlike Masaryk, Beneš never really learned to work with the Pětka.[47] Additionally, Pětka leaders were displeased by Masaryk's unconditional support of Beneš. Kramář particularly resented the changes wrought by Masaryk to the presidential articles in the constitution, paving the way for Beneš to succeed his mentor. Senators were required to be forty-five years old; the president, however, had only to be thirty-five. This stipulation ensured that Beneš, thirty-four years old in 1918, would be eligible for the presidency whenever Masaryk decided to resign.[48] Kramář and other Pětka leaders had suspicions about Beneš's foreign policy. Finally, Beneš was simply a safer target than the country's beloved father-president. Masaryk was protected by his august age, personal charisma, service to the nation, and even legislation: paragraph 11 of the 1923 Law in Defense of the Republic threatened citizens with imprisonment for insulting the president, exposing him to public ridicule, or publicly incriminating him.[49]

All this said, quite often the Castle and the Pětka (and the Pětka's successors, such as the Šestka [the Six] and the Osmička [the Eight]) held their collective noses and worked together, even while attempting to lessen each other's influence and power. Generally, the Castle's relationship to Parliament and the Pětka can be characterized as a combination of cooperation and mutual challenge. They struggled throughout the 1920s over the makeup of government cabinets, the passage of important legislation, and the participation of the country's national minorities in the government. But there was considerable common ground. Masaryk, while frustrated at having his will thwarted, trusted Švehla, the leading Pětka member, and was willing to delegate domestic questions to him. After 1928, Švehla's successors seemed willing to defer to Masaryk: for example, before the 1929 elections, Masaryk essentially dictated to Agrarian Prime Minister Udržal the makeup of the new ruling coalition, and got his wish, as well as the ability to select and dismiss cabinet ministers until 1932.[50] With the onset of the Great Depression, which devastated the Czechoslovak economy as it did the rest of Europe, as well as the increasing threat to Czechoslovakia from abroad, the Castle-Pětka conflict virtually ceased.[51]

The Castle thus operated against a relatively predictable parliamentary backdrop, tightly controlled by the ruling parties. The parties' refusal to brook genuine debate or opposition on the floor of Parliament allowed the Castle to position itself as the country's only loyal opposition. Both sides claimed to be truer to an ideal democratic practice. Švehla, for example, once chided Castle ally Karel Čapek for being "one of those intellectuals who preach freedom and democracy, and who at the same time would want to get rid of parties. . . . Removing the parties would mean dictatorship; democracy is based on the parties."[52] Of course, the Pětka could be seen as a dictatorship of the parties. Masaryk and Beneš were no more interested in true populism, believing democracy to follow from a set of philosophical principles and to be best enacted by efficient elites. In this view the importance of a democratically structured state disappears.[53]

The Presidential Chancellery

Masaryk's presidential chancellery (in Czech, the Kancelář presidenta republiky, or KPR) was a central Castle institution. In fact, the chancellery's importance to Masaryk was such that he insisted on its creation almost immediately upon his 1919 return to the country, when his authority was practically limitless. The chancellery was located physically inside Prague Castle, near the president's residence. Masaryk tended to choose close friends to direct it. In 1919–1920, it was headed by a triumvirate of Masaryk allies: Otakar Webr, Josef Koschin, and Augustín Popelka. Realist and former *gymnasium* instructor Jiří St. Guth-Jarkovský helped craft official court ceremony. In 1920, Masaryk chose friend and former Realist colleague Přemysl Šámal as chancellor, who oversaw a substantial expansion.[54] Webr stayed on as head of administrative affairs for the chancellery, working with legislative and political head Josef Schieszl and František Blažek, responsible for the KPR and Castle's physical plant, police guard, and archive. The chancellery also added a military affairs division. By 1925, the chancellery employed 213 people.[55]

Aside from these official staffers, there were others who collaborated with the chancellery—or played more influential roles—without a title. Foremost among these was Vasil Kaprálek Škrach, the president's librarian, secretary, and most important confidant. Disliked by other Castle personalities, Škrach's influence over the president was marked, particularly after the late 1920s.[56] Masaryk's children were also at the heart of the Castle. His son Jan helped establish the chancellery, then joined the presidium of the Foreign Ministry, eventually becoming ambassador to Great Britain. Upon the death of Masaryk's wife, Charlotte Garrigue, in 1923, his younger daughter Alice took on the role of Czechoslovakia's First Lady, devoting herself to her father and to the Castle.[57] Finally, Masaryk's close friend Václav Bouček, a Prague attorney and former *Čas* writer, also entered chancellery affairs.[58] Conversely, some highly ranked officials within the chancellery bore their positions in name only, such as Josef Patejdl, a former Legionnaire who was named head of Slovak and Subcarpathian Rus affairs in 1920. That same year, he became the head of the Union of Czechoslovak Legionnaires, with some 40,000 members. Patejdl did little for the chancellery but ensured a close relation between the Castle and the Legionnaires.[59]

Like the Republic itself, the chancellery staff was divided by nationality, political affiliation, and generation. Masaryk required that the chancellery staff contain Slovaks and, after 1926, when some German-speaking parties entered the governing coalition in Parliament, Germans as well. They did not always succeed. Chancellor Šámal complained that the most capable were alienated by the relatively low salary, and that the selection process was "politically hellish." In March 1927, the Slovak L'udak (Populist) Party made an official visit to Šámal to request that at least the head of the division for Slovak issues be a Slovak. (They also brought along their own candidate, who was refused.)[60] Party affiliation mattered less. Šámal and Josef Schieszl were not the only KPR staffers to abjure party membership and identify themselves as the president's men.[61] Observers noted that the real divisions within the chancellery were not based on nationality or party but rather between the newer employees, who called themselves Czechoslovaks and felt they better understood the needs of the new republic, and the older, more highly ranked employees, who considered themselves more capable, but whom the younger ones labeled Austrian (*Rakušák*)—an insult to Czech patriots. The self-described "old soldiers" were more politically conservative; some observers called them "centers of reaction" and warned that there were many of them within the Czechoslovak government, not just within the chancellery.[62] One of these was Masaryk's trusted political chief Schiezsl, who by the 1930s was writing in his diary about the bankruptcy of liberal democracy.[63]

Parliamentary leaders were from the beginning concerned about the chancellery as a possible alternate center of power. Upon approving its budgetary allocation for 1919, parliamentary leaders cautioned that the chancellery should not become a shadow government. But the law did little to prevent this from happening. It specified only that the chancellery ought to concern itself with "issues which fell to the sphere of competence of the president of the republic." Parliament also allowed Masaryk and the heads of the chancellery essentially unlimited power over hiring and firing.[64] Despite these initial fears, chancellery staff often spent considerable time on the floor and in the back rooms of the parliamentary building, obtaining information for the president.[65]

The most important characteristic the chancellery staffers shared was unconditional loyalty to Masaryk. This sometimes came at a price, making the KPR into an echo chamber in which Masaryk was told what he seemed to want to hear, or what he himself had already said. Contemporaries complained that the chancellery was staffed with cold bureaucrats who hid behind the president's authority. Some called the chancellery a camarilla, protecting Masaryk from real engagement with the government and country he led. Ironically, the party most opposed to the chancellery was the Social Democrats, who tended to support the Castle in most other issues and for whom Masaryk himself was rumored to vote.[66] The party leaders consistently complained that the chancellery abetted Masaryk's tendencies to act like a monarch, and that chancellery staffers engaged in political scheming and prejudiced the president by giving him false information.

In 1922, in response to parliamentary roadblocks impeding Castle initiatives, the chancellery began actively soliciting journalists, high-ranking officials, representatives of various political parties (including those opposed to the Castle), members of important organizations and associations, and Masaryk's and Beneš's intimates: thus came into being the "highly effective and dreaded" informational network that helped the Castle maintain its power.[67] Castle agents and informants reported on activities within each political party and in the personal lives of politicians, at times even acquiring medical records. The Castle was also able to draw on intelligence departments in other ministries, such as the Ministry of the Interior. These activities were paid for by Masaryk's and Beneš's considerable discretionary funds, in addition to their own personal wealth.[68] Masaryk and Beneš did not hesitate to use the information they gathered, to the point of publishing it when deemed necessary.[69] Castle agents sometimes even attempted to "directly [buy] the sympathy or allegiance of individual politicians or even whole parties," as in an abortive attempt to purchase the support of the Živnostenská strana (Tradesmen's Party) in 1925.[70] Newspapers provided information and logistical assistance: informants dropped envelopes into accessible mailboxes in the editorial or advertising offices of various Castle-friendly newspapers, from which the messages would be quietly taken up to the Castle.[71]

The chancellery played a crucial, and independent, role in Czechoslovak interwar politics. It quickly grew to a substantial institution and the center of Castle activity, coordinating and monitoring the press and political culture; its staff advocated for the Castle in the cabinet, in the back rooms of Parliament, and the drawing rooms of the powerful. Few interwar politicians ignored a summons to the Castle. The Social Democrats' fears were fulfilled: the chancellery did function as a parallel government, one entirely within Masaryk and Beneš's control.

Zamini: The Ministry of Foreign Affairs

Another significant Castle center of power was Beneš's Foreign Ministry, located on Loretánské náměstí, a short uphill walk from Prague Castle. Among its other responsibilities, the ministry took up the two tasks the Castle regarded as having created the Czechoslovak state: foreign relations and propaganda abroad. Beneš's ministry, like the French Foreign Ministry on which it was modeled, was divided into six sections. The First Section included Beneš's office, as well as the protocol and personnel departments. The Second, or political, Section, the "executive arm of foreign policy," controlled the diplomatic network. The Third Section dealt with propaganda and intelligence gathering, both defined quite widely, as well as supervision of the ministry's discretionary funds.[72] The economic, consular, and legal divisions of the ministry all had their own sections as well. The ministry was known to political insiders by its Italianate nickname, Zamini, in fact a compression of its full Czech title: Ministerstvo zahraničních věci.

Beneš and Masaryk kept tight control over the Foreign Ministry and handpicked its staff. Beneš had to build a new foreign service, immediately and from the ground up, in a state whose peoples had previously had little contact with the world outside the empire. The Czechs, viewed as problematic under the Habsburgs, had with a few exceptions been barred from entering diplomatic service. The few Czechs who had worked for the old regime could not be counted upon to be loyal to the new state. Relatively few citizens of the new Czechoslovakia were even fully bilingual in Czech and German at an educated level; knowledge of foreign languages was rarer still. Since Beneš did not return from Paris and Geneva until 1920, President Masaryk began staffing the Foreign Ministry. Rudolf Künzl-Jizerský, ambassador to Romania during the latter part of the interwar period, describes being interviewed for the diplomatic corps in late 1918 by the president himself.[73] With Beneš frequently gone on diplomatic business, Masaryk remained actively engaged in the activities of Beneš's ministry, especially the undertakings of the Third Section.[74] The ministry's daily administration was left to an elite group of diplomats and bureaucrats, among them Masaryk's son Jan before his elevation to ambassador to Great Britain.

Zamini staffers were overwhelmingly Czech, drawing from the professoriate, the domestic and foreign wartime resistance, and notably from the ranks of Legionnaires from the Russian, Italian, and French fronts.[75] A few local civil servants were boosted into the ministry's ranks, as were a select group of appointees from the larger political parties or financial institutions. But as in the KPR, politics, ethnicity, and prior professional background were relatively unimportant.[76] Zamini employees were expected to be, above all, competent, dedicated to the Czech national cause as manifested by the creation of the Czechoslovak state, and loyal to the Castle. For example, Jan Hájek, a former writer for *Čas* and an important colleague for Beneš throughout the war, became the Third Section's chief officer and the head of the Czechoslovak propaganda effort.

The Third Section was one of the Castle's most important centers of publicity, information gathering, and strategizing. It also strove to be an important voice shaping postwar civil society at home. Its goal was to help delineate a new Czechoslovak identity, in terms supportive of Castle policies, particularly foreign policy; this makes Third Section propaganda an important, and as yet overlooked, source of information about Castle policy and practice. The Third Section wanted to orient Czech domestic opinion toward the democratic West. To be a Czechoslovak, according to the Third Section, meant thinking in terms of Western Europe instead of the East. It meant comparing oneself to a Frenchman instead of an Austrian or a Serb; it meant being able to knowledgeably discuss the new British government or the latest League of Nations initiative at parties. The Third Section's task was to teach Czechoslovaks—especially influential businessmen and political figures who had previously supported the monarchy, Pan-Slavism, or the Young Czechs—about themselves and about the world. The Third Section's other intended audience was West European public opinion. Beneš planned to target especially the French and the British, whom he hoped to secure as Czechoslovakia's Western guarantors. Since the new League of Nations was to be housed in Geneva, the Swiss were also involved. Finally, the Third Section was to encourage the efforts of Czechoslovaks abroad, especially in the United States, in making their new homeland part of public discussion.

As the needs of the state became clearer, the Third Section's sense of its mission widened accordingly. By 1923, the Third Section described its tasks grandly: it was to be "the best and safest source of information about the Czechoslovak Republic," responsible for entertaining visiting foreigners, acting as a clearinghouse of information for visiting journalists, and publishing foreign-language magazines, brochures, and other information for foreigners. The Third Section was also responsible for following antistate propaganda at home and abroad, and "paralyzing" or at least countering it. Finally, the Third Section was to concern itself with improving direct, personal relations between Czechoslovak citizens and foreigners. It was to help create relationships with leading personalities abroad, in politics, academics, art, journalism, industry, and finance; it was to send leading Czechoslovaks abroad as much as possible, encouraging trips for study as well as for openly propagandistic purposes.[77]

The Third Section also served as the government's semiofficial publishing house, crafting newspapers, pamphlets, and other publicity materials in all the major European languages. These efforts in cultural diplomacy had their roots in Masaryk's and Beneš's wartime experiences. Beneš's *Gazette de Prague* became *L'Europe Centrale* in 1927. Zamini created the German-language *Prager Presse* in 1921, followed by the English-language weekly *Central European Observer* in 1923, and the Russian monthly *Tsentralnaia Evropa* in 1927.[78] The Third Section also published the Czech-language *Zahraniční politika*, with essays on foreign politics, international law, and the world economy, intended for academics and policy aficionados, and edited by Hájek himself.[79] Many of its contributors were Foreign Ministry employees, themselves former academics. In addition to print materials, the Third Section ran Radio Central/Central European Radio/Radio de l'Europe Centrale, an Orbis-controlled radio syndicate based in Geneva, Switzerland.[80]

Of these efforts in cultural diplomacy, Zamini was most worried about the *Prager Presse* as a counterweight to the anti-Czech propaganda pouring out of Reich German and Czech German papers. The worst of these, the Third Section concluded, were the Viennese *Tschechenspiegel*, the *Völkerbund* published in the Czech spa town of Karlový Vary (Karlsbad), the Sudeten German Union's *Zeitschrift*, and *Bohemia*, published in Prague itself, which the Third Section feared would make a particularly strong impression in France and London. Still worse, Max Brod's *Prager Tagblatt* and the Viennese *Neue Freie Presse*, long one of Europe's most respected German-language dailies, were running inaccurate economic statistics (claimed a worried Third Section analyst), which might dissuade potential investors. In fact, because the Czech state lacked other mouthpieces in major languages, the *Prager Tagblatt* was being circulated by Czechoslovak consulates.[81] This early concern about the *Prager Tagblatt* resolved itself relatively quickly. The *Tagblatt*, published by center-Left German Jews (most prominently Brod, known for his later efforts on behalf of Franz Kafka's literary works and reputation and his interest in Czech culture), remained the republic's most important German-language newspaper, and tended to support the Castle. In fact, some *Prager Tagblatt* correspondents worked directly with Zamini.[82]

Still, Zamini wanted to found its own German-language paper. Its *Prager Presse* provides a useful window into the Third Section's belief in rational exposition at the heart of successful propaganda. As in the First World War, the Czechoslovaks would once again position themselves as a source of truth for the unenlightened at home and the suspicious or mistaken abroad. "The state needs a means of protecting its interests against Germans abroad, [who are] prejudiced and one-sided," wrote a Third Section analyst, defending plans to produce the *Prager Presse*. The language here directly recalls Masaryk's and Beneš's understanding of wartime propaganda: simply expose the facts, to awaken readers to their prior blindness. "Especially in Germany and Austria it is necessary to [make public] . . . the true international standing of [our] Germans after the war, so that they can recall their prewar thoughts and have the opportunity to understand the errors they made."[83] As the paper's reputation grew, the Third Section hoped, so too would Czechoslovakia's reputation for reputable journalism. Czechoslovak analysis of Central European relations would counter those of Germany, Austria, or Hungary in European opinion.[84] Zamini would distribute the paper free of charge, at least at first, to leading political, literary, and financial figures in European countries.

The Third Section planners intended the *Prager Presse* to remain distant from the Prague political press, which they saw as coarsened by polemicizing and scandalmongering. If the *Prager Presse* entered the fray, it might interest a foreign audience less and would inadvertently publicize abroad Prague journalism's worst characteristics. Instead, the Third Section authors wrote, the *Prager Presse* would strive to present information unbiased by partisan stances or lowly arguments over domestic trivia. Its overall goals were, in typically didactic Castle fashion, to "make a vivid and genuine impression abroad, and morally to improve [society] at home."[85]

The *Prager Presse* appeared on the scene with an appeal for tolerance, unity, and energetic commitment to Czechoslovakia and the new Europe. The Third Section's hopes of attracting Czechoslovak Germans are subtly apparent. "[S]ubscribe to a cutting-edge daily newspaper embodying a new spirit," its advertising flyer exhorted. In the new postwar era, "it behooves us all, finally, to abandon all the old animosities, disputes, and differences—whether national, social, political, economic, or cultural—and with common strength to serve the reconstruction of our communal life." The paper called "all honest, capable, hard-working, and creative people to the great task of uniting in cultural brotherhood," and promised to avoid Czech chauvinism in favor of an "intelligent nationalism." The *Prager Presse* would be a truly European daily, equally useful for "the worker; the bureaucrat; the white-collar worker; the industrialist and entrepreneur; the intellectual [*der Geistes-Arbeiter*]," and concentrating on economics and foreign affairs.[86] But the *Prager Presse* was immediately identified as Zamini's organ by other Prague newspapers, which were horrified by the prospect of government-sponsored competition with seemingly bottomless financial resources. The *Prager Tagblatt* remained the most important German-language paper in the country, although the *Prager Presse* did develop a dedicated audience of loyal readers abroad, and respectable circulation figures as well as influence in Prague elite circles.[87] Still, after 1927, the paper stopped publishing a Prague evening edition and focused overwhelmingly on its foreign audience.[88]

The Third Section published its newspapers, and much else besides, through Orbis, its semiprivate publishing house established in 1923. Zamini had hoped to collaborate with one of the established Prague publishing houses, but when that proved impossible, it created its own, studding Orbis's board of trustees with leading figures from Czechoslovak finance and industry, academic, political, and bureaucratic circles.[89] The Third Section intended to keep Orbis partly private, funded and controlled by the state but with the appearance of a private press. No one was fooled. In early 1923, *Rudé právo*, the Communist daily, informed its readers about the ministry's new publishing firm. It had spent 15 million crowns just in its first year of existence, *Rudé právo* claimed, most of that going to the hemorrhaging *Prager Presse*. Orbis and the ministry were going to pour another 10 million into the *Prager Presse* in 1923, wrote the *Rudé právo* reporter, and the directors of Orbis were said to receive king's ransoms for salaries.[90] But Orbis was a far more modest business enterprise than *Rudé právo*'s feverish prose might indicate, and the continuing debts of the *Prager Presse* strapped it still further.[91] The Third Section was forced to defend expenditures on the paper and Orbis more or less continuously throughout the interwar period. Even its own employees were divided. A pessimistic Third Section analyst from 1928 claimed that the ministry's involvement had proved problematic for Orbis and had destroyed the *Prager Presse*'s chances of exercising true influence; the ministry's insistence that the *Prager Presse* avoid partisanship meant that the paper lacked any real character.[92]

In fact, the Third Section's original goal in forming Orbis had been to protect the *Prager Presse* and its other newspapers, which were likely to lose money, with profitable activities and publications.[93] Orbis imported "newspapers, journals and contemporary magazines from the entire world," engaged in distribution for booksellers, owned its own stalls and kiosks in railway stations, and offered "leading foreign newspapers; fashion magazines of all kinds for the home, for seamstresses, fashion designers, and gentlemen's tailors." Many of Orbis's popular fashion and lifestyle journals were glossy apolitical lifestyle magazines, containing handsome photographs and relatively sparse text.

Orbis also published pro-Czechoslovak propaganda texts of all kinds. Its works described the republic's political system, minorities, history, and artistic and literary achievements, as well as the Little Entente and other facets of the post-Versailles system in Central Europe. Beneš's and Masaryk's memoirs were important Orbis books; other Orbis authors included feminist Františka Plamínková, philosopher Emanuel Rádl, professor Evžen Štern, journalist and Masaryk biographer Jan Herben, and economics professor Josef Macek. Some, although not many, Czech Germans saw their works in print thanks to Orbis: Max Brod's 1923 *Sternenhimmel* was one of them.[94] The ministry also kept in print works by foreign authors on Czechoslovakia, such as Robert Seton-Watson and Lewis Namier; various romanticized biographies of Masaryk in English and French; and reference sources, such as French-language editions of an encyclopedia of the Czechoslovak Republic. In 1926, the Third Section claimed that Beneš's ministry had had a hand in almost every book published outside Czechoslovakia on Czech topics; it had suggested topics, assisted with editing or publication, and supported authors financially, not to mention keeping unprofitable books in print while hiding this from both foreign and domestic readers.[95] "[F]oreign propaganda has greatest success if [our] bureaucratic collaboration in individual actions remains hidden[;] it is understandable that it is impossible to inform the domestic public about the breadth of this activity."[96]

In addition to publishing its own papers, the Third Section remained very involved with the Czech and foreign press. It supported Castle-loyal papers all over the republic, in particular those aimed at the country's non-Czech nationalities, and in part to counter political extremism among those nationalities. Foreign journalists on Czechoslovak soil received discounted rail travel and were regularly sent information and useful photographs from the Zamini archives.[97]

The Third Section also concentrated its efforts on social relations and friendship. Creating and improving personal relationships between influential Great Power intellectuals and representative Czechoslovaks had been a subject of concern since 1920, when it became apparent that conservative

German political cliques were using social occasions to their advantage. Rudolf Künzl-Jizerský recalled that "relations with foreign countries and mainly with diplomatic circles were almost nonexistent. . . . [T]he socially more advanced German circles [made] their way into the embassy salons and [rained] down fire and brimstone on the absent Czechs."[98]

After returning from Paris in 1920, Beneš held afternoon teas in his private apartment for foreign diplomats and prominent Praguers. Later, as Prague Castle was renovated, it was used for receptions and banquets. But unofficial socializing was important as well, as a 1923 internal Third Section document noted.

> Unfortunately, thus far [we lack] an appropriate large social center, which might concentrate the flower of our cultural, public and social life, and where this [process of] acquaintanceship might be easier and more rapid. . . . [T]he founding of a large club is under preparation; [the club] will be [organized] on an all-national [*všenárodní*] basis, after the model of an English club. [The club will include] reading rooms, writing rooms, a restaurant, rooms for conversation and gambling, top-notch service, comfortable and elegant decor.[99]

By 1925, some of the country's most prominent political and cultural figures had united behind the cause of a state-run gentlemen's club. The leaders of the movement, Castle stalwarts all, were Josef Schieszl, Beneš's wife Hana, and Vílem Pospíšil, director of the National Bank. A 1925 letter from these three, noting the participation of some fifty other notables, informed the recipient that such a club would benefit the state not only in terms of international propaganda but also in smoothing over partisanship at home: "If our social life were more cultured, our partisan battle would not take such a coarse and vulgar form. . . . In battles over public questions we are gruff and harsh only because we do not know one another."[100] In 1927, Zamini succeeded in creating such a club, another "private" institution in fact sponsored by the state. The club was simply called the Společenský klub (Social Club) and located on the stylish National Avenue, in the heart of downtown Prague.

The Third Section's activities, exemplified by the *Prager Presse*, Orbis, and the Společenský klub, demonstrate some central tenets of Castle political education. In all these activities, domestic politicking and Czechoslovakia's international standing were understood to go hand in hand. In both arenas, moral improvement and education were necessary. Finally, as during wartime, propaganda and cultural diplomacy were more effective when the state's hand was hidden. All three of these institutions were introduced to the public as private; only after they were revealed as government supported and

Castle controlled was the truth made available. Castle cultural diplomacy mirrored its assumptions about democratic politics. Electorates, whether Czechoslovak or European, needed to be led. Deception was unfortunate but often necessary, albeit only on behalf of the public good.

Prague's Partisan Press

The domestic Czech-language press was another crucially important arena of contestation. The Castle leaders, both former journalists, believed wholeheartedly in the importance of the written word in shaping attitude and action. It was in the pages of the interwar partisan press that Masaryk and Beneš defended their ideas and legacy, attacked their opponents, and reached out directly to the electorate, beyond the parties and the Pětka. The Castle also founded and tried to take over many papers and journals throughout the interwar decades, more proof of the centrality of the press to their political vision.

Czech-language journalism had burst into vibrant development in the late nineteenth century.[101] By the interwar period, the Czechoslovak press constituted a thriving, multilingual journalistic marketplace for all readers, from high- to lowbrow. Czechoslovakia's tabloid, or yellow, press did an energetic business. Fashion magazines for both men and women flourished along with Prague's budding couture *ateliery*. Journals serializing or commenting on literature, art, and even linguistics found a faithful audience.[102] In 1920, there were 2,259 periodical publications in Czechoslovakia, of which 1,521 were Czechoslovak while other ethnic groups, such as Germans, Hungarians, and Poles, published 759. By 1930 the total number of publications had risen to 3,933.[103]

However, politics had traditionally provided journalism's foundation in the Czech lands. The Czech press before the First World War had been both overwhelmingly contentious—described as "a battle of all against all"—and highly politicized. Nor did that change after the war: a 1920 survey reported that at least one-third of interwar papers identified themselves as being political.[104] The number actually sponsored by political parties was no doubt higher, since most parties published semiprofessional papers aimed at attracting different occupational groups, such as teachers or the employees of large firms like the Škoda works in Plzeň. Moreover, Czechoslovakia did not outlaw any political party, even the most extreme, until 1938; nor did the government fully repress any party's political press.

Most of the interwar political press was enthusiastically partisan, and interwar politicians viewed their party's press apparatus as acutely important.[105] Each party possessed its own daily, its own evening paper—usually closer to a sensationalist tabloid than the more august morning edition—as well as weekly opinion journals and cultural magazines aimed at women and youth, published in different cities and directed at various regions and linguistic groups all over the country, from North Bohemia to Subcarpathian Ruthenia.[106] The powerful Agrarians, by the mid-1920s the country's largest political party, owned thirteen printing houses in all by 1928, and published thirty-eight newspapers, including six dailies.[107] The Communists in 1921 published fifty-three periodicals, including seven newspapers, four of them in Czech.[108] Of the country's three largest newspaper printing firms, two of them were dominated by political parties; the Agrarians supported Novina, while the National Democrats dominated Pražská akciova tiskárna.[109] Czech-language press factionalization was mirrored by the country's other ethnicities, which also had their own well-developed partisan presses.[110]

The republic also saw "independent" newspapers, dailies that were not supported by party funds: among these were the Stránský family's *Lidové noviny*, based in Brno, and the Prague Legionnaire daily *Národní osvobození*. Independence had to do with ownership rather than American assumptions about journalistic objectivity: independents often took strong political stances, often in defense of the Castle.[111] Independent Prague German papers such as the *Prager Tagblatt* also maintained a general support for Masaryk and the center. However, journalists at independent papers were free to espouse whichever political platform they chose, rather than having to toe a party line. The support of independent newspapers could be very valuable for many reasons: these papers could of course defend particular policies, but they also were useful in creating a particular ideological atmosphere and bringing ideas into common currency. Perhaps most important, the Castle's lack of overt political control over these papers meant that support from the independents allowed the Castle to claim its ideas were attractive to a wider public.

The president and his chancellery staff paid the republic's newspapers careful attention. The KPR monitored the newspapers, evening editions, and magazines of each established governing party, in addition to those papers which represented groups hostile to the state or its public order. Papers were important political bellwethers. Information about party newspapers, whether about subscribers or a change in editorial positions, could offer valuable information about the parties themselves, and therefore about the Castle's ability to craft lasting political coalitions that might support Castle policy. Some of the Castle informants on the world of Prague journalism included such cultural luminaries as Arne Laurin, redoubtable chief editor of the government's *Prager Presse*, and Karel Čapek, novelist, playwright, and journalist-of-all-trades for *Lidové noviny*.

For the intellectuals writing in and reading its pages, the world of journalistic politics offered a chance to articulate and defend points of view, to work with like-minded writers and editors, and perhaps to develop political influence, all the while maintaining a gentlemanly distance from the electorate. The journalist, unlike the parliamentarian, could maintain intellectual independence and was not required to follow instructions or vote the party line; while he was expected to hew to it in his articles, he could at least choose the issue and the time. Also, Prague journalism—like Prague politics—was quite an intimate endeavor. Most leading politicians and cultural figures in Prague knew one another. Friends reviewed friends' novels and plays; old enemies rehashed old grievances in columns and feuilletons. Such intellectual intimacy, common in small countries with equally small intelligentsias, mirrored Prague's political incestuousness, in which bitter enemies on the floor of Parliament would chat happily at social occasions just a few hours later.[112]

Yet this discussion neglects perhaps the most important characteristic of interwar journalism: endemic financial insecurity, both for journalists and for the papers themselves. The major partisan dailies—as well as the independents with which they competed—were sold at a loss to attract readers. This kind of competition was especially fierce among evening editions. Every newspaper thus developed massive deficits, which sometimes threatened not just the existence of the newspaper but also of its sponsoring political party.[113] The editors of the centrist daily *Tribuna*, almost bankrupt by 1926, defended its precarious financial condition in a letter to President Masaryk by asking rhetorically, "What daily [paper] these days isn't in the red?"[114] As with the papers, so with their employees. Commentary in memoirs and correspondence indicate that debt was commonplace among journalists in interwar Prague. Arne Laurin was reportedly in the habit of saying to his newsroom staff, "Austrian officers had to have syphilis, so as not to flee before the enemy: a reporter has to have debts for him to do any [work] at all."[115] Internal documents from Stránský's *Lidové noviny* indicate that many reporters and editors remained in debt for the entire interwar period, often to their employer, who covered their debts or vouched for their reporters' ability to pay.[116] Even renowned journalist and editor Ferdinand Peroutka was mired in debt for much of the interwar period thanks to his expensive tastes, which included travel to Paris, furniture from the Prague atelier of Adolf Loos and Mies van der Rohe, and steady patronage of Prague's nightlife.[117]

If newspapers were financially precarious and their reporters living beyond their means, politicians with deep pockets or highly placed connections might be able to sway them. Thus the press's finances were both a political issue and a political opportunity. The creation of new newspapers, and the takeover or even closure of others, as well as the loyalties, placement, and replacement of reporters and editors, remained politically significant throughout the interwar period. Both the Castle and its foes worked to obtain journalistic support this way; for example, the late 1920s saw a Castle attempt to wrest *Národní listy* away from the National Democrats, while *Tribuna* fell briefly to the right and then ceased publication.[118]

The Castle-loyal *Lidové noviny* (*People's News*) was the First Republic's flagship newspaper, called Prague's *Le Monde*—the only interwar Czech paper with world-class reporting and literary journalism.[119] *Lidové noviny*'s literary quality and association with the Castle lent it symbolic importance well beyond the interwar period. In 1988, playwright Václav Havel and other dissident writers titled their new *samizdat* liberal opinion weekly *Lidové noviny*, deliberately evoking both interwar democracy and the Castle. More than one historian has called "*Lidové noviny*... one of the symbols of Czechoslovak democracy."[120]

Lidové noviny began within the progressive wing of the nineteenth-century Czech national movement. It was founded in 1889 as *Moravské listy* (*Moravian Pages*), a Moravian counterpart to the Prague-based Young Czech *Národní listy*, by Adolf Stránský, a young Jewish lawyer who moved to Brno from Havlíčkův Brod (then Německý Brod), and converted to Christianity to further his political career.[121] The paper was a standard provincial Young Czech daily, sharply partisan, reprinting competitors' news reports. But then Stránský hired Arnošt Heinrich as editor. A college friend of Stránský's son Jaroslav, Heinrich hailed from Prague and had worked on *Čas* between 1902 and 1904 with Masaryk, who personally recommended him. Heinrich loosed the paper from its political affiliation; inspired by Vienna's *Neue Freie Presse*, he made belles lettres an essential part of the newspaper, rather than just a Saturday supplement as was then typical.[122] Heinrich published essays and feuilletons by his Prague literary friends and their friends, reimagining *Lidové noviny* as a forum for the best in fin-de-siècle Czech letters. The paper gained popularity, sent its own correspondents to Prague and Vienna, and shifted to a morning edition. Both Adolf and Jaroslav Stránský busied themselves with politics and business, leaving the paper to Heinrich, editor in chief by 1919 and as brusque with Adolf Stránský as with the paper's reporting staff: eyewitnesses recalled him saying, "Grandpa, this senile editorial you sent down today, do you actually think I'm going to allow this to be printed?"[123]

During the First World War, Heinrich and both Stránskýs worked with the *Maffie*, and participated in the provisional national assembly in 1919. Heinrich returned to the newsroom after the war; both Stránskýs joined Kramář's National Democratic Party but resented its attacks on the Castle. Jaroslav abandoned his legal training to remake his father's publishing enterprises after the war, creating a Brno publishing house, Polygraphie. In 1920, he established a Prague *Lidové noviny* newsroom on Štěpanská ulice, and provided a staff of young, dynamic writers for his bureau boss, K. Z. Klíma, *Lidové noviny*'s former Vienna correspondent. The Prague edition of *Lidovky* (the paper's nickname) was more expensive than its competitors, who used their contacts with Prague municipal authorities to throw obstacles in the paper's way, but it overcame these initial difficulties.[124]

Of the writers for *Lidovky*—a prominent group, given Heinrich's continuing emphasis on literary excellence—Karel Čapek was by far the best known. He began his career at *Národní listy*, but left in late 1920, to protest its constant attacks on the Castle. He had already earned a national reputation by then, thanks to his prolific work. His doctoral dissertation on pragmatism, published in book form in 1917, introduced Czechs to a school of philosophy still relatively unknown in Central Europe. Čapek's 1919 translation of Apollinaire and his 1920 collection of French poetry still serve as the standard translations for Czech students of European literature, and opened the door to the West for the famed Czechoslovak avant-garde artistic group Devětsil.[125] Despite his continued literary success as a novelist and playwright, Čapek remained on *Lidové noviny*'s staff from April 1921 until his death in 1938.[126] He "loved *Lidovky* with fanatical devotion," filling in for vacationing staff members and writing just about any kind of column, feuilleton, editorial, or article, in addition to his post as literary and theater critic. Čapek could write in any style, including sports reporting; he would often write five contributions to a single day's issue, many signed with pseudonyms.[127] His *Lidovky* experience especially marked his novels, particularly the 1922 *Factory for the Absolute* and the 1935 *War with the Newts*.[128] In his 1936 comic essay *Jak se dělají noviny* ("How Newspapers Get Made"), Čapek introduced his readers to the busy, highly structured life of a Prague newspaper, clearly based on *Lidovky*. His depiction helps further illustrate the world of the Prague political press.

A Czech newspaper's administrative hierarchy began at the top with the *šéfredaktor*, or editor in chief, who directed the paper's overall operations and tried—in Čapek's ironic portrayal, usually with little success—to order the newsroom's chaos. Another important position was that of *odpovědný redaktor*, a position directly linked to the Austro-Hungarian, and later Czechoslovak, legal system.[129] This editor, whose position literally translated as "responsible editor," was to respond to accusations of libel, and print corrections and apologies, seemingly a full-time job. The managing editor (referred to variously as the *noční*, or night editor; the *denní*, or daily editor; and the *strejček*, "little uncle") oversaw the coordination of the entire day's newspaper and served as the link between its editorial and production components.

> At his desk gather on the one hand all the manuscripts which are supposed to go into print, on the other hand all the members of the newsroom staff [*redaktoři*], who at that moment neither are writing nor making telephone calls. Rather, they are complaining of the flu, exchanging opinions and anecdotes, . . . sitting at desks, eating sausages, taking apart cameras, cursing about their damn lives, reading evening editions, and generally contributing to the newsroom's lively din. In the middle of all this confusion sits the night editor, who edits reports from the Czech Press Office; dispenses medical advice; reads newspapers; instructs the younger *redaktoři*; receives the mail and representatives of various groups, who deliver reports of plenary meetings or forthcoming benefit evenings; throws them (that is, the reports) into the trash; sends material to the teletype or to the composing room; surveys the proofs; generally dislikes parliament, panels, ministerial proclamations, celebrations . . . , who knows everything and can speak on any topic with not insignificant expert knowledge, primarily about his own health, which is always shaken by [his] demanding and complicated service. . . .[130]

Finally, the editorial office manager or *redakční sekretář* dealt with the world outside the newsroom. The *redakční sekretář* opened and distributed the paper's mail; he read letters to the editor and readied that section of the paper for publication; he read unsolicited manuscripts and returned most of them politely to their authors, and received the various visitors who vainly attempted to gain the ear of the editor in chief. Čapek described these visitors as primarily being insulted persons who demanded the newspaper print public retractions of perfectly factual stories, muckrakers who wanted the newspaper to clean out or at least announce the existence of one or the other political Augean stable, and gently deranged readers who wanted the attention of, if not the head of state, at least the editor in chief of an important Prague daily.[131]

The journalistic pecking order followed a generally understood hierarchy. At the top of the heap were the editorial writers, the paper's mandarins, the author of the Sunday editorial being primus inter pares (in the case of *Lidovky*, this meant Ferdinand Peroutka). Close on the mandarins' heels followed the writers on political affairs, among whom foreign affairs commentators enjoyed slightly more prestige than analysts of domestic issues. Similarly, the parliamentary reporter was held in higher regard than the senate reporter, as most legislative business was done in the lower house. The "politicals," in Čapek's words, were the newsroom grandees, often entering politics themselves. Other rubrics included economics, culture (whose writers were referred to also as *běloručky* or *milostpáni*, translating loosely to "soft-palmed/white-collared ones" and "gracious gentlemen"), sports, court reporters, and the *lokálu*, reporters covering local news.

Lidovky was only one of Jaroslav Stránský's efforts to support the Castle. In 1924 and 1925, Stránský acquired F. Borový, a venerable Prague literary publisher, and agreed to put out Ferdinand Peroutka's opinion journal *Přítomnost*, founded in collaboration with Masaryk. In 1928–1929, when Stránsky moved his Prague print enterprises to Národní třída 117, his businesses filled the building: *Lidové noviny* had the second and third floors, *Přítomnost* the fourth, and Borový, the fifth, sixth, and the basement.[132] Borový and the National Socialist–owned Melantrich were widely considered Castle publishing houses; other than Orbis, Stránský's holdings constituted the closest thing the Castle had to a party press.[133] And journalists for Stránský's papers—particularly Čapek—worked with Orbis personnel to help the Castle strategize and to expand its influence in the realm of Czech letters. The Castle's intimate involvement with the interwar press is more evidence—beyond its engagement in and emphasis on propaganda—that Masaryk and Beneš believed passionately in the political power of the written word.[134]

Other Allies

Beyond these cultural organizations, the Castle hoped for, used, or took for granted the support of many other groups and individuals within Czech society. Personal friendships and connections dictated many of these political alliances. Others came from ideological conviction or historical experience, such as the Castle's relationships with different Legionnaire groups and feminists. The Castle's main concern was always the expansion of its power and influence. For its allies, motivations varied, ranging from a desire to serve the state to the hope for continued protection or assistance.

Leaders in finance and industry called frequently on the Castle; the best-known example is Masaryk's close personal relationship with Jaroslav Preiss, the president of the powerful Tradesman's Bank (Živnostenská bánka).[135] Preiss was undeniably one of the most influential figures in interwar Czech finance; at times quite close to Masaryk and Beneš, his initial cooperation with the Castle faded during the 1920s as his opportunism and ambition became clearer. By the 1930s, Preiss collaborated with Castle opponents, including the Fascists, although he maintained contact with Beneš.[136] Historians have also noted the Castle's closeness to the Legionary Bank (Legiobánka), the English Bank (Anglobánka), and the Škoda Works, Czechoslovakia's equivalent to Krupp and Mercedes, which manufactured both automobiles and weaponry.[137]

Also important to the Castle were political and religious organizations. Clubs and associations constituted a central part of Czech civic life, from sports and Sokol to literary discussions, feminist circles, and professional and religious organizations. Each political party offered its members women's, youth, teachers', and various other organizations within the party structure. The Castle could not emulate them; instead, it drew on independent organizations, such as the Teachers' Union and leftists and centrists within Sokol, the powerful nationalist organization devoted to physical activity.[138]

One of the most steadfast sources of Castle support came from Jews, although Masaryk's relationship with Jews and Judaism was far from simple. He had been hailed as a champion of the Jews for his response to the Hilsner affair of 1899, in which he condemned a ritual murder trial and called on Czechs to leave superstition behind. He was inspired not by philosemitism but by the desire to save the Czechs' international reputation and to guide his nation away from superstitious bigotry. Masaryk decried popular or political antisemitism; but in private, he identified himself as "emotionally antisemitic," retaining an instinctive dislike for and prejudice against Jews. This combination of political support and private distrust and prejudice characterized Masaryk's attitudes to Judaism until his death.[139]

During the Republic, Masaryk's relationship to Jews remained complex. He and Beneš ensured that religious minorities were constitutionally granted equal civil rights and were allowed but not forced to identify themselves as Jewish in the census and elections.[140] Still, Masaryk found Czech Zionists' declarations of difference more intellectually and emotionally congenial than the efforts of assimilationist Jews to "become Czech." He had believed Jews to be a separate nation from the Czechs—and indeed the rest of Europe—since 1883.[141] Yet he continued to support Czech Jewry politically at least in general, if not in every specific effort.[142] His efforts gained him the accusation, found frequently in the right-wing tabloid press, of having "sold the republic to the Jews." Jews returned the favor and support; both assimilationist and Zionist groups tended to ally themselves with the president and Beneš.[143]

Feminist organizations and women's groups also hailed Masaryk as a defender of equal rights for women. Masaryk had long made "astounding claims" about women and their place in the world, lecturing for example in 1904 that "women were just as intelligent and reasonable as men, . . . that 'women's nature' did not justify their subordination to men" and that not just Czech but all of European society needed to be restructured to right this historic wrong.[144] He had shocked members of the Czech women's movement by acknowledging the difficulty of housework and child rearing, noting that men worked "only" eight-hour shifts and then felt entitled to an evening in the pub, while women bore a child yearly and spent eighteen hours a day maintaining a home and the people in it.[145] When the First Republic was founded, feminist and women's groups looked to the Castle as a guarantor of women's equal rights, both inside and outside the home. Masaryk made equal civil rights based on gender part of the Washington Declaration of Czechoslovak independence: this platform was accepted without comment or resistance by the Czech political leaders at home and enshrined in Article 106 of the Constitution a few years later.[146] However, Article 126 enjoined lawmakers to protect "marriage, motherhood, and the family," presumably in its traditional incarnation. This ambivalence led to years of battles over women's rights to employment in the civil service, abortion, and whether married women should have to take their husbands' citizenship. Women's rights' advocates looked to the Castle for support but were not always satisfied with the Castle's response. In fact, Hrad allies Karel Engliš and Jiří Beneš were among those rebutting the positions of women's rights advocates.[147]

One of the most important relationships the Castle had was with the different groups of Legionnaires, veterans from the Great War "battle abroad" on behalf of Czechoslovak independence. The Legionnaires' heroic effort supposedly helped clarify the ideological concepts on which Castle policy and self-understanding were based: the "intelligent Czechoslovak nationalism" the Castle wished the country to espouse, and the founding myth the Castle hoped to propagate.[148]

> The Legionnaires put their lives into play for the embattled state; they embodied the revolutionary and the warlike aspects of the Hussite tradition . . . [they] fought against the oppression of the Czechs by Austria-Hungary, against German bureaucracy and the [imperial] aristocracy, against the Catholic Church, against German predominance in [the Czech lands], against Communism.[149]

The Castle deliberately allied itself with the Legionnaire tradition, both politically and symbolically. The guards at Prague Castle were dressed in the uniforms of the Russian, Italian, and French legionary divisions.[150] Returning Legionnaires were greeted as the first citizens of the republic. The anniversary of the Legionnaire victory at the 1917 Battle of Zborov was celebrated as one of the First Republic's state holidays.[151]

But the Legionnaires could be unpredictable. They returned home armed, and not all of them were prepared to accept parliamentary rule. In 1919 and 1920, different Legionnaire groups called for Masaryk to become dictator, ending socialist domination of Parliament, and tried to "cleanse" Czechoslovak society by threatening local Jews with expulsion.[152] They had to be propitiated. Law 462, propagated on July 24, 1919, defined who was to be designated a Legionnaire and set aside posts within the state, local, and regional administrations for them; in the end some 20,000 Legionnaires took positions as bureaucrats and public employees, some in very high-ranking Castle positions. Former Legionnaires held prominent ambassadorial posts: for example, Stefan Osuský in London and later in Paris; Lev Sychrava in Paris; Lev Borský in Rome; Karel Pergler in Washington; Bohdan Pavlů in Omsk.[153] Others returned to their prewar trades or, after receiving preferential treatment and subsidized loans in Czechoslovakia's land reform, became small farmers. Many entered the young state's armed forces, particularly in the officer corps and as noncommissioned officers: by the end of the interwar period, one source estimates, "Legionnaires essentially led the army."[154]

Legionnaire life in the First Republic was as highly organized and internally subdivided as the rest of Czechoslovak society. In 1919, two main Legionnaire political groupings emerged: the left-leaning League of Czechoslovak Legionnaires and the rightist Czechoslovak Legionnaires' Collective. In May 1921, with state support, centrists formed the Union of Czechoslovak Legionnaires to try to bring the two wings closer together. A year later they created the Czechoslovak Legionnaire Community, an organization intended to coordinate the three groups on issues of common importance, which possessed its own publishing house, Čin (Deed), and published three newspapers. This organization was generally regarded as being close to the Castle. There were also smaller groups, such as the more radical League of Socialist Legionnaires and the hard-right Independent Union of Czechoslovak Legionnaires. There were also two Slovak Legionnaire groups (one autonomist, one not), a group for ill or handicapped Legionnaires, and various smaller groups from each front. By the mid-1920s, roughly twenty-five distinct Legionnaire groups had formed, representing different political, ethnic, and socioeconomic affiliations.[155]

Opinions about Legionnaires varied widely, both within and outside their ranks, even as the patriotic cult around them grew. Masaryk's own writing, in particular his 1918 *The New Europe* (*The Slav Standpoint*), is said by some to represent the beginning of the Legionnaire cult.[156] Some Legionnaire authors worked to ennoble the Legionnaires as superhuman heroes, without error or weakness, and entirely loyal to Masaryk and Beneš as the leaders of the wartime struggle abroad. A genre of Legionnaire art sprang up to support this notion: novels by Castle allies František Langer, Josef Kopta, and Rudolf Medek, František Kupka's visual art, and Otto Gutfreund's sculpture, among others. Others resisted the Legionnaires'—and the Castle's—deification. František Zuman's 1922 *Osvobozenecká legenda* (*Legends of Liberation*) alleged that the work of all Czechs on behalf of the country's independence was being unfairly disputed, and that all the credit was being attributed to the "Great Leader Masaryk" and the Legions. Similarly, a 1924 debate in the pages of *Přítomnost* raged over the Legionnaires' level of education (implicitly, whether they were just a bunch of uneducated belligerents who happened to be in the right place at the right time), and also over the alleged holy or untouchable Legionnaire cult.[157] Former Legionnaire and diplomat Lev Borský in his 1929 memoirs attacked Masaryk and Beneš for betraying the Legionnaire ideal. Masaryk had committed treason to the warlike, nationalist Legionnaire spirit, Borský wrote, by describing Czechoslovak independence as a moral victory more than a military one, by withdrawing the Legionnaires from Siberia to France where they were just "another little troop," and by bringing German political parties into the governing coalition in 1926.[158]

While the Legionnaires served as a powerful and contentious symbol throughout the interwar period, concretely they also served the Castle. For most Legionnaires, Masaryk's political and moral authority was unshakable; Beneš's position as Masaryk's hand-picked successor granted him a similar status. Masaryk and Beneš attended Battle of Zborov commemorations, approvingly observing extensive military formations and displays.[159] Legionnaires played leading roles in public state ceremonies; they helped create both the physical memorials and the public rituals associated with them, such as the Memorial of the National Liberation on Žižkov Hill in Prague (see figures 2.1 and 2.2). They even wrote plays and films romanticizing Legionnaire exploits.[160] When the Legionnaires' noble deeds were lauded, so was the President-Liberator. Still, Masaryk remained dubious of the Legionnaires' commitment to the new democratic republic.

The Castle leaders also cultivated prominent writers and intellectuals, particularly those a generation younger. The two best-known Castle writers and helpmeets, essential popularizers of the Castle's mythology, were among the most significant literati of the interwar era: playwright, journalist, and novelist Karel Čapek and master essayist and journalist Ferdinand Peroutka. These two writers set the intellectual tone for the younger Castle intelligentsia, frequently referred to as the lost generation, the generation of pragmatists, or, most tellingly, the Čapek generation, a term first used by Czech literary critics in 1913 to describe the generation of artists born between 1880 and 1895.[161] In a 1931 set of essays, František Goetz described the Čapek generation as powerfully influenced by the Great War, the formation of Czechoslovakia, and Tomáš Masaryk. Previous generations had engaged in destructive revolt; the Čapek generation had overcome its early nihilistic tendencies to devote itself to the representation of Czech culture on the world stage and the good of the state and nation. "[T]he most essential foundations of Czech national life . . . [are] simultaneously personified in the fundamental

Figure 2.1. November 8, 1928: Celebration to mark the beginning of construction of the Legionnaire "Pantheon" and mausoleum on Žižkov Hill in Prague. Masaryk is in the center of the photograph, hatted, looking downward. He is flanked by an uncomfortable-looking Edvard Beneš to his left and Karel Kramář to the right. Source for this and figure 2.2: AÚTGM fotografické oddělení, VIII/47/2*389/1–3, 3741, 3742, 3745.

Figure 2.2. Masaryk during the same event, reviewing soldiers (some of them former Legionnaires) at arms.

experiential, social, and artistic opinions of this generation, which has never denied that [these opinions stem in large part] from Masaryk's work."[162]

Peroutka agreed that his generation owed Masaryk a political and intellectual debt. Unlike Masaryk, Peroutka wrote, the Čapek generation lacked a metaphysics, drawing instead on Henri Bergson's "vitalism," American pragmatism, and Nietzsche's "antimetaphysical radicalism." The focus of their gaze and their art had been the world: they sought inspiration and joy in what they could see, and found the past irrelevant. Despite their differences with him, Masaryk was a crucial exemplar of passionate praxis, idealism translated to reality. Masaryk's philosophies—political realism and existential humanism—were close to the Čapek generation's vision of the world, although they and the president had traveled utterly different paths and continued to differ, Peroutka wrote. "[We] do not link humanity with being Czech, or even with being a Slav, but rather with being a good European." For Peroutka, Masaryk was the last and greatest of the Czech Awakeners: his vision of Czech history, linking the Hussite past to the republican present, offered the Czechoslovak nation a new, enlightened, powerful vision of itself.[163]

Peroutka personally introduced Masaryk to the group of intellectuals and literati at Čapek's Friday evening salons (Friday is *pátek* in Czech; the group was dubbed the Pátečníci, or Friday Men). Just before the war, Čapek began holding weekly gatherings with a few friends at Prague cafés to drink black coffee and expound on their art. In April 1925, when Čapek, his father, and his brother's family moved into a double "villa" in the Prague suburb of Královské Vinohrady, a room was reserved for the Friday meetings, which grew to include more participants (figure 2.3).[164] First-time guests to Čapek's salon had to be escorted by a regular attendee. If the new guest seemed congenial, he was welcomed back into the group on his own. "Karel Čapek sat at the door of the little room. . . . He did not get up when a new guest entered. He just extended his hand. 'So, take a seat somewhere!' "[165] Regular attendees tended to sit in the same easy chair, or next to the same people. A table held drinks and refreshments, and Čapek solicitously poured coffee and offered food, libations, and cigarettes.[166] Friday Man Adolf Hoffmeister described the room where the Friday Men met as the "kitchen of conversations; they cook all afternoon." Hoffmeister's Čapek was a "small, black-haired, rosy-cheeked host, with a coffeepot in hand and half a cigarette in his holder, attentive to ideas and to guests."[167] Discussion topics ranged widely, from issues in the public eye to wine, women, and song. Friday Men would kid one another about female companions or attending séances, and mock academic politics.[168] The group's custom was to treat one another with blasé courtliness. Not even those who had known each other since boyhood addressed one another with the intimate *ty*; all Friday Men used the formal

Figure 2.3. Adolf Hoffmeister's cartoon of the Friday Men. First row, from left: Ferdinand Peroutka, J. B. Kozák, Arne Laurin. Second row: Karel Kraus, František Langer, Karel Čapek, Josef Kodíček, Josef Macek. Third row: Josef Čapek, Vladimír Vančura, Masaryk, Edvard Beneš, Karel Poláček. Fourth row: František Kubka, Josef Kopta, Dr. L. Procházka, Vilem Mathesius, Josef Šusta.

vy, and last names. No women, not even Čapek's housemaids, were allowed save on rare occasions such as New Year's Eve celebrations.

> Tolerant Čapek wanted to . . . bring opposing views closer to one another. Only he could have managed to surround himself with such heterogeneous talents and ideological opponents, and create for them a reconciliatory atmosphere in which communist writers and Marxist aesthetes sat companionably alongside Legionnaires, militant Catholics next to liberals.[169]

There were many overlapping groups and generations within the Friday *assemblées*, which drew on some forty members, although no more than twenty generally appeared any given Friday. Among the Communists, many of whom also participated in the Left avant-garde group Devětsil, were journalist and artist Adolf Hoffmeister, novelist Vladimír Vančura, and more occasional visitors such as poet Vitězslav Nezval and journalist Ivan Olbracht, writer for *Rudé právo* and editor in chief of *Rudý večerník*. There was a *Lidové noviny* contingent, including publisher Jaroslav Stránský, reporters Karel Poláček, Eduard Bass, and Jan Herben, and Prague editor in chief Karel Zdeněk Klíma. (Ferdinand Peroutka, one of the earliest members, stopped coming to the Fridays by the 1930s.) František Langer and Josef Kopta, Legionnaire novelists and writers for *Národní osvobození*, came, as did publisher Bohumil Přikryl of the centrist Legionnaire publishing house, Čin. Other journalistic members included *Prager Presse* chief editor Arne Laurin and reporter František Kubka; Josef Kodíček, *Tribuna* drama critic and theater director; and friendly reporters from hostile papers, such as *Národní listy*'s Karel Scheinpflug.[170] The older generation of Friday Men generally came from the professoriate or the civil service, and sometimes both. Among them were Germanist Otakar Fischer, historian Josef Šusta, philosopher J. B. Kozák, and Anglicist Vilém Mathesius. Fischer, also a poet, would eventually head Prague's National Theater; Šusta and Mathesius engaged in various kinds of government service, Šusta serving briefly as minister of education. Mathesius was the group's link to the well-known Prague Linguistic Circle of the 1930s; articles by Čapek and other Friday Men appear in the early issues of the Linguistic Circle's journals.[171] Otokar Vočadlo, who taught Czech language and literature at the London School of Slavonic Studies, attended when in Prague.[172]

But the most famous Friday Man was President Masaryk. Beginning in 1926, Masaryk, Beneš, and other KPR and Zamini leaders—Vasil Škrach, Josef Schieszl, Václav Bouček, and Masaryk's son Jan—occasionally visited the Fridays.[173] When Masaryk was to attend, Čapek placed a vase of flowers on the table near the president's chair, otherwise kept ceremoniously empty, and served only black coffee. Masaryk rarely spoke much, according to Friday Man memoirs, and heightened the group's formal air by addressing each member according to his profession: "Mr. Reporter [*pane redaktore*]," and so on. Peroutka recalled that when he attended, "Unfortunately a few people spoke 'presidentially,' always positively and in defense of the state: 'And, Mr. President, just as the sun shines above us, etc etc.' This was hideously irritating." But the Communist members of the group openly baited the president and were met with good-natured humor. "Once [poet Vitězslav Nezval] with his customary enthusiasm declared to Masaryk, 'The petiter the bourgeois, the worse! [*čím menší buržoa, tím horší*]' Masaryk smiled widely; this was more pleasant for him than hearing serious opinions."[174] But the president recalled things differently. During a 1934 visit from Friday Man Josef Macek, Masaryk commented that he had stopped attending the Friday meetings because they were a waste of time. Macek explained that the Friday Men wanted to enjoy tranquil conversation, not exhaust themselves with problems. "Entirely wrong," Masaryk responded acidly. "Nothing's more tiring than talking about nothing."[175]

The president's presence intimidated most attendees into careful conversation or awkward silence. František Kubka wrote, "We did not speak about women in front of the president, nor did we tell each other anecdotes, curse about politics, or use words which were inappropriate for conversation."[176] If Masaryk dampened the Friday discussions, Beneš enlivened them. Peroutka wrote that "Beneš was a debater. He led argument, would discuss absolutely anything, and argued openly, as was his habit."[177]

Masaryk considered the Fridays to represent a political grouping, and once told some of the Friday Men, "Your 'Friday' is already a [political] program in and of itself." František Kubka disputed this: "The Friday Men in fact had no political program, and were unwilling to organize themselves as a political unit. Especially when even the host, Karel Čapek, was unenthusiastic about the matter."[178] Although the Friday Men did not in fact take up the president's call as an organized group, many responded individually, especially Čapek, Peroutka, Stránský, and the many Friday Men working for Zamini. Masaryk's impression was strongest on the younger members, as Čapek explained in a grateful letter after the president's first visit:

> I can say for almost everyone you saw at my house on Friday that we had been prepared for you in our youth; you had ceased teaching when we were at university, and thus we missed [contact with] the single philosophical figure who affected us directly and vividly. How we came to find you despite this, not just from books but from our lives, is another story; but, along with our sincere thanks, I wanted to say to you, that last Friday you gave our generation back what we had missed then.[179]

After 1926, the Friday meetings became a locus for Castle intellectuals and the center of a constellation of Castle-loyal cultural institutions, from newspapers to political parties to publishing houses. The Friday Men's close personal relationships with Masaryk and Beneš, their centrality to interwar Czechoslovak culture, and their willingness to take up political activity made them uniquely placed observers and actors in interwar Prague political life. And although the group welcomed diverse members, its members shared the same basic political assumption: "loyalty from one human being to another, and... to Czechoslovak democracy, and to the so-called humanistic ideals on which it relied."[180]

Not a single German speaker or Slovak, much less a Hungarian, attended Čapek's Fridays: their absence was not coincidental. The Castle's relationships to Czechoslovakia's subject nationalities were among the trickiest to negotiate. Masaryk and Beneš wanted the country's nationalities, especially the Germans, involved in parliamentary coalitions; the Castle helped bring German "activist" (pro-Czechoslovak) parties into the "gentlemen's" or "all-bourgeois" governing coalition of October 1926 through

October 1929. The National Democrats publicly accused them of betraying the new republic's ideals, calling out "Germans into the government—we into revolution!"[181] The Castle had reliable German and Slovak allies, among them Samuel Saenger, chargé d'affaires in the German embassy in Prague; professor and Christian Socialist leader Robert Mayr-Harting; German Social Democrat Ludwig Czech; German Agrarian leaders Franz Křepek and Franz Spina (also a Slavic studies professor at the German University in Prague); Slovak Agrarians Vavro Šrobar and Milan Hodža (although Hodža's relationship to the Castle alternated from opposition to close collaboration and back); and Slovak Social Democrat Ivan Dérer.[182] Non-Czech intellectual figures also associated with the Castle or accepted support from Zamini to act as cultural ambassadors for the new state: among these were German writers Max Brod, Otto Pick, and Pavel Eisner, and the Slovak and Hungarian members of Czechoslovakia's P.E.N. Club.[183]

Still, the Castle frequently played both ends against the middle when it came to the minorities. Robert Mayr-Harting can stand as an example: even as the Castle relied on him, they also reported on him, monitoring his activities through 1936.[184] Masaryk and Beneš considered Czechoslovakia's creation a "national"—that is, Czech—revolution. They defended Czech interests, assuming that the minorities had little real justification for complaint, and that their caviling would ebb in a generation or so. Historians have discussed Masaryk's relative popularity in Slovakia; the Castle-sponsored National Labor Party polled surprisingly well in Bratislava in 1925.[185] But Slovaks voted consistently throughout the interwar period for the autonomist Slovak L'udak (Populist) Party (SPP) led by outspoken Castle critic Father Andrej Hlinka; the SPP criticized Masaryk for supposedly promising Slovaks autonomy in the Pittsburgh Agreement of May 1918 and then reneging upon his return to Czechoslovakia. They also disagreed with Beneš's reliance on the West and his hostility to right-wing, but Catholic, states like Poland and Austria.[186] The SPP occasionally sparred directly with the Castle throughout the interwar period, for example in 1925, when Hlinka was sentenced to eight days in jail for insulting the president.[187] Nor did the Castle possess widespread popular support among the country's Germans or Hungarians. The Czech-led land reform, described as an instrument of social justice but administered as a tool of nationalist retribution for mythologized losses—specifically White Mountain, in 1620—angered these groups throughout the interwar period.[188] Although Zamini argued before the League of Nations committee for minority complaints that Czechoslovak land reform had been fair, Beneš later admitted to the British minister to Prague that "Before the war, the Germans were here [pointing to the ceiling] and we were there [pointing to the floor]; now, [reversing the gesture] we are there and they are there. . . . The lesson had been necessary, and land reform had been necessary if only as part of it."[189] German-Castle disputes on this and other matters continued throughout the interwar years, within domestic and international politics.[190]

Conclusion

Ferdinand Peroutka once recalled longtime Prime Minister Antonín Švehla as "a politician of small rooms." The much-vaunted democracy of the First Republic was clearly a democracy of small rooms, since most important decisions were made there, among a small circle of leaders, rather than in the voting booth.[191] Neither parliamentarians nor the electorate had any real say over policy in the interwar period. Since the judiciary had little power or independence, "the fate of Czech democracy was solely in the hands of the executive, i.e. the government (and the parties backing it) and the President."[192] The Pětka, particularly the Agrarian Party, also wielded power, frequently in opposition to the Castle. But historians have been far less kind to the Pětka than to the Castle, despite their commonalities.

While claiming to represent transcendent European ideals, Castle political methods were decidedly earthbound: they included the questionable and the unsavory. Certainly Castle political infighting was no less forceful than the Pětka's. Masaryk and Beneš created the KPR and Zamini as their de facto political organization, staffed by their closest supporters and with control of "dispositionary funds." It was within these institutions that Castle priorities were established, Castle contacts and attempts at persuasion made, information and policy assembled. The press was also central, not just for the Castle but for interwar Czechoslovak politics overall. The Castle tried to buy out oppositional newspapers, and was not above bribery of individuals or of entire parties. Castle personnel cultivated literati, but rewards for loyalty were infrequent.

The Castle's political philosophy was probably closest to the Social Democrats: reformist moderate socialism. Yet the Castle leaders were able to look farther afield than most other Czechoslovak political groupings, never losing sight of Czechoslovakia's place in the new European order and how incidents at home might appear from abroad. The Castle's legitimacy rested on several different foundations: their standing and success abroad, their links to groups at home capable of supporting them symbolically (especially the Legionnaires and the press), and their ability to exercise real power through institutions and financial or personal relationships. The Castle's foreign policy depended on its strength at home; its strength at home depended at least in part on the success of its foreign policy. In this sense it was far more than a Czechoslovak political institution: we might view the Castle as a European political and propaganda organization with a Czechoslovak arm.

For these reasons, the Castle remained preoccupied with control of and representation in the Czechoslovak and European press. For Czechoslovakia to remain the heart of the postwar European order and Europe's new Switzerland, with Masaryk and Beneš as ideal democrats, Czechoslovakia's reputation in the West had to be spotless. The entire country had to be viewed as solidly behind the Castle; its flaws had to be made to disappear, or at least to be overshadowed by those of Czechoslovakia's enemies. Domestic Czech political squabbles—especially what seemed to be the rising power of the Czech far right—might echo across the continent. The Castle would have to find a way to contain them and to gain symbolic legitimacy as well as actual political power. The next chapter details various efforts at gaining actual and mythic power at home by the Castle.

3

Battles of the Legend Makers

Taking over the stage requires keeping other people off it.
—*Milan Kundera*

The American diplomat George Kennan once famously compared interwar Czech politicians to "small boys dividing a stolen melon," obsessed only with the size of their share.[1] In fact, Prague could never turn its back entirely on the rest of Europe, or the world. After all, the First Republic owed its existence to international political upheaval; its continued security depended on the West's commitment to Central Europe. For that reason, Czech newspapers avidly, if solipsistically, followed any mention of Czechoslovakia in the international press. The shadows of the Great Powers and the Soviet Union, of Italy and Japan, played across the surface of Czechoslovak politics throughout the interwar decades.

The Castle leaders understood this perhaps more clearly than any other Czech political faction. International approval had always been Masaryk and Beneš's greatest trump card, although they had to play it carefully. Neither at home nor abroad could they afford to appear a Great Power pawn. In the eyes of the world, no other Czech politician could compete with Masaryk or Beneš for authority. Their political legitimacy depended on their Great War legacy, on the success of their foreign policy, and on Masaryk's popular status as a kingly president and beloved father figure. These factors meant that international issues and the Great War served as the basso profundo note underscoring domestic Czechoslovak politics.

The Castle fought two related battles with its domestic opponents, referred to by one historian as the "anti-Castle [Protihrad]," as if it were a unified bloc.[2] One conflict focused on concrete political power; here the Castle's enemies were the Pětka and the country's increasingly radical Right, manifested in the National Democratic party, the right wing of the Agrarians, and the Czech fascists, led by former Legionnaire and general Radola Gajda (Rudolf Geidl) and former Castle ally Jiří Stříbrný. The other, less familiar conflict involved "mythic politics"—the Castle's efforts to discredit this same set of opponents in the realm of myth, narrative, language, and symbol, predominantly through the media and popular culture. Both the Castle leaders and their adversaries fought to dominate public discussion of the nation and its past. Who and what comprised Czechoslovakia, who should lead it, who should protect it, who created it in the first place: control of this discursive symbol translated to symbolic legitimacy as well as to political power.

The most overt challenge to the Castle leaders consisted of Czech nationalists Kramář and Viktor Dyk hurling epithets at Beneš as a surrogate for the president. Meanwhile, Brno lawyer and Castle publishing tycoon Jaroslav Stránský attacked Stříbrný, the Czechoslovak National Socialists' power broker, who had argued with Masaryk, then tried to boot Beneš from the party leadership and from his position as foreign minister. Stříbrný sued, and Stránský's attempt to discredit Stříbrný in the resulting trial took the newspaper audience back to the waning days of the Great War. Real power was at stake in these seemingly arcane historical disputes—influence within Parliament and in prominent financial circles, continued Castle control over foreign policy (and therefore closeness to the West European Great Powers)—as well as the possibility of transforming Czechoslovaks into the Castle's idealized Western-style democrats.

This symbolic warfare was waged in part via the mass media. The republic's journalists, press, and publishing houses were crucial allies. Equally important, and somewhat independent from these other issues, was the personality cult the Castle crafted for Masaryk. That, too, depended on the press and publishing houses: pamphlets of his writings, children's plays in typically didactic Castle style, hagiographic discussions of the "President-Liberator" in secondary school textbooks, and souvenir photograph books showing Masaryk on horseback reviewing troops, with his family at home, or looking august amid other European leaders. All these symbolic disputes draw attention to the central role played by Castle intellectuals. They joined the Castle's information network, reporting on developments within the media and arbitrating disputes. They helped Masaryk and Beneš negotiate for control of some newspapers. They helped the president strategize attacks and responses, serving as an unofficial brain trust. They also offered him their newspaper columns as platforms and allowed him editorial control over interviews, ensuring the finished piece would read as a polished statement of the president's views.

The debates featured here bring to light the Castle's use of mythmaking, propaganda, and image manipulation, as well as its reliance on literary intellectuals, within domestic political conflicts. They also help identify tendencies within mythmaking. For example, Castle figures often deployed the Castle myth of a near-perfect Czechoslovak democracy in response to accusations of undemocratic practice. Additionally, the Castle's high-minded, complex vision of Czechness was one of many combative national myths in a very crowded field. The National Democrats, the Czech Fascists, the right wing of the Agrarian Party, the Czechoslovak Communists, and the Slovak autonomist parties each had their own. Thus the Castle had to craft and defend its myth as well as legitimate its leadership. Competing political parties, libel and treason trials, and pitched battles on editorial pages, both within and outside Czechoslovakia: these symbolic battles between the Castle and its opponents married old personal arguments to profound disagreements over the new state's political structure and international orientation, and were fought tooth and nail.

The Czech Radical Right

By the mid-1920s, authoritarianism had begun its sweep of the European continent. The Castle was acutely aware of the Right as a threat at home almost from the moment of the young republic's birth. The Czech Right believed the country would be best served by an aggressive Czech chauvinism; Masaryk and Beneš understood "Czechoslovakism" as an enlightened, gentler Czech nationalism. The Czech Right saw Germans as a permanent threat to the Czech nation. The Castle believed that the Versailles accord, although fragile, would last; that the West would control Europe's pariahs, Germany and Russia. Their traditional appetite for small Central European states would ebb with full membership in the League of Nations and increasing integration into the postwar order. This ideological rivalry between the Castle and the Right translated into political problems. The National Democrats and Agrarians were old hands at Czech politics, commanding considerable authority and between them a substantial percentage of the electorate.

The Agrarian Party was the true center of parliamentary power and the most significant potential opponent to Castle plans. However, the party believed it could achieve its goals within the parliamentary system by dominating it. Castle parties and factions were increasingly forced onto the defensive; the Agrarian right wing collaborated more or less openly with the National Democrats and the Fascists. Still, the Agrarian leadership worked with the Castle until the republic's demise.[3] The more outspokenly anti-Castle National Democrats were a more important target: a government party, still commanding much influence in high financial and industrial circles, moving slowly toward affiliating itself with the radical, anti-state right. The right-wing Agrarians might still be tamed by the more moderate elements within their own party, trusted by the Castle. No such group remained within the National Democrats by the mid-1920s. Also, the National Democrats were vulnerable financially and at the voting booth, and might prove a less costly object lesson than confronting the Agrarians.

One means of sapping the National Democrats' strength was an electoral challenge. *Lidové noviny* publisher Jaroslav Stránský, a Castle ally within National Democratic ranks, had chafed at the party's ideological constraints and attacks on the Castle leaders. As early as autumn 1919, Stránský had publicly requested that the Prague party leadership "critically reevaluate and correct its policies."[4] Soon Stránský left, taking with him prominent intellectuals and leaders. He began holding political meetings, agitating among prospective voters, and writing inflammatory editorials. In April 1923, Masaryk offered Stránský a million crowns, half to found a new political party publicly espousing Castle ideals, half to found a new journal of ideas, edited by journalist Ferdinand Peroutka.[5] Peroutka's *Přítomnost* (*The Present*, or *The Presence*) appeared six months later and launched a tirade against the Pětka, calling for moral reform of Czechoslovak politics. Meanwhile, domestic intelligence reports noted the creation of a new party, headed by Stránský, affiliated with Zamini, the centrist Czechoslovak Legionnaire Community, and the newspaper *Národní osvobození*.[6] Prime Minister and Agrarian leader Antonín Švehla, a frequent opponent of Beneš, believed that Beneš had given Stránský funds for the new party, to be called the National Labor Party (Národní strana práce, henceforth NLP).[7]

Although its name referred to the British Labor Party, the NLP hailed Masaryk as its political and moral model. It pledged to "uphold Masaryk's republic, not Švehla's" and made its intellectual debt to the Castle clear. "Our program: do not fear and do not steal. Our model: T.G. Masaryk. Our tactics: honor, even in politics."[8] The party advocated moderate socialism, vowing to "complete and ground political democracy in economic democracy."[9] Concerned about the NLP and other splinter parties, Pětka leaders responded by sponsoring an electoral reform effectively doubling the number of votes required for parliamentary representation. The NLP never managed much of an electoral showing, though it did shear away much of the National Democrats' traditional voter base, especially in Moravia, Silesia, and parts of Slovakia, before conceding defeat and folding itself into the National Socialists in 1929.[10]

The NLP emerged at a moment of stress for the young republic. Before the 1925 elections, the three strongest coalition parties (the Agrarians, the Social Democrats, and National Socialists) had repeatedly betrayed agreements to pass one another's legislative priorities and had withheld their support for Pětka projects. Relations between the main parties and their smaller collaborators, such as the Czechoslovak Populists, also deteriorated. After the elections, Prime Minister Švehla and President Masaryk spent months working to form new governing coalitions, Švehla with the goal of strengthening the center, Masaryk the left. For a time, both the Pětka and the coalition seemed powerless—and with their decline came also the end of the consensus that had marked the previous system. The president created a nonpartisan cabinet, which served until October of that year.[11] During this time, Slovak Milan Hodža took interim control of the Agrarian Party, substituting ruthless power plays for Švehla's usual patient negotiation. Hodža created lasting enemies on the Left. This period was also marked by increasing vituperation in the partisan press.

Vojtěch Tuka, strategist for the Slovak L'udak (People's) Party, whose autonomist wing was strengthened in the 1925 elections, later recalled that 1926 was a year of great political nervousness and increased radicalism on both Left and Right. It seemed to Tuka, as it did to many observers, that the parliamentary system would not be capable of resolving these crises.

> A revolutionary mood flared up again in 1926. There were wild rumors: "The leftist parties are planning a coup," "The Czech fascists are preparing a coup . . . " I could understand either possibility. I met with the Czech fascists about taking power together, with the condition that Slovakia would receive autonomy under the new regime, and I met with the Communists, to see whether we might not coordinate some kind of action. It did not matter to me.[12]

Politicians and political analysts circulated ideas, ranging from constructive to innocuous to authoritarian, about the future of Czechoslovak democracy. Some wrote quite favorably of Marshal Józef Piłsudski's May 1926 "cleansing" coup in Poland, and raised the possibility that Masaryk might grant himself similar powers. NLP leader Jan Herben was among those discussing the possibility:

> Many have been calling for a long time on President Masaryk to lead some kind of coup as Piłsudski did in Poland. Many call for his dictatorship. Fools! If he had wanted to do so, he would have done so. Nothing, however, is more removed from the spirit of Masaryk's politics than experiments.[13]

In fact, Masaryk and Beneš did contemplate a Castle coup. Internal Castle conversations on this topic took place during April 1926 between the president, Beneš, and Jiří Stříbrný, then still just barely a Castle intimate. Masaryk was deeply disquieted by what appeared to be an extraordinary spike in fascism's popularity among Czechs. A coup, he hypothesized, might be necessary to control nationalist sentiment and hold the country together. The Castle's envisioned leader of the coup would be the National Socialists, specifically Beneš, Stříbrný, and Václav Klofáč. Beneš believed a coup was justifiable only as a last attempt to save the state, after every parliamentary means of resolving conflicts had failed. He interpreted authoritarianism in a seemingly democratic manner: he discussed the importance of the German socialist parties' support and wanted to permit the press and all political parties to function freely. He also imagined how he might defend himself after the rule of law was restored, when a court would hold him accountable for his actions.[14]

Czech fascism's sudden, seemingly explosive entrance into Czech politics explains the Castle's concern. A small group of National Democrats and other discontented political observers, including members of Charles University's legal faculty, formed the "Red-Whites" in 1922, and grew steadily, uniting with other groups throughout Bohemia and Moravia, and numbering 20,000 supporters by 1925.[15] These groups joined to form the National Fascist Community (Národní obec fašistická, or NOF) in March 1926. NOF ideology combined Czech chauvinism with prejudice against Germans, Magyars, and Poles, as well as idiosyncratic notions of Pan-Slavic brotherhood (evidently excluding the Poles). Czech fascism's enemies were Jews, socialists, Communists, and the Castle. Its supporters came predominantly from urban areas, specifically Prague, and included artisans, white-collar workers and lower-level civil servants, former Legionnaires, students, and businessmen; fascism also attracted members of Sokol.[16] The fascists' numbers seemed to be increasing rapidly: Castle informant Ludvík Hených wrote on June 2, 1926, that in Prague alone there were 40,000 organized NOF members, in Moravia and Bohemia together roughly 200,000.[17] The NOF made little headway in Slovakia, where Dr. L. Bažovský's Slovak National Fascists, and paramilitary groups associated with some of the larger parties, already operated.[18]

Meanwhile, the Right readied a "counterputsch" should the Castle try to take power. The plotter who worried the Castle most was adventurer Legionnaire general Radola Gajda.[19] Like the National Democratic leaders, Gajda resisted the Castle's leadership and ideology; he espoused integral Czech nationalism, expressed hostility to Germans, and insisted on the importance and interwar leadership of the Legionnaires.[20] Rumors began to circulate that the fascists and Gajda would attempt a coup d'état during the upcoming Sokol congress in Prague on July 4–6, 1926. (In the fall of 1925, the Brno police had obtained other coup plans naming the 27th and 28th of October 1926 as the date. The Rodobrana, a Slovak paramilitary group, would support the NOF; martial law would be imposed, the borders closed, and parliamentarians jailed.)[21] It was during this tumultuous season that Masaryk met the young intellectuals of Čapek's Friday salons and invited them to visit the presidential villa at Lány, outside Prague.[22] During their stay, the president and Beneš discussed Piłsudski's coup in neighboring Poland and the threat that Czech fascists might try to emulate him later that summer. Over after-dinner coffee, Masaryk read the Friday Men an article about Gajda. The article argued against the necessity of any kind of dictatorship in Czechoslovakia, constitutional or otherwise—in essence, a response to the rumors circulating about a Castle-directed "constitutional coup." When he finished reading, Masaryk asked the group, "What do you say to that?" Kubka recalled that no one spoke. The president said grimly,

> Gajda! . . . This summer there will be a Sokol congress. Thousands of people will pour into Prague. Gajda has teamed up with Stříbrný and could use the congress for a fascist putsch, as Piłsudski did yesterday in Warsaw. But unfortunately even Kramář supports these things. . . . I am for parliamentary democracy. I asked you all to come visit me here and, later, where you can, to write and speak in this spirit. We must not fear the fascists. But we must counter their . . . heckling with our arguments.[23]

The leading Friday Men, including Čapek, Peroutka, and Josef Kopta, had already entered Castle politics, writing on behalf of the NLP before the 1925 elections and even placing themselves on the party's list of candidates.[24] Masaryk's warning politicized them further. František Kubka recalled that, after Masaryk's words,

> we all were affected. In that moment we felt that it was necessary to enter the battle in defense of the democratic republic. Not just to watch, not to write whatever occurred to us, but to lend a hand to the common task. It was something more than just a mood among us.[25]

The Castle forced Gajda off the army's general staff on July 2, and immediately charged him with having passed secret French military information to the Soviets while in Paris.[26] That December, a military court convicted him of a related crime and forced him to retire from the army. The government handled the case very secretively; Gajda's supporters concluded that it was to hide Gajda's innocence.[27] In 1927, the Castle launched another suit against Gajda, charging him with ten different related crimes. A special military court of appeals convicted him in February 1928 of the dubious espionage charges, of negotiating secretly with the Soviet Union, of cooperating with the Czech fascist movement, and of plotting to overthrow the Czechoslovak government, a charge unsupported by evidence even at the time. The appeals court demoted him to the status of private, in effect barring him from future political life by keeping him in the army. From this point on, Gajda appeared in public not in a Czechoslovak uniform but in that of a tsarist general.[28]

The fascist threat continued, and the Castle remained vigilant. In a fall 1926 *Prager Tagblatt* interview, Masaryk linked fascism to the internal difficulties of the National Democrats, calling the fascists the "pathological scum" of the party. Kramář responded that he did not consider fascism pathological.[29] Especially in Moravia, NOF members would attend and violently disrupt NLP meetings, correctly viewing Stránský's party as a Castle surrogate. A March 1927 meeting in the Prague suburb of Královské Vinohrady became so violent that the gendarmes fled (Czechoslovak law mandated the presence of gendarmes at all political meetings).[30] At a 1927 meeting in Beroun, a small town outside Prague, NOF supporters attacked NLP leader Vaclav Bouček with a chair. Thirty-five people, most of them fascists from Prague, were arrested; their confiscated weaponry included knives, wooden clubs, various types of guns, rubber truncheons, and brass knuckles. Other NLP members were also hurt.[31] Threats to Vaclav Bouček and Jaroslav Stránský became so common that state ministries granted both men continual bodyguards and protection.[32] In December 1927, the NOF discussed throwing potassium nitrate or aniline at Peroutka and Stránský at an NLP meeting, to blind and disfigure them. Gajda told the members not to talk much about it.[33]

Karel Čapek abandoned active work for the NLP in 1926, turning instead to a close personal relationship with Masaryk. Čapek became a frequent presence at Castle strategy meetings. The president discussed with him the case against Gajda, writing to him about new evidence and requesting, "Keep this strictly to yourself and please think about how best to use it."[34] Čapek also joined Masaryk's informal intelligence network, in particular aiding efforts to form a "leftist bloc" within the media—a group of Prague dailies, unified by the Castle to attack Gajda and to help promote the Castle agenda before the May 1927 presidential elections. The press bloc was modeled after the socialist parties' formation, in March 1926, of a parliamentary bloc, generally understood to include the NLP although it lacked parliamentary representation.[35]

Čapek hoped the bloc's partisan press might operate with a similar unity. In an August 1926 letter to the president, Čapek informed Masaryk that various editors of journals friendly to the Castle had met at Čapek's house to discuss how to proceed. Čapek credited the idea of a bloc—which he called a "democratic bloc"—to Arne Laurin. The well-connected Laurin had long provided information for the president. Other participants were longtime Masaryk ally Bedřich Hlavač, chief editor of the then-floundering daily *Tribuna*; Josef Kopta, representing *Národní osvobození*; Hubert Ripka from *Přítomnost*; Čapek, standing in for K. Z. Klíma, Prague editor of *Lidové noviny*; and an editor from the Social Democratic paper *Právo lidu*. Representatives of the Democratic Center, a dissenting group within the National Democrats, had pledged their "silent solidarity." The meeting, Čapek wrote, went quite well.

> We promised to leave one another in peace . . . It should not be allowed to happen that within the nation, leftist versus rightist blocs should come to be, because the president cannot run [with the support of] any single bloc, but rather [with that of] a wide democratic majority. . . . All . . . agreed on the necessity of ceasing scandalizing and "affair-ism" and turning the attention of the public to serious political issues. A daily center will be created for the practical relations of editors of each paper, and once a week they plan to meet, for the interim at my house. . . . I would be glad if something permanent came from this.[36]

Although Castle opponents wrote venomously about the "leftist cartel," the powerful Social Democrats never participated, robbing the democratic bloc of much significance.[37] But its members continued to aid the Castle, especially focusing on the affairs of the press: in October 1926, Čapek wrote to the president, "Even in *Národní Osvobození* things are worsening; Kopta tendered a symbolic resignation, because the editorial board is meddling in the newsroom's affairs. The last decent people are fleeing *Nár. listy*. . . . Indeed there is some kind of journalistic crisis and it is not yet clear what good might be gotten out of it."[38] Variants on this organizational theme continued through 1927: Stránský called a May 1927 meeting not just for the NLP but for the Progressive Confederation, which included the Czechoslovak National Socialists and the Czechoslovak Union of Legionnaires.[39] But Masaryk's reelection to the presidency that month robbed the bloc of its raison d'etre. The leftist bloc did inspire similar blocs elsewhere in Prague journalism, such as the Club of Czech Economic Journalists, sponsored by captains of industry and finance such as Jaroslav Preiss, former professor and head of the Czechoslovak Industrialists' Union František Hodáč, director of the Škoda Works Bedřich Loewenstein, and other prominent figures. Participating journalists came from all over the political spectrum and were treated to lush banquets as well as the occasional financial reward. The Communist daily *Rudé právo* called it the "club of purchased journalists" in December 1928, and was sued for its troubles.[40]

Just a few weeks after his "democratic bloc" meeting, Čapek wrote to Prime Minister Švehla, asking him to take the Agrarian press in hand and work with the Castle. Even *Venkov*, the august Agrarian daily generally regarded as under Švehla's influence, was tilting dangerously toward the right:

> Allow me to speak directly: Ugly things are happening, and they are happening in newspapers which the public is accustomed to understanding as your[s]. *Večer*, and to a certain extent even *Venkov*, are helping to maintain and to feed this unsightly disquiet in our political life.... Their behavior in the Gajda affair, their ambiguous attitude toward fascism, their thoughtless attacks on minister Beneš, all this provides grist for the mill of people to whom you, the creator and premier of the democratic coalition, should not even extend your hand. The issue becomes very serious as long as the public assumes that the opinion of your papers is your opinion.

Equally serious, Čapek wrote, were the increasing ideological gaps in Czechoslovak political life. "[Something] is beginning here, which thanks to you had never existed before: the sharp division of journalism, parties and the nation into the 'rightist bloc' and 'leftist bloc.'" Čapek warned Švehla that the growth of fascism would be attributed not to the fault of police or administrators, but to him: "If fascism grows now, it will grow among the wealthy farmers of your party, with the complicity of your press and those who direct it.... Today this depends only on you." Čapek ended by pleading that Švehla return to public life: "We would be so glad if you returned... we apolitical people have at least one right: that of demanding to be led well."[41] Švehla evidently responded positively to Čapek's letter, for the two maintained a friendship up until Švehla's death in 1933.[42]

Political tension also marked the run-up to the 1927 presidential election. Masaryk had been abroad in the eastern Mediterranean, recuperating from illness, for several months; Švehla, too, had spent time away from Czech politics following a heart attack. Slovak Agrarian leader Milan Hodža, who would later become a Castle ally, actively opposed the Castle; he, together with Kramář and the right wing of the Agrarians, saw the 1927 elections as their first real chance to limit or end Castle influence. They planned to nominate Švehla for president against Masaryk, and to enlist the support of the German "activist" Christian Social and Agrarian parties. (Weimar politicians also involved themselves in this episode: Gustav Stresemann encouraged the Bohemian German parties' participation in this plan, while the German foreign ministry refused to sanction any efforts against Beneš.) In a letter to Beneš, Masaryk insisted that his election was crucial given rising international tensions: "if a majority had to be scrabbled together for a runoff election, I would refuse the election." Meanwhile, Švehla sharply refused to go along with the Castle opponents' plans: "You can't be writing [to tell] me that Masaryk is dead?" he wrote, implying that Masaryk's death would be the only condition under which he would consider becoming a presidential candidate. In the end, Masaryk won the first round of voting with a solid majority. But this episode indicates the continuing tensions of the mid-1920s.[43]

President-Liberator?

The Castle's effort to discredit the political Right—particularly Karel Kramář, who had openly expressed sympathy with Gajda and fascism in September 1926—was related to the effort to establish Masaryk, Beneš, and the Legionnaires (collectively referred to as "the resistance abroad") as the republic's only true founders. Through a series of contentious newspaper and magazine articles, many anonymous but bearing obvious hallmarks of the president's style, Masaryk argued that he and Beneš were the country's authentic liberators and the true Czech nationalists. The "domestic resistance"—those who fought at home on behalf of the Czech nation—was tainted, in this view, by having compromised with the Austrian imperial government. These debates over the war and the country's founding raged throughout the interwar decades and caused lasting rancor. Collectively known as the *Boj legendistů*, or Battle of the Legend Makers, they concerned concrete power far more than abstract values: wartime service to the nation became the ultimate means of legitimating power during the First Republic.[44] The *Boj legendistů* debates helped establish Masaryk's and Beneš's historical legacies. The debates legitimated both the power they exercised and the policy they crafted.

Kramář was the Castle's most prominent opponent. Married to a Russian, he had long espoused variants on Pan- and Neo-Slavism, and was less familiar with the languages and cultures of the West than the Castle leaders.

He was frustrated by Masaryk and Beneš's decision to observe the Bolsheviks warily, while covertly aiding White Russian groups in Prague and Western Europe. Certain that Czechoslovakia would need Russian support to ward off inevitable German aggression, Kramář still hoped to oust the Bolsheviks and bring to power a Russian government willing to play protector of the Slavs. When Beneš and Masaryk refused to work against the Soviets, and did not aid the Poles during the Polish-Soviet war, Kramář accused them of fomenting Bolshevism abroad and at home. Kramář distrusted the new country's ethnic minorities; his ideal Czechoslovakia would ensure permanent Czech supremacy over the country's substantial German and Hungarian minorities, avenging centuries of presumed oppression under Austria and Hungary.[45] Kramář also mistrusted Masaryk's reliance on Beneš, who for his part had resented, and publicly criticized, Kramář's wartime refusal to join or do much to aid the resistance abroad. Kramář's representative Josef Dürich had tried to sabotage the National Council's Russia policy, on Kramář's instructions. Kramář, meanwhile, insinuated that Masaryk and Beneš had somehow come upon misbegotten funds to subsidize their wartime activities, and misappropriated those funds for their own use.[46]

Thus various factions vied for the liberators' mantle, and with it moral high ground and political legitimacy. For the Castle, protecting Masaryk's legacy as President-Liberator also meant protecting Beneš's chances of presidential accession and Castle policy. For Kramář and fellow National Democrat Viktor Dyk, as well as former National Socialist Jiří Stříbrný, highlighting their wartime courage and leadership meant the possibility of limiting the Castle, reestablishing their own political power, and shifting the country's international orientation away from the West. The National Democratic party press, and later Stříbrný's tabloid press, became the main arena for these figures to defend themselves. After May 1927, they were joined by a pointedly nationalistic journal titled *Fronta* (*Front*), edited by former Castle ally and diplomat Lev Borský. Dyk wrote for it, as did Karel Horký, Josef Dürich's embittered son-in-law. *Fronta* brought together writers and thinkers opposed to the Castle. Its primary target was what it termed the Castle's "liberation legend," especially as embodied in Masaryk's memoir *Světová revoluce*.[47]

Kramář threw down the glove in 1922, with the publication of *Five Lectures on Foreign Affairs*. The lectures addressed the previous forty years of European history in broad outline, centering on Central European events and emphasizing his own significance to Austrian foreign policy. Kramář claimed that he had spent the previous twenty years participating in foreign affairs as a member of delegations; much of the book responded to criticism of his "Slavic" politics before the war, praised the actions of the *Maffie* in 1914 and 1915 (when he had been a member), and pointedly avoided much mention of Masaryk or Beneš.[48] A review published in *Čas*, Masaryk's former

Realist daily, criticized the book. The author identified himself only with the initials V. S., soon to become one of Masaryk's standard pseudonyms; Kramář deduced immediately that his critic was the president. Another anonymous article in *Čas*, published November 3, 1923, reacted to one of Kramář's *Národní listy* articles about October 28, 1918 (the country's founding day) with the following terse condemnation: "[the National Democrats under Kramář's leadership] must one day be silenced in the interest of internal peace."[49] These articles created immediate bad blood. Jiří Stříbrný likewise "believed that Masaryk was the author of the anonymous articles in journals such as *Čas*, *České slovo*, and *Národní osvobození*, which criticized Stříbrný, Kramář, and other defenders of the role of the domestic resistance."[50] The Masaryk and KPR archives in Prague, as well as the recently reissued series of Masaryk's writings titled *Cesta demokracie*, contain anonymous manuscripts proving Stříbrný right.[51]

In a series of anonymous articles written between July and October 1924, intended for *Národní osvobození* and the *Prager Presse*, Masaryk continued the argument. He claimed to be a Legionnaire, responding to Dyk's assertion that a wall shut the Legionnaires away from the rest of Czech political life. Masaryk blamed Dyk and his party for building it, claiming that they had begun a battle over the relative worth of the two wartime struggles for independence. The author defended the contribution of the struggle abroad, writing that "the entire nation, and the entire world" understood the Legionnaires' achievements—and, implicitly, the Castle's.[52]

While his anonymous articles demonstrate respect for some of the domestic leaders, such as Stříbrný and Social Democrat František Soukup, Masaryk persistently questioned the value of their wartime work. Without the exiles' work for Allied recognition, he argued, Austria might have been able to conclude a separate peace, and Czechoslovakia would never have existed. Moreover, even on October 28, 1918, the very day of glorious independence, Masaryk implied, the country lacked an exact recounting of the domestic leaders' actions. Masaryk quoted the Austrian wartime military governor, Count Maximilian von Coudenhove, who recalled in his memoirs that the Czech domestic resistance had agreed to cooperate regarding the new republic. Was the supposedly revolutionary National Committee of domestic leaders, then, in fact collaborating with the Habsburgs, possibly strengthening the eleventh-hour Austrian attempt to retain the empire in federated form? This criticism was aimed most bluntly at Karel Kramář. Masaryk reported that Kramář, as he traveled with the representatives of postwar Austria in 1919 to Paris, to attend the peace conference at Versailles, was said to have confided that he was a monarchist. Neither Kramář nor the other members of the domestic resistance adequately refuted Coudenhove's version of October 28.[53]

In another anonymous article, Masaryk claimed that their refusal to do so was important not just for their personal political legacies but for the young republic as a whole. By keeping information from the historical record, they were preventing the country from fully understanding itself; they were damaging the nation they claimed to found. The members of the National Committee, Masaryk revealed, had agreed among themselves not to divulge details of their revolutionary activities. Why was the Austrian military governor left to set his memories into the historical record uncontested? For the sake of history and country, these political questions had to be laid to rest, Masaryk insisted. But "Dr. Kramář has tried for years now to elaborate our national liberation in a manner which is purely partisan and directly personal."[54]

At roughly the same time, the president asked Stříbrný to critique chapters of *Světová revoluce*. Stříbrný expressed deep frustration with the president's characterization of the Prague uprising in late October 1918. Without the uprising, demonstrating de facto Czech territorial control, the Czechs would not have been entitled to representation at Versailles, Stříbrný argued. In addition, Stříbrný emphasized that the domestic leaders were risking execution under martial law.[55] But the president responded intransigently, refusing to amend his text. Masaryk reminded Stříbrný of National Democrat Alois Rašín's comment that the Prague uprising was not as decisive as other events from the nation's liberation. He also cited a letter from French minister Stéphen Pichon that Beneš had been invited to Versailles without having had to demonstrate a right to be there.[56] His conclusion seems less than sincere:

> I see from [your notes about our discussion] that you do not respond in fact to my chapter and its tendencies, but rather to the journalistic discussion of issues. For example, you defend yourself against the assertion that the relationship in Prague with some representatives of Austrian power was [the result of an agreement]. This I myself have never said anywhere, and I have never thought it.[57]

One of the last prominent *Boj legendistů* arguments took place in 1929 between Masaryk and Dyk, who had moved far to the Right since the republic's founding. Dyk's Czech chauvinism was mystical: "he viewed national consciousness as a fundamental, powerful, and enduring force all but inaccessible to scientific inquiry or interpretation, and in Dyk's view difficult, if not impossible, for a foreigner to understand."[58] He was a dominant force in the party and on *Národní listy*, defending Gajda and fascism and attacking the Castle. Because Dyk died unexpectedly in 1931, his 1929 exchange with the president, much publicized in the Castle and far-Right press, was one of his last contributions to Czechoslovak political life. An excellent encapsulation of the *Boj legendistů* arguments, the Masaryk-Dyk debate is worth recounting not just for its content but also for its process, which relied on mutual friends as intermediaries and textual critics.[59]

In the spring of 1929, Dyk published a political pamphlet titled "Ad usum pana presidenta" (For the Use of the President). He dedicated the book to Masaryk: "I do not know whether the president will read these lines or not; but I wrote them for him to read during the period [that witnessed] a debate over the methods of Dr. Eduard Beneš. *Ad* his *usum*, in no way *ad usum delphini*."[60] The dauphin in question was, of course, Beneš himself, in Dyk's view responsible for inexcusable moral corruption within the government and for the antipathy between the country's political Right and Left. Dyk reminded Masaryk that at the beginning of the Great War he had had no quarrels with Beneš, and had in fact welcomed Beneš's decision to join Masaryk abroad. Beneš had asked Dyk to come as well, and tried unsuccessfully several times to help him leave the country. Soon after these attempts failed, Dyk was arrested for anti-imperial activity; throughout the war he publicly opposed the empire and supported the resistance abroad. However, Dyk complained, after the Castle leaders returned home in 1918, they began to attack those who had remained, bringing disharmony into Czech politics. Dyk accused Beneš of using this conflict to strengthen his own position: for example, Beneš had ensured that the age of presidential eligibility had been lowered. Dyk also criticized Castle policy, particularly its beneficent treatment of the country's Germans, which he viewed as near-treasonous. He accused the Castle of attacking Kramář, Stříbrný, Švehla, and Milan Hodža, sharpening political stridency after 1925, and planning an executive coup. "Must all within the republic suffocate so that one person can breathe?" Dyk pleaded. "Is Dr. Edvard Beneš more than Czechoslovakia?"[61]

Masaryk responded to Dyk's pamphlet with deliberation, rather than another fiery anonymous editorial. The president drafted a personal letter and enlisted various Castle colleagues to read it and strategize, including presidential chancellor Přemysl Šámal, Karel Čapek, Beneš, and František Udržal, the newly appointed prime minister.[62] Šámal recommended that Masaryk enlist friendly National Democrats, such as Jaroslav Preiss, chair of the Živnostenska Bank. Preiss suggested Masaryk invite Dyk to his regular autumn meeting with Castle allies and prominent political leaders, which might mollify Dyk by making him feel more important.[63] Capek also offered his home.[64] But Masaryk and Dyk do not seem to have met: the rest of their conversation took place via correspondence.

Masaryk's response addressed Dyk's points and other questions from the nation's first ten years. First, the president defended his activist policy of bringing the country's Germans into the government, and rejected Pan-Slavism as a basis for Czechoslovak policy.

> I want to say that our policy towards the Germans cannot be structured by chauvinism; it cannot be revengeful. . . . That we must lead the Germans is a matter of course; the question can only be, how we will lead them. . . . Who, please, is for a non-national state? . . . And [Pan-Slavism]: Beneš, now in Belgrade, has done more for Slavic politics than a heap of your Slavs, who content themselves with Slavic speeches and preaching without deeds.[65]

Masaryk refused to accept the idea of a Castle clique: "You reproach me for byzantine-ness [byzantinism], that I have forgotten how to hear the truth, you accuse [me] of [participating in] a camarilla, [in] attacks and intrigues, and that I am surrounded by people who have cut me off from a great part of the nation. Pardon me, Mr. Senator, all of this is falsehood and untruth."[66] Though the Castle had suppressed or eliminated certain people from political life, Masaryk admitted, these actions had been necessary to stem corruption and to purge the less able from leadership. Gajda, Stříbrný, and Hodža were not patriots but dangers to the nation. Why, the president asked, was Dyk, as a leading politician, not educating himself more fully?

Masaryk reserved his strongest rhetoric for Beneš's defense. "Without Beneš," Masaryk thundered, "the republic would not exist, and despite this you and the rest of his opponents recite political fairy-tales about Beneš, who has slaved morning till night for years [in the name of] the republic . . . pardon me, these are—bluntly stated—hyperbole and entirely unproved condemnations." Could Dyk provide him with a single concrete example of Beneš's wrongdoing? The president rejected outright Dyk's suggestion that Beneš retained his position out of sentimentality or loyalty. On the contrary, no one but Beneš was capable of resolving the problems still facing the republic, and Masaryk would not countenance replacing him. He also rejected Dyk's accusation that Beneš had at his disposal suspiciously large discretionary funds. "From this purely trifling amount he [Beneš] could never make a single bribe; inform yourself, please, what kind of funds the Yugoslav and German foreign ministers have, for example."[67] Finally, Masaryk acknowledged that Beneš's cabinet position was an odd one, given that his party was in the opposition, but that both Prime Minister Švehla and leading financial advisers had recommended that Beneš remain in his post.[68]

Masaryk turned to attack the National Democrats, although he claimed that he did so reluctantly. For a long time, he wrote, he had hoped the National Democrats could serve as the republic's true conservative party. "Mr. Senator, I assure you, I wish I had a decent and politically adept party of the bourgeoisie, that I wish I had a party of the real intelligentsia, which could lead its opponents, in a businesslike manner, both in parliament and [through its] journalism." But the National Democrats' anti-Castle politics had in fact strengthened factions, such as the Communists, who wanted to destroy the state entirely. The National Democratic leaders had acquired their political habits under Austria, Masaryk wrote: "they are used to the jargon of opposition." But National Democratic politicking had become dangerous, the president argued. National Democratic papers and leaders called him a Bolshevik and claimed that he created the state for the Jews. They falsified both domestic and foreign news reports, and even maliciously edited his name and Beneš's out of official news reports.[69] Dyk's accusation that the president refused to speak with him or with the leaders of his party was sheer nonsense, Masaryk countered. He had approached Dyk himself various times, through various mutual acquaintances, and had spoken with many National Democrats about their activities, which Dyk well knew.

The president's letter ended with a challenge, calling on Dyk to prove out his accusations—even to demand an official government investigation on the floor of Parliament, so that Masaryk and Beneš could defend themselves publicly.

> I would not be being entirely direct, were I not to say to you openly a few words about your special polemical method. . . . I have seen in the past how frequently you aid yourself with half-truths; *Ad usum* is also a half-truth. [Y]ou in fact have said nothing, for you have not indicated even a single piece of evidence [behind] your polemical insistence.[70]

Dyk and Masaryk corresponded for the next several months, touching upon two main issues of difference: Masaryk's attitude toward the National Democrats and the president's involvement in political life. Dyk identified a 1920 interview with the president in the Viennese *Neue Freie Presse* as the beginning of ill will between the Castle and the Right. In the interview, Masaryk had called the National Democratic antipathy for the country's Germans a source of danger for the young republic. Since then, Dyk complained, all dissenting or separatist factions within the National Democrats had named the president as their source of authority and legitimacy.[71] Masaryk argued that the *Neue Freie Presse* interview constituted only one among many public statements he had made. Then, shifting approach, the president noted that the journalist had not even bothered to sign his name to the piece, implying that anonymity in this case meant carelessness with the facts—in other words, that Masaryk had not spoken as harshly as the reporter recorded. As for dissenters within the National Democrats, he wrote, he had in fact advised dissatisfied National Democrats to remain in the party. He repeated his earlier hope that the National Democrats could have been the country's much-needed bourgeois, urban-centered conservative party, commanding the respect of the nation's intelligentsia, professoriate, and bureaucracy. In the National Democrats' belligerence toward the president and flirtation with fascism, Masaryk saw a nationwide crisis of the intelligentsia made manifest. But Masaryk's response also betrayed his continuing worry that a government party, with real influence over powerful sectors of society, harbored resentment toward the state's leaders and its rapprochement with its national minorities. "As for your accusations about lacking empathy for the National Democrats, how can you expect me not to respond to direct attacks on myself and Beneš, which have continued for a decade?"[72]

Masaryk and Dyk differed strongly on what Masaryk labeled chauvinism, and what Dyk defended as appropriate national loyalty and self-defense. "We do not apotheosize our own state," Dyk claimed, "nor do we hate other [nationalities] or try to destroy them." But, he warned, the Germans did. They had tried to extinguish Czech nationality; they would always want to dominate Central Europe. The Czechs' only defense was an assertion of national strength. Dyk and the National Democrats worried that Masaryk's tacit definition of Czechness as enlightened European humanism—leavened with affection for Czechoslovakia's language, geography, and history—in fact ruined healthy Czech patriotism and weakened the republic. Dyk's view invoked social Darwinism: for him, nationalism was associated with the ability to defend the nation, spiritually, physically, and economically, against competitors or aggressors. Peaceful coexistence was unlikely: Masaryk's visions of pan-Europeanism and world citizenship were chimeras. Neither Masaryk nor Dyk made any real effort to bridge this ideological chasm; Masaryk tried only to lessen the amount of finger-pointing by writing that his remarks on chauvinism in 1920 had not implicated only the National Democrats but also other groups and events, such as the Red-and-Whites (an early protofascist group), the illegal occupation of the German-owned Estates Theater by Czechs, and random local shootings of Germans. Can't we have differing ideas of patriotism, the president asked Dyk, without accusing the other of nonpatriotism?[73]

They also continued to differ over Masaryk's public presence and the existence of the Castle organization. Masaryk maintained that his presence in public life was necessary, and that rumors of some Castle political grouping were largely exaggerated. Dyk rightly pointed out that the presidential chancellery functioned as a political institution; he repeated his comment that it was a camarilla and insisted that the president surrounded himself with informers and yes-men.[74] Masaryk, again dabbling in half-truths himself, wrote back that he had no informers; rather, he spoke with appropriate ministers, leaders, and party figures. As for the putative camarilla, he rejoined, "my chancellery is a purely administrative office."[75]

But a plaintive request by Dyk highlighted the sticking point of their disagreement: "Finally, please, admit that liberation is a collective work."[76] The Castle had rejected this possibility as early as 1919; it seemed even less possible by 1929. As long as the National Democrats' "patriotism" was an integral, aggressive nationalism, the president would not allow them to share the mantle of liberator with himself and with Beneš. Masaryk and Dyk never came to any kind of rapprochement. Their correspondence trailed off. Unlike Karel Kramář, who socialized with Masaryk in 1926 even as they attacked one another in the media, Dyk and the president never met privately.[77] Given the divergence of their beliefs and a decade of forceful arguments, perhaps reconciliation was impossible.

These and other *Boj legendistů* debates articulated the causes of enduring antipathy between the Castle and the Right: competing claims to the liberator's mantle, the diminution of the National Democrats' electoral successes, Beneš, the Czech-German relationship, Czechoslovakia's Western orientation, and the Castle structure. They also proved yet again the centrality of journalism to interwar Czechoslovak political culture. Moreover, the *Boj legendistů* had concrete political ramifications. The country's rejection of the moderate socialist parties at the polling booth meant increased insecurity for the Castle, who viewed the socialists as the country's natural leaders. Given an overall shift rightward between 1922 and 1930, the growing extremism of the National Democrats might have poisonous domestic repercussions, among them the alienation of the country's German minority and a foreign-policy shift away from the Western democracies. Thus the *Boj legendistů* represents more than haggling over a place in the history books: for the Castle, it offered the opportunity to discredit a group of influential, and possibly dangerous, political opponents. It was one of many ways the Castle worked to isolate the National Democrats, defend Masaryk and Beneš, and iterate the values underlying Castle policy.

The Unpredictable Jiří Stříbrný

Jiří Stříbrný, hailed almost unanimously by historians as one of the First Republic's most talented, ambitious, well-connected politicians, began his career on the side of the angels. Before the war, Stříbrný joined the Czech (later Czechoslovak) National Socialists, founded in 1898 by Alois Simonides and Václav Klofáč, and rose quickly through the ranks. He was a member of the domestic resistance, representing his party on the Prague National

Committee and contributing to Czechoslovakia's founding in 1918. That very year, Stříbrný began challenging Klofáč for leadership of the party.

Stříbrný's political career in the republic's early years matched his promise. He served as minister of postal and telegraph services in the first coalition government under Kramář (1918–1919), of railroads under Prime Minister Vlastimil Tusár in 1919–1920, in various positions under Švehla (1922–1925), and as minister of defense from 1925 to 1926. Stříbrný helped found the Pětka and remained a member until 1925.[78] Despite Stříbrný's continual involvement in scandals and his resistance to Beneš's program in foreign affairs, Masaryk remained cordial to him. In fact, in 1925, Švehla chose Stříbrný for minister of defense, a cabinet office Masaryk usually controlled; certainly the president's approval for such an appointment would have been sought.[79] During his brief absences from government Stříbrný consolidated his position within his party, and began to dominate the National Socialists' executive committee, packing it with loyalists who had joined the party in droves after the war.

But the Castle was watching Stříbrný carefully. In 1923, Edvard Beneš had joined the National Socialists and quickly allied himself with Klofáč against Stříbrný.[80] Stříbrný had long personally disliked Beneš; he resented Beneš's treatment of the Pětka leaders in the early 1920s and disputed Beneš's position as Masaryk's successor. Like Agrarian Prime Minister Antonin Švehla, Stříbrný thought the next president should be a Slovak, specifically the Slovak Agrarian and then-Castle foe Milan Hodža. Stříbrný began trying to alter the National Socialists' previously predictable pro-Castle orientation.[81] But Stříbrný's power within his party was also shifting. His ostentatious lifestyle, questionable personal affairs, rightward political shift, and "dictatorial tendencies" from his years as a *pětkář* (Pětka leader) had cost him support.[82]

Spring 1926 saw the decisive break between Stříbrný and the Castle. In April of that year, Masaryk, Beneš, and Stříbrný discussed the possibility of an executive coup to repress Czech fascism and any nationalist responses by the country's minorities. Stříbrný's envisioned coup, a standard-issue authoritarian putsch, differed profoundly from the Castle's more legalistic suggestions. Stříbrný intended to arrogate all power to the executive, allowing Parliament to flounder into irrelevance. He proposed to alter the electoral code, suppressing the Communists, and quelling the minority parties entirely.[83] This seems to have been the last time the Castle consulted Stříbrný on issues of governance. But the Castle's obvious antipathy notwithstanding, Stříbrný and the Castle differed more in degree than in kind. Masaryk himself had lauded NLP leader Karel Engliš's idea of restricting the electoral rights of younger men and soldiers, who voted Communist in large numbers, and completely denying the franchise to women, viewed as likely to support clerical parties.[84] At this same time, Stříbrný hosted a meeting of anti-Castle right-wing politicians at his villa in Káraný; Kramar and Gajda were among the participants.[85]

In March 1926, Švehla's governing coalition was replaced by an "experts' cabinet." Beneš had served before in Masaryk's nonpartisan cabinets, but this time, Stříbrný's loyalists on the National Socialist executive committee insisted that Beneš resign, to prove his loyalty to the party. Instead, Beneš left the National Socialists, supported by Masaryk, and retained his portfolio as foreign minister.[86] Stříbrný moved into open opposition against the Castle, publishing a brochure, "Kdo je vinen [Who Is Guilty]," that accused the Castle—particularly Beneš—of plotting against himself and Gajda. Meanwhile, Klofáč, Beneš, and other National Socialists loyal to the Castle launched a counterattack, including publishing unverified accusations in *Lidové noviny* that Stříbrný suffered from syphilis.[87] By the fall of 1926, Klofáč had regained control of the executive committee and presidium. At the party's congress that September in Brno, the National Socialists expelled Stříbrný by a vote of 90 to 42.[88] His supporters also left the party, and Beneš reentered it. Klofáč defended Stříbrný's ouster and the National Socialists' support of the Castle by stating simply that only Masaryk and Beneš could adequately lead and defend Czechoslovakia and avoid another White Mountain, alluding to the 1620 battle in which Habsburg forces defeated the Czechs.[89]

As the party congress opened, National Labor Party leader and Castle publisher Jaroslav Stránský waded into the fight on Beneš's side. Stránský bore Stříbrný a grudge held over from the NLP's 1925 electoral defeat. In an April 1925 letter to Zamini Third Section chief Jan Hájek—a letter Stránský could safely assume Beneš would see—Stránský complained that Beneš's own party was supporting a reform that would doom the NLP's chances. The only imaginable reason for this, Stránský wrote, was Stříbrný.[90] Stránský revenged himself just days before the September party congress with a *Lidové noviny* story accusing Stříbrný, the heroic "man of October," of collaborating with Austrian officials. Stránský claimed to have documents proving that Stříbrný and another National Socialist deputy had gone in 1914 to the Austrian military governor in Prague, Count Franz von Thun, offering obedience in exchange for exclusion from the draft and permission to publish their party newspaper, *České slovo*. The documents, transcripts of telephone messages to and from Vienna about their visit and what they had promised, seemed quite damning. Stránský's article was clearly intended not just to persuade the National Socialists still supporting Stříbrný of his lack of character, but also to tarnish Stříbrný's political legitimacy and burnish that of the Castle. A few months later, Stříbrný sued for libel, insisting on a correction and the restitution of his good name.

When the libel trial began in early January 1927, Stříbrný denied that Stránský could possibly have any kind of proof: "neither [I] alone, nor with deputy Vojna, neither directly nor indirectly approached the military governor's office in Prague on such matters." Pointing to the timing of the article, Stříbrný emphasized that Stránský was obviously attempting to ruin his political career.[91] Stránský proudly concurred:

> I noticed that deputy Stříbrný, and especially his party, had long been supporters of the new regime [the postwar Czechoslovak state] and the leaders of the revolution abroad, but that increasingly he was coming to the side of those who set themselves in opposition. . . . And in this . . . , I saw his harmfulness and [the] danger [he posed] for our state and national interests. . . . I grew to be convinced that he is a dangerous enemy of this new regime and I said to myself that my duty . . . was to engage in battle with him, . . . and at an opportune moment strike a blow against him.[92]

The trial's highlight was Stránský's and Stříbrný's mutual cross-examination. Both men knew one another personally from their years in Parliament, and their closeness to Masaryk and the Castle. Stránský, trained as a lawyer, skillfully questioned Stříbrný and defended the Castle in heroic cadence. Stříbrný, flamboyant by nature and at ease before a crowd, blithely defended himself and missed no opportunities to jab at the Castle along the way. The burden of proof was on Stránský, and Stříbrný's evasions were masterful. If proving that Stříbrný had approached the governor was in fact impossible, Stránský asked, how was it that he could produce these documents? Stříbrný replied:

> The history of our documents has a peculiar character. Both true and false documents exist. [As for the real documents,] after Austria, we [Czechs] were given five carloads of documents . . . to be handed out to the individual ministries. However, the Ministry of Foreign Affairs hastened to take all five carloads. On the way many truthful documents were lost. . . .[93]

In other words, Beneš's ministry had begun the postwar era with theft, making both minister and ministry untrustworthy. Stříbrný continued with an artful suggestion:

> Then there are also false documents. In Vienna and in Lvov exist[ed] entire offices where for a mere trifle—from 100–200 crowns—it was possible to obtain documents with official stamps and forms. . . . I had

> the impression that in my case [the issue concerns] false documents. This could also [account for] some changes in the names.[94]

That is, Stránský, like his benefactor Beneš, played fast and loose with the evidence. Stříbrný then produced several witnesses, all of whom swore that they had spoken or eaten with him at his summer residence in provincial Bohemia on the day mentioned in the documents. Stránský's only eyewitness was the Czech staff member at the governor's office, who did not remember having seen Stříbrný or Vojna, although he mentioned that he did not usually see every visitor who passed through the governor's office. But the specter of doubt had been raised, and Stránský could not prove his case definitively. Stříbrný simply, effectively outmaneuvered him.

And yet Stránský did not quite lose his case, which dragged on until 1929. The court clearly shared the Castle's dislike of Stříbrný; it awarded no punitive damages to Stříbrný other than repayment of legal costs. Nor did it ask Stránský to publish a retraction of his initial charges or any other admission of error. Rather, he was instructed to publish the court's verdict, praising Stránský and the Castle and casting aspersions on Stříbrný. The court implicitly dismissed Stříbrný's complaint that Stránský's documents ruined his political career. It defended Stránský's decision to publish the documents until just before the National Socialist party congress.

> [The court] can only agree with the opinion of the defendant Dr. Stránský that it is not the journalist's duty—and Dr. Stránský is without question a journalist—to publish immediately every matter he discovers. This is the habit only of another kind of journalism, desirous of any [kind of] sensation, perhaps even those it plans itself. ... [This] has nothing to do with the common good.[95]

The journalism "desirous of sensation" named by the verdict was clearly that of Stříbrný himself, who published several tabloid newspapers through his firm Tempo. All in all, the Stříbrný-Stránský cause célèbre ended in a draw—or, given Stříbrný's ouster from the party, a win for the Castle.

Jiří Stříbrný was far from finished with Czech politics. When he left the National Socialists, he took his financial backers and attracted sympathy from some National Democrats, although others viewed Stříbrný as a dangerous rival for the allegiance of rightist voters. Stříbrný also had important journalistic allies, including Ferdinand Kahánek, editor of the weekly magazine *Pondělník*, whose anti-Castle prejudice extended to printing Hungarian propaganda. Kahánek's extensive contacts throughout Czech politics included anti-Castle Agrarians (including *Venkov* editor Josef Vraný and Milan Hodža) and Zamini's ambassador in Rome. Stříbrný's tabloids—particularly *Polední list*—and printing firm Tempo guaranteed him a political platform.[96] He soon began collaborating with Gajda, attempting to make the leaders of the domestic resistance into the "martyrs of October 28" and to attract a force of dissatisfied voters behind them. In late 1927 and early 1928, Stříbrný contemplated creating a new movement called "neofascism," under which he hoped to unite voters from all the fascist factions as well as from the party he was trying to strengthen, his Radical National Socialist Party.[97] The party's cofounder, Karel Pergler, had been Masaryk's assistant in America during the Great War and had wanted to be the Czechoslovak ambassador to the United States after the war; Masaryk sent his son Jan instead. Stříbrný's party joined Gajda's NOF to form the National League just before the October 1929 elections.[98] Stříbrný, Gajda, and Pergler won three seats in Parliament, funded secretly by the anti-Castle right wing of the Agrarian party.[99]

In 1931, the Castle tried once again to use the courts to rid themselves of the Fascist irritant. Karel Pergler was found to be an American citizen and thus ineligible to serve in the Czechoslovak Parliament; he was expelled from Parliament and summarily deported. Gajda was convicted of libel and also lost his seat. Stříbrný, however, managed to survive. Accused once again by Stránský of corruption, this time during his tenure on the cabinet in the early 1920s—of which, historians have concluded, he was no doubt guilty—he threatened to publish embarrassing information about his accusers.[100] He went free. The 1929 electoral victory remained Stříbrný's, and fascism's, most notable achievement between 1928 and 1934. Stříbrný remained loudly aggrieved until the republic's very end: in the spring of 1938, Stříbrný published *TGM a 28. Říjen* (*TGM and the 28th of October*), reiterating his complaints about *Světová revoluce* and Masaryk's alleged lies.[101]

The 1926 Castle efforts against Stříbrný kept the National Socialists in the Castle camp, where they steadfastly remained through 1948. But Stránský's cause célèbre against Stříbrný did not win him the Castle's trust. His continuing desire to best Castle enemies frequently exceeded that of the Castle leaders, and sometimes his own abilities. In late summer 1926, for example, just before the Stříbrný trial, Stránský accused Milan Hodža of corruption. Here, too, Stránský could not make his case stick; this time, a court forced him to print a lengthy apology to Hodža along with a correction. When this ran in *Lidové noviny*, presidential chancellor Přemysl Šámal told Masaryk that many in Prague thought the NLP had been weakened by Stránský's actions. The president responded tersely that he had never hidden his opinion: Dr. Stránský did not have the qualities necessary to lead a political party.[102] A year later, Masaryk noted in a letter to Beneš that he had spoken with Karel Čapek and Antonín Švehla about the possibility of creating a cooperative that would take over *Lidové noviny*, limiting Stránský's influence on the paper.[103] In April 1928 Masaryk wrote Beneš, "That Brno professor who works for you is polit[ically] naïve and, I hear, impossible tactically. You're going to have to choose someone else."[104]

The significance of Stříbrný's trial, and his ongoing public antipathy with Stránský and the Castle, lay in the trial's outcome and arguments. The judge publicly supported the Castle and Stránský's effort to eliminate Stříbrný from national politics. Stříbrný accused the Castle of deception and theft, implying that Beneš had stolen documents or created false ones. Stránský, meanwhile, accused Stříbrný, and by implication the rest of the men of October 28, of outright collusion with Austria during the war. Stránský also tried on the role of Castle knight, tilting at the domestic resistance in the name of ensuring the Castle leaders' historical legacy.

The Husbandman: Masaryk's Leader Cult

During his lifetime and long after, Masaryk was one of the most famous Czechs in world history. He was nominated at least twice for a Nobel Prize and lionized by noteworthies across the globe. However, that esteem paled compared to the adoration expressed for him at home. During and after his lifetime, Masaryk was held up for Czechs as the embodiment of moral rectitude, cosmopolitan erudition, and democratic egalitarianism. By the end of the 1930s, Masaryk's association with the state he had helped found was impressively total. But it was not accidental. Many different groups and factors conspired to position Masaryk as the only man capable of superseding Czechoslovakia's ethnic and political divisions, a devoted democrat to lead Europe's self-styled ideal new democracy.

In fact, admiration for Masaryk rapidly became a complex and expansive personality cult. The cult, intended to integrate Czechoslovakia's diverse nationalities and to legitimate the young state, also constituted a central element of the national mythology crafted by Masaryk, Beneš, and other Castle personalities. The Masaryk cult, like the Castle's version of the Czechoslovak national myth, was a useful political tool both at home and internationally. Public devotion to Masaryk strengthened his political position, and that of the Castle, particularly against the leading Czech political parties. Abroad, the cult situated Masaryk as the quintessential representative of his state and the values it supposedly manifested, such as a love of liberty, dedication to truth and justice, and adherence to Wilsonian democratic ideals. His international reputation in turn greatly strengthened his hand at home. Many historians have noted the cult's existence, but less is known about its creation and propagation.[105]

Leader cults are ancient, and some scholars argue their origins can be found in sacred myth. Many religious myths feature a "culture hero," generally not a god but a human whose brave deeds make the world habitable.[106] Joseph Campbell's analysis of comparative mythology presents the archetype of a hero "who ventures forth from the common world into a region of supernatural wonder; fabulous forces are there encountered and a decisive victory is won; the hero comes back from this mysterious adventure with the power to bestow boons on his fellow men," and to awaken or recreate his society.[107] Masaryk's writing and political work under the Habsburgs, and especially his wartime activity abroad on behalf of an independent Czechoslovakia, certainly made him a persuasive candidate for drawing on universal symbols and narratives like these. But Masaryk's cult was predominantly civic rather than sacred, although his ecumenical Christian faith comprised an element of it. The cult's main purpose was to create an emotional bond between the inhabitants of Czechoslovakia's fractious new polity and their new president. The other new postwar East and Central European states faced similar challenges and similarly tried to persuade their publics to identify with their new leaders and governments, to approve of their regimes' policies and goals, and to take pride in their regimes' achievements. Leader cults were central in almost all cases, most obviously in the elaborately constructed cults of Vladimir Lenin and Joseph Stalin in the Soviet Union.[108]

Leader cults reach beyond simple glorification. Cults require the leader's involvement in public ritual; the use of the leader's image on stamps, coins, and everyday objects; the public celebration of dates or events from the leader's life or achievements (birthdays, liberation, etc.); the public display of the leader's image; a leader-sanctioned version of the state's history, presented in text and ritual; and the participation of the state's mass media in helping create, disseminate, and comment on the leader's cult.[109] Leader cults also manifest the functions of power. Texts and rituals surrounding leaders personalize the state's abstract power, simplifying the inherent complexity of a government and bureaucracy into a mythologized presentation of that government's leader or president.[110]

The cult most frequently presented Masaryk in a role alluded to in this section's title, taken from a poem by Vitězslav Nezval: the "husbandman" of a grateful nation. That term lends itself to multiple interpretations: master of the estate, father of the family, caretaker of the nation. In fact, Masaryk was frequently referred to as "Tatíček," for which the closest English translation is "Daddy." Within the Czech political context, Masaryk's cult drew on Palacký's, and paralleled the cult of Austrian Emperor Franz Josef. Like these other cults, Masaryk's cult contained biblical or religious references and historical allusions to previous great Czechs as well as to early modern folk beliefs about kingship. At the same time, much about the Masaryk cult—above all its twinning Masaryk with democracy—was unique to the First Republic.

Likenesses between the Masaryk cult and that of Emperor Franz Josef, in the waning years of the Habsburg Empire, helped maintain a sense of continuity between the old empire and the new state. Echoes of Franz Josef were probably not deliberate: the Castle viewed Czechoslovak democracy as entirely displacing, not replicating, the imperial order. Nevertheless, the two men possessed common habits and personalities; the cults featured these characteristics in similar ways. For example, the emperor was always depicted in military uniform, even when at home in the imperial palace. Masaryk's "uniform" was the stylized garb of the country gentleman: riding jodhpurs, a plain fully buttoned equestrian-style jacket, and a peaked hunting cap, black in winter, white in summer.[111] His fondness for military parades and his frequent public appearances on horseback at an advanced age mirrored the imagery of the emperor in his last years. Also like the emperor, Masaryk was famed for his ascetic lifestyle, rising early to work for the good of the people, practicing regular physical exercise, and abstaining from rich food and alcohol.[112] Souvenir photograph books of both men posed them at their writing desks (the emperor's a baroque glory of gilt, beveled edging, and black lacquer; Masaryk's of simple wood) and holding lovable grandchildren, thereby crafting images of servants to the state as well as of devoted family men (figure 3.1).[113]

Public expectations and governing style also linked Masaryk to the emperor. One Prague newspaper characterized Masaryk's elaborate welcome, on his return to Prague in December 1918, as "a royal welcome for our first president."[114] In 1919 prominent National Socialist Emil Franke criticized the National Democrats, who then led Parliament, for refusing to treat Masaryk as a "son of the people" upon his return. Rather than inviting the president to the Parliament, to be welcomed by the people's representatives, Franke complained, "we all had to go to the Castle, as if to [visit the] monarch."[115] This effect was enhanced by the complex, minutely articulated interwar presidential ritual crafted by KPR personnel. For example, the members of Masaryk's entourage were directed how to respond if, when leaving the Castle, they might encounter a working-class family, whose small child might happen to run toward the president.[116]

Masaryk's civic apotheosis was initially a collective effort, building on a largely spontaneous popular outpouring of jubilation and gratitude at the end of the war. Those who had admired Masaryk's reputation before the war were still more inclined to salute him after it, as in these verses from a poem by Karel Čapek that ran in the magazine *Nebojsa* on January 2, 1919, comparing Masaryk to St. Nicholas, who in early December brings Czech children small presents—in this case, national independence:

Figure 3.1. A complement to the family photographs in *Masaryk ve fotografii*: this 1931 Castle publicity still shows Masaryk (in his summer suit) with his grandsons, Herbert and Leonard Revilliod. *Source*: AÚTGM fotografické oddělení, VIII/47/2*145/19–20, 1210.

Thomas's blessed day
Merrier than Christmas
What you wanted, what you prayed for,
nation mine, you have it here!
Thomas here! Four years gone
Now come from apostolic paths
bringing in your (yellow) bag
a new blessedness.[117]

In 1919, Čapek was a noted young journalist and author, not yet the Castle intimate he would become by 1926. The themes of this poem, linking Masaryk to St. Nicholas and other saints ("apostolic paths"), were common.

Masaryk was frequently portrayed as the culmination of Czech history and a means of linking that history to biblical or European greatness. In the 1920 poem "President Masaryk. Song for His Seventieth Birthday," Jan Rokyta compared Masaryk to Moses (and not coincidentally, the Czechs to the Jews, the ultimate martyred people), Jan Hus, Jan Žižka, fifteenth-century king of Bohemia Jiří z Poděbrad (George of Podebrady), and Jan Amos Komenský. In Rokyta's poem, Masaryk "enters the castle of Czech kings as if it were his home."[118] Other contributors to the cult invoked the nineteenth century, while still others drew on the Bible. In 1926, a self-identified worker from Osík u Litomyšl sent a poem, titled "To Our Dear President," to the presidential chancellery; all six verses begin with "Our Tatíček, Mr. President," and compare Masaryk to Christ.[119]

But whatever his great predecessors, Masaryk was the greatest of all. Many of these comparisons, after the early years of the republic, were made by Castle adherents in Castle-loyal journals. For example, in a 1930 article for *Národní osvobozeni* (*National Liberation*), František Kubka imagined a future Czechoslovak president addressing schoolchildren in an assembly at the Castle in the year 2000. Kubka's imaginary future president recalled, as a schoolchild himself, seeing Masaryk speak at the Castle: "he was as simple and kind as one's own grandfather, but at the same time he was a hero from a real-life fairy tale about the miraculous resurrection of the nation. . . . After Jan Hus and Komenský he was the greatest man of our history. And indeed he was greater than those two martyrs, because he had luck and success. Jan Hus only hoped that the truth would prevail; Masaryk's truth prevailed!"[120]

Masaryk's cult emphasized his humble origins and his connections to the *lid*, or people, thus drawing on a powerful element of Czech romantic nationalism dating back to the nineteenth century. The cult also tried to establish Masaryk, with a Slovak father and Moravian, German-speaking mother, as the literal embodiment of Czechoslovakism. Masaryk's souvenir photograph books always included pictures of him in discussion with timid, smiling Moravian or Slovak peasants, often in folk costume. His many biographers dwelt on his humble childhood home, and his youthful apprenticeship as a blacksmith.

Masaryk's cult always had detractors. The National Democrats, for example, tried to promote a similar cult for Kramář.[121] The Czech Populists tried to substitute Czech Catholic tradition, such as the medieval missionaries Cyril and Methodius and Saint Václav/Wenceslas, for Masaryk's preferred ecumenical Protestantism and celebration of the "national" religious martyr Hus. Many Slovaks were also alienated, while Germans viewed Hus as anti-German; both groups were frustrated with Masaryk for promoting what they saw as a cult of Hus.[122] Some Germans actively resisted the Masaryk cult, scrawling graffiti on empty pedestals that had once held statues of

Habsburg Emperor Joseph II: "Kaiser Joseph steht auf und regiere, dummer Masaryk liegt da nieder und krepiere! [Emperor Joseph, stand up and rule; stupid Masaryk, lie down and die!]"[123] In December 1920, Germans in Cheb shot a portrait of the president.[124] In short, the Castle myth's reference to Czechoslovaks did little to cement over the very real national divides that continued to characterize public life in the new republic.

Resistance notwithstanding, the esteem granted the office of the presidency anchored and magnified Masaryk's personality cult. Just as the emperor's image had adorned public institutions and private homes, Masaryk's visage gazed benevolently throughout the new republic, hanging in stores, homes, schools, and government buildings. On state holidays, "[Masaryk's] busts and portraits . . . somewhat kitschily looked out from between goods in shop windows at the customers and grocers."[125] Even émigré Czechs displayed Masaryk's image. Religious historian Jaroslav Pelikan, whose parents emigrated to the United States in 1923, recalled that "we used to observe two Independence Days in our home, the Fourth of July and the twenty-eighth of October; and the photograph of Masaryk hung like an icon alongside the usual Christian images."[126] The president's public presence involved his name, not just his august personage. "Military troop units, streets, squares, the largest Czech battleship, public institutions, but also for example the wheezing paddle-wheel tourist steamship on the Vltava . . . were all named after him."[127] Even Brno's university renamed itself Masaryk University—while Masaryk was still in office—as did many other schools, ranging from elementary to high schools, all over the republic.

The presidency helped maintain another aspect of the Masaryk cult. Interwar workers, among many other groups in Czechoslovak society, viewed Masaryk as the "good king" who would enact justice. This understanding of Masaryk was widespread, as the interwar Czechoslovak presidency maintained imperial traditions regarding personal appeals to the state's highest authority. Ordinary citizens could walk into the Castle and ask to see the president; they also wrote him asking for help, whether it was financial assistance or appeals for judicial clemency. Workers sent a steady stream of "petitions, appeals, and memoranda," not to mention workers' delegations, into the presidential chancellery, requesting help with various kinds of conflicts.[128] In fact, the vast majority of letters entering the Castle chancellery requested financial support; their writers ranged from the indigent to former Legionnaires and even former senators. The Castle chancellery seems to have written to regional police and social organizations to verify claims, as a basis for awarding financial assistance.[129]

Both the Castle and private citizens promoted and produced Masarykiana. Czechs could buy books, pamphlets, brochures, commemorative plates, cups, and ashtrays bearing the president's likeness, and of course portraits abounded. Many publishers hastened to produce short, cheap works on the president for a mass public. One such piece was Arnošt Caha's 1921 brochure "Tatíček Masaryk—Osvoboditel [Daddy Masaryk—Liberator]," part of a series titled *S vědomím českých dějin: Sbírka rozprav pro nejširší vrstvy lidové* (*With an Awareness of Czech History: A Collection of Treatises for People from All Walks of Life*). Printed quickly on a low-quality machine (many letters are unclear or almost doubled), the pamphlet provides many pictures of Masaryk from his early years, as well as the area where he grew up. Words of Western derivation are defined in the margins, such as *akademický* as opposed to *vysokoškolský*.[130] Ordinary citizens crafted presidential folk art for Masaryk's birthday or for other symbolic occasions. Journalist Ivan Herben recounted an outpouring of such goods for Masaryk's eightieth birthday in 1930.

> Along the wall stand countless presidential pictures and . . . portraits. . . . In one, painted by a simple worker, the president stands holding his grandson on his shoulders, exactly as in the famous photograph [taken at the family villa in] Topol'čianky. But behind the president stands not the Topol'čianky villa, but the Alps. Beneath it is the symbolic caption: the great one among the great ones. A barber with artistic inclinations sent . . . a portrait of the president created out of hair of all colors. . . . A bakery worker managed to place in a bottle . . . a tiny cake with eighty candles surrounding a bust of the president in the center.[131]

So much of this folk art poured into the presidential chancellery that the Masaryk Institute, founded in the early 1930s, opened a Museum of Gifts. This collection was divided up in the 1950s, and most of it was destroyed. The few photographs that remain show rooms overflowing with busts, portraits, collages, watercolors, and other artistic representations of the president, among gifts as varied as embroidered textiles and violins (figure 3.2).[132]

A version of the Masaryk cult was directed at children, in the spirit of Mircea Eliade's "exemplar history," in which a myth and its main protagonists are paradigms, "both a model *of* and a model *for* reality."[133] Masaryk's portrait adorned each school and sometimes individual classrooms. Classes put on patriotic tableaux to celebrate state holidays, with Masaryk prominently featured; typical is Josef Koudelák's juvenile patriotic drama *T.G. Masaryk*, which portrays a hungry family with two young children at the end of the Great War. The father, a Czech Legionnaire and survivor of the Battle of Zborov, comes home, and the happy children are chosen to welcome President Masaryk as he visits their village on his way back to

Figure 3.2. Taken in the Museum of Gifts in 1930, this picture shows various busts of Masaryk, as well as busts of others given to the president. Several violins hang in the cabinet at the back. *Source*: AÚTGM fotografické oddělení, VIII/47/2*411/10, 4823.

Prague.[134] Schoolchildren could also read juvenile fiction about Masaryk—lightly "improved" historical depictions of his boyhood—as well as accounts of Masaryk's growth from boy to man, emphasizing his morally superior qualities and his devotion to family and country.[135]

Schoolbooks often presented Castle ideology as history. The most popular text used to teach high school history was written by Josef Pekař, known for publicly challenging Masaryk's romantic-nationalist interpretation of Czech history. Yet Pekař's book could have been written by Castle publicists. Its 1921 edition described the medieval German colonization of Bohemia as an "especially great danger for the Czech future."[136] Pekař's depiction of the Great War emphasized the importance of Masaryk and Beneš for Czechoslovak independence; they and their allies and colleagues abroad are almost the only independent actors discussed in Pekař's text until the fall of 1917. The Czech politicians who remained home hardly appear in the book. Pekař disingenuously described all Czechs of the time as "almost without exception [being] aware that a German-Hungarian victory would without question make their lives more difficult and extinguish all hopes for achieving their national goals," an obvious recasting of the Castle's present back into the nation's past.[137]

The president energetically helped create the visual imagery presented to the public. Masaryk never refused artists' requests and posed for least sixty-four different artists; the president sat for the artist V. Hynais ninety-four times. He did not object to film, or to "acting" in repeated takes; "in the archives of the Plzeň firm Škoda, there are clips of Masaryk posing in a Škoda-Hispano-Suiza car the firm had given him. . . . The president was aware . . . of the effect of his person, and he had no inhibitions about using it."[138] Among the books Masaryk crafted with Karel Čapek was a souvenir book of presidential photographs, *Masaryk ve fotografii* (*Masaryk in Photographs*, 1931). The book presents Masaryk in various mythologized guises: as a man of the people, marching through fields of wheat in his customary black suit and speaking with a kind smile to the usual Slovak and Moravian peasants; deep in thought in his libraries at Lány and in the Castle; the great statesman, meeting with foreign leaders and diplomats; the family man, hoisting laughing, naked grandchildren on his shoulders. In every setting Masaryk is uniformly dapper, dignified, kind, and reserved (figures 3.3–3.6). One theme is strikingly absent from the book, and from most of the visual depictions of Masaryk as president: there are few pictures of Masaryk on the floor of Parliament or voting.[139]

Figure 3.3. Masaryk on the country's tenth anniversary (October 28, 1928), on a white horse at the charged site of Bílá hora, the hillside outside Prague where Czech forces lost to the Habsburgs in 1620. Masaryk took other publicity shots at this same site on a black horse. *Source*: AÚTGM fotografické oddělení, VIII/47/2*396/8, 4087.

Figure 3.4. Masaryk photographed from below, at Židlochovice in Slovakia, July 15, 1931. *Source*: AÚTGM fotografické oddělení, VIII/47/2*145/19–20, 1203.

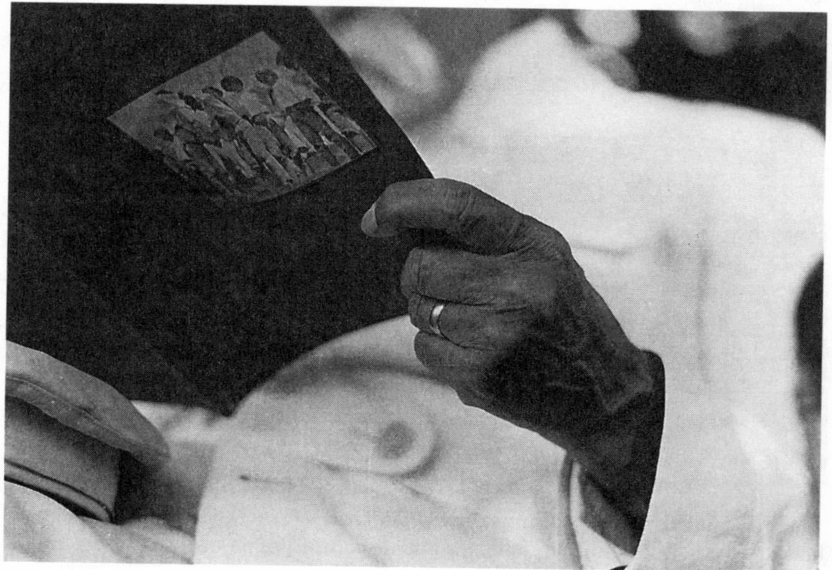

Figure 3.5. Masaryk's body was part of the cult: here, the beloved president's hands. *Source*: AÚTGM fotografické oddělení, VIII/47/2*105/14, 801.

Figure 3.6. Three-quarter profile of Masaryk, in his dark winter suit, taken in September 1931. *Source*: AÚTGM fotografické oddělení, VIII/47/2*1081/17, 839.

Masaryk's visual iconography was often deliberately militarized, thus visually linking him to the Legionnaires. In fact, the Masaryk cult rested at least in part on the correlated cult of the Legionnaires and their brave national service during the Great War. Masaryk and the Castle drew on Legionnaire support to buttress the presentation of Masaryk as military hero, adored by all soldiers who served him. Meanwhile, the Legionnaires energetically crafted and promoted their own cult, abetted by the president in his writings, in public rituals, and in novels, films, and memorials written, designed, and planned by Legionnaires, to which the Castle lent support.[140] The two cults used similar language and imagery, for example comparing Legionnaires to the fifteenth-century Taborites; but much Legionnaire writing was antisemitic, unlike the Masaryk myth.[141] Legionnaires published popularizing pamphlets and photograph books about their wartime exploits.[142] But non-Legionnaires also contributed to the Legionnaire cult, as in composer Leoš Janáček's composition *Osvoboditelům* (*To the Liberators*, 1918), which set to music a poem by Antonín Horák.[143] Many souvenir picture books of the president, including *Masaryk in Photographs*, include photographs of Masaryk's participation in military parades or smilingly shaking soldiers' hands.[144] Castle promotion of the Legionnaire cult and the Masaryk cult went hand in hand, reminding citizens at regular and public intervals of the basis of Castle power and the importance of continued Castle predominance within Czechoslovak politics (figure 3.7).

The cult also relied on words, not just images: its basis in the 1930s was various longer works of political prose. Masaryk himself was one of the most important propagators of his cult, particularly through text. His wartime pamphlet *The New Europe*, his 1925 war memoir *World Revolution*, and the 1933–1936 *The Path of Democracy* series, a collection of his writings and speeches, all communicated the cult's (i.e., the Castle's) main ideological tenets and availed themselves of any opportunity to bolster Masaryk's and Beneš's reputations. Masaryk's considerable body of anonymous journalism did the same. Also important to the cult were the many Masaryk biographies, often published by Orbis, Čin, and other Castle-friendly publishing houses, which tended to bathe the Czechoslovak state and its leaders in a rosy light. These biographies were written by Czechs as well as foreigners; the foreign writers were often hosted by the Castle-sponsored Social Club and given translated copies of Czech-language Masaryk biographies. Hence a certain

Figure 3.7. Masaryk riding out of the Castle gates to participate in the July 1926 Sokol *slet*. Riding with him are three Legionnaires. Note the different uniforms, each representing a different fighting front. *Source*: AÚTGM fotografické oddělení, VIII/47/2*396/6, 4074.

uniformity of presentation and information prevails in these texts, from Jan Herben's 1926 three-volume *T.G. Masaryk* to British propagandist Cecil J. C. Street's 1930 *Thomas Masaryk of Czechoslovakia* to German journalist Emil Ludwig's slightly more critical 1936 *Defender of Democracy: Masaryk of Czechoslovakia.*

The Masaryk cult's evidentiary remains are ubiquitous; this discussion has treated only a fraction of the available materials, translated into at least eight languages. But while we know much about the cult's production, historians can only generalize about its reception or public function. Since cults, like political myths, "offer charters, warrants, validations, legitimations, and authoritative precedents for beliefs, attitudes, and practices," the Masaryk cult can be understood as an attempt to legitimate the Castle and its interpretation of the country's history.[145] Akin to leader cults in the rest of Eastern Europe, Masaryk's cult was "intended as cement, to cover over . . . divisions, to reinforce a sense of purpose and unity." The cult positioned Masaryk to represent various transcendent ideas: he embodied the Czechoslovak state, the very notion of democracy, and a tolerant, cosmopolitan Czechness.[146] This last element helps emphasize the extent to which the cult was Czech first and foremost, implicitly equating the Czech national legacy with Czechoslovak citizenship. Through Masaryk's cult, Czech leadership of the Czechoslovak state and a supposedly ideal democracy were symbolically joined.

The Masaryk myth in fact was both a signifier of Czechoslovak democracy and somewhat distant from it. The myth was vigorously rejected or contested by Czechoslovakia's national minorities and some Czechs as well, particularly Catholics, National Democrats, and Communists. While influential, Masaryk's cult was never equivalent to leader cults in totalitarian states, buttressed by censorship and an obedient mass media.[147] Yet mythic politics and leader cults are to be found in all states, whether dictatorial or democratic. The existence of a Masaryk cult in the interwar republic did not make the state less democratic; the cult's insistence on the primacy of democracy did not make the state more so. However, the kingly emphases in the cult might have legitimated the speedy dismantling not just of Masaryk's republic but of its democratic structure in 1938–1939, under the Nazi-collaborationist Second Republic.[148]

Masaryk's cult was part of the Castle's engagement in mythic politics, linking the Castle, its leaders, and its ideas to the best in the Czech and European traditions. Despite being constructed as a set of symbols, the Masaryk cult, and Castle mythic politics more generally, was always related to the direct exercise of real political power. Masaryk himself understood his cult this way. In a May 1927 letter to Edvard Beneš, he wrote, "Švehla is correct in telling the parties that I [personify the state]; this is how I have regarded my election [to the presidency] since the beginning. . . . Any party against my [re]election cannot be in the government. In other words: either I am the representative of the state, or the parties are."[149]

The Masaryk cult shifted over time, reaching out to different groups within Czechoslovak society (including émigrés) during and after the interwar period. This ability to appeal to all onlookers is a characteristic of the most successful leader cults, which embody elements of different national or popular traditions, the better to speak to disparate groups. E. A. Rees notes that the Stalin cult in the Soviet Union

> drew on Russian traditions, the tradition of authoritarian leadership, a deep étatist tradition with its own bureaucratic culture, and even a tradition of popular monarchism.... [I]t may also have drawn on the strong patriarchal peasant culture with its respect for the elder [*starosta*].... [The cult also] sought to link itself with the popular classes.... For the elite it could be seen as a guarantee of their power. For the disadvantaged the Stalin cult offered the hope of redress.... [T]he cult came to symbolize the new social order that had been created.[150]

The parallels with the Masaryk cult are by now clear. The husbandman, the father of the nation and state; the humble man of the people; the man of ideas, or philosopher-king; the great democratic statesman; the family man; the military leader: within the cult, Masaryk was all these things and more. Particularly, he was Czech—Czechness itself—embodying Czechoslovak virtue, truth, and national identity, not just within a particular historical moment but for the ages.

Conclusion

Castle conflicts tended to focus on three themes: the consolidation of concrete power; efforts at integrating the state, primarily by promoting the Masaryk cult and hoping to use him to draw each citizen into a greater personal commitment to the republic; and finally, more abstractly, the nature of legitimate political authority in the postwar era. Those conflicts played out in part within the expected arenas of Parliament, personal relationships, and the press. But they also operated symbolically as competing interpretations of Czech history, from the fifteenth century to the First World War. Taken cumulatively, these conflicts can represent the Castle's agenda at home: defang the political Right, claim the mantle of liberator, and associate itself inextricably with the Czechoslovak state as well as the Czech nation. The Castle lauded Masaryk, Beneš, and the Legionnaires as Czechoslovakia's founding fathers and symbolic representatives. Parliamentary leaders (some of them, at any rate) strove for similar status, but never acquired it.

The Battle of the Legend Makers exemplified the basic arguments between the Castle and the Czech Right, its most significant opponent mythologically, if not quite politically (the anti-Castle right wing of the Agrarian party was a more direct threat). The Dyk-Masaryk and Kramář-Beneš polemics crystallized the conflicts growing between the Castle and the Right for the republic's first decade: the direction of the country's foreign policy, Beneš's closeness to Masaryk and his position as anointed successor, the creation of the Castle and Masaryk's politically active presidency, the Castle's attempt to claim the mantle of liberator and limit the historical credit granted to the domestic resistance, and the Castle's open efforts to counter the Pětka and silence the political Right. These same issues played out in the creation of the National Labor Party, the Gajda and Stříbrný trials, and the creation of leader or hero cults for Masaryk and the Legionnaires. Particularly in the last, the Castle attempted to present its own form of civic patriotism, different from the Right's integral nationalism. In every case, the Castle worked to disseminate its own values and narrative, the basic postulates of Castle ideology.

The *Boj legendistů* debates and correspondence also helped articulate the fiercely loyal relationship between Masaryk and Beneš. As in his letters to Dyk, Masaryk's letters to Beneš bluntly rejected criticism of his protégé: "The main thing: You will remain as [foreign] minister; not just the international, but also the domestic, situation demand[s] that. It is pure nonsense [to generalize] from the internal [political] crisis to a crisis in the foreign ministry."[151] Masaryk helped corral leading politicians on Beneš's behalf; in 1933 he wrote that he had spoken to allies of ambassador to Paris Štefan Osuský, and that Osuský was now "100 percent for you, that you become the second president."[152] In addition to political strategizing, the letters reveal more personal concerns: Masaryk worried often about Beneš's health, repeatedly suggesting that he consult doctors and take vacations.[153]

The Castle's conflicts with the right emerged during a period in which political consensus seemed to have broken down. From 1919 to 1925, the established parties had done their share of squabbling, and occasionally aimed sallies at Minister Beneš. But after 1925, these arguments became more direct, more public, and far more shrill. Prime Minister Antonín Švehla had been the only politician who could convince the Prague partisan press to keep its gloves on. Even his brief return to politics from 1926 through 1928 did not change matters; Masaryk, by nature a fighter rather than a conciliator like Švehla, did not calm the situation. An increasingly sharp polarization and fractiousness came to characterize Czechoslovak political life, even as the Castle became increasingly powerful and active behind the political scenes, where Masaryk and his chancellery frequently brokered conflict.[154] Both inside and beyond the political elites, there was a shared sense of crisis in 1925–1927, arising again in 1928 and 1929. Yet the basically conservative nature of interwar Czech politics meant that the established parties and leaders were able to fight off challenges to the status quo, such as the National Labor Party and the fascists. And F. Gregory Campbell notes that no domestic politician could truly confront the Castle.

> [I]t soon became apparent that Masaryk's personal prestige and popularity—and hence his political power—was so great that no group could openly and effectively oppose him and his supporters. . . . [T]he opposition was not united behind any man or program that offered a viable alternative to the logically conceived and executed policies of "the Castle." . . . To be sure, there were alienated elements among Kramář's National Democrats, Hlinka's Slovak populists, the Communists, or the extreme nationalists from the national minorities, but . . . Masaryk's power lay in the fact that the majority of citizens of diverse social stations revered him as the liberator of the country.[155]

Thus the Castle's contestation over historical legacy had direct political ramifications.

These internal Czech political disputes echoed beyond Czechoslovak borders. The Western powers' warm wartime reception of the Czechs had stemmed from their seeming Westernness—their rationalism, their high-mindedness, their dedication to the values animating the postwar era—and the unity of the resistance abroad with Prague political leaders, at least for the war's final year. If Czechoslovakia were seen abroad as a hotbed of fascism or an inefficient government dedicated to maintaining sinecures, rather than as a hardworking democracy; if internecine squabbling prevented sane policy from being enacted; if Castle opponents won the upper hand at home, and then succeeded in redirecting Czechoslovak foreign policy; Czechoslovakia's enemies would be heartened, and its Western guarantors alienated. The Castle feared, and worked to prevent, these scenarios from coming to fruition.

At the heart of Castle conflicts lay propaganda and the media. Election sloganeering, managing of newspapers and message, the creation of a personality cult, and mudslinging via pamphlet and anonymous editorials were all crucial elements of Castle strategy. Moreover, Castle allies in the media were central in battling the chaos of the late 1920s. Čapek helped strategize and mediate differences among high-ranking officials and tried to form a Castle-friendly press bloc. Masaryk published freelance editorials in

Castle-friendly journals. Stránský and Bouček tried, through the NLP, to create another Castle-friendly parliamentary grouping and to oppose the growth of the Right. Stránský's journals became a crucial arena for Castle propaganda, mythmaking, and defense during the political trials of Gajda, Stříbrný, and the other far-Right leaders, not to mention the Battle of the Legend Makers. These were only the most prominent; other journalists and newspapers allied with the Castle were no less active during these years.

The domestic Battles of the Legend Makers had their parallels abroad. Just as the Castle struggled for moral legitimacy at home, so in the eyes of Europe the Castle and its allies also conducted an argument about history, moral worthiness, and contemporary political power. This time its enemies were other post-Habsburg states and Nazi Germany. Once again, the weapons were propaganda and cultural diplomacy, testing the Castle's contacts and resources. It is to that parallel set of battles that we now turn.

4

Difficulties Abroad

No nation likes to be told where its duties lie, least of all by foreigners with foreign accents.

—Philip M. Taylor

Czechoslovakia's international position made it a vulnerable victor. At Versailles, Beneš had alternated among various related arguments for conjoining the disparate peoples who would make up the Czechoslovak state. The Czechs of the Bohemian lands deserved liberation from Austria according to the principle of self-determination, Beneš explained, and their innate egalitarian, rational tendencies made them ideal allies for the democratic West. Beneš invoked arguments made by Czech nationalist societies, the *Národní jednoty*, that throughout Czechoslovakia, Germans were intermingled with Czechs, making a Swiss-style solution of federated cantons impossible in the Czechoslovak context. Czechoslovakia's Germans would have to be folded into a Czech-led state to maintain the Bohemian kingdom's historic boundaries, mandated by historic right and economic necessity—or so went the story. Similarly, Beneš justified Slovakia's detachment from Hungary (bringing with it many preponderantly Hungarian districts) with arguments about ethnic self-determination, economic considerations, and supposedly natural boundaries.[1]

Beneš received most of what he asked for, but at a cost. Most of its neighbors bore Czechoslovakia territorial grudges. The heart of the cordon sanitaire, meant to shore up France by containing Germany and blocking Bolshevik radicalism, itself needed shoring up by the West. In particular, the British elite, which had long found the Versailles treaty distasteful, soon became less than sure of its new ally. Inside the republic, many Slovaks—deemed a "state-creating" nationality—and much of the country's sizable German community evinced misgivings about the Czechoslovak republic. The supposed epitome of Wilsonian national self-determination was almost as multiethnic as the empire it replaced; the republic's leaders alternated between presenting "Czechoslovakism" as a fait accompli and as a slow process needing several generations for completion.[2]

The Czechs began the interwar era with some advantages. Masaryk and Beneš had won the ear and attention of the Great Powers. The French government in particular viewed Beneš and the Czechs as the lodestone of their new Central European order. Even the Americans, uninterested in European entanglements, sent ministers to Prague who were forthright proponents of the Czech view abroad. Beneš involved himself deeply in the affairs of the League of Nations and had quickly formed the Little Entente, an alliance among Czechoslovakia, Yugoslavia, and Romania, by 1921. This alliance was meant to serve as an extension of Western power and values in East-Central Europe; Beneš hoped it would become a regional counterweight to Germany, Austria, and Hungary, all aggrieved and resentful former powers. Czechoslovak stability and economic conservatism seemed all the more impressive as chaos enveloped other Central and East European states in the early postwar period.

Yet the Czech position was never sure, and relied centrally on propaganda and cultural diplomacy in maintaining its all-important ties to the West. This chapter is devoted to Czechoslovakia's, and the Castle's, relationships abroad: the challenges of preserving them, the different methods they employed in doing so, and the threats they faced. As during the Great War, Castle strategy concentrated more on elites than on electorates, focusing on journalists, newspapers, cultural figures, and political leaders. But interwar cultural diplomacy was a more dangerous game than its Great War predecessor, as exemplified by various international cultural imbroglios between Czechoslovakia and neighboring states or those claiming to speak for them. Masaryk, Beneš, and Castle intellectuals were deeply involved in these conflicts, whether in international associations, such as the supposedly apolitical International P.E.N. Club, or on the pages of newspapers like London's *Daily Mail*.

The Czechs were far from alone. Each fragile new state between Germany and the Soviet Union waged a continual cultural relations and propaganda battle, resting above all on a discourse of Europe. The East-Central Europeans claimed that they knew and loved the West's art, belles lettres, and political culture; most important, they claimed to embody European values. East-Central European states had of course used similar gambits to attract Western attention since the early nineteenth century, when Greeks struggling for independence from the Ottoman Empire learned they had a rapt audience among well-educated young British men—among them the dashing Lord Byron—infatuated with the romance of ancient Athens and determined to rescue the birthplace of Europe from the infidel Turks. Similarly, calling part of Europe "East" had long been a way to disparage it. Diplomat Klemens von Metternich, defending Austria against its rebellious territories in 1848, justified continued absolutism by noting that Asia began at Vienna's Landstrasse.

But the aftermath of the First World War put a new spin on this old conversation. East-Central Europeans argued that they were central to the new European project of collective security, transparency in national and international affairs, and adherence to the Wilsonian ideals that dictated the structure of the postwar peace, such as protection of the rights of minorities. They were, they claimed, on their way to becoming the energetic, prosperous, tolerant New Europe hoped for by the signers at the Paris peace talks. But, they sighed, their neighbors were not. Often, East-Central Europeans could and did use almost identical arguments against one another. The Hungarians, for example, claimed that they were the only people in the Danube basin capable of building a state and administrating it effectively, while the Czechs discussed their historic dedication to what would now be called civil society, or democratic civic norms. Those making counterclaims were dismissed as barbarians or, worse, Orientals: Ante Trumbić, arguing for the worthiness of the Croat nation, scolded a French writer: "You are not going to compare, I hope . . . the Croats, the Slovenes, the Dalmatians whom centuries of artistic, moral and intellectual communion with Austria, Italy and Hungary have made pure occidentals, with these half-civilised Serbs, the Balkan hybrids of Slavs and Turks."[3] As historian Maria Todorova argues, for most Europeans, "East" is elsewhere—that is, it is east of where they are.[4]

A Dangerous Europe

An old joke bewails Mexico's geographic location: "Poor Mexico: so far from God, so close to the United States." The First Czechoslovak Republic faced a similar problem. Whatever its distance from the divine, Czechoslovakia's proximity to so many hostile or unstable states presented reasons for concern. Many Czechoslovak ethnic groups could look to national homelands just across the border, making domestic Czechoslovak minority policy into foreign policy, and complicating both. Meanwhile, Western Europe was swiftly turning its back on the rest of Europe. European international relations during the interwar era were vexed; East-Central international relations were characterized by a variety of relationships, ranging from veiled competition to outright hostility. A brief discussion of interwar European international affairs, from the Czechoslovak perspective, makes clear not just Czechoslovakia's challenges but those facing its allies and opponents.

The First Republic's most significant neighboring state, Germany, experienced a vast array of postwar problems, discussed elsewhere in more detail than this book can offer. Despite them, the postwar German state slowly built a measure of domestic stability while negotiating its new status as Europe's democratic pariah. One method of reestablishing equilibrium involved defying the West—for example, the secret sections of its 1922 Treaty of Rapallo with the equally feared Soviet Union, enabling weapons testing and military expansion and flouting Germany's Versailles obligations. But Germany could not afford to alienate France and Great Britain, as France's 1923 occupation of the Ruhr made clear. Czechoslovakia's relationship to the Weimar government was initially constrained by German-French tensions. The Czechs expressed to the Americans and British their frustration with French pressure on Germany, they had to defer to their most important Great Power ally. American ambassador to Prague Lewis Einstein reported in 1923, "Already last winter President Masaryk in private conversation with me referred to the occupation of the left bank of the Rhine as a mistake, and Dr. Beneš has often criticized the French policy toward Germany as lacking in magnanimity."[5]

Weimar German interests abroad directly threatened the small states of East-Central Europe. Even before unification in 1871, German political elites had discussed union (if only in terms of trade) with Austria-Hungary, often invoking as a corollary military and colonial expansion into eastern and southeastern Europe. During the Great War, Friedrich Naumann's book *Mitteleuropa* brought these ideas into popular discourse, arguing that Germany could and ought to exert political and economic control and cultural hegemony over the European continent from Belgium's western frontier to the border of the Russian Empire and beyond (specifically, the Vistula/Wisşa River), and from the Baltic Sea to the Balkans.[6] Such ideas retained their allure through the interwar period. Weimar's leaders assumed the Czechoslovaks would be forced economically to join an Austro-German union; once they did, Germany could pressure Poland regarding border revision.[7] (Significantly, the 1925 Treaty of Locarno guaranteed Germany's borders with Belgium and France, not with its eastern neighbors.)[8] Both these steps would begin to undo the postwar peace settlement that had brought the new post-Habsburg states into being. Thus the smaller countries of East-Central Europe intensely resisted intermittent German hopes for an Austro-German economic union, such as the 1925–1926 policy of *Angleichungspolitik* (steps to bring closer to one another the trade, economic, and legal structures of Germany and Austria).[9] Weimar also cautiously tried to block the creation of regional alliances intended to constrain Germany.

Czech-German conflict arose at home as well. Of Czechoslovakia's 13.3 million citizens in 1921, more than 3 million spoke German.[10] Czechoslovak Germans—soon labeled as Sudeten Germans after the Sudeten mountain range dividing Czechoslovakia from Poland—were divided when the Great War ended. Most either wanted to join Czechoslovakia, or were too indifferent to protest against it. A minority hoped Austria or Germany would annex Czechoslovakia's ethnically German regions; still others wanted independence based on the new Wilsonian tenets of national self-determination, hoping eventually to join the Reich and create a pan-German state.[11] But the anti-Czechoslovak attitude prevailed. On March 4, 1919, in the interwar era's deadliest set of confrontations, some fifty-four Germans and two Czechs lost their lives, and German civilians battled the Czechoslovak army throughout Bohemia and Moravia.[12] Sudeten political leaders refused to cooperate with the new government until the Treaty of St. Germain, dissolving the Austro-Hungarian Empire, was signed in September 1919, one of several reasons the Czechs gave for not consulting the Germans while writing the country's constitution.[13] New language laws established "Czechoslovak" as the national language (33,000 German bureaucrats were fired in 1926 when the law went fully into effect); new education laws mandated that German schools with fewer than thirty students close; postmen refused to deliver letters without Czech street names; the first postwar National Assembly roll call rendered into Czech the names of the German delegates.[14] Even President Masaryk made an infamous comment in December 1918 labeling Germans in the Czech lands as "settlers and colonists," although the following day, at the traditionally German-language Estates Theater in Prague, he encouraged them to "perform" along with the Czechs in the country's "great political drama."[15] Beneš's foreign policy was considered detrimental to German interests as well, although the Castle promoted Czech-German cooperation, suggested German ministers for cabinet positions, and encouraged German party participation. The Castle counted the entry of activist German parties into the governing coalition in 1926 among its greatest political successes.[16] Still, Sudeten German popular discontent with Czech rule remained a problem throughout the First Republic's lifetime, occasionally making its presence known internationally.[17] Czechoslovak Germans particularly disliked the Castle's reliance on France; the American envoy in Prague quoted a German senator in 1923 as saying that "German Czech soldiers would refuse to fight on behalf of such an alliance if it came to a war."[18] Beneš's hope seemed to be that Czechs and Slovaks would outnumber Germans in the Czech lands within a generation or two, and that Czechoslovakia's Germans would accustom themselves to life in a Czech-led state.[19]

Czechoslovak-Austrian relations during the interwar period began badly, but quickly stabilized. Austria tried unsuccessfully to claim two Bohemian border districts full of German speakers (the Allies also refused it German-settled border districts from Hungary and Italy) and took in hundreds of trainloads of Czechoslovak coal daily during 1919. Radically truncated, devastated by war, Austria was a "state no one wanted."[20] By 1920 Austria was a conservative autocracy.[21] Czechoslovak policy toward Austria tended to focus on attempts at preventing an *Anschluss* with Germany, and blocking attempts by Karl and Otto von Habsburg to return and claim the dynastic throne.[22]

The Soviet Union was, at first, a conundrum on Czechoslovakia's eastern border. Masaryk and Beneš disapproved of the Bolsheviks. Both rejected violent revolution as a political tactic; Masaryk's travels in Russia before and during the war had introduced him to many Tsarist generals and political leaders, such as Pavel Miliukov, a fellow academic and member of the provisional government overthrown by the Bolsheviks.[23] Meanwhile, the Soviets experienced what one historian has called "the Masaryk trauma"—not only that Masaryk had been one of Marxism's important intellectual opponents during the late nineteenth century, but that he was understood as "a protagonist, if not the architect, of the Allied intervention in Siberia" during the Russian Civil War.[24] Beyond these issues, the Czechoslovaks were constrained by the other members of the Little Entente. The Romanians were quarreling with Moscow over Bessarabia, while the Serbian royal family of Yugoslavia was concerned about the treatment of the Romanov dynasty. Beneš could not establish diplomatic relations with the Soviets before his Entente partners. At home, almost all the leading Czech parties were anti-Bolshevik.[25] Masaryk, the Czechoslovak Social Democrats, and Karel Baxa, the anti-German and pro-Russian mayor of Prague, helped make Prague a center of the anti-Bolshevik Russian exile, supporting a population of 20,000 Russian expatriates with material and legal assistance through 1922 (Prague's Russian community lasted well into the 1950s) and hoping for the restoration of democratic Russia.[26] Czechoslovak de jure recognition of the Soviet state was postponed until 1929, long after most of the rest of Europe had normalized relations. Not until Hitler's accession to power, which brought to light British willingness to abandon Versailles and the state system it created, did the Czech attitude toward the Soviets undergo a change.

Hungary and the Hungarians presented a more obvious problem for the interwar Czech government. Hungary's extreme postwar upheaval—the establishment of a Bolshevik regime by Béla Kun, the failed invasion of Slovakia in 1919, the conservative response of the "White Terror," and worst, the country's profound truncation at the hands of the Paris planners, reducing it from 18 to less than 8 million people—left it a constant source of fuming revanchism and propaganda abroad. Interwar Magyar politics focused on restoring the entirety of the crown lands of St. Stephen. The Hungarians had lost territory to each of the Little Entente states. But no Great Power would countenance revanchism against Romania. Yugoslavia was more promising, as Italy also coveted Yugoslav territory and could assist Hungarian interests there. But Croatia had never been considered a crucial part of the prewar Hungarian lands, and had seceded of its own accord. That left Czechoslovakia, which was also widely understood to symbolize the postwar order in Central Europe.[27] If the Magyars succeeded in getting the Western Powers to consider treaty revision of Czechoslovakia's Hungarian-populated borderlands, other treaties might also be revisited, and Czechoslovakia's territorial integrity might be seriously threatened. Czechoslovakia's democratic structure and closeness to the West was also seen as a rebuke to the more feudal, oligarchical interwar Hungarian state, which one observer has labeled "neobaroque."[28]

After 1919, between 750,000 and 1 million Hungarian speakers found themselves Czechoslovaks.[29] Czechoslovakia granted its Magyars political and educational opportunities, but there were complaints. For example, the 1919 land reform, designed to break up large estates and distribute holdings to small- and medium-scale farmers, adversely affected many Czechoslovak Magyars (as it did Sudeten Germans, who along with the Hungarians complained that the land reform's purpose was to weaken the minorities and strengthen Czechs and Slovaks) and led to the objection that the Czech government had simply robbed ethnic Hungarians of their land.[30] Overall, Czechoslovakia's Magyars were, like its Germans, both a domestic and an international problem: a frequently discontented minority at home (albeit one that overall adapted relatively well to, and participated politically in, the Czechoslovak state) and a potential embarrassment, or even danger, abroad.

Czechoslovakia and Poland, its northern neighbor, shared little save the support of the Great Powers and a precarious geographical position. Poland appreciated the Habsburgs as the most progressive of their three partitioners; the Czechs dismissed their Habsburg years as their "dark ages." Similarly, the Poles loathed the Russians in any guise, Tsarist or Bolshevik, while the Czech Right for years had cherished Pan-Slavic dreams of a Romanov on the Bohemian throne. Each state dismissed the other as a multiethnic hodgepodge; the Czechs thought little of the Poles' annexation of Belorussians and Ukrainians, while the Poles were skeptical of Czech promises of brotherhood with the Slovaks. Poland's 1919–1920 conflict with Czechoslovakia over Těšín (Cieszyn, Teschen) seemed to epitomize each state's vulnerabilities. Těšín was ethnically Polish, the center of a coal-rich industrial region and the transportation hub through which ran the only railroad connections linking Bohemia, Slovakia, and Ruthenia. Both countries claimed it. The Czechs tried unsuccessfully to occupy Těšín in January 1919, when it seemed that the Paris Peace Conference would cede it to the Poles. Despite this embarrassment, later diplomatic shifts went in the Czechs' favor, and Poland never forgave them for it.[31] The country's internal political tumult, resolved by the executive coup d'etat of General Józef Piłsudski in 1926, occupied considerable energy, but even once Polish policy stabilized, Polish-Czech relations were at best formal, at worst icy. Poland maintained friendly relations with suspect Hungary, and was in "latent conflict" with Germany and Russia. Despite Franco-Polish cooperation and Czechoslovakia's long Polish border, Beneš remained aloof from the Poles and was alleged to have referred to Poland as a "Northern Balkan."[32] Even in the 1930s, both under threat by Germany, the two states worked against one another, hoping to persuade the Nazis that the other state would prove a richer prize.

Czechoslovakia's ties to its Great Power patrons vacillated during this period. British irritation with the Czechs began at the Paris peace talks and grew from there.[33] The Foreign Office's frustration with the French, and their seemingly endless desire for vengeance on the Germans, exacerbated dislike of the Czechs, the centerpiece of the French cordon sanitaire.[34] Their exasperation focused on the person of Edvard Beneš, despite his moderate policies. In response to a proposed 1923 visit by Beneš to London, Foreign Secretary Lord Curzon was said to have replied "that he was always glad to meet Beneš as it saved him the necessity of speaking."[35] In 1924, after the Czechs concluded a treaty of friendship with the French, the *Berliner Tageblatt* attempted to smear Czechoslovakia by accusing it of creating secret military pacts within the treaty. Even after the *Tageblatt* comments were exposed as a forgery, the London press opined that Beneš's attempts to exercise leadership in Central European international politics were dangerous, bullheaded, or both.[36] Meanwhile, the Czechs' most important British sponsors during the Great War, historian Robert Seton-Watson and journalist Henry Wickham Steed, had also irked the Foreign Office, provoking a description of their collaboration as "a dangerous combination of megalomania, self-righteousness and crusading spirit."[37]

Certainly the Czechs could claim some success. Jan Masaryk, ambassador to Great Britain, was highly regarded within British society and by some within the government. Masaryk cultivated, for example, figures like Allan Leeper, a Foreign Office bureaucrat and a friend to the Czechs since the Paris Peace Conference, for which he prepared the British briefing materials placing Czechoslovak claims in a favorable light. Leeper was described by Jan Hájek, chief of the Czechoslovak propaganda effort, as "the most knowledgeable [person] in the Foreign Office on Central European affairs," and a significant influence on his brother Rex, assistant to the Foreign Office's press director. Hájek created an Allan Leeper Fund with the help of the other members of the Little Entente after Leeper's death in 1935; Hájek wrote, "We mainly have him to thank that Hungarian revisionist propaganda never gained an audience among the top administrators in the Foreign Office."[38] Sir George Clerk, the first British minister to Czechoslovakia, was a stalwart, if unromantic, supporter of the republic. In 1921, regarding the establishment of the English-Czech Bank (Anglobánka), Clerk wrote to Sir Eyre Crowe, "If any of the Succession States . . . is going to last, it is this hard-headed unpleasant unmannered country, and its stability is the greatest factor for peace in Central Europe." A year later, when the bank had been established with difficulty, Clerk wrote to Miles Lampson, head of the Central European Department at the Foreign Office,

> The whole lot, Czechs, Magyars, Poles, Jugos, Rumanians, should be put in a bag and shaken up, and then handed over to a decent Briton to administer. . . . Czecholand today may not seem worth more than a casual, though perfectly friendly nod when we sit next to it at luncheon . . . but one day it is, or should be, our best bridge into Russia, and even now it is the lynch-pin of central Europe. . . . [L]ittle though I like [Beneš] as a man and a brother, I am sorry to see him unnecessarily rubbed up the wrong way.[39]

But the Foreign Office lost patience with and interest in the Czechs, and the internecine disputes of the Habsburg successor states. By the mid-1920s, an Austro-Hungarian nostalgia spread through the ranks of the senior diplomats; Jan Masaryk called it "the ghost of the Habsburg Empire."[40] The Czechs' patrons could no longer exercise much influence: a friend in the Foreign Office rebuked Robert Seton-Watson for being "deaf to any criticism of the Czechs."[41] When Wickham Steed wrote in 1930 to suggest the unusual step of sending a special mission to Czechoslovakia to congratulate Masaryk on his eightieth birthday, Sir Orme Sargent, counsellor of the Foreign Office, practically snarled in response: "In the case of an unimportant country like Czechoslovakia . . . certainly not worth the trouble and expense." Another Foreign Office bureaucrat wrote on the document, "This proposal opens up alarming vistas. How about Pilsudski and Mustafa Kemal? And heaven only knows where we could stop. . . . Moreover, . . . the real creators of Czechoslovakia are the principal Allied Governments who . . . destroyed the Austro-Hungarian Monarchy. Without that victory, M. Masaryk would still be another exile in the United States."[42] Foreign Office bureaucrats writing in 1920 would not have denigrated Masaryk's wartime work abroad or dismissed his country. Times had changed.

British foreign policy had undergone a thorough reorientation. By the 1930s, the Foreign Office was divided between pro–League of Nations idealists and isolationists, who insisted on disengagement in continental Europe.[43] The traditional fear of Bolshevism, especially within the Tory party and the London *Times*, trumped any concern about Hitler. The British financial sector was substantially invested in the German economy. A group around Lord Lothian believed that Hitler would stabilize Germany and bring about peace on the Continent. Meanwhile, many powerful Britons disliked the French and felt sorry for the Germans, whom they considered a "conquered but honorable foe."[44] Similarly, Chamberlain and Churchill both admired Mussolini and wanted to give him a free hand in the Balkans.[45] The new British minister in Prague, Sir Joseph Addison, was scathingly anti-Czech.[46] As British sympathy for the Germans, Italians, and Hungarians deepened, Little Entente states began creating bilateral ties with the Germans and Hungarians.[47] All this left the Czechs, and to a lesser extent the French, alone.[48]

The French, Czechoslovakia's main ally, were of relatively little help. Franco-German rapprochement under Briand and Stresemann allowed the Czechs to normalize relations with Weimar, although the French retained their cordon sanitaire, along with military missions in Czechoslovakia and Poland through 1932.[49] Officers at the missions were said to have embezzled funds, leaked details of international treaties, and concocted schemes about detaching Ukraine from the USSR and making it a French protectorate, under mostly Polish control.[50] France also encouraged and sponsored private financial interests in East-Central Europe, although French national economic policy remained relatively uninvolved.[51] When the German threat reemerged in 1933, the logistical difficulties of French commitments in East-Central Europe were undeniable. France's growing military and economic dependence on Great Britain lessened the likelihood of true support for the East-Central Europeans. In the end, the British were militarily and economically of greater significance, suspicious of the Czechs and determined to avoid war with Germany.

Paying for Positive Opinion

Against this problematic backdrop, the importance of Zamini's Third Section, focused on propaganda and the press, becomes clear. One of the Third

Section's most significant tasks was organizing journalists and newspapers in Great Power states to write favorably of Czechoslovakia. Through its embassies in Paris, London, Geneva, Vienna, and Belgrade, the Third Section supported a tremendous number and range of publications, including business periodicals, news dailies, opinion and special-interest weeklies, and academic journals. Jan Hájek sent checks regularly to twenty-eight dailies, journals, and press agencies in France alone.[52] The Third Section also carefully monitored the European press and book publishing. It used whatever allies it could to intervene behind the scenes when foreign papers accused the Czechs of scandalous behavior. And it kept in print, through its publishing house Orbis, works that emphasized Czech honor, rationality, and dedication to democracy, and argued that Czechoslovakia was the mainstay of Central European peace and prosperity. The Third Section's vexing task was to combat West European indifference and ignorance, as well as the active propaganda efforts of other successor states.

Zamini supported journalists, editors, freelancers, and academics all over Europe—and a few in New York—but by far the largest number went to Paris. The French press of the time was "not only frequently manipulated but . . . notoriously venal," characterized by deliberate leakages and highly susceptible journalists.[53] This meant trouble for the Czechs. A 1933 Zamini internal summary of "Foreign Propaganda in France" noted that the Italians, the Japanese, and the Nazis were the main influences on the French press; the Hungarians and the Little Entente states played far lesser roles. The Japanese were a particularly powerful corrosive force: "even minor journalists were offered . . . tens of thousands," and the former chief of French diplomacy headed a firm importing Japanese goods.[54] The Hungarians' brash activity took Zamini aback: the Zamini author noted that the Hungarians had urged France to abandon its Little Entente allies and create a Danubian federation instead, with Hungary at its center. Budapest was once again becoming one of the great cities of Europe, claimed the Hungarians, and to demonstrate it they proposed to fund a trip for forty French members of Parliament.[55] The Hungarians had already invited a host of French journalists as well. Finally, the Hungarians asked that the spirit of the peace treaties with regard to national self-determination be fully applied: in other words, the Hungarian-inhabited districts within Slovakia ought to be given back to Hungary. French parliamentarian Ernst Pezet, ruefully described by Zamini as highly skilled and intelligent, was perhaps Hungary's greatest proponent in France, and highly dangerous: "his intelligence gentles and impedes the outrageousness of Hungarian propaganda."[56] The Hungarians had crafted agreements with *L'Oeuvre* and *La Republique*, Zamini reported: with funding that seemed to come from London, the Hungarians were publishing their own journals, *Les Nouvelles Danubiennes* and *Le Danube*. Both boasted multinational contributors and argued for Transylvanian independence, Slovak autonomy, and plebiscites in mixed districts.[57] The Nazis, reported the Zamini author, relied on émigré Germans in Bordeaux, Paris, Alsace, and North Africa; they could count on positive press in the *Paris-Soir* and *Midi*, which they had recently "purchased," as well as *La Volonte, Le Matin*, and *Notre Temps*.[58] This game was one the French themselves played: the Zamini author noted that under Briand, the French had paid a good 50 percent of the expenses of various reviews and cultural enterprises to help ensure the success of the Briand-Stresemann rapprochement.[59]

The Czechoslovaks had their hat in this propagandistic ring. The Zamini author recommended that the Czechs respond to the Nazis and Hungarians by recruiting at least eight young, smart French writers and publicists, and paying them handsomely, along with a host of French papers across the political spectrum.[60] Third Section documents list twenty-six French papers, press agencies, and radio agencies on the Czech payroll, including *Journal des Dèbats, Paris Soir*—presumably the same paper claimed by the Hungarians and Nazis—*Le Temps*, and *Volonte*.[61] Similar to the Hungarian effort to fund the travel of French parliamentarians, French academics and journalists were brought to Prague on Zamini stipends, including Fuscien Dominois of the Institut d'Études Slaves in Paris.[62] The Third Section sent a regular stipend to various French academics, including Geouffre de la Pradelle, French expert on international law and director of the Institut des Hautes Études Internationales, who published *Revue de Droit International* and *La Vie des Peuples*.[63]

Some of the Czechs' opponents were enormously impressed by what seemed like total success. The Hungarians and Romanians, for example, were "awed" by the supposed impact of Czechoslovak propaganda on the Great Powers.[64] But the Czechs could not compete with the sums paid by Great Power states. In 1933, Germany spent 256 million francs on international propaganda, and the French 74 million francs; in contrast, Poland could only muster 26 million and Czechoslovakia 18 million.[65] (The Little Entente states sometimes combined forces, collectively hiring journalists like Jules Sauerwein, accused by a Nazi collaborator of having served both Prague and Belgrade between 1928 and 1938.)[66]

As in Paris, so too in London. Jan Masaryk, as embassy staff and later ambassador in London, played a central part in funneling Czech monies to writers and journalists in England. He also worked at charming prominent politicians and bureaucrats into supporting the Czechoslovak cause.[67] Masaryk's friends Seton-Watson and Wickham Steed were stout advocates for Czechoslovakia, while their influence lasted. A pro-Czechoslovak concentration of scholars worked at the King's College London School of East European and Slavonic Studies. Loyal journalists were important and were treated well. Wickham Steed, who left the *Times* in 1922 to found *Review of Reviews*, received considerable advertising support from the Third Section and was paid for contributions to the *Prager Presse*.[68] In 1928, with Steed's fortunes in disarray, the Third Section hired him to write a biweekly article, to run simultaneously in the *Prager Presse*, the *Neues Wiener Tagblatt*, and Belgrade's *Politika* and to be aired on Radio Central/Central European Radio/Radio de l'Europe Centrale, Orbis's Geneva-based radio syndicate.[69] In 1930, when Steed's magazine went under, Beneš and Masaryk personally granted him funds.[70] Some journalists in Britain were hired not just by the Third Section but by other Castle-loyal papers as well. For example, Polish émigré Vladimir Poliakoff, writing under the name "Augur," published articles as well in Stránský's *Lidové noviny*.[71]

The media was just one element of recruiting prominent allies abroad to espouse each country's virtues. Some of these intellectuals were émigrés; others were Great Power citizens who for academic or personal reasons had signed on as protectors of a particular state; still others were paid. Another element of creating positive impressions of Czechoslovakia abroad involved Orbis and the texts it disseminated. By the 1930s, Orbis published a wide range of materials itself and sponsored other publishing houses. Among the works it ensured were in print were travel brochures and maps of Czechoslovakia in Spanish, Dutch, and Lithuanian; art books on Czechoslovak glassmaking in Swedish; economic atlases of Central Europe, prominently featuring Czechoslovakia; and German texts on Czechoslovak minority rights. Orbis translated Alois Jirásek's romantic nationalist stories and Karel Čapek's witty travelogues into many European languages; they even translated a piece by Masaryk's old colleague from *Čas*, Jan Herben, into Esperanto.[72]

Some examples from English-language texts illustrate Orbis's most constant themes. Cecil J. C. Street's affectionate 1924 travelogue *East of Prague*, as well as his 1930 biography *Thomas Masaryk of Czechoslovakia*, was on Orbis's distribution list, along with journalist Henry Baerlein's 1925 historical romance *Here Are Dragons*, set in Czechoslovakia's ethnically mixed border regions. Street's *East of Prague* depicts a long journey by rail and car from the German border in northern Bohemia down through Prague and Brno to Vienna, from there to Bratislava and through the Tatra mountains to Kosice, to Užhorod, and throughout Ruthenia to the republic's easternmost town of Jasina, with a detour to Marmonošska Sihot in northern Transylvania. The Czechs and Slovaks are the clear-sighted heroes of Street's book, the Czechoslovak Magyars only slightly less so; Czechoslovak Germans and irredentist Hungarians are portrayed as entertainingly unrealistic and untrustworthy, in need of good Czech tutelage. Street's discussion of Czechoslovakia's minorities could have been written by the Castle:

> Geographically and economically Bohemia is an indivisible unit . . . while there are certain districts in which the Germans are in a definite majority, there are many others in which the Czech and German inhabitants are so mingled as to be inextricable. . . . The Swiss cantonal system cannot be applied to Bohemia, owing to the intermingling of the races. Meanwhile, the Germans, despite remarkably fair treatment on the part of the Czech leaders of the Republic, stand out from all participation in the affairs of the State.

Any problem on the part of the Czechoslovak Germans, Street explains to his readers, is "really more psychological than material."[73]

Likewise, the Hungarian claims on Slovakia were entertaining, if unjust. Street depicted Hungarians as lazy, greedy, excitable, and excessively passionate. Unlike the hardworking Czechs, the Magyars wanted handouts from Europe.

> [I]n the old days, . . . Hungary included a number of territories whose inhabitants were content to do most of the hard work of the state for them [the Magyars]. . . . Now . . . they spend much valuable time and money in standing like beggars before the chancelleries of Europe, bewailing their sad fate. . . . They declare with tears in their eyes that they are a peaceful people, who only want a little charity to set them on their feet once more.[74]

But the Magyars had treated the Slovaks ("a hardy and independent race") with great cruelty. The Slovaks "endeavored to free themselves from the Hungarian bondage," and "turned naturally to their brother Slavs," the Czechs, from whom the Slovaks "received every form of sympathy."[75] The history of Slovak repression under the Magyars explains why the Slovaks are not as advanced as their brothers, the Czechs, although the Slovaks are "extremely intelligent and ready to learn."[76] This portrayal of the average Slovak as a bright child or noble savage, common in Czech depictions as well, continues throughout Street's work, for example in a 1927 propaganda pamphlet, *Slovakia Past and Present*, published and distributed by the Czech Society of Great Britain.[77] Street dismisses entirely any complaints on behalf of the Hungarian minority within Czechoslovakia: they "are almost to a man perfectly contented with their lot. . . . [T]he grievances of the Magyar minority in the Republic are without any real foundation, and exist not so much in the minds of the individuals . . . as in the scheming brains of the propagandists."[78]

The Czech government of Street's pages was benevolent, fair, efficient, moral, and determined—an analogue for the most idealistic depiction of

British government. Street explained to his readers that in this the Czechs had little company among their neighboring states. Street recounted an anecdote about another travel writer, determined to photograph a pedestal in Bratislava on which a statue of Maria Theresa had once stood; the statue had been torn down by returning Legionnaires in the early days of the republic. The author was certain he would be harassed by the authorities, but no one was watching him; Street patronizingly noted that the author had to console himself with the hope that a man following him in the street might have been a detective.[79] Moreover, Street wrote, the Czech and British peoples were remarkably similar in many important ways. On the streets of the Bohemian town Kutná Hora, the Czech soldiers Street encountered were "startlingly like British soldiers in appearance and cheerfulness . . . that contented and care-free appearance which one associates with our own men, but is distinctly uncommon on the Continent."[80] Similarly, the landscape, "indescribably homely," "reminds one of the atmosphere of our own country. . . . The people are very like the people of the English countryside, lacking the excitability of the Latin or the apparent lethargy of the Teuton."[81] Like the British, the Czechs devoted themselves to their work, as Street repeatedly reminded his reader: "The Czech population has fully realised that the surest way of consolidating their State is to set down to work."

> [I]t is not until one has viewed the spirit of work that pervades the country at close quarters, and compared it with the general air of *laissez faire* which prevails in other European states, that one understands fully the enormous lead which Czechoslovakia is gaining over her neighbours and competitors.[82]

All in all, "The Czechs have waited long and struggled hard for their political liberty, and now that they have gained it, they seem to know how to use it for the benefit of all concerned."[83]

Orbis also distributed British journalist Henry Baerlein's 1925 historical novel *Here Are Dragons*, set in the ethnically mixed Bohemian borderlands.[84] *Here Are Dragons* tells the story of the inhabitants of a few small villages and their reactions to Czechoslovak independence. Every character is a simplistic political archetype: Jan Klafka, the brave, practical, humble Legionnaire; the aged Prince Condorotti, afire with support for the German-Bohemian cause; the kind, beautiful German, Countess Mary, and her husband, Condorotti's nephew Frederick, representing a new generation of Bohemian Germans who support the Czechoslovak state. For example, Mary refuses to accept Bohemian German stereotypes about the onset of Czech rule. "Here are the two people in the same country," she argues with Frederick.

Wouldn't it be far, far better if they tried to understand each other? . . . [D]o you remember those mediaeval maps that your uncle has got in his library? . . . When the people who made the maps didn't know anything about one of the remoter districts they inscribed upon the parchment "Here are dragons." . . . [But] if they had gone to those parts they would have found, very likely, that it was not so different from their own region.[85]

Later in the book, Mary is seen sitting in an inn, the only German in a roomful of Czechs singing "a choral song by Smetana." Mary is singing "heartily" with the Czechs. Prince Condorotti's gardener says, in a voice "hoarse and quavering," "O thou dear God, . . . canst Thou permit this crime, a German girl among the Czechs?"[86]

Mary stoutly insists that Czechs are equal to Germans, and touts Czech virtues: "The Czechs didn't do like the old Russian Nihilists. Instead of bombs and secret meetings and exile to Siberia, the Czech leaders kept alive the spirit of the people by means of music and the study of history and the comradeship of their gymnastic societies, the Sokols."[87] Frederick agrees with her. While chatting with Jan Klafka, he notes, "Of course there are excesses. Your young men who pull down the statues of Joseph II—I'm sorry they do it because our side try [*sic*] to put them up again." Regarding controversy over "national" schools, Frederick states simply, "[T]here are faults on both sides."[88] The old Prince Condorotti does not share his nephew's sanguinity. He rails against the Czechs for not consulting the Germans in drafting a constitution; his interlocutor, a local Czech named Zlatnik, then asks the prince about the German-Bohemian army he is helping to create. " 'We have not had much time,' said the Prince, 'but we are doing our best. A useful consignment of machine-guns is expected from Vienna. . . . and we are drilling, drilling . . . ' He looked flushed and resolute. 'I should have thought,' said Zlatnik, 'that you are too busy to assist them with their constitution.' "[89]

The Third Section tried to create a global Czech presence, whether personal or textual. The Ministry of Education and Culture helped the Third Section send Orbis books to schools, universities, museums, institutions, and newspapers all over the world. Among hundreds of recipients were the Romanian ministry of education; the Portugese ministry of agriculture; a Russian *gymnasium* in Tallinn, Estonia; seminars on East European history and law at the universities of Hamburg and Ljubljana; St. Procopius College in Lisle, Illinois; the Detroit Museum of Art; Stanford University; and the *Chicago Tribune*.[90] In addition to books, the Third Section sent abroad at state expense a parade of authors, journalists, and intellectuals, of different political affiliations and ethnic backgrounds, to learn about other countries, to develop relationships with political journalists and leading cultural and economic figures abroad, and to represent Czechoslovakia. Many (though not all) were loyal to the Castle, such as Max Brod of the *Prager Tagblatt*, or Hubert Ripka of *Lidové noviny* and *Přítomnost*.[91] The Third Section also sponsored exhibitions of Czech art and concerts by Czech musicians (which it dubbed "musical propaganda") in European capitals, and further afield to Rio de Janeiro.[92] The Third Section sent Czech and Slovak scholars and politicians to international conventions and congresses, and aided groups of foreigners traveling to Czechoslovakia.[93]

Zamini closely monitored European publishing as well as the European press. Embassy staffs reviewed books on political topics and sent the Third Section regular reports on recent publications and their potential significance for Czechoslovakia. For example, in late 1931 a staffer in the Vienna delegation sent to Prague an assessment of Gerhard Schacher's *Die Nachfolgestaaten/Österreich, Ungarn, Tschechoslowakei/und ihre wirtschaftslichen Kräfte*. He wrote reassuringly that the author, who had published a highly praised book on the Balkans in 1930, emphasized the importance of sustained relationships among the title states and with Germany. The Czechoslovak diplomat contentedly noted that the author dismissed the notion of an Austro-German customs union. The author advised Austria to focus its attention on southeastern Europe, which would not be aided by a customs union: for that matter, Austria would find reasons just as solid to unite with Czechoslovakia.[94]

A brief examination of the Hungarian propaganda effort helps place Zamini's work in comparative perspective. Like the Czechs, the Hungarians had proponents in Great Power capitals and academic circles. Prominent historian C. A. Macartney advocated for them as secretary of the League of Nations Minority and Labor Committees, as assistant vice-consul in Vienna, at the Royal Institute of International Affairs (Chatham House), and later at All Souls College, Oxford.[95] Already at Oxford was the Oxford League for Hungarian Self-Determination, created in the 1920s by a group of Hungarian citizens working with the Hungarian Foreign Ministry.[96] The Hungarians also had their journalists. For example, Fleet Street denizen Dudley Heathcote, author of a travel diary about the Balkans, offered his journalistic services to the Czechoslovak Foreign Ministry in the mid-1920s; after they refused him, he went to work for the Hungarians.[97] The Hungarians had trouble initially establishing themselves in Great Power capitals, but by 1926 were paying regular subsidies to *Le Temps* and the agencies MTI and Havas in Paris.[98]

Hungarian propaganda aimed at the West began during the Paris Peace Conference, far later than the Czechoslovak effort, and was initially private rather than state sponsored, relying on organizations such as TEVÉL (Magyarország területi épségének védelmi ligája, or the League for the Defense of Hungary's Territorial Integrity) or faculty at Hungarian universities. Hungarian arguments paralleled those of the Czechs, claiming both moral worthiness and political experience. They claimed that the Hungarians had hospitably received and taught Western civilization to the other nations on Hungarian territory, but that for a thousand years the Hungarians had proven themselves the only people in the Danube basin capable of organizing and maintaining a centralized state. Still, the Hungarians were willing to re-create the kingdom on a federalized basis, as long as it was retained in full, since Hungary "naturally" formed a "perfect" territorial unit.[99]

As the Paris conferences continued, the Hungarian Foreign Ministry took over more propaganda work, publishing brochures in English and French on such topics as the division of Hungary, possession of the port city of Fiume, Croatia's "martyrdom," and Czechoslovakia's "geographical impossibility."[100] The Hungarians also made overtures to the European mass media, establishing press offices in Switzerland and Great Britain. TEVÉL combined brochures with a wide range of materials, including three magazines beginning in 1920: *The Hungarian Nation, Les pays du Danube*, and *La Transylvanie enchaînée.*[101] After the signing of the postwar peace treaties, both TEVÉL and the Foreign Ministry focused their attention on the British press—contrary to Czechoslovakia's focus on the French—and shifted to economic arguments.[102] Edmund Morel, editor of *Foreign Affairs*, published pro-Hungarian essays dripping with bathos, such as propagandist Karoly Rácz's "Hungary under the Treaty of Trianon. 'Hopeless, Heart-Breaking Bondage,' " in which he wrote, "The Hungarian of to-day knows very well that he has to struggle very hard for the piece of wood out of which the cradle of his child will be made, and for the wood out of which his coffin will be made one day.... [I]t is his only desire to be left alone with his work to be capable of redeeming posterity through his sufferings."[103] Morel and others portrayed the Habsburg successor states as outposts of French militarism, run amok on the Continent.[104] Rácz published other pieces in the London press, including glowing reports about Hungary's economy in *The Economist.*[105]

Tacitly politicized social relations remained crucially important throughout the interwar period; here the Hungarians had rather more success than the Czechoslovaks. TEVÉL invited writers and political leaders to visit Budapest, entertained them elegantly, and squired them around the "Hungarian lands."[106] Many British Foreign Office professionals grew close to members of the Magyar aristocracy; the Hungarian ambassador in London was a fixture on the social circuit. Judit Márffy-Mantuano, a relative of Count Pál Teleki, married Lord Listowel, and carried messages from Teleki at various points.[107] F. Alexander Szarvassy, a Hungarian émigré and chairman of the British Foreign and Colonial Corporation, was said to have been foremost among supporters of Trianon Hungary in London's financial sector.[108] Hungarian advertising and journalistic subvention also bore touristic fruit. Britons traveled to Budapest and the fertile *puszta*, and skied in the Carpathians. The Prince of Wales traveled twice to Hungary in 1935.[109]

The Venomous Lord Rothermere

The British press tycoon Harold Harmsworth, better known as Viscount Rothermere, was a former minister of aviation and a prominent anti-Communist conservative, and owned the *Daily Mail* as well as other papers throughout Britain. In the summer of 1927, Rothermere loosed what would prove to be a decade-long campaign on behalf of Hungarian revisionism in the British press.[110] Calling for the revision of the Treaty of Trianon, and the other postwar treaties to boot, Rothermere's essays defended the Hungarian revisionist cause mainly by aiming systematic attacks at Czechoslovakia, its leaders, and its people, not to mention the Great Power states that had brought it into being. Rothermere's rhetoric and arguments are worth examining as evidence of European conservative hostility to Czechoslovakia and its fellow Little Entente members. Rothermere's writings also manifest the competing romantic national mythologies and stereotypes at work in interwar cultural diplomacy. All of these mythologies rested on claims to morally "European" qualities such as bravery, tolerance, or gallantry, or to having been Europe's defender at a moment of weakness.

The attacks began on June 21, 1927, with Rothermere's shrill "Hungary's Place in the Sun" in London's popular *Daily Mail*. Rothermere decried the postwar peace treaties as a "blunder," East-Central Europe as a region "strewn with Alsace-Lorraines" and new, angry minorities, ready to begin a new "conflagration."[111] Of the flawed postwar treaties, Trianon—the treaty establishing the borders of a truncated Hungary—was by far the worst. Hungary had to pay for losing the war, and ought not to return to its prewar size, but should not be cut off from so much of its prewar population. He advised the Great Powers to award Hungary various narrow strips of Hungarian-inhabited border territory from Czechoslovakia and Yugoslavia, with internationally supervised plebiscites in other, mixed areas. The article was accompanied by a map, containing various obvious errors of fact, indicating the areas to be returned to Hungary.[112] The Great Powers and Western financial firms could ensure Little Entente cooperation by threatening to call in loans or tighten the money supply.[113]

The tone of a second essay on August 30 was still more venomous. In "Europe's Powder-Magazine: Gross Injustices Making for War," Rothermere dismissed Czechoslovakia as a "hybrid state," an "artificial operation only carried through by outraging the principle of nationality which it was supposed to serve," a "spoilt child of fortune," the "powder-magazine of Europe."[114] The moment it got its hands on "its" Hungarians, Rothermere wrote, Czechoslovakia "adopted toward its Hungarian minority population a deliberate policy of expropriation of property, which has continued unchecked.... If only half the stories that are told about these land deals are true, the Czech Government is responsible for tolerating some of the worst frauds that have ever taken place in the public life of Europe."[115] Not only had the Czechs cheated the poor Hungarians, Rothermere wrote, but they had also swindled all of Europe; they had only pretended to help the Western powers during the Great War, and had misrepresented themselves since then. Rothermere claimed: "Apart from a handful of Czech 'legionaries' who came over to the Allies, the Czechs fought on the side of the Austrians to the last. It was thus a curious freak of fortune which enabled Czecho-Slovakia... to assume the role of a triumphant conqueror." The Czechs were also ingrates, since Rothermere alleged that the *Daily Mail* "and its associated newspapers" were the first to suggest Czechoslovak independence to Western readers. Without the *Daily Mail*, he stated, the Czechoslovak state would never have existed.[116] They would do well, then, to heed his words.

Rothermere's 1927 articles began a long anti-Czechoslovak campaign for Central European border revision. In March 1929, he wrote in the *Daily News and Westminster Gazette* an essay, "The Next War." This time it was the Austrians who had suffered on the Czechs' behalf: "that other Peace Treaty of St. Germain by which the territory of Austria was carved up, principally for the benefit of Czecho-Slovakia, in such a way that the great city of Vienna, with two million people, was left practically without national territory to supply its needs or consume its products."[117] In 1930, Rothermere predicted that German national pride would never be satisfied with mediation by the League of Nations; when a Nazi government came to power, it would move decisively to remedy "injustices." The first remedy would be Czechoslovakia's destruction, Rothermere predicted. "Czecho-Slovakia, which has so systematically violated the Peace Treaty, both by its oppression of racial minorities and its failures to reduce its own armaments, might be elbowed out of existence overnight."[118] Seven years later, Rothermere once again doomed the Czechs to a "baneful and fraudulent existence" as a "synthetic and spurious State."[119] The Hungarian minority in Slovakia in 1920 "were handed over to the Czechs with no more consultation than if they had been cattle... as captives of a race notorious for petty meanness they have been subjected to cold-blooded expropriation and oppression. Every effort has been made to suppress their languages, and the Czech police have tried to break their spirit by systematic persecution."[120] But now that the Nazis were making noises about the Sudeten Germans, the Hungarians' claims were also in the public eye: "The dragon's teeth that the Czechs have sown are sprouting all around them in a crop of deadly dangers."[121]

European reaction to Rothermere's writing varied widely. Evidence suggests Rothermere was not acting on behalf of the Hungarian government, which was notably circumspect about the essay. The first 1927 articles called for the return of only narrow strips of territory, whereas Hungarian propaganda had consistently demanded the entirety of prewar Hungary.[122] Hungarian Prime Minister Bethlen played both sides of the issue, at home celebrating that the essay had made treaty revision "the focus of the world press," while emphasizing to the British and the French that he had not encouraged Rothermere but could not contradict his electorate.[123] Popular Hungarian adulation of Rothermere reached such ecstatic heights that he and his son Esmond were named as possible candidates for the Hungarian throne: when Esmond traveled to Hungary in May 1928, he was received almost as a visiting head of state.[124] Meanwhile, the British Foreign Office was startled and embarrassed. Joseph Chamberlain, the foreign minister, immediately made it clear to the Hungarians that Rothermere had acted on his own initiative; the semiofficial London *Times* publicized the Foreign Office's irritation. "Right or wrong, the peace treaties have got to stand for at least another twenty years," wrote one anonymous analyst in 1927.[125] When Beneš rushed to London to see whether Rothermere's ideas were widely shared, "King George made such cutting remarks on the pro-Magyar British tycoon that in Prague Beneš 'dared not even repeat' them."[126] But the Foreign Office never openly repudiated Rothermere's article, much to the Little Entente's frustration. In fact, by the mid-1930s, when discussion of treaty revision had become public and common, ideas similar to Rothermere's found their way into the discourse of Ramsay MacDonald and Winston Churchill.[127] Beneš was right to be concerned.

Why was Rothermere so agitated on behalf of the Czechoslovak Magyars and Hungary? His frustration seemed to play on a romantic sense of nobility likening the aristocratic Hungarian nation to the imperial British. In his memoirs, he wrote indignantly of "the injustice to such a noble people as the Hungarians . . . it seemed to me that we were tending to attach Britain to an unworthy ally against an ancient friend . . . to perpetuate a situation in which a people to whom Europe owed much were to be placed at the mercy of a cruder and more barbaric race." The Hungarians had historically proven themselves to be a "chivalrous and warlike aristocracy" worthy of defense and international justice; they had responded to Empress Maria Theresa's desperate plea for aid in 1741 just as they had saved Christendom in 1526, and for centuries had been Europe's "bastion against which the forces of Mahomet vainly hurled themselves."[128] Meanwhile, the historical nonentities the Czechs had "bamboozled" the Great Powers in 1919.[129] He reminded his readers repeatedly that there were more Germans in Czechoslovakia than there were Irishmen in the newly free republic of Ireland. He also argued that Great Britain should turn its back on the Continent: the British, "descendants of the Vikings," were a seafaring people with no interest in Central Europe.[130]

Czechoslovakia was not the only parliamentary democracy Rothermere found frustrating. He spared no criticism of his own, full of "pinhead pacifists," or of the League of Nations. Hitler and Mussolini, however, fascinated him, particularly their decision to rule "without the delays and encumbrances of the Parliamentary machine."[131] Hitler, with whom Rothermere boasted a private correspondence, was a former "gallant man of the trenches" who "exudes good fellowship . . . simple, unaffected, and obviously sincere . . . supremely intelligent."[132] "Italy and Germany had been re-taught the lessons of an earlier generation," he admonished his readers. "They believed with Napoleon that God is on the side of the big battalions. They believed with Caesar's legions that it is sweet and glorious to die for one's country. The so-called Democratic States had been rendered soft-fibred. The Dictatorships were high-mettled," he wrote.[133]

The attitude Rothermere represented was among the Czechs' most prominent concerns. The significance of the Rothermere episode lies in its demonstration of the myths and countermyths at work in European cultural politics. The Castle myth claimed that the Czechs were right-minded European democrats, inspired by the ideals of the Enlightenment and the Wilsonian postwar era; Rothermere accused them of being corrupt, abusive autocrats, repressing the noble Hungarian dream. Versailles, in the Czech formulation, represented the victory of democracy and national self-determination; in Rothermere's, it represented Czechoslovak barbarism, the ascent of slick hucksters who successfully wooed international opinion while abusing minorities at home. European cultural affairs between the two world wars entertained both these discursive possibilities: the work of the Czechoslovak propaganda apparatus was to ensure the Czech variant won out.

International Relations at Home

Clearly, Czechoslovakia's relations with its dissatisfied minorities made for problems abroad. Castle leaders tried at least to some extent to address these problems at home, both to burnish the country's international image and to improve domestic political harmony. One means of improving domestic relations was the Castle's cultivation of activist German parties, politicians, and literati; it was somewhat less successful with Slovaks and Hungarians.

Another method of dealing with minority issues at home was interpretative: presenting Czechoslovak internal affairs carefully and positively to influential foreign cultural figures, particularly embassy staffers and journalists. Whether speaking to the minorities or about them, venue and relationships mattered greatly. Sociability and personal connections between influential Great Power intellectuals and representative Czechoslovaks remained a subject of Castle concern throughout the interwar period.

The Castle's most important unofficial gathering place was the Společenský klub, created in 1927, one of the most elegant social spaces in interwar Prague. Modeled on British gentlemen's clubs, its luxurious environs were famed among Castle-friendly politicians, artists, journalists, and intellectuals. Edvard Beneš's wife, Hana, KPR political chief Josef Schieszl, and National Bank director Vilém Pospišil had agitated for the club's creation since 1923; they served on its first board when it opened its doors and membership rolls in February 1927.[134] Zamini Third Section chief Jan Hájek was assigned as the club's "archivist"—perhaps an inside joke acknowledging that a considerable amount of Společenský klub documentation found its way to the Third Section, which paid for roughly one-third of the club's operating expenses. It also bought and refurbished the club's building, a "palace" on the stylish National Avenue in the heart of downtown Prague, just down the street from Jaroslav Stránský's publishing offices and the *Lidové noviny* newsroom.[135]

In fact, the club had been established in part to ease the Third Section's burden. Previously, Third Section bureaucrats had attended to visiting foreigners, researching their background and needs, making tourism arrangements, and squiring them around on weekends and during the evening. Predictably, many "important foreigners" neglected to inform Zamini of their arrival, complicating matters further. "Care for foreigners" thus became the Společenský klub's purview. A committee of Zamini bureaucrats and Prague professors was charged with organizing itineraries, arranging translation, connecting foreigners with like-minded Czechs, and informing the press of their visits. The club would also host Czech friendship societies: the British Society for Czechoslovakia, the Czechoslovak Italian Society, the All Peoples Association, and the American Institute.[136] Bohumil Markalous, the club's honorary administrator, was also connected to the Third Section; he edited *Pestrý týden*, an Orbis magazine.[137] The magazine popularized Castle-style Czechoslovak patriotism; its first issue, on November 2, 1926, took Czechoslovak independence as its theme.[138]

At the end of 1927, the Společenský klub's board bragged that in just eight months it had already acquired 1,032 members; sponsored forty-eight dinners, twenty-seven lunches, eight teas, a salon, two receptions, six evening debates, fourteen dances, two lectures, a literary evening, and a dance class;

and hosted 912 visiting foreigners. Its library housed eighty-six periodicals, thirty-three of them foreign, along with a small allotment of books, mainly contributed by Orbis and friendly diplomats (its titles were overwhelmingly in Czech, French, and English, with a few in Slovak, German, and Romanian). The club also provided mah-jongg tiles and a ping-pong table.[139] This rate of activity continued. In 1929, in addition to large groups of visiting academic Slavicists, the club hosted hundreds of other foreign professionals: businessmen from Halle and Cleveland, Swedish porcelain manufacturers and British rubber tycoons, various members of European parliaments and current or former ministers, and actors, translators, writers, publishers, priests, professors, and librarians from all over Europe and the United States. Attention was particularly lavished on American and West European journalists and writers; they were given free opera and symphony tickets, escorted on day trips to Prague sights, and allowed to meet personally with Beneš and Masaryk. All were wined and dined at, and offered free entry to, the Společenský klub. Many were sent home with Orbis materials in their suitcases.[140]

During the long, hot summer of 1932, the Společenský klub became the meeting place for a small number of Karel Čapek's Friday Men, adrift in Prague as most of the group fled for the cooler countryside. Julius Firt was the business director of Jaroslav Stránský's publishing house, F. Borový; he began meeting two friends regularly for lunch there. They formed the core of what was dubbed the Táflrunda (Round Table), joined by many others at summer's end. The Táflrunda did not meet on a particular day, but nonetheless had its internal rules and habits. Many Táflrunda members were fanatical players of the popular card game *mariáš* (a complex multihanded game similar to bridge, or to the Hungarian game *ulti*) around which revolved many group jokes. The group's "leader and dictator," according to Firt, was Ferdinand Peroutka, who usually adjourned the group by retreating to another table to edit *Přítomnost* or occupy himself with other work, including his historical masterwork, *Budování státu* (*Building the State*). However, the "chairman" was Karel Steinbach, nicknamed Kadelík, whose wit and charm governed the Táflrunda's evenings. Other Round Table attendees were actress and legendary *raconteuse* Olga Scheinpflugová, Karel Čapek's companion and wife after 1935; Friday Man Karel Poláček; actor and director Hugo Haas; Prokop Herben (Jan Herben's youngest son, who worked for Zamini); theatrical and literary critic Edmond Konrád; and various other professionals and politicians. Celebrities such as actress Adina Mandlová sometimes sat at the table, usually at the invitation of Táflrunda stalwarts.[141]

Noteworthy, however, is the relative absence of minority names on the Společenský klub registers. The initial 1925 invitations discussing the club's formation were not sent to a single German or Hungarian speaker; there are no more than five Slovak names or Bratislava addresses on the list of fifty people.[142] Czech National Socialists and Social Democrats dominated its rolls. The Společenský klub, like most of the rest of the Castle institutional apparatus and mythic narrative, benignly ignored the country's other nationalities. As the Castle myth went, Czechoslovakia's creation was a Czech national revolution; the Czechs built Central Europe's healthiest democracy. The nationalities were still in a Habsburg hangover, the myth narrated, and had yet to enter the modern state as active citizens. In particular, the Germans found it difficult to divest themselves of their old repressive, aristocratic habits. Only when they did would the Společenský klub—and fuller participation in the life of the Castle-led state—open to them. In the meantime, the Společenský klub would demonstrate to foreigners the joys of Czech social life. The minorities would remain guests, not members.

The Castle and the P.E.N.

Similar issues dominated the life of Czechoslovakia's P.E.N. chapter. P.E.N. International began as an intellectual supper club. Its idealistic London founders envisioned the group as a writerly League of Nations, allowing intellectuals from around the world to discuss cultural concerns and to support one another's work and freedoms.[143] Given the chance to meet socially, writers from every country could overcome political animosity and establish common ground. P.E.N. was also to support "the internationality of art," as well as freedoms of artistic production and communication. In short, the British leaders of International P.E.N. hoped that P.E.N. members would return to their home countries inspired to spread the values of cooperation and goodwill, and to use their cultural prominence to influence their political leaders.[144] But writers from the new East-Central European states viewed P.E.N. as a political arena for defending the interests and needs of their insecure countries. Writers from the Habsburg successor states jockeyed for power and wooed Great Power intellectuals in P.E.N. just as their diplomatic corps did Great Power politicians in Geneva, Paris, and London. Geopolitical alliances and hostilities played out in P.E.N., despite London's continual attempts to purge P.E.N.'s yearly congresses of "political" discussions.

Castle intellectuals, most prominently Karel Čapek, created a Prague P.E.N. chapter hand in hand with Zamini's Third Section, explicitly dedicating it to propagating the Castle myth abroad and acting as cultural diplomats on their state's behalf. Almost immediately, the Prague chapter found itself embroiled in ethnic or nationality conflicts mirroring those facing Czechoslovakia.[145] Prague German writers accused Czechoslovak P.E.N. of excluding them and argued with the club's decision to use only Czech as its official language. Later, Hungarian P.E.N. accused Czechoslovakia and other Little Entente states of censoring and otherwise mistreating their Hungarian minorities. Prague P.E.N. fell back on the standard tropes of the Castle myth in defending its country; it also demonstrated the Castle's tin ear for national sensitivities within the Czechoslovak state. Finally, these debates demonstrate the ubiquitousness of propaganda of all kinds in interwar Europe. Propaganda leaflets are intellectual property and raise questions about the free circulation of ideas across borders: thus P.E.N. was one of the organizations dealing most forthrightly with how to address propaganda and its effect on international relations.

Nominally, Prague P.E.N. existed before Čapek and the Castle became interested. In late 1923, British writer and P.E.N. president John Galsworthy had his publisher contact František Khol, a theatrical agent and playwright, to ask him to create a Czechoslovak P.E.N. Jiřina Tůmová, who worked with Khol in his agency and served as P.E.N.'s longtime secretary, noted, "None of us was very sure at that time what exactly a P.E.N. center was, nor how it might have significance for the Czechoslovak Republic."[146] Still, Khol complied with Galsworthy's request, bringing onto the board well-known older literati who had fought for Czech independence during the First World War, such as Viktor Dyk and Legionnaire author Rudolf Medek. But that was the extent of Prague P.E.N.'s activity. Jiřina Tůmová recalled, "[W]e did nothing aside from providing [the London headquarters with] . . . information. It seemed that the [London] leadership thought it sufficient that a P.E.N. chapter existed . . . in the Czechoslovak Republic."[147]

In 1924, Otakar Vočadlo, a Czech teaching at the London School of Slavonic Studies, was asked by London P.E.N. to exhort Prague P.E.N. to become more active. But Czech intellectuals seemed almost wholly indifferent.[148] Vočadlo's tone grew urgent after Prague Germans contacted the London center, offering to form a Prague P.E.N. chapter: this was precisely what Vočadlo feared. Were Czech Germans to create lasting contacts with British intellectual circles, their already substantial influence among the British elite might increase. The Czechs could not compete with these important personal contacts:

> We hoped that with time, we would develop a[n ally] out of one of our scholars [at the University of London], who would defend us against enemy propaganda; but instead of this, wealthy German circles won them over to their side, one after the other, through sociable relations . . . and elegant hospitality.[149]

In the summer of 1924, after months of Vočadlo's pleading, Čapek finally agreed to visit London P.E.N., funded by the Third Section. Čapek was an obvious choice for Prague P.E.N. leadership: his plays had already received international recognition by the early 1920s and, unlike most Czech intellectuals, he spoke and read passable English and French. Čapek's trip impressed him greatly, and inspired the first of his many beloved travelogues, *Letters from England* (*Anglické listy*, 1924), serialized both in *The Manchester Guardian* and in *Lidové noviny*. He met H. G. Wells, Rebecca West, G. B. Shaw, and John Galsworthy, among other writers. He was predisposed to appreciate his British hosts, but also realized quickly that it might be politically advantageous for the Czechs to emulate British-style clubs and British upper-class social relations.[150] Upon his return to Prague, Čapek moved quickly to create an active Prague P.E.N. for propaganda purposes: P.E.N. could, like the London club, provide an unofficial space for politicized socializing. Čapek was certain that the government would fund P.E.N. At the board's first official meeting on February 19, 1925, Čapek told the other members that Masaryk would attend their first evening gathering—before the club had even invited him.[151] P.E.N. committee meetings were initially held at the Prague *Lidové noviny* newsroom. By 1928, P.E.N.'s permanent meeting place was the Společenský klub.[152]

Prague P.E.N.'s membership spanned professional and political divides. Czech-speaking literati and journalists attended alongside professors, Zamini bureaucrats, and prominent Castle allies and enemies. Conservative National Democrats were part of P.E.N., such as literary agent František Khol, *Národní listy* journalist Vincenc Červinka, author and feuilletonist Karel Matěj Čapek-Chod, and literary historian and poet Hanuš Jelínek, close friend of Castle foe Viktor Dyk.[153] So were novelist Marie Pujmannová and short-story writer Božena Benešová, prominent in the Czechoslovak Communist Party until 1929 and outspoken leftists thereafter. Zamini personnel from legations all over the world, from Budapest to Argentina, joined the Prague chapter. Many Zamini employees were also former academics, and perhaps on this basis many other government employees and professional politicians were solicited for Prague P.E.N., including KPR political chief Josef Schieszl, Social Democrat Rudolf Bechyně, Slovak Agrarian Milan Hodža (then minister of education), speaker of parliament Dr. Jan Botto, Masaryk's personal secretary Vašil K. Škrach, governor of the National Bank Vilém Pospišil, Tradesman's Bank president and powerful financier Jaroslav Preiss, and Ambassador Karel Krofta in Berlin (later minister of foreign affairs during Beneš's presidency).[154] In short, membership in Prague P.E.N. became a badge of national honor, a mark of attachment to and service of Masaryk's republic. Čapek's official letter to the Third Section made P.E.N.'s domestic and international political significance clear. He hoped that P.E.N. would bring "Czechoslovak"-speaking writers into regular contact with Czechoslovak Germans. This contact, and the mutual understanding that might result, could mean a kinder reception for Czech speakers in German circles abroad. Moreover, P.E.N. would bring outstanding foreign literati to Prague, the better to impress them with Czech kindness. Like the Společenský klub, P.E.N. could entertain visitors previously hosted by Zamini, in an ostensibly private setting. Čapek wrote, "The club will act in full consciousness of the great propaganda significance of its actions, which, not possessing an official or administrative character, will be able to work much more freely and often even more effectively."[155]

Čapek was right to preoccupy himself with the Prague Germans. London P.E.N. had contemplated two Prague chapters, one for Czech writers and one for Germans. The Czechs reacted with panic: granting the Germans equal representation might constitute a rebuff, in the realm of international letters, of Czechoslovakia's legitimacy and of Czech culture. Vočadlo's worried letter of December 31, 1924, to the secretary of London P.E.N. demonstrates Prague's alarm:

> As P.E.N. Club is an instrument of unification, spiritual unity, it ought to avoid everything tending to disunion. . . . [W]hy shouldn't our co-citizens of German tongue join their confreres and try to pull together? . . . German literature is represented [in P.E.N.] not only by Germany but also Austria and Switzerland (partly). . . . Between ourselves, there are very few German writers in our country who are any good, the best among them being Jews. There is one really great or at any rate very interesting poet Rilke who was born in Prague and loves Prague as a Czech would. But he lives in Switzerland and hates the Pangerman attitude for which our Germans became notorious. But it is only a question of one generation. Then it will be all right! And I think it would be wrong to encourage the "wild spirits" who are in the way of ultimate reconciliation instead of promoting co-operation.[156]

This emphasis on coexistence and the passing of time—"it is only a question of one generation"—is very much akin to the Castle's hopes for ethnic integration within the Czechoslovak state. London seemed satisfied by this suggestion.

But the Prague Germans were not. Two weeks after founding the chapter, Čapek announced to the executive committee that Max Brod, editor of the

Prager Tagblatt, and other Prague German writers were angered at not having been immediately invited to join P.E.N.[157] Not a single member of Prague P.E.N.'s executive committee suggested full, complete collaboration between Czechs and Germans. The younger, Castle-oriented writers—Čapek and his friends—advocated compromise: inviting a few German writers to participate immediately as guests at the steering committee meetings. The older, more nationalistic members of the committee were reluctant to include any Germans at all, even stating at one point that "Germans will never rid themselves of their aggressive nature," and fearing that the German "element" would dominate the committee: a *Drang nach Osten* within P.E.N.[158] In the end, the committee agreed that Čapek should consult with two pro-Czechoslovak German intellectuals: Otto Pick, reporter and editor at the*Prager Presse*, also a translator and poet; and Rudolf Fuchs, translator of Czech poets Petr Bezruč and Otakar Brežina.[159]

Two months later, the Germans again contacted Prague P.E.N., demanding full membership rather than guest status, and asking that German accompany Czech as Prague P.E.N.'s official language. The Czechs rejected this request out of hand. Literature professor and drama critic Václav Tille spoke for the group: "the Czech chapter of an international society can only be *Czech*. The question of the Germans in this case isn't political but literary, and the Germans will have to sort this out themselves." That is, politically, the Germans deserved equal representation within Czechoslovakia; but German culture had already gained a hold within P.E.N., thanks to the Austrian, Swiss, and German chapters. The Sudeten Germans would have to negotiate with P.E.N.'s other German speakers. Again, Tille, echoing the Castle's basic approach to the country's minorities: "The Prague chapter was conceived by the London headquarters as a Czech center; [but] the club is willing to make a go of it with the Germans, and they will always receive courteous treatment."[160] Brod refused to be pacified and continued to print negative notices about Prague P.E.N. in his *Prager Tagblatt*.[161]

The Germans made one more attempt. In late November 1926, the Czech chapter received a letter from Hermon Ould, International P.E.N.'s general secretary, informing them of complaints that Germans were not allowed to participate in representative numbers. Galsworthy had himself visited Prague in May 1926: Ould noted that Galsworthy's impression had been that Germans were present and appropriately represented. Nonetheless, he wrote, "it has been proposed that there should be two centers in Czecho Slovakia—one for those writing in Czech and another for those writing in German."[162] Čapek's brief, vehement response stated:

> [W]e beg to inform you, that you have received incorrect informations. . . . Our German members have been asked several

> times to nominate [their] representative to serve on the committee and thus to take part on all managements and functions of the Club. If they have not as yet done so it is only by their proper omission. One of the chief purposes of the P.E.N. Club is to promote the bringing together of the different nationalities. We are afraid that the establishment of another center of Prague would make this astrangment but durable. [*sic*] On the other hand we may rightly be proud that in the bringing together of both the nationalities we have done a considerable deal of work.[163]

London accepted this interpretation and never mentioned the matter again.[164]

After 1926, Germans entered Prague P.E.N., just as they had the Czechoslovak Parliament: as in Parliament, their numbers in P.E.N. were never representative. In May 1926, out of 117 total members, only 10 identified themselves as ethnically or linguistically German. Five other self-identified German speakers did not receive invitations to the general assembly meeting, having failed to pay their dues.[165] Among the few German speakers who did join P.E.N. were Paul/Pavel Eisner, another *Prager Presse* staffer, and Johannes/Jan Urzidil, cultural attaché at the German embassy.[166] Others were journalists for the larger German newspapers; some professors from the German University in Prague; and a few civil servants or party members, in particular officials Bloch and Ebel, who worked in Zamini's press office, and Dr. Emil Strauss, an influential Sudeten German Social Democratic Party journalist.[167]

A few years later, the Hungarian P.E.N. chapter accused Prague of literary nationalism. Strict censorship in Slovakia had been in force since 1920, justified by the Czechoslovak government as a response to a troubling inflow of Hungarian irredentist propaganda, insinuated into Magyar schoolbooks, dictionaries, grammar books, atlases, and belles lettres alike. The Czechoslovak authorities responded by barring most texts from entering through Slovakia, although their entry into Bohemia, Moravia, and Silesia was allegedly guaranteed.[168] Between 1929 and 1935, the Budapest P.E.N. club repeatedly claimed that Czechoslovak censorship of Hungarian materials entering Slovakia was overly restrictive, threatening the intellectual freedom of the Hungarians in Slovakia. The dispute began in earnest at the 1929 P.E.N. congress in Vienna, where the Hungarian chapter raised a general question about intellectual freedom for minority Hungarians in the Little Entente countries (Czechoslovakia, Yugoslavia, and Romania). A P.E.N. committee, in which the Czechs were supported by the Poles and Romanians, decided that free circulation of intellectual products applied only to belles lettres, and that the Little Entente countries had the right to block propaganda.[169]

In the spring of 1930, Radó Antal, member and later president of the Budapest P.E.N. chapter, wrote Prague lamenting Czechoslovak censorship:

> [T]he pettifoggery with which [Czechoslovakia] has sought to suppress Hungarian books has become more serious than in the past, given that [Czechoslovakia] has organized veritable "razzias" [raids] in some bookstores, . . . [the state] has confiscated books which do not contain a single word of politics, nor any kind of allusion to your state.

Antal asked the Czechs to look into the problem.[170] Other, less conservative Hungarian writers also took up the cause. Jenö Mohacsi, writer for the important Budapest cultural journal *Nyugat*, visited Prague later that year. Upon his return home, he wrote a cordial letter to Prague P.E.N. in which he reported that he had given a communiqué on censorship in Slovakia, drafted by himself and Čapek, promptly to the Budapest newspapers *Az Est* and *Pester Lloyd*, as well as the Prague *Prágai Magyar Hirlap*, as Prague P.E.N. had requested him to do. He then asked pointedly whether the Prague chapter had received word from its government with regard to anti-Hungarian censorship in Slovakia.[171]

Prague P.E.N., led by Karel Čapek and historian and former cabinet minister Josef Šusta, had written immediately upon receiving Antal's letter to Minister of the Interior Juraj Slávik, who coordinated censorship policy. Čapek and Šusta distrusted the Hungarian charges, but worried that Budapest might use these complaints to public relations advantage, especially in front of Great Power colleagues in P.E.N.:

> We . . . ask you to kindly turn your attention to this issue and help us make possible its resolution, which would thoroughly protect the interests of our republic against Hungarian irredenta. We have no doubt of [the irredentists'] seriousness and treacherousness, concealed behind various products of belles lettres and academic literature; [a solution] would deprive our enemies of a welcomed opportunity to attack these assumed obstructions, [and] grant our republic a desirable freedom of international intellectual relations.[172]

Slávik ignored P.E.N. for a year. When they wrote a third time in May 1931, they sent a similar letter to their patron Beneš, asking for help with two "delicate and urgent" matters: the infiltration of Hungarian propaganda onto Czechoslovak soil, and what increasingly seemed like an overly draconian censorship policy in Slovakia. P.E.N. asked Beneš to inform them confidentially whether the state's policy could be changed, and whether P.E.N. might initiate discussion on this topic. Čapek and Šusta assured Beneš that they knew just how deviously Hungarian irredentists exploited belles lettres and academic work; in fact, P.E.N. had learned that the Ministry of the Interior had collected some astounding exemplars, which P.E.N. wanted very much to see, and which it planned to show Budapest and the rest of P.E.N. International, thereby gaining the moral high ground for Czechoslovakia. Prague P.E.N. ended the letter by asking Beneš to intervene with Interior Ministry officials, so that P.E.N. could get the evidence and information it needed.[173]

In the spring of 1932, Prague P.E.N.'s luck turned. First, Jiří Ježek, an employee of the university library in Bratislava, helped establish a Slovak section of the Prague club in February 1932.[174] Thus Slovak members of Czechoslovak P.E.N., along with Czechs and Germans, would represent Czechoslovakia at that year's international P.E.N. congress in Budapest. P.E.N. Slovaks could serve as a useful source of information and supportive testimony about censorship policy in Slovakia; they would also demonstrate the inclusive, tolerant nature of the Czechoslovak state as opposed to Hungary. Second, P.E.N. finally received the information it needed—not from the Interior Ministry but from Zamini. From April 1932 through 1935, the Third Section sent Prague P.E.N. the Hungarian sections of its internal intelligence reports, the *Daily International Media Summary*, which reviewed Hungarian newspaper commentary on Czechoslovakia.[175] Third, an April communiqué from the Czechoslovak diplomatic legation in Budapest suggested that Zamini could support the pro-Czechoslovak faction within Budapest P.E.N. by ensuring that before the Budapest congress, distribution of Hungarian printed material would be loosened in Slovakia and Subcarpathian Ruthenia—the very change in policy Prague P.E.N. advocated to Ministers Slávik and Beneš.[176]

In the end, Prague P.E.N. got the policy change it wanted: the Ministry of the Interior finally approved increased circulation of apolitical Hungarian printed materials in Slovakia. The new policy would go into effect June 1, a week after the Budapest P.E.N. congress, thereby giving the Czechs the opportunity to trumpet their success before all of P.E.N. Edmond Konrád, head of the Prague delegation, brought information from Zamini and the Ministry of the Interior, including the long-sought exemplars of censored harmful material, translated into English and German for the benefit of the Budapest and London P.E.N. clubs.[177] Intellectual freedom was much discussed at the Budapest congress, but little direct pressure seems to have been applied to the Czechs or other Little Entente nationalities, judging from Zamini and other Czechoslovak intelligence reports, as well as the accounts by Prague P.E.N. members. In this sense, the congress was a success.

But not completely. Those mixed results, and their possible consequences not just for Prague P.E.N. but for Czechoslovakia, are apparent in several postconference articles that ran in Prague newspapers. Some delegates struck an optimistic tone about the congress, emphasizing the Czech public relations success and excellent relations among the East-Central European delegates: the pro-Czechoslovak Hungarian P.E.N. members, such as Jenö Mohacsi and Deszö Kosztolanyi, and the Czechs, the Yugoslavs, and Poles evidently got on famously.[178] But Prague delegate Adolf Hoffmeister in *Literární noviny*, writing just a few months before "Magyar racial chauvinist" and radical rightist Gyula Gömbös took office as Hungary's prime minister, bluntly described Hungary as a haven of reaction and a state relying on terror to control its people.[179] Yet the writers of the West seemed ignorant of or deceived about real conditions in Hungary. In fact, French novelist Jules Romains, who became P.E.N. International's president in 1935, proclaimed support for Hungarian irredentism. Hoffmeister made Romains out as an embarrassed naïf, perhaps trying to turn the speech into a victory for the Czechs:

> After Marinetti's speech, . . . Jules Romains spoke, [his] speech, quite tainted with revisionism, which all the Hungarian pro-government newspapers reprinted with joy: but, oh, poor Jules Romains! The moment he had finished, Slovaks, Romanians, and Croats pounced upon him, began scolding him, and emphatically presented a very different portrait of reality. . . . Mr. Romains apologized and disavowed [his earlier speech] until even his "good evening" stuck in his throat. . . . Jules Romains recognized very well that he had overstated his gratitude.[180]

But Hoffmeister probably recognized quite well that Romains's praise of Hungary might bode poorly for the Czechs.

Budapest was not finished with Prague. Only a month after the congress, Radó Antal sent another letter of complaint to Prague P.E.N.; reports questioning Czechoslovak goodwill appeared in many major Budapest newspapers during the late summer and early fall.[181] One Zamini report quotes the Budapest daily *Magyarság* from September 24, 1932, reminding its readers that Prague delegate Edmond Konrád and the Czechoslovak interior minister had announced a change in Czechoslovak censorship policy, which the paper characterized as a "general ban on the import of Hungarian printed material into Slovakia." But the Prague Hungarian daily *Prágai Magyar Hirlap* had recently declared that the ban on Hungarian material continued in full force. Hungarians were not surprised, reported *Magyarság*: on the contrary, they would have been surprised had the minister kept his word.[182]

Adding insult to injury, Prague newspapers also roundly criticized Prague P.E.N., blaming it for potentially dangerous Hungarian propaganda now infiltrating Slovakia. Even the centrist *Lidové noviny*, Čapek's own paper, advised caution. In November 1932, it admonished that of the books Hungarians wished to export to Slovakia, "many, even those of artistically very high quality, . . . are written with tendencies which ignore post-1918 conditions. . . . Popular scientific works and academic dictionaries are imbued with the same spirit." The article mentioned the example of one historical dictionary, recently sent en masse into Slovakia, that excluded most Czechoslovak politicians, including Masaryk, and all postwar peace treaties—in particular Trianon, which had given Slovakia to Czechoslovakia and truncated Hungary.[183]

From 1932 to 1934, the Hungarians hurled charge after charge at the Czechoslovak P.E.N. chapter and government. As soon as the Czechoslovaks responded to one accusation, generally by providing statistics or documentation absolving their government of wrongdoing, Radó Antal would fire off yet another letter citing a new complaint. His allegations were impressively varied. One letter charged the Czechoslovak government with targeting financial legislation against the Hungarians; another letter complained that all Hungarian literature entering Slovakia was forced to go through a single Bratislava customs office.[184] Prague P.E.N. duly requested assistance and documentation regarding each issue from various government officials and institutions.[185] They also attempted to use as intermediaries their allies in Budapest P.E.N.[186] Meanwhile, the Prague chapter prepared an appeal to Paris and London, summarizing all the events and policies mentioned in and leading up to the complaints made by the Hungarians, all the steps taken by the Czechoslovak government to improve the situation, and—adding a charge of their own—the censorship experienced by Slovaks in Hungary.[187]

In an anticlimactic final confrontation at the 1935 P.E.N. congress in Barcelona, Antal and the Hungarians finally insisted on publicizing their complaints. Czechoslovak delegate Edmond Konrád arrived at the congress ready to plead Czechoslovakia's case in front of P.E.N.'s International Steering Committee. He was armed with a speech rebutting the latest Hungarian complaints and the dossier of materials prepared by P.E.N. and the Third Section.

Zamini's dossier rooted the P.E.N. conflict in the aftermath of the First World War, when Hungary used both military and propaganda efforts to try to regain Slovakia. "In general, the whole of the post-War Hungarian literature, both belletristic and academic, was permeated with the spirit of irredentism," the dossier concluded, "and all of it had to be placed at the service of propaganda in favor of treaty revision."[188] As time went on, considerable numbers of Hungarian books were imported into both Slovakia and Subcarpathian Ruthenia. In June 1932, after the Prague P.E.N. club petitioned the government to relax conditions still further, only political periodicals were censored. However, all publications were still required to enter the region through the Bratislava customs office, which ascertained whether they were harmful, with the help of the P.E.N.-affiliated Hungarian Society for Science, Literature and Art in Czechoslovakia.[189] The report mentions that in the second half of 1932, fourteen publications were censored; in all of 1933, only seventeen were censored.

Then Konrád moved from defense to offense, castigating the Hungarians and their government. Konrád claimed that Czechoslovak censorship law in Slovakia derived from the laws of the antebellum Hungarian kingdom: that is, these censorship policies were in essence Hungarian policies, which the members of the Budapest chapter ought to recognize. In fact, those very policies and others like them were applied to the Slovak population in Hungary. The Hungarian government canceled Slovak cultural evenings and barred Slovak artists from visiting Hungary.[190] Finally, Konrád stated, Hungarian revisionism had long posed a real threat to Czechoslovakia; the Czechs needed to be able to address it effectively. Konrád's case stuck. When the Hungarian demand that Little Entente countries not censor imported Hungarian materials came to the floor, no delegate seconded it.[191] Čapek, the Prague P.E.N. leadership, and Zamini had won this battle for their nation's honor. In the eyes of P.E.N., they had successfully defended their country's good name.

In the end, Prague P.E.N.'s long argument with the Budapest P.E.N. chapter says more about the Castle's use of Prague intellectuals for European cultural diplomacy than about Czech-Hungarian relations. P.E.N. was a stage on which Karel Čapek and other P.E.N. members defended the Castle and its vision of Central European minority relations, and communicated relevant elements of the Castle myth abroad. For P.E.N. and the Castle, Czech actions against Hungarian propaganda in Slovakia were purely defensive and always had been. Moreover, Czechoslovakia's Hungarians aided the censorship endeavor, changing it from Czech repression of Hungarian intellectual life to a Czechoslovak effort. Thus, as usual, the tolerant, inclusive Czechoslovaks were in the right, while the Hungarians were rabid nationalists, as were the Czechoslovak Germans who had earlier tried to interleave nationalist politics into P.E.N. Čapek's last newspaper column, in fact, bemoaned European nationalism, from which he evidently excepted the Czechs:

> What can one do, it is terribly far from nation to nation; all of us are increasingly alone. Might be better now to never step a foot out of one's house; better to lock the door and close the shutters, and let all do as they please. I no longer care. And now . . . close your eyes and say very, very quietly: How do you do, old gentleman from Kent? Grüss Gott, meine Herren! Grazia, signor! A vôtre santé![192]

Conclusion

The Castle's propaganda apparatus, including the Společenský klub, did have its intended effect, at least on some foreign journalists. British writer John Gunther's 1938 *Inside Europe*, for example, contains a map of Europe as an overleaf, with brief depictions of each country. The thumbnail sketch of Czechoslovakia reads, "'The master of Bohemia is the master of Europe.' Here a great man, Thomas Masaryk, set up a free republic; here a great man, Eduard Beneš, rules it wisely." The chapter on Czechoslovakia is titled "Masaryk and Beneš," and begins with these words:

> Masaryk—what grandeur the name inspires! The son of a serf who created a nation; the blacksmith boy who grew to have "the finest intellect of the century"; the pacifist who organized an army that performed a feat unparalleled in military annals—the Czechoslovak legions who marched across Siberia to the Pacific; the philosopher who became a statesman in spite of himself; the living father of a state who is also its simplest citizen; an unchallengeably firm democrat who, in the *débâcle* of the modern world, still believes in rule by tolerance; the man who more than any other smashed the old Austro-Hungarian empire, so that Czechoslovakia, a free republic, rose from its ruins—the stablest, strongest, and most prosperous of the succession states.[193]

A more perfect summation of the Castle message was not to be wished. Moreover, Gunther complimented not just Masaryk but Castle propaganda: "The press bureau in Prague is so well run that it is often accused of 'propaganda.' Of course, propaganda is what it exists for. What enemies of Czechoslovakia object to is that Czechoslovak propaganda is so friendly, efficient, and, in general, honest and accurate that rival countries are outrun."[194]

But Gunther was an optimist. Czechoslovakia's rivals outpaced it in the race for Great Power approval. In the end, the Castle message could not outweigh Britain's distaste for engagement on the Continent (or for Beneš),

French dependence on Britain, or American reluctance to involve itself in European affairs. The Castle's myth had its main victory in the realm of discourse, not realpolitik. Still, Czechoslovak and East-Central European cultural diplomacy and propaganda highlight previously neglected aspects of interwar political culture. Like their neighbors, the Czechs reiterated and adapted nineteenth-century romantic nationalist tropes. Like their neighbors, they insisted that they were the most quintessentially European of the Habsburg successor states, devoted to the postwar order's values and stability, while their revisionist neighbors and national minorities were at best chaotic and unsophisticated, at worst autocratic and violent.

Edvard Beneš wrote that the struggle for Czechoslovak national existence meant trying to Europeanize Czechoslovakia.[195] Beneš meant persuading Czechs to see themselves as Europeans; Castle propaganda demonstrates that he also needed to persuade Europeans to see Czechs as Europeans. The Castle myth worked at persuading Europeans that Czechoslovaks were identical to themselves, using familiar terms: the Czechs were practical, hardworking, attached to the land, tolerant, and humane. Some West Europeans—mainly cultural elites in Paris and London—responded. In 1925, George Bernard Shaw called Masaryk the natural choice to serve as president of a United States of Europe, should the European states overcome their historical differences. French public opinion was willing occasionally to "exalt" Masaryk as "a great humanitarian; Beneš as the unflinching ally and collaborator." But for the most part Castle rhetoric met with West European suspicion or indifference. Articles in the important *France Militaire*, a specialized journal directed at members of the armed forces, contained "'childish errors' and fantastic stories." In October 1929, *L'Illustration* ran a map of East-Central Europe on which Yugoslavia was labeled Czechoslovakia.[196] Great Britain differed little. British financial interests trusted the Hungarians more than they did the Little Entente states, complaining that the Romanians and Yugoslavs were unreliable debtors.[197] Prime Minister Ramsay MacDonald instructed the smaller nations as early as 1924 that "Pacts or no pacts, you will be invaded.... The certain victim of the military age and military organization of society is the small nationality that trusts upon its moral claim to live."[198] In 1938 John Gunther described British policy as essentially committed to pacifism and isolationism—and to "playing for time, until its own tremendous rearmament program is complete."[199] During the 1938 P.E.N. International Congress in Prague, the British writer H. G. Wells and French novelist Jules Romains had requested an interview with Edvard Beneš. Storm Jameson, British P.E.N. member, predicted their comments: "They are saying that the only people in France and England who admire you for your reasonableness and honesty are middle class liberals and intellectuals, of no importance and without any influence."[200]

Throughout the interwar period, the foremost goal of Czechoslovakia's leaders, in particular Beneš, was to strengthen the state's ties to its Western patrons, the better to ensure Czechoslovakia's survival.[201] The European press, international organizations, and other forums for cultural diplomacy were crucial for the Castle effort. East-Central European revisionists understood that if Czechoslovakia fell, the entire system of postwar treaties and the post-Versailles order in Europe might be called into question; the Czechs worked from the same assumption. The Czechoslovak cultural relations war was continuous and hard-fought, but propaganda could not overcome all the challenges the Czechs faced. Castle arguments for moral worthiness and European similitude confronted ignorance, disinterest, or suspicion that idealized Castle claims about relations between Czechs and their subject minorities might not be entirely accurate. The gap between Czechoslovakia and Western Europe remained—in fact, it widened—and could not be closed by myth.

5

A Time of Iron and Fire

Anyone who understands how to read will find me between the lines of my books.

—*Tomáš Garrigue Masaryk*

As the 1930s progressed, fewer and fewer Europeans believed another war could be avoided. The postwar peace and the era of collective, democratic security it had supposedly ushered in were under profound threat from the Depression and rightist regimes throughout the Continent. Liberal parliamentarism, in retreat even before the Great War ended, seemed to belong to a distant, happier age. Of Europe's "dirty torrent" of dictators, Hitler posed Czechoslovakia the most direct threat.[1] The May 1935 parliamentary election indicated that Czech and Slovak support for the state and the main political parties remained constant. But the tallies in the German communities of Czechoslovakia's highly industrialized border region indicated a groundswell of support for aggressive German nationalism, and revived frustration with the Czechoslovak state.

Germans in Czechoslovakia seemed, between 1925 and 1932, to have reluctantly reconciled themselves with the First Republic, despite intermittent demonstrations and protests. But "German nationalist civil society" had long distanced itself from Czech or Czechoslovak affairs.[2] Then the German-settled border regions, housing most of the country's light industry, were hit early and hard by the Depression; Czechoslovak exports never recovered, even after a devaluation of the crown.[3] Nazi nationalism worked successfully on Sudeten German economic misery, reminding Germans of their lingering resentment at perceived slights like the Czechoslovak land reform, the 1926 language law, and Beneš's systematic rejection of Czechoslovak German petitions to the League of Nations.[4] The Sudeten German Fatherland movement (Sudetendeutsche Heimatsfront), led by former gymnastics teacher Konrad Henlein and bookstore owner Karl Hermann Frank, transformed itself into an organized party (the Sudetendeutsche Partei, or SdP) in 1935, to take part in parliamentary elections. Nazi Germany funded its campaign, although historians have cautioned that the SdP was "overwhelmingly authoritarian" but "only partially Nazi," maintaining an ambiguous relationship with Nazism through 1938 and beyond.[5] SdP lieutenants Heinrich Rutha, Richard Goldberg, and Walter Brand worked assiduously and successfully to create a leader cult around Henlein's bland personality.[6] The SdP polled 15.2 percent of the total vote (a full two-thirds of the German vote), garnering more votes than any other party, even more than the powerful Czechoslovak Agrarians. The German activist parties now no longer represented the majority of Sudeten Germans. Meanwhile, the SdP emulated Masaryk and Beneš in taking their plaint abroad to Hungary, Italy, Austria, and Sweden before fixing their gaze on Great Britain. Rutha, Brand, and Henlein traveled to London at least four times between late 1935 and May 1938, relying on aristocratic Bohemian Germans to reach members of the British aristocracy, such as Robert Vansittart, foreign under secretary for Central Europe, and Winston Churchill.[7] Even moderate Czech Germans like Wenzel Jaksch of the German Social Democrats complained in London and Paris: for example, Jaksch, in November 1937, told an audience at the Institute of International Affairs at Chatham House that progress aside—more Germans had entered the civil service—Czechoslovakia's nationalities conspicuously lacked mutual trust.[8]

By 1937, thanks to a defense-based public works program, the Czechoslovak economy—including the German-settled border regions—had begun to extricate itself from the Depression. The government hoped to quell German unrest by granting greater regional autonomy and waiting for national economic gains to make themselves felt in the Sudeten areas. At this same time, Karl Hermann Frank's radical right-wing faction within the SdP gained ascendancy, and the party moved closer to Hitler. On Hitler's advice, Henlein made progressively greater demands on the Czechoslovak government. By 1938 the SdP was increasingly open about its opposition to the Czechoslovak state and its ties to Hitler; it attracted some 85 percent of German voters in Czechoslovakia in that year's communal elections. Meanwhile,

Czechoslovakia's Great Power allies were increasingly uninterested in the country they claimed credit for creating. Sir Joseph Addison, the pessimistic British minister to Prague from 1930 to 1936, expressed to London doubt about the Czechoslovak state's viability. In January 1932, he called it an "artificial country"; in late 1933 he described it as a hastily sewn patchwork quilt, needing only a tug to collapse into pieces. Addison blamed the Czechs for "needlessly provoking" the Germans, even refusing to ameliorate the Depression's effects in the German-settled areas, thereby forcing the Czechoslovak Germans into a hostile posture and forcing Hitler to defend his fellow nationals. In Addison's eyes, the Czechoslovak government was guilty of "acts of petty tyranny."[9]

The Czechs themselves had contributed to their growing distance from the West. The Little Entente effectively dissolved, as Yugoslavia and Romania turned to Germany to buy their agricultural goods and exports. Beneš believed that Hitler's seizure of power meant that the Versailles order, predicated on a weak Germany, had been overturned. Czechoslovakia was therefore fundamentally endangered unless a new European balance of power could be achieved. The Soviet Union, Czechoslovakia's only potential savior, represented potential danger as well, since the British remained preoccupied with Bolshevism.[10] Beneš and French Foreign Minister Louis Barthou both wanted to bring the Soviets fully into European international relations: the USSR joined the League of Nations in 1934. But that same year, Barthou was killed, leaving Beneš isolated.[11] In 1935, the Soviet Union signed a mutual assistance pact with Czechoslovakia similar to that which it had signed with the French; the Soviets were only obliged to help Czechoslovakia once the French fulfilled their own commitment to do so. After the pact was concluded, Edvard Beneš gave an interview to *Pravda* in which he effusively praised both the treaty and Stalin's USSR. Propagandists in Germany, Hungary, and Poland promptly and gleefully painted Beneš and Czechoslovakia as a Soviet fellow traveler or lackey. Worse still, later that year, Beneš—always surprisingly loquacious for a diplomat—lectured Addison for almost two hours about Stalin's reliability and the trustworthiness of the Soviet Union.[12] Previous British reserve toward the Czechs now became open impatience, combined with growing interest in Konrad Henlein. The Foreign Office found him moderate and reasonable, and saw him as a potential counterweight to Hitler; they also believed that without the Sudeten Germans, Czechoslovakia was doomed to disintegrate. Czechoslovakia therefore had to be "realistic" about its relationship to its Germans and to Nazi Germany. Vansittart repeatedly discussed the possibility of recreating Czechoslovakia as a "state of nationalities" with substantial autonomy for German speakers; Ambassador to Britain Jan Masaryk agreed that such a step would be necessary.[13]

Within Czechoslovakia, now Europe's lone democracy east of the Rhine, even Castle stalwarts expressed considerable doubt about the virtue and security of Czechoslovakia's democratic system. Prominent National Socialist Emil Franke noted, "our democracy is suitable for normal conditions, quiet times, and relative wealth. If conditions are extraordinary, one cannot exclude equally extraordinary measures."[14] Similarly, Václav Klofáč, Beneš's coleader of the Czechoslovak National Socialist Party, argued on September 30, 1933 that the "parliamentary system, and everything connected with it, needs a thorough revision, because . . . it is a relic of the old capitalist/liberal trends." Josef Schieszl, political chief of Masaryk's chancellery, wrote in a personal letter dated from mid-1933 that "liberalism can work only in a liberal society . . . and liberalism is on its last legs."[15] At one of Karel Čapek's Friday meetings in 1934, the attendees argued about Czechoslovakia's problematic relationship with Poland. Josef Šusta blamed Beneš for it, and for his blind confidence that Mussolini and fascism would disappear. "We are completely isolated," he despaired.[16] Beyond the Castle, readiness to move rightward was even more widespread.

By the 1930s, the Czechoslovak parliamentary system had remade itself as a "disciplined democracy," willing to suspend the constitution in the name of the state.[17] In 1933, Parliament passed a *zmocňování zákon* or Enabling Law, allowing the government to make economic policy by decree during the crisis years of the Great Depression. Crafted by the Agrarians, who used it to harass the Social Democrats, the scope of the law gradually grew beyond economic policy and was used to rule by decree, even to replace existing legislation; many experts believed this violated the constitution.[18] Other means of bypassing full parliamentary sessions had been in place since the republic's birth, such as the *stálý výbor* (Permanent Committee) of sixteen representatives and eight senators, granted power to deal with parliamentary matters when Parliament was not in session and used frequently, especially in the 1930s.[19] In 1935, Masaryk's designated successor Beneš won the presidency with difficulty. In the initial voting, the Czechoslovak and German Agrarians, the National Union (the National Democrats, Jiří Stříbrný's National League, and the semifascist National Front led by Prof. Františšek Mareš), and the Fascists united against Beneš, denying him a majority. Beneš refused to turn to the SdP for the necessary votes. Milan Hodža, prime minister and a former foe of the Castle, placed the Slovak Agrarians in Beneš's camp; thanks to Hodža's suasion, the Slovak Populists joined them, tipping Parliament toward the Castle. In the final vote, Beneš won by a substantial majority. But the negotiation process—the open split within the Agrarian Party, the Agrarian right wing opposing the Castle, the Slovak autonomists' increasing importance—was unnerving.[20] The Castle had claimed for seventeen years to represent democracy itself, and Beneš was Masaryk's chosen disciple. Dissension and challenge within Parliament, against an increasingly hostile international context, augured badly for the Castle and perhaps the republic.

The Castle propaganda apparatus remained extremely active during these arduous years. Increasingly, the Third Section supported Castle-loyal papers all over the republic, in particular non-Czech papers, in an effort to build the bridges not constructed a decade earlier. The Third Section sent funding to the German Christian Social publications *Bund der Landwirte, Deutsche Presse*, and *Landpost*, as well as the German-language magazines *Zeit im Bild* and *Die Brücke*. After 1933, Jan Hájek and the Third Section became an important source of support for German Jews and leftists fleeing Nazi Germany, working in coordination with the presidential chancellery. Zamini sponsored publications by émigré Germans, such as *Der Montag*, published by Walter Tschuppik in Prague, and *Wahrheit*, published by G. Mannheim and Bela Rév, respectively German and Hungarian journalists living in Prague. The relatively liberal Bratislava Hungarian daily *Magyar Újsag* also received Third Section funds in the late 1930s.[21] The Castle's increasing sense of threat was reflected in Orbis titles. By the mid-1930s, Orbis materials loudly iterated the Czechs' contributions to European culture and post-war politics, and the importance of a stable, democratic Czechoslovakia at Europe's heart. Historian Kamil Krofta, Beneš's successor as foreign minister after 1935, published with Orbis his *Europa im Scheideweg/Europe at the Cross-Roads/L'Europe au Carrefour* and *Czechoslovakia and the Crisis of Collective Security*. Beneš contributed *The Problems of Czechoslovakia*. Orbis published many other texts, in French, English, and German, on Czechoslovakia's German "problem," its strategic importance, and its relationship to the Third Reich and the Soviet Union.[22]

At home, Czech expressions of steadfast devotion to the state and its leaders continued, at least as quantified by a steady stream of books, magazines, brochures, gadgets, photographic portraits, and other items allowing Czech consumers to support the Castle. Not just Masaryk but also Beneš now received his share of propagandistic popularization. The Castle myth-making apparatus responded to the country's increasing political insecurity by emphasizing the old nineteenth-century oppositions, reinvigorated by a dangerous new era. The Czechoslovaks were once again noble martyrs as their Hussite predecessors had been, threatened by the Germanic onslaught. But at no point did the Castle extend a symbolic hand to the country's minorities.

Masaryk died in 1937; Karel Čapek and the First Republic expired in 1938. As the republic was forced to its end, an onslaught of text about and by its foremost symbol and popularizer bolstered the Castle myth. Čapek's

Conversations with Masaryk was published in installments from 1927 to 1935; a companion volume, *Silences with Masaryk*, about the circumstances of creating the *Conversations*, came out in 1935. Čapek also helped Legionnaire novelist Josef Kopta and Masaryk's secretary, Vasil Škrach, compile *Days of Sorrow*, a collection of photographs and writings about Masaryk's death from within and outside Czechoslovakia. And Ferdinand Peroutka's four-volume history of the republic's early years, *Building the State: Czechoslovak Politics in the Postrevolutionary Years*, was published between 1932 and 1937. The *Conversations* and *Building the State* focused on the immediate post-war aftermath, when the nation had emerged victorious from the chaos of the war and, with the blessing of the civilized West, moved forward to take its place among the nations of Europe. The books emphasized the role of Masaryk and Beneš in this jubilant process, and in steering the state through the waters of the relatively calm and prosperous 1920s (Čapek's book mentions the 1930s only glancingly). Čapek and Peroutka created a narrative of Czechoslovakia through their work, a Czechoslovakia that had Masaryk and Beneš to thank for its very existence, which rested on tolerant and inclusive multiethnicity, democracy, and the support of the West.

Beneš's capitulation to Hitler's 1938 Munich *Diktat*, and the Czech experience of Nazi occupation during the Second World War, changed both the presentation of the myth (now coming from the exile government in London) and public reception of the Castle myth at home. At home, especially after the Nazi invasion of March 1939, most Czechs continued to believe in Beneš as Masaryk's heir, an important symbol of continuity with the prewar era. At the same time, few wanted to return to the First Republic. The interwar democracy was now seen as a luxury ill afforded in difficult times, weak, corrupt, perhaps mistaken to have relied on the West, and certainly wrong to have tried to accommodate the country's minorities, now viewed as uniformly belligerent. The party system, not the Castle, received much of the blame for the First Republic's inadequacies. In exile, Beneš reiterated most of the Castle myth, but its themes changed in response to wartime developments. The new Castle myth slowly eliminated any potential coexistence with Czechoslovak Germans, and began to emphasize Czechoslovakia's ties to the Slavic world, particularly the Soviet Union. While the myth still hailed democracy as the Czechoslovak ideal, now invoking "economic democracy" and social egalitarianism, Beneš's wartime writings never clarified what exactly democracy entailed. Like Masaryk, Beneš tended to discuss democracy in terms of personal morality rather than just institutions. By war's end, the Castle myth had shifted considerably, although its terminology had not. While still discussing "democracy," Beneš's postwar variant on the Castle myth defended a socialist approach to the country's economy and social problems, and invoked the "Slavic" Soviet Union as protector and model.

This chapter analyzes text—books, journalism, and correspondence—as well as cultural diplomacy and political activity to sketch out the shifting parameters of the Castle myth at the end of the republic, during wartime, and between 1945 and 1948. Response to and participation in the myth shifted notably, in three disparate phases: heightened intensity through 1938, complex adherence between 1939 and 1945, and critical analysis between 1945 and 1948.

Conversations with Masaryk: *Myth as History*

Books by and about Masaryk had always stood at the center of Orbis publishing efforts. The 1933 Zamini analyst describing the French press's venality and cooptation by Nazi and Japanese propaganda concluded his report with a set of suggestions, among them that the Czechoslovaks send more texts by Masaryk, as if his shining moral example could magically compensate for Czechoslovakia's financial limitations and strategic concerns.[23] A central Orbis text, granted great importance by the Castle, was Karel Čapek's *Conversations with Masaryk*.

The *Conversations* were conceived as propaganda, to secure Masaryk's place as founder and symbol of the state. Čapek and Masaryk discussed the idea of a cowritten autobiography during a 1927 visit with Masaryk at Topol'čianky, the president's home in Slovakia. Čapek wrote his companion Olga Scheinpflugová that the book would be "a politically good thing, . . . tremendously valuable: I'd like to have it finished as a gift for the republic's tenth anniversary."[24] Only the first third of the book was finished by then; the entire work did not come out until 1935.

The *Conversations* were a collective Castle effort. The writing process began with the eponymous conversations: Masaryk and Čapek would typically talk together for hours, Masaryk answering a series of questions Čapek put to him, Čapek taking notes (figure 5.1). Čapek would then write up an initial draft and send manuscript pages to the president, leaving a wide left margin in which Masaryk made comments or suggested changes.[25] Once Čapek wrote up a manuscript incorporating Masaryk's recommendations, Masaryk's intimates and family became involved. Čapek's work did not always please Masaryk; the president had noted, after reading the draft of the second volume, *Life and Work*, "Often it is him in there and not me."[26] Alice Masaryková, with the help of family archivist Anna Gašpariková and Masaryk's personal assistant Antonín Schenk, edited

Figure 5.1. Masaryk chatting with Karel Čapek at Bystrička in Slovakia. From left: Jan Masaryk, Alice Masaryková, Masaryk, Čapek. *Source*: AÚTGM fotografické oddělení, VIII/47/2*107/16, 826.

the manuscript to "preserve the 'pure Masaryk' . . . [and] tried to erase the traces of the, according to them, rather unimaginatively materialistic author. . . . [T]hey also censored alleged vulgarisms."[27] Čapek complained to his friend Julius Firt that Alice Masaryková was "puritanical" and wanted to keep her father on a pedestal, rather than show the world the living man.[28] Masaryk's correspondent Olga Sedlmajerová sent him suggestions for improving the *Conversations*.[29] Beneš, too, requested to see the manuscript, which frustrated Čapek.[30]

Most of the *Conversations*' three sections presented Masaryk's life, told in a charming, gently self-deprecating tone purporting to be Masaryk's own. *The Era of Youth* (1928) contained Masaryk's remembrances of his childhood. *Life and Work* (1931) took Masaryk's story up through his 1919 election to the presidency. The final section of the book, *Thought and Life* (1935) was a philosophical interview, in which Masaryk expounded on abstract issues from suicide to cognition, metaphysics, ethics, religion, and culture. This material would be largely familiar to Czechoslovak patriots, thanks to the welter of previous Masaryk biographies. The main difference here was the singular narrative voice, since Masaryk's old-fashioned constructions and occasional use of Moravian dialect were left intact. Like other biographers, Čapek made much of Masaryk's peasant childhood in a Slovak village, his moves to Brno, Vienna, and Prague to pursue schooling, his career as an outspoken university professor and public gadfly, his bravery during the First World War, his incessant efforts on behalf of his nation, and his fatherly concern for the young Czechoslovak democracy. Čapek admiringly noted Masaryk's personal virtues: his teetotaling, his adoration for his American wife. In the *Conversations* as in the other presidential biographies, Masaryk frequently departs from the story of his life to issue virtuous declarations about social issues, particularly feminism and education.[31] Czechoslovak political life appeared infrequently in the *Conversations* and generally presented the standard Castle narrative. For example: "Our politics are . . . essentially rationalistic, enlightened. In this, we are like France—hence those national sympathies with her." Or, underscoring the link between Czechoslovakia and democracy: "In virtue of our history and nature, we are destined for democracy. . . . [W]e are a nation democratic in body and soul."[32]

The heart of the *Conversations* is, of course, the president. The *Conversations'* Masaryk is nothing like the canny, frequently aggressive politician contemporaries knew. Čapek's Masaryk represents an ideal of gentlemanly masculinity, willing to move boldly when the situation demands it but preferring an unassuming, contemplative life. The *Conversations'* Masaryk practically has to be begged to describe his glorious deeds to the public, let alone to explain their significance or extol his own bravery. For example, Čapek complained in the foreword to the fourth edition of *Life and Work* of his subject's modesty. "Press questions on him, how it was then, what he did, how it was for him in this or that difficult moment. He barely waves a hand and says: 'Yes, well, that's long past.' . . . It would be difficult for you to find another man who is so reluctant to speak about himself."[33] The sheer number of Masaryk biographies written during the interwar period, many of them based on interviews with Masaryk himself, belies this comment. Nevertheless, Čapek's characterization is compelling.

Masaryk's recollection of revolutionary Moscow exemplifies the *Conversations'* presentation of heroism and courteous reserve. The Legionaries had told Masaryk to go to Moscow, believing it would be safer than St. Petersburg. But within moments of his arrival, Masaryk heard gunshots. He left his Legionnaire-assigned bodyguard at the train station to collect the baggage and went off alone to the Hotel National on foot, then found his way blocked by a row of soldiers. Masaryk asked to pass, and was told (and saw) that the Bolsheviks and Kerensky's forces were exchanging gunfire in the streets. He went instead to the Hotel Metropol, where the gate was shut in his face. "I banged on it and called out, 'What are you doing? Open up!' 'Are you a guest?' the porter called back. 'We can't let you [in] if you're not; we're full up.' I didn't want to lie, so I yelled out to him, 'Don't be an idiot and let me in!' " Gunshots were being fired at the hotel as well. The guests and Masaryk fled to the cellar, and were confined to the hotel for a week. But Masaryk recalled that he seldom felt fear. "I wasn't afraid, and if I was, I didn't let myself know it, because of our boys. How on earth could I have commanded them if they'd seen that I was afraid?"[34] This anecdote neatly conveys the mythic Masaryk's greatest qualities: his refusal to lie, even to protect his own life; calm in the face of imminent danger; and a constant attention to the collective good, effectively commanding his men, extricating them from Bolshevik clutches, and returning them to the Czechoslovak state they were working together to create. Masaryk's depiction as the personification of honesty itself, along with the comment, "I didn't want to lie," appears in his other biographies and memoirs; in *Světová revoluce*, for example, he noted that even propaganda must be honorable: "exaggeration and outright lies never succeed."[35]

One might assume a president's biography would discuss politics, but Čapek's Masaryk discussed domestic and international politics almost entirely in the realm of theory, as if his own considerable political praxis did not exist. When Masaryk mentioned his difficulty in adjusting to the role of president and notes that he made mistakes, the example he offered is in the end somewhat flippant: in early 1919 he agreed to meet some friends at a café, only to find himself surrounded by crowds.[36] The book's final section did refer obliquely to current events, specifically Czechoslovakia's minorities. For example, Masaryk stated:

> [N]ational and racial minorities have been part of human development since the beginning. . . . Every European state contains linguistic minorities; little states and nations are minorities among the larger states, and even the largest states and nations are in the end minorities when compared with the human world. Thus the just resolution of minority politics is a precondition for better and more cosmopolitan organization of the world.[37]

In this way Masaryk tried to defuse the calls from Czechoslovakia's minorities for better treatment with an implicit request that Czechoslovakia's larger neighbors extend her the same courtesy.

Similarly, the final section contained an uncharacteristically topical statement about Czechoslovakia's German minority. "The state is ours, it is ours by historical right, by the majority principle and by the [fact] that we created it," Masaryk stated, "but we have significant minorities. . . . [I]t is our task to [win over] for the idea of our democratic republic the minorities with whom we live . . . Their numbers and their cultural advancement charge us, and them, [to create] a democratic compromise." Masaryk then called on the (presumably Czech) reader to be inspired both by the noble Czech past and its ignominy under Austria:

> Our procedure with the minorities is practically given to us by our own experience under Austria-Hungary. What we did not like to be done to us we shall not do unto others. The program of Palacký, the father of our nation, applies for us and for the future. Our history, the politics of the Přemyslid dynasty, of saint Václav, of [Kings] Charles and George [of Poděbrady] must be a model for our politics regarding our Germans. The fact that we are encircled by our large German neighbor forces the thoughtful Czech to a wise and circumspect politics.[38]

This passage indicates that at least discursively, even in the mid-1930s the Czechs were still essentially separate from "their" Germans, still suspicious of German allegiance to the state even after almost twenty years of largely peaceful coexistence. Wisdom and circumspection were forced on the Czechs by admiration for German culture or (more likely) the powerful German Reich, not by any sense of shared rights or responsibilities within a common state. Masaryk focused his attention on the Czech past, using ideas and phrases quite similar to his depiction in *Světová revoluce*, published almost ten years earlier. As a statement of Castle myth, this speaks volumes.

Čapek wrote of his text, "It in itself is more than a document or a biography; rather, it is—what else could we call it?—*an example*."[39] This comment's religious overtones suggest religion's central role in the *Conversations*, similar to the generalized Christian spirituality featured in Masaryk's prewar writings. More than half of *Thought and Life* (1935) addresses topics like "*Sub specie aeterni*," "Spirit and World," "The Religion of Jesus," "The Religion of Love," "Religious Development in the Czech Lands (*u nás*)," and "Faith and Science." Masaryk repeatedly emphasized his own reverence for and intimate, loving relationship with God, from which he derived his relationship to humanity. "[Y]ou would like to hear my creed: its last word is *reverentia*; a conscious honoring of God and man; implicit in this honoring of those close to me is love; I mean by that a love that is also conscious."[40] This love for God naturally implied a love for one's fellow citizen, in Masaryk's understanding: "love, sympathy, synergy—such is the law of life whether it be for the couple, the family, the nation, the state, or humanity."[41] This late presentation of Masaryk's ideas implies that the individual's relationship to God provides the basis for his political sensibility and participation; the individual, rather than institutions, constitutions, parties, or administration, is charged with transforming civic culture into a culture of *reverentia* and love. These statements seem startlingly similar to those he expressed in his major works of the 1890s, and like them evade analysis of democratic discourse and interaction by emphasizing individual civic religiosity.

Since 1926, Čapek and Masaryk had worked closely together: Čapek had become Masaryk's admiring confidant and one of the Castle's most important popularizers. The *Conversations* was far from his only contribution to the Castle's work or to Masaryk's personality cult. As he was writing the *Conversations*, Čapek also produced a great number of Castle-friendly articles and interviews with the president in *Lidové noviny*, some of which he allowed Masaryk to edit.[42] Čapek was the main force responsible for the popular mass-audience picture book, *Masaryk in Photographs*; he suggested it to the president, took some of the photographs, shepherded the book through production, and wrote its foreword. Some of the best-known images of Masaryk, such as the president holding his happy, naked toddler grandson on his shoulder, come from this book.[43]

Čapek's newspaper articles from the 1930s reveal other, related concerns for the state, as in the 1932 piece "Your Masaryk." Čapek explained to his readers that "any educated foreigner," even those who knew little about Czechoslovakia, knew about Masaryk: "your Masaryk," they allegedly said, "you're lucky!" This was true, Čapek avowed, even though the world press wrote little about Masaryk or, by extension, Czechoslovakia. This worrisome development—that Czech propaganda efforts to attract the world's attention were unsuccessful—was in fact a sign of good fortune and lasting fame, Čapek explained: "[O]ur public and state life . . . never appears . . . in a sensational light. . . . Masaryk's world popularity is not current, because it is permanent. . . . That same foreigner who says to us 'your Masaryk' knows factually little about him, just as he knows little about George Washington."[44] Masaryk was more than a human being, Čapek wrote after Masaryk's final, unanimous reelection to the presidency in 1934: "Masaryk is a *principle*. Masaryk is for us and for the entire educated world the embodiment of certain moral and political ideals, which can be called *democracy*." The Czechs, Slovaks, and the country's national minorities had chosen Masaryk, and democracy, at a moment when Europe was abandoning it, Čapek wrote: "In Germany, in Austria, in Bulgaria. Everywhere around us. . . . [We are] a little island in the center of Europe. Or perhaps God's soldiers, strengthened by their faith rather than by power. . . . as Antonín Švehla said just before he died, 'We are clearly the bastion of Western democracy; that means that we must *hold on*. . . .' Call it our fate, . . . or the meaning of history."[45] Čapek's journalistic output increased in the weeks after Masaryk's death in mid-September 1937, when he wrote long articles every few days about Masaryk's funeral arrangements, the country's respectful participation, and Masaryk's meaning for the country. "T.G. MASARYK

STILL WATCHES OVER US," Čapek emphasized: Masaryk was "eternal"; in him his grateful citizens saw "courage and wisdom, beauty and greatness, a classical model of man and spirit"; he was "an instrument in the hand of God." At the foundation of the state, as built by Masaryk, was God himself.[46]

Čapek's service to the Castle went beyond his prose. At home, he often acted as the Castle's intermediary, defending Masaryk publicly and privately, even to Castle allies whom the president abandoned. He helped to orchestrate state visits, using his experience as a playwright and dramaturge, and represented the Castle at the bedsides of ill allies and enemies alike. A rueful letter from early September 1929 indicates the extent of his services:

> I have been devoting myself to . . . charitable deeds; I visited the ill *Scot Viator* [nickname for Robert Seton-Watson], I went to visit [Slovak Agrarian Milan] Hodža; [and] in the last few days I directed the arrival and welcoming of marshal Petain. In short, . . . I have not left myself any peace and quiet, what with my damned usefulness.[47]

And from 1927 until his death in 1933, Čapek also befriended powerful Agrarian Antonín Švehla. Initially formed at the Castle's behest, this friendship eventually ended Čapek's close collaboration with Masaryk. Both Švehla and Čapek frequently took rest cures in the spa town of Karlovy Vary (Carlsbad); Masaryk occasionally traveled there to speak informally with the prime minister, and Čapek shuttled between them, smoothing out grievances. "I have had many good conversations with Švehla," wrote Čapek in July 1927: "he is an interesting and strong person and he means well towards the president."[48] But it soon became clear that Čapek found Švehla more than "interesting." In 1928, Robert Seton-Watson asked Čapek to contribute a brief celebratory article for Czechoslovakia's tenth anniversary. Čapek responded, "I assume that if someone talks about Czechoslovakia, he should talk about Masaryk—or about Švehla."[49] He wrote: "[Švehla], beyond all others, is deserving of being known and appreciated as much outside, as inside, the country which for ten years he has ruled more than anyone else." Švehla's enthusiasm when discussing the germination of a grain of corn was "poetic," his vocabulary "Rabelaisian," Švehla himself "ruthlessly and passionately practical," with an "uncanny knack of mastering situations and people." Švehla's name, Čapek wrote, was written "not only in the annals of our country, but in the annals of world democracy."[50] Masaryk's and Beneš's names appear nowhere in the essay; Švehla is essentially granted sole credit for having carved the republic out of the chaos of postwar Central Europe.

Čapek's closeness to Švehla deepened as his distance from the president grew. In late 1930, when Švehla seemed to be recovering, Čapek wrote to him, in language as adoring as that with which he had addressed Masaryk in 1926:

> You gave me great pleasure last Monday . . . seeing you recovered and actually returned to us all. I have not had such pleasure in many years. . . . If I speak with you, I gain more than if I were to scribble or read something; therefore I ask you candidly to avail yourself of my time whenever it should be convenient for you.[51]

Meanwhile, the president was aging. He had taken office at the age of sixty-eight in 1918; by 1932, Masaryk was frequently exhausted, repeatedly ill, and becoming querulous and capricious. Government and Castle colleagues were resigned to the fact that the president's age was affecting his judgment, making him less flexible and more prone to favor his personal likes and dislikes over pragmatic concerns.[52] Masaryk's influence, and his ability to bring together erstwhile opponents or otherwise exert the force of his personality combined with his place as the country's founder, slowly began to weaken. Čapek found himself between two increasingly opposed mentor figures. In February 1932, for example, during an evening with Masaryk, Čapek acknowledged that once Švehla had urged him "to position himself against 'Masaryk's' politics. He recalled as well 'a certain antagonism against Beneš.' "[53]

The distance between Švehla and Masaryk grew as Švehla seemed to recover his health. In 1932, he had given some energetic speeches and warned against the personality cult developing around his name. By early 1933 Švehla had begun involving himself again in Agrarian party activities, and during his stay in Karlovy Vary, he even addressed the public, speaking in September 1933 in support of the current Agrarian prime minister, Jan Malypetr. Švehla's return to national politics seemed imminent. Castle intellectuals recalled that Švehla tried to court Čapek and the other Friday Men in 1933, openly requesting their support for his policies and discussing Czech intellectuals' new challenges given Hitler's accession to power, which dramatically altered Czechoslovakia's domestic and international politics. Švehla confided that he was very worried about the republic's future, particularly Czechoslovakia's parliamentary system and the relatively large number of political parties, which made rapid reaction and decision impossible. Švehla wanted to change the electoral code to force parties with similar programs to unite, so that consensus would be easier to orchestrate.[54] Most threateningly, he openly expressed suspicion of Castle foreign policy. "[We are] a small state and an unprepared, untried nation. Strong minorities, that means international . . . politics on our own land, in our own backyard." Beneš did not want to recognize the imminent crisis, or even destruction, of the system of collective security on which his politics were based, meaning the League of Nations' irrelevance and the Little Entente's probable demise. Beneš was altogether indifferent to the situation of the pro-government German parties, known as the activists, Švehla charged, and dismissed the inevitable conflict between the activists and German nationalists who might be inspired by Hitler.[55] Masaryk also tended to underestimate the Nazis as hooligans and fanatics. Finally, Švehla believed Masaryk held a low opinion of him and did not believe he would reenter (much less lead) Czechoslovak politics; he sensed Beneš behind recent press allegations of corruption within the Agrarian party.[56] Švehla told Čapek that when he returned to the government, he would insist on Beneš's resignation.[57] The prospect of a divide between the Castle and the powerful Agrarian party, led by a resolute and healthy Švehla, seemed unavoidable.

Čapek carried this unpleasant news to Masaryk at Topoľčianky in September 1933; the result was the end of their seven-year collaboration. Čapek did not record his views of their parting of the ways, but those close to Masaryk did. Švehla died of pneumonia on December 12, 1933; that evening, Masaryk reminisced about his argument with Čapek months earlier. His assistant Antonín Schenk recalled him as saying,

> I never believed that Švehla would return to politics. . . . Not even when Čapek got so excited about it last summer. And it irritated me about him [Čapek] that he was so unobservant. I let him know about it. And also that I don't believe his novels. All of them are somehow affected. Like a machine. Čapek had visited Švehla at Karlovy Vary and later reported to me about it. But he didn't tell me everything. . . . I found out about it later. Švehla [said] that . . . [Beneš] was the misfortune of the republic and that his politics would bring the nation to ruin! Or something like that . . . Evidently Čapek told him that I was a good person. But Švehla said: "Masaryk's a hard man. He has kind eyes, but look at his mouth!"[58]

(Čapek also reported to Beneš that Švehla planned to replace Beneš as foreign minister, appointing him minister of the posts, then excluding him from government altogether.)[59]

Masaryk's attacks on Čapek's political engagement and belles lettres changed Čapek's relationship not just to the Castle but to politics more broadly. The Friday Men noticed his new distance from the president. Julius Firt observed,

> A wholehearted devotion remained; nevertheless I sometimes caught him, during intimate conversations . . . [engaging in] previously unthinkable critical views and perceptions. As if suddenly in Čapek's

> eyes a slightly different Masaryk had appeared, [other] than the way we know him from the *Conversations*.[60]

Yet neither this argument nor his relationship with Edvard Beneš, far more distant than his relationship to Masaryk, ended Čapek's work for the Castle and his state, particularly abroad. Through the 1930s, Čapek traveled through Europe as a Czechoslovak cultural diplomat, discussing literature and his homeland.[61] During these travels he befriended Zamini embassy personnel, so much so that after his trips he would write asking for local items for his garden.[62] He presented a series of radio lectures to British audiences in 1934.[63] In June 1936, Čapek traveled to Budapest as Czechoslovakia's representative to the League of Nations' international committee on literature and art. A month later, Čapek and his wife Olga Scheinpflugová journeyed to Sweden, Norway, and Denmark, again on Zamini's payroll. In each country, the Czechoslovak embassies arranged lectures, meetings with publishers and academics, and meals hosted by various intellectuals. Zamini also sponsored his driving tour in the summer of 1937 to France (that year's P.E.N. International Congress was in Paris) and Switzerland.[64] Orbis translated Čapek's novels, his children's stories about his puppy Dašenka, and the *Conversations* into English, Dutch, Swedish, and German, among other languages.[65] They also translated his many travelogues, illustrated with his own idiosyncratic pen-and-ink drawings, describing Italy (1923), England (1924), Spain (1930), Holland (1932), Scandinavia (1936), and Czechoslovakia (1938). All save the first were produced with Zamini's financial assistance or were published by Orbis.[66] More ominously, Čapek and Ferdinand Peroutka served as diplomatic couriers in late March and early April 1938, between President Beneš and Ernst Eisenlohr, the Nazi ambassador to Prague, transmitting Eisenlohr's warnings about Hitler's desire "to physically eliminate the Czech nation."[67]

In late summer 1938, a group of German émigrés invited Čapek to Switzerland, which would have guaranteed him safe harbor in a neutral country.[68] Čapek refused the offer and turned to Zamini, asking what he could do for the country as part of a coordinated effort. In fact, at roughly this same moment Third Section leader Jan Hájek, Beneš, and foreign minister Kamil Krofta were beginning to plan for another government in exile either in Paris or Toulouse, and were ready to smuggle out various high-ranking officials from the Third Section to head and staff a fully functioning propaganda effort.[69] Hájek's response indicates that he had already assumed this staff would include Čapek:

> When we created a theoretical plan for the propaganda service in exceptional circumstances, we counted on your cooperation, without having asked you. Now, [after thinking about your letter,] in my

> opinion the most advantageous solution would be to combine both of your suggestions as long as domestic radio [programming] is possible, but to be prepared to embark on a journey abroad. In that case we would, of course, take on ourselves [the necessary preparations.] I assume that . . . [we will probably arrange] a freight truck. It will be harder with the driver, for whom of course we cannot advertise ahead of time.[70]

Čapek's work for Masaryk and the Castle in the First Republic's final decade was of tremendous importance. Čapek was not Masaryk's only biographer, but he was the most emotionally persuasive. He was not the Castle's only popularizer, but he was the best-known, in Czechoslovakia and in Europe. He was not the only writer to call Masaryk "eternal" or Czechoslovakia a democratic "island in the center of Europe," but his essays ran in *Lidové noviny*, by the late 1930s considered Czechoslovakia's paper of record, and his work was known throughout the Continent. Čapek's formulations of Castle tenets proved durable and influential. Certainly his carefully crafted image of Masaryk, as presented in the *Conversations*, took on a life of its own, one difficult to dismantle.

Building the State: *Complicating the Myth*

Ferdinand Peroutka's *Budování státu: Československá politika v letech popřevratových* (*Building the State: Czechoslovak Politics in the Postrevolutionary Years*) never attained the level of acclaim that Čapek's work garnered, nor did its depictions enter conventional wisdom in quite the same way. Circumstances denied Peroutka's magisterial history the place it deserves in Czech letters. *Building the State* was never finished. Like the rest of Peroutka's work, it was never translated out of Czech. And it was published in its (incomplete) entirety only as the republic itself came under direct threat, at a moment when the world of letters was much less important than the world beyond them. Still, Peroutka's masterwork deserves attention, not just for its deft prose but also for its role in perpetuating the Castle myth. A subtle, complex, less sentimental historical portrait than Čapek's biography, *Building the State* was also a central element of the Castle myth's propagation at the end of the republic.

Several oddities marked *Building the State*'s composition. First, the book was serialized, but on its own rather than in a newspaper. It came out in "notebooks," or installments of thirty-two pages, every two weeks beginning October 5, 1932.[71] The series boasted 5,000 subscribers, a surprisingly large number for a book of this kind and in this format, indicative of Peroutka's prominence.[72] But critics necessarily withheld reviews until the entire work had been published, limiting its impression on Czech letters. Peroutka later explained that the book's distinctive nature came from journalistic habit. "I always wrote everything at the last moment... under the pressure of necessity.... I remember that sometimes,... I wrote an entire installment in two days."[73] Second, as previously stated, Peroutka never finished the book. He had intended to cover the years from 1918 to 1926, when the national minorities entered the government. For Peroutka, 1926 was a crucial moment for the Czechoslovak state: it signaled that the Czechs had rejected the oppositional, overly nationalized political culture they had inherited from Austria: "I was convinced that building the state was a psychological problem. That people... had to educate themselves in some kind of state consciousness."[74] But Peroutka's record went only through the Czechoslovak municipal elections of September 1923. He abandoned the book in 1937, when the growing tension between Czechs and Germans persuaded him that Czechoslovakia had in fact failed to integrate its minorities. The state had not, in the end, been built.[75]

Peroutka had the Castle's blessing and assistance while researching and writing *Building the State*. In 1930, after culling parliamentary records for material, Peroutka spoke with Masaryk about his new project. "He asked me: 'how old are you?' I was about 33 at that time, and he said, 'well, you have time to begin something larger, so start.'" A month later, Peroutka recalled, he spent a week with the president at Topoľčianky reviewing Masaryk's personal archive and the early history of the republic; the two men met repeatedly thereafter. Beneš also contributed memories and documents to Peroutka's project. "[T]he meetings with Beneš lasted until three, four in the morning. He was indefatigable, far more so than I."[76]

Peroutka had long been an authoritative figure in Czech political journalism. He had first gained notoriety from a 1921–1922 essay series in the journal *Tribuna* titled "Jáci jsme [What We Are Like]." In these polemics against Czech romantic nationalism, Peroutka criticized Masaryk's portrayal of the Czech past: he called for more thorough contextualization of Czech history within European history, and defended the contribution Austrian culture had made to Czech development.[77] The ensuing controversy—an unknown young journalist arguing publicly with the president—brought him to Masaryk's attention. In April 1923, Masaryk asked Peroutka to edit a new journal, to be published by Castle newspaper tycoon Jaroslav Stránský. *Přítomnost* (*The Present* or *Presence*) was an immediate critical and intellectual success if not a financial one.[78] Peroutka also wrote the Sunday editorial and other political analysis for *Lidové noviny*.[79]

Přítomnost covered sixteen pages with tiny print, analyzing the most important questions and events of the week, but also dealing with ongoing questions. It proved to be a journal of ideas, rather than the week-in-review journal Masaryk had intended.[80] The front-page editorial was usually written by Peroutka or someone equally prominent, generally on politics. Other rubrics addressed national economics, European economics and politics, social issues, literature, and occasional commentary on women's issues. But Peroutka was the journal's heart, as Julius Firt, director of Stránský's enterprises in the 1930s, recalled:

> Peroutka read and edited every contribution to every issue himself. . . . [He] had mastered the ability to make a meaningful text out of an average draft. It would happen [sometimes] that one of [*Přítomnost's*] hardworking writers would wander to another magazine. . . . At that point . . . the brief, accurate, pointed contributions by this *Přítomnost* author suddenly were prolix, loquacious, lacking the ability to make . . . [comments] aimed precisely at the heart of a problem.[81]

Peroutka's refusal to create Masaryk's desired weekly review irritated the Castle. He also assailed sacred Castle tenets. In January 1930, for example, Peroutka wrote that Beneš ought not to become president, due to the country's polarized politics and Beneš's long history of conflict with party leaders.[82] Peroutka was aware that the journal vexed the president.[83] In 1927, when Stránský's publishing firm was in financial trouble, Zamini's Jan Hájek offered to purchase *Přítomnost*—but without Peroutka.[84] Stránský's affairs improved, and Masaryk sent some anonymous editorials to *Přítomnost*, but a certain degree of distance continued. In 1932, even as Peroutka was drafting the early chapters of *Building the State*, Masaryk complained that Peroutka "is lazy and has lost his touch; he is uninformed and subject to moods. . . . I don't like how he twists things in *Přítomnost* these days. . . . I don't expect much from that book of his, either."[85]

If Masaryk expected an uncomplicated repetition of the Castle mythology and personality cults, then he was no doubt disappointed. Peroutka did not write hagiography. *Building the State* drew on memoirs by the leaders of the domestic resistance as well as on Castle materials.[86] He lionized Antonín Švehla as "the master of reconciling difficult situations."[87] Peroutka lauded National Democratic finance minister Alois Rašín's insistence on revaluing the country's finances as an example of quiet heroism, an unpopular but desperately necessary step. A long chapter depicts Rašín himself as an energetic man of action for whom the republic should have been grateful.[88] Even Peroutka's presentation of Karel Kramář was balanced. Peroutka admired Kramář's wartime heroism, citing it as the reason for Kramář's largely symbolic position at the head of the National Committee: "In that Austria condemned this man to death, it was to be shown that such a judgment in the eyes of the nation was an honor and a qualification [for leadership]."[89] Yet Peroutka did not shy away from detailing Kramář's postwar mistakes. He listed Kramář's vain hope, even after the war ended, that a member of the Russian royal family might yet sit on the Bohemian throne, as well as his (to Peroutka, groundless) allegation that the Castle had rudely ejected him from Czech politics.[90] Švehla, Stříbrný, and Rašín had eclipsed Kramář thanks to his decision to attend the Paris Peace Conference; the Castle had nothing to do with it.[91] In traveling to Paris, thus ignoring domestic affairs and trying to play the statesman, Kramář demonstrated that "he lacked the correct temperament to be prime minister," Peroutka argued. He also painstakingly recorded Kramář's fury over his ouster from power, and his impolitic comments to Allied diplomats at the peace talks about the "Bolshevistic and Germanophile tendencies" of the incoming Czechoslovak government.[92]

Although Peroutka allowed other Czech politicians their moment in the sun, Castle myth is certainly present in his pages, and Masaryk and Beneš were the most creative and powerful protagonists of his story. Peroutka situated Masaryk against a backdrop of great Czechs, comparing him to Komenský, Palacký, and Havlíček, as in this passage, purporting to show Masaryk's thoughts in 1914: "Palacký . . . did not believe in the possibility of independence . . . : is Palacký right, or am I? . . . Independence . . . is possible to maintain if the nation, as Havlíček demanded, is morally educated and always resolved to defend its freedom, if it obtains the world's sympathy and if, finally, democracy is strengthened in Europe."[93] The bold Masaryk of the *Conversations* appeared here as well:

> The former theoretician became capable of the kind of practical work, particularly diplomatic, no Czech had ever undertaken, and which remained the most prized source of international experience for the new state. He who had spoken of nothing so frequently as of humanity and love for one's neighbor became the leader of revolutionaries not just with his heart and head, but with rifles and grenades. When imprisoned Legionnaires were executed, he spoke in hard tones: "We will have the opportunity and the power to revenge ourselves on those who fall into our hands, and I hope that many such Germans and Hungarians will. An eye for an eye, a tooth for a tooth."[94]

Peroutka quickly put paid to the dispute between the domestic resistance and the resistance abroad. His depiction of October 28, 1918, is telling. Švehla, Rašín, Soukup, and Stříbrný of the National Committee went to see the Austrian governor, who had gone to Vienna; they met his deputy instead and asked whether he had instructions to hand over power. When he revealed that he had none, they encouraged him to telegraph Vienna and ask for permission for the committee to take over Bohemia's administration. Peroutka commented acidly, "When one stands on the barricades, one does not ask the opponent on the other side what his instructions are."[95] Masaryk's leadership was necessary after the war as well, Peroutka explained. "The people's vision picked out Masaryk as the strongest, most sensitive and wisest man [in the chaotic situation of 1919]." But Peroutka's Masaryk refused to serve as absolute ruler, preferring to be his country's wise father. "The people who offered Masaryk dictator[ial powers] did not understand that they offered him that which he could never accept if he wished to remain who he was.... He believed that the people must teach themselves how to govern.... [H]e did not conceal from himself that not much was agreeable in the portrait of the era's democracy; but he was convinced that these were the illnesses of infancy, through which it was best to move without stopping."[96]

Peroutka's Beneš was also a hero awaiting his time. "If the war had not come,... the larger part of his actual abilities would have remained undeveloped. This man, occupying himself with papers without noticeable success, was *au fond* a man of action.... All these characteristics... almost exploded the moment he secretly crossed the Austrian border."[97] Peroutka defended Beneš's foreign policy, rebutting the common critique that Beneš was overly pedantic and intellectualized, and asserting instead that his policy stemmed from experience in and knowledge of the West.[98] In fact, Beneš's clinical politics were the reason he had prevailed in Paris. "Kramář's activity was more emotional, Beneš's more rational.... Kramář was prouder (of his nation and of himself), Beneš more modest. Kramář's impression was that of a pathos-laden nationalist, Beneš's of a cold calculator."[99]

Peroutka's portrayal of Czech politics focused on, and criticized, the parties and Parliament. Peroutka claimed that Parliament's fundamental passivity and inaction in the realm of foreign affairs "forced Dr. Beneš to take all the weight of decision-making on himself" and noted that as early as 1920, parliamentary leaders were already beginning to oppose Beneš and Masaryk—mainly, Peroutka implied, out of jealousy.[100] A chapter in the second volume, "Nervous Nation," contains letters and commentary from many Castle figures about the shockingly low level of Czechoslovak parliamentary life and its effect on the country as a whole. Vojta Beneš, brother of Edvard Beneš and leader of American Czech exile groups during the war, is quoted despairingly about his observations during a visit home: "A general thoughtlessness and decrepitude, terrible striving after sinecures,... not just a mere distaste for work but something far worse, an incapacity for constructive, creative work, a genuine moral [*characterový*] decline.... [P]olitical partisanship at home has changed into political loathing [*nenávist*]. . . . It will be a national calamity."[101]

Peroutka tended alternately to obscure or praise the Castle's extensive participation in the daily affairs of Czech politics. In 1919, for example, given the weakness of Kramář's successor Vlastimil Tusar, Peroutka wrote that "Masaryk's direct leadership . . . was welcomed by all," although Švehla and some of the other party leaders frowned on his tendency to write each of the ministers long letters, and requested especially that the president present himself to the public as infrequently as possible.[102] Castle involvement was necessary not just for good governance but for the state's very foundation. In Peroutka's telling, Masaryk's former colleague and Castle adherent Jan Herben suggested, on the floor of Parliament, the precise phrasing for the Czechoslovak constitution's preamble, ending with the words "we wish to take up our membership in the society of nations as . . . civilized, peace-loving, democratic, and progressive." Herben's suggestion brought the chamber to enthusiastic agreement, Peroutka recounted, with members rushing to shake Herben's hand.[103]

Peroutka's assessment of democracy, the partisan organization of Czechoslovak politics, and the general Czech failure to consult the country's minorities reflected basic Castle policy. Peroutka justified the creation of the Pětka, as well as the Czech political parties' ironclad discipline over their members, by noting the "tendencies toward anarchism" of a "Slavic nation," and the need for "strong authority at a crucial moment . . . [of] almost unappreciable [importance] for a young nation without tradition and without experience with independence." Whether or not the Czech system was "politically aesthetic," Czechoslovakia was the only Central and East European democracy to withstand the great crisis of the 1930s. Overall, Peroutka concluded, the party system did Czechoslovakia more good than harm.[104] Although he dismissed the Czechoslovak rhetoric of the domestic leaders' National Committee—"Czechoslovak it was not. Not a single Slovak occupied a position on it."—Peroutka noted that the "terror of the Hungarian government" in Slovakia would have made it almost impossible for Slovaks to have participated.[105] In Peroutka's portrait, the Castle rarely erred; when it did, some parliamentary shortcoming or manipulation was usually to blame. In discussing Czechoslovakia's early rapprochement with Austria, for example, Peroutka noted that the Castle leaders—especially Beneš—were slow to realize that the Czech man on the street, goaded by nationalist politicians such as Kramář, opposed Czechoslovakia's granting of economic aid to a starving Austria under pressure from the Allies. Beneš's rationale, however, was entirely praiseworthy. "[Beneš] relied on the tenacity which has always characterized him," Peroutka wrote. "Active engagement in the ordering of Central European relations—this was Masaryk's and Beneš's program."[106]

Historians of the republic's early years have relied on Peroutka's work, and for good reason. Its characterizations are pointed and memorable. Even when less than accurate, Peroutka was rarely boring. But despite its relative balance and subtlety, *Building the State* has defending the Castle as its clear goal. For a journalist as innately oppositional as Peroutka, who so frequently opposed the Castle himself, it is clear that the growing external threats of the late 1930s influenced his assessment of the early 1920s. *Building the State* is equally interesting for what it reveals about Peroutka's intellectual and ideological shifts away from his earlier stances. The man who criticized Masaryk for excessive romanticism and for his insistence on Beneš as his successor, who in the early 1920s tried to defend liberal parliamentarism as Czech society's golden mean, who hurled invective at the Pětka for not allowing a truly democratic loyal opposition, had now concluded that democracy was a relative luxury and that the nation needed strong leadership and only a semblance of democratic form. Soon his country was devoid even of sham democracy, and of Peroutka. Unlike Čapek, Peroutka was not offered the opportunity to escape the country with the Castle leadership. He spent the war in Nazi concentration camps.

A Second Exile: The Myth Abroad, Again

In September 1938, after a spring and summer full of threats, Adolf Hitler insisted that the Czechs grant Germany the Sudetenland. As the Czech emissaries waited despairingly in an anteroom, Hitler, Mussolini, Édouard Daladier, and Neville Chamberlain decided together to carve up Czechoslovakia. If the Czechs refused the terms and decided to fight, the Great Powers agreed, they would fight alone. After anguished consultation with parliamentary leaders, Beneš concluded that attempts at defense would be tantamount to national suicide, and reluctantly acceded to the Nazi demands while crowds outside the Castle begged the president to fight for Czechoslovak independence. The Munich *Diktat* granted the Nazis roughly one-third of Czechoslovakia's population and territory. Six months later, in March 1939, the Nazis invaded the rest of the country and placed Bohemia and Moravia under direct occupation. Slovakia seceded and became an autonomous state and Axis ally. Hungary received Ruthenia. Czechoslovakia no longer existed.

Although Zamini had reckoned on war, Hitler's skillful intimidation of the French and British took the country by surprise, including Karel Čapek. Čapek poured into his writing his heartbroken shock at the West's betrayal: the *Lidové noviny* editorial he wrote after Munich, and also read on the radio, described Czechoslovakia in torture, as a "man caught between cogwheels; aware in that first and most dreadful moment of pain that he still lives."[107]

Privately, Čapek wrote Beneš, urging him to flee immediately and devote his energies to rescuing the state through work in exile, just as he had created it twenty years earlier.

> Our dear Dr. Beneš: the first thing I could do after a sleepless night was to write you at least a few words. Not you, but all of us have lost our faith; not just you, but all of us move away and depart from that which we were. What I feel now is a vehement and directly painful sense of solidarity with you and with all whose moral world was vanquished. I believe that we were morally right; I believe that we will be right, despite all that is happening in the world. I am sure that ahead of you lies another work of liberation, and I will live with my eyes fixed on your future deeds. . . . [B]e calm and strong. . . . Save your strength: you will yet have need of it.[108]

This October 1938 letter became the center of the last scandal to erupt around Čapek while he still lived. Another letter, supposedly Beneš's response to Čapek, began to be circulated around Prague in November 1938, as the Agrarians and fascist collaborators dismantled the First Republic and created an authoritarian Second Republic in its stead. Praguers wrote out copies and distributed them to friends. On November 21, Jiří Stříbrný's tabloids and the Agrarian paper *Pražský vecer* published excerpts from the letter, trying to paint Beneš as an extreme leftist. Modern historians agree that the Beneš letter was a fake, part of a campaign to discredit Beneš and liberal democracy in general, echoing Hitler's rhetoric by labeling Beneš a Bolshevik. It was part of the Second Republic's attempt to demean the First, and its leadership.[109]

Beneš's continued presence in the Czech lands was unacceptable both to the Nazis and to the rightist leaders of the Second Republic. Beneš had abdicated the presidency after Munich and retired to his country home at Sezimovo Ustí, exhausted. But by the end of October 1938, he fled Czechoslovakia for the second time. He would spend the majority of the war in London, surrounded by the young Castle academics and intellectuals who had worked with him at Zamini and during his short presidency, as well as friendly politicians: Edvard Taborský, Hubert Ripka, Social Democrat Jaromír Nečas, Agrarian Ladislav Feierabend, National Socialist Jaroslav Stránský, Czech Populist leader Jan Šrámek, Social Democrat Rudolf Bechyně, and Agrarian Milan Hodža.

Before Beneš's time in London, the University of Chicago's sociology department offered him the Walgreen Visiting Professorship, to spend February through July of 1939 lecturing on "the development of democracy and its problems . . . up to the present day."[110] Asked by the State Department to avoid public appearances, he obliged until mid-March. But when Hitler's annexation of the remnant of Czechoslovakia he had pledged to protect caused international outrage, Beneš responded with his first public wartime address, in which the interwar Castle myth appeared in a new guise. The Czechs were still egalitarian, progressive, hardworking, tolerant, and cosmopolitan; Czechoslovakia still represented freedom and democracy. But now Czechoslovakia symbolized the West's blindness. The Czechs were noble martyrs, suffering for all of Europe.

> [Our] land was, simply, violently attacked.... For ten centuries—from the time of the princely saint Wenceslas—this little nation was forced to struggle for its national existence and its freedom.... In the sixteenth century we were enslaved [*ujařmeni*] by the Habsburgs... for three centuries we lived under the yokes of the Germans and Hungarians.... [D]uring the last twenty years Czechoslovaks... built their own state; they created an enviably balanced, even social structure, progressive system of law, mature national economy.... [W]ithin the state [its people] lived in genuine political freedom and religious tolerance. Although it had minorities—a problem with which all of Europe has had difficulties... Czechoslovakia was known as a refuge for citizens of free nations and as the League of Nations' most enthusiastic supporter. There was no religious or sectarian persecution; Jews were not persecuted; nor was there racial persecution of any kind. It was truly one of the most enlightened, developed and progressive democracies east of the Rhine. It was the republic of that great humanist, T. G. Masaryk.... The conquest of Czechoslovakia must be the destruction of the very idea of freedom in Central Europe.... The entire world was willing to sacrifice Czechoslovakia.[111]

Beneš reiterated this new Czech national narrative as he crisscrossed the country, speaking at other universities throughout the East and Midwest.[112]

When Beneš returned to Europe, he found organizing an exile government to be far more difficult the second time around. For one thing, British Prime Minister Neville Chamberlain and French Prime Minister Édouard Daladier, the architects of Munich, remained in power as the war began. Czechoslovakia did not gain de jure ally status until July 1941.[113] Another problem was the large number of potential cooks to stir the émigré soup, in stark contrast to the First World War. Challenges to Beneš's authority came from Štefan Osuský, Czechoslovak ambassador in Paris, and Milan Hodža, Czechoslovak foreign minister 1935–1936 and prime minister

1936–1938, in London; both made deliberate efforts to undermine Beneš's position and that of the London-based Czechoslovak National Committee he had created.[114] Hodža formed his own separate Slovak and later Czecho-Slovak National Councils, which competed with Beneš's organization and rebuffed Beneš's efforts at fence mending.[115] Jaroslav Stránský thought that Beneš's plans for expelling Czechoslovakia's Germans were "cruel," and openly criticized many of his other initiatives as well.[116] Disputes emerged between Rudolf Bechyně, recalled by Beneš's chancellor Jaromír Smutný as "witty, nervous, now seriously ill," and Jan Šramek, "skilled, patient, with a Jesuitical memory."[117] Other members of the Czechoslovak effort abroad accused one another of furthering their own careers and desires at the expense of Beneš's policies. These "petty, myopic quarrels and . . . odd political allegiances" within a "confined, hot-house" ambiance were termed *emigrantština* by the émigrés themselves, who frequently admonished one another to avoid them.[118]

Some of these differences stemmed from competing beliefs about the future of Czechoslovakia and Central Europe. Hodža and Beneš disagreed about Slovakia's place in a postwar Czechoslovak state, and on foreign policy. Before Munich, Hodža had tried unsuccessfully to bring the Little Entente states, Austria, and Hungary into a customs union; he had long believed in a Central European union and a unified Europe, as opposed to Beneš's reliance on Great Power states and the League of Nations.[119] Beneš initially seemed amenable to a variant of this approach, and worked with the émigré Polish government headed by Władysław Sikorski toward a Czech-Polish federation. Beneš wrote that such a bloc would represent a first step toward a larger goal of a European union, itself part of a larger international world organization.[120] But in practice Beneš was far more concerned with Czechoslovakia finding a Great Power patron, whereas Hodža insisted that an effective, democratic Central European federation would be the small states' only means of countering the Great Powers.[121] In the end, Beneš's 1943 agreement with the Soviets rendered efforts at regional organization meaningless.

Another fundamental change was Beneš himself, at the helm of the government in exile. Beneš had never aroused the kind of personal devotion or leader cult Masaryk had, no matter how diligently some Castle colleagues had tried to create one. After Beneš's 1935 election to the presidency, Jan Hájek asked Karel Čapek to edit a book to celebrate the occasion: *Beneš in Photographs*, akin to Čapek's 1931 *Masaryk in Photographs*. Čapek "politely declined" to perform the same service for Beneš as he had for Masaryk.[122] Beneš was not as photogenic as his predecessor: shorter, with a rounder, clean-shaven face and more prominent ears, Beneš lacked Masaryk's eccentric nineteenth-century grandeur. He was more at home behind a desk or in a diplomat's frock coat and tie than on horseback leading a parade. But Beneš's limitations were often perceived as more than visual, as evidenced by the wartime recollections of Jaromír Smutný, head of Beneš's presidential chancellery.

> We lack a spiritually great [leader.] Beneš is an outstanding tactician and strategist, the greatest Machiavelli of our day, but he is not able to captivate the masses, to inspire them with pleasure in their work, conscious unity.... [H]e does not inspire trust. Instinctively people who approach him sense that there is something left unsaid, that Beneš will make use of them for a plan of his.... [H]e stands above us thanks to his great intelligence, his doggedness, his appetite for hard work.... [H]e is a machine for thought and work, without human feeling, but with human failings.[123]

For these reasons, Hubert Ripka's propaganda operation was crucial for Beneš in maintaining his power during wartime. Ripka, a former *Lidové noviny* and *Přítomnost* writer, organized "official publications, radio broadcasts over the BBC, public lectures," and other events intended to position Beneš as Czechoslovakia's voice abroad. Bruce Berglund has identified Ripka as "the chief ideologue of the exile movement... one of the most important figures... after the president."[124]

The legacy of the First Republic proved complex during Beneš's years abroad. The First Republic was the source of his own legitimacy; Beneš and Ripka drew on it and memories of the Castle to rally Czechs and Slovaks behind the government in exile. In Beneš's memoirs and radio addresses, in the pages of official journals like the *Central European Observer* and *Čechoslovák*, even in the Communist journal *Nové Československo*, and private letters, Czechoslovakia would always be "the republic of Masaryk."[125] Still, Beneš had no desire to re-create what he viewed as the First Republic's structural flaws. Like many other wartime observers of the First Republic, Beneš publicly blamed its failures almost entirely on Parliament rather than on the Castle. During conversations with Smutný, Beneš criticized Masaryk for allowing the Agrarian Party so much power, which he linked to the growth of the Henleinists. "Masaryk allowed [the Agrarians] full freedom not just with the executive but also politically... that is why they wanted Masaryk to remain president until his death, at any cost.... [T]hey knew I would not allow them to do that."[126] Beneš's colleagues in the government in exile tended to agree. In June 1942, Jaroslav Stránský spoke to a joint meeting of the Czechoslovak P.E.N. Club and the Syndicate of Czechoslovak Journalists in Exile, in which he excoriated the

First Republic partisan press, particularly its behavior in 1938. Stránský, and the many audience members concurring with him, blamed the party leaders who controlled their newspapers' content. Some of the Social Democrats present, such as publisher Josef Bělina and State Minister Jaromír Nečas, blamed the citizenry for failing to demand unbiased information. Either way, the Castle (and the press) escaped reproach.[127]

Beneš's intellectual postulates and organizational work during the Second World War demonstrate many similarities to his efforts abroad during the First. He retained, at least to some degree, his faith in the West, despite Munich: "I...did not consider the security guarantee which the Western Powers gave to Czechoslovakia during the Munich crisis to be wholly worthless."[128] As before, Beneš concentrated on providing the Allies with a Czechoslovak fighting force, in this case the Czech unit within the British Royal Air Force and an infantry division, initially part of the French army, that escaped to Great Britain after the French capitulation to the Nazis.[129] Masaryk believed that the Great War had helped move the world from theocracy toward democracy; Beneš wrote about the Second World War as part of that same larger historical development, helping to bring about a truer, "economic" democracy.[130] Beneš's earlier moral claims on the West continued, now premised on Czechoslovak sacrifice: "[T]wenty years of liberty and all that had happened since September 19, 1938, entitled us to this, while on the British Empire and all others it imposed an enduring, weighty moral and legal duty until our liberation was complete."[131] And once again, as opposed to the other European peoples organizing in Great Britain to help liberate their states, the Czechoslovaks would be the voice of reason and democracy: "[We will] give to the whole movement, order, respect, coherence, and most important of all, a *democratic character and spirit*.... [We will] demonstrate our political experience and maturity."[132]

That very political experience, however, meant that Beneš's plans for postwar Czechoslovakia also involved some fundamental differences from the interwar era. First among them was a changed approach to minority issues. At least rhetorically, Beneš was friendlier to the idea of greater Slovak autonomy; more Slovaks were on his National Council (five out of thirteen positions) than any prewar government had ever included. In private conversations, Beneš criticized Masaryk for ignoring the Slovaks. "He said, they're a nasty lot, corrupt. I always had the opposite opinion, but he put me off, it was at Topoľčianky, waving his hand: 'you don't know them.'...We left the Slovaks to arrange their own affairs among themselves, and they never managed it. Masaryk never had any interest in Slovak affairs. The fact is, we erred in Slovakia....Slovakia became the property of twenty families" and never emerged from Hungarian influence, Beneš concluded.[133] To a certain extent, Beneš's wartime pro-Slovak position also constituted a defense against criticism by Štefan Osuský, who struggled with Beneš over leadership of the effort abroad and attacked him for failing to acknowledge publicly that "the brotherly coexistence of Czechs and Slovaks . . . demands [that Czechs] respect the Slovak language, Slovak schooling, Slovak culture, and Slovak administration in Slovakia."[134] After the war, two Slovak parties (along with two Czech parties and the Czechoslovak Communists) were included in the National Front.

But Beneš portrayed the Czechoslovak Germans with unalloyed hostility. "[M]ore than 80 per cent of our Germans . . . had gone over to Hitlerism and . . . during the war, were always ready to do anything they could to help destroy our Czech people."[135] The new Castle myth emphasized German aggression, a threat not just to the Czechs but to Europe itself: "The German 'Drang nach Osten' must always be a 'Drang nach Westen' too. Unfortunately this fundamental element of German policy was . . . not understood."[136] Reconciliation was impossible: instead, Beneš continued to promote population "transfer." In 1938, in a last-ditch response to Henlein, Beneš had suggested that one-third of Czechoslovakia's Germans and the border regions they inhabited could become part of Germany; one-third, specifically democrats, socialists, and Jews, could remain in Czechoslovakia; and the other third would be "resettled." But by mid-1942 Beneš had decided that Czechoslovakia's Germans would have to leave the country entirely.[137] This policy, he wrote, would be for the good of all of Europe, indeed all of humanity: "Though this would mean a grave . . . crisis for the persons actually involved, it would nevertheless provide a *better and more humane solution than fresh inhuman massacres in the postwar period . . . and brutal vengeance causing the continuation of nationality struggles for centuries* thus frustrating . . . the social and economic progress of mankind."[138] Despite Beneš's rhetoric, massacres and vengeance indeed occurred after the war, in part encouraged by his policy.

The war also changed Czechoslovakia's geopolitical alliances. Beneš continued working with the British, and to a lesser extent the French. His war memoirs emphasized his contacts with de Gaulle, stating, "It was in the interests of Czechoslovakia—and of Europe—that a new and strong France should be reconstructed again as soon as possible. . . . I still believe firmly in its new and great future." But the Soviets and Americans figured far more prominently in his calculations. Beneš blamed the war on the West's fear of the Bolsheviks; future world wars would be averted only by greater mutual understanding. Beneš was in near-constant contact with Ivan Maisky, the Soviet ambassador in London, and believed wholeheartedly that the promises he had received from Stalin in his December 1943 visit were genuine. "The growth of a new Soviet Empire . . . in the spirit of a new popular democracy, is undeniably and definitely on the march," Beneš predicted. "A new Soviet Union will . . . stand at the head of the Slavs and will exact . . . an entirely new position in the world." After this visit, in which Beneš signed a treaty of friendship with the Soviet Union, he began touting his idea that the postwar era would see greater convergence between the Soviets and the West, with Czechoslovakia serving as a bridge. He also appealed to the Americans, calling Czechoslovakia "the god-child of the great and glorious Republic of the United States."[139]

Finally, Beneš's earlier distrust of parliamentary democracy had deepened into an almost total rejection. His 1939 treatise *Demokracie dnes a zitra* (*Democracy Today and Tomorrow*) focused primarily on democratic leaders' personality and governing style, hardly mentioning popular participation in government or the development of efficient, fair institutions. Rather than blaming legal structures, Beneš blamed individuals—leaders and citizens—for democratic or civic failures.[140] Therefore, postwar rebuilding efforts also necessitated creating a new citizen. This ideal *Homo democraticus* would avoid prewar mistakes, such as "insufficient civic courage; unacceptable utilitarian opportunism when it came to applying democratic principles and constant attempts at impossible agreements with fascist enemies; selfishness, at the level of class, party, and person . . . ; inadequate and false knowledge of concrete international problems."[141] Czechoslovaks and Europeans alike had refused to educate themselves and had failed morally as well. It would be the postwar state's obligation to re-create the citizenry, rather than the electorate's duty to craft a postwar state.

All these ideas appeared in Beneš's last radio address from London before returning to Prague via Slovakia. His vision was stark and simplistic. Czechs during wartime had been victims at the Germans' hands: Beneš listed Nazi crimes committed on Czech soil, from torture of individuals to destruction of entire villages, and then reminded his listeners, "Hitler did all of this to us, and also our Germans [did it]." The Soviets figured as the Czechs', and Europe's, saviors. "For the Red Army stands practically before the gates of Berlin and with it comes . . . real and unavoidable justice and retribution, awaited by us for six years." The Soviets would prove trustworthy allies and allow Czechoslovakia independence, Beneš reassured his audience: "We value highly [our treaty of alliance with the Soviet Union] and we will always comply with it in letter and spirit, just like the Soviet Union itself. The Soviet Union wants only for us to be its dear friend and faithful, but independent, strong, firm, and prosperous ally. And we ourselves wish the same."[142]

The new Czechoslovakia would differ considerably from its predecessor. "I know that our people at home do not wish to return to prewar partisan relations; and I am convinced that after the war partisan life in

Czechoslovakia will take, must take, new forms and undergo fundamental changes, both in the formation of the parties themselves and in individuals." Postwar local politics would be based on Soviet-style "national councils," to be organized in each city and region as they were liberated. The postwar government would consist of a national front, representing workers, farmers, the middle class, and the intelligentsia; the Slovaks would have a prominent role. Beneš opened the door to critical discussion of the First Republic: "we must . . . learn from the mistakes and inadequacies of the past." And, as at the close of the Great War, the new state called for revolutionary change. "Our new house must be politically and socially rebuilt with new content, new people, and in many cases new institutions." The new state would not be Masaryk's republic: it would be "popular-democratic [*lidově demokratický*] . . . a new, fresh democracy."[143]

Life Under the Swastika

Beneš's listeners at home had undergone their own wartime metamorphosis. For a brief moment at the beginning of the war, Nazi rule seemed as though it might mean Habsburg-style incomplete repression. True, thousands of intellectuals, priests, leftists, and other leaders had been arrested and sent to concentration camps as early as 1939; the chief of the SS in Prague told a gathering in Old Town Square, "Whoever is not with us, is against us. And whoever is against us, will be pulverized."[144] But some resistance to the Nazis was initially possible. Clubs in the Protectorate served as gathering centers for Czech (i.e., non-Nazi) public life, such as the Czech Aviation Club, the National Auto Club, and the Sokol movement. Czech Catholicism also took on a patriotic role. The Czech Communists survived underground, remaining in contact with Communists abroad and even printing a few clandestine copies of *Rudé pravo*. The *Politické ústředí*, or Political Center, a group comprised of members of the prewar parties in contact with Beneš, were able to publish twenty-seven issues of *V boj!* (*Into Battle!*) in 1939.[145]

Even *Přítomnost* was allowed to continue publishing. In the early days of the Second Republic, Ferdinand Peroutka joined in the chorus blaming the sins of the First Republic on its Parliament. On November 9, 1938, Peroutka wrote dryly that after fifteen years of criticizing the parties in *Přítomnost*, he now found that the very politicians who had founded the parties were joining him. In fact, they were scathingly castigating not just the parties, their failings, and their corruption, but the First Republic in toto and anyone who had lived through it. "All was in error; and therefore there was nothing honorable in [all of] your past," Peroutka mockingly echoed the party leaders. "[S]piritually you lived in vain. . . . [Y]ou have squandered the best years of your life." This was obviously foolish. Some of the party system would remain: if the Czech nation wanted to retain democracy, the country would need more than one party, and "the wholehearted decision of this country [to have] a democratic system is too clear." The First Republic had not been composed totally of errors, of course: but, Peroutka concluded, the country now needed an authoritative (*autoritativní*, not *autoritářský*, or authoritarian) government that could decide and act quickly. "Our previous democracy was a system for an era of calm and prosperity, . . . when mistakes . . . did not have fateful consequences."[146] A week later, in "A Hard Word," Peroutka portrayed the interwar party system as an utter mess, about which neither Masaryk nor Beneš could do much. Rule by a single strong party was now "an internal necessity." Peroutka praised the proposed two-party system, even though the smaller party would exercise no real power: "its role will be honorable; it will be a sign that we have not lowered our democratic flag."[147]

Peroutka continued to discuss the Castle, aligning it with democratic values and the best in the Czech national spirit while reinterpreting the Castle ideology and legacy for wartime circumstances. "What would Masaryk do now?" Peroutka wondered on Masaryk's birthday in 1939. He would, Peroutka hypothesized, remain true to his political philosophy of realism, and insist on clearsightedly analyzing the nature of European power relations as a basis for action. He would remain an activist, involved in public life, and would remain a fundamentally oppositional politician. And, probably, he would return to his Habsburg ideology of small-scale daily work (*drobná práce*) as appropriate for a nation under the thrall of a stronger one. The word *democracy* does not appear in this article.[148]

But a Nazi crackdown in November 1939, in response to a student demonstration, quelled further efforts at popular resistance at home. As Sudeten German leader and Protectorate administrator Karl Hermann Frank explained to a crowd in České Budějovice, the Nazis were not the Austrians; the old approaches of passive resistance and subtle displays of Czech national allegiance would not be tolerated.[149] Most Czechs put their heads down and endured. Yet the Nazi leaders remained deeply concerned about continuing loyalty to prewar Czech values and leaders, particularly the Czechoslovak government in exile. The Nazi Gestapo chief in the Czech lands was reported to have told General Ježek, minister of the interior in the Hácha collaborationist government, "I know, the Czechs are quiet now, but only because Beneš tells them [to behave that way] from abroad."[150] Historian and former resistance leader Radomír Luža wrote, "[Beneš's] popularity in the country . . . soon reached an all-time high," and noted the president's prestige was "immense" in 1943; the resistance in April 1945 without exception "backed the authority of President Beneš."[151]

The domestic resistance agreed with the government in exile about the structure of a postwar Czechoslovak state. The largest Czech resistance group, the ÚVOD (Ústřední výbor odboje domácího, or Central Committee of the Domestic Resistance; it was later known as the Rada tři, or Council of Three) was "convinced that the prewar party structure had failed badly," and called for a democratic socialist state structure as well as true "economic democracy." This group also demanded that the country's Sudeten Germans be removed, like Beneš rejecting the Castle's earlier nominal Czechoslovakism.[152] By 1941, almost all domestic resistance groups agreed on this agenda.[153] The Czechoslovak Communist Party, after various shifts, also supported an independent Czechoslovak state, and over the course of the war supported the trend toward anti-German chauvinism.[154] Only Vlajka, a hard-Right Czech nationalist group collaborating with the Nazis, continued to promote its own version of the Czech national future.[155]

After 1942, wartime exigencies rendered meaningless prewar arguments over the Castle and the content of Czech nationalism. Nazi persecution of any potential social leaders, from intellectuals and academics to businessmen and politicians, effectively silenced most of Czech society. So did the annihilation of the villages of Lidice and Ležáky in retaliation for the government in exile's May 1942 assassination of Reinhard Heydrich, military governor of the Protectorate and one of the architects of the Holocaust. Beyond Nazi oppression, denunciations internally divided Czech society. Czechs in the Protectorate understood their daily existence as a battle against Nazi Germanization and oppression, to preserve Czech culture and the Czech soul.[156] That battle was mainly fought passively. Czech workers obediently produced roughly 10 percent of the Nazi Reich's industrial output in exchange for handsome salaries, and a skeleton crew of 2,000 Nazis oversaw an efficient Protectorate bureaucracy of 350,000. By 1945, only thirty partisan groups—most of these tiny and internally fragmented—were operating in the Czech lands. In short, resistance was very limited. Czech Communist partisans worried that this would stain the national honor.[157] The same issue vexed Edvard Beneš, for first the British and later the Soviets wanted evidence that the Czechs were fighting with them against the Nazis—hence Beneš's 1942 decision to assassinate Heydrich, despite the pleas from resistance groups to target a Czech collaborator instead. The government in exile's radio broadcasts throughout the war called for acts of material sabotage, to no avail.[158] Meanwhile, Karl Hermann Frank met every call for resistance with arrests and murders, publicly announced, and Czech informers from home demanded of Beneš that his broadcasts contain only facts, not incitements.[159]

The First Republic and the Third

In autumn 1944, the war in Europe was drawing to a weary, bloody close. The Allies were pushing east from the Atlantic coast, the Soviets moving steadily westward. By February 1945 Allied and Red Army troops were in Paris and Budapest. In the Protectorate, the impending Nazi loss made itself felt: Czechs worked twelve to fourteen hours a day, six days a week, and clothes, food, and medicine were difficult to obtain. Chaos and public violence increased daily. Thousands of former concentration camp inmates and ethnic Germans fled into the Protectorate from the northeast. Forced laborers returned home. A retreating Wehrmacht division moving through Moravia brought with it "tens of thousands of prisoners of war, slave laborers, and East European SS divisions." The SS troops still in the Czech lands burned down entire villages, killing their populations.[160] The Slovak National Uprising shook Nazi control over the Protectorate as well, and gave courage to the splintered Czech resistance movement. Despite Nazi reprisals, the Czechs were ready in April 1945 when the Soviets entered Czech territory and liberation was imminent. The Prague uprising began on May 5; bitter street and house-to-house fighting killed roughly 3,700 Czechs, wounding some 3,000 more.[161] On May 11, the last military operation in Europe took place east of Prague, as the Red Army cut off the last German Army Group and took its 800,000 troops as prisoners of war. Meanwhile, Czech hostilities against Czechoslovak Germans, encouraged by Moscow, by Beneš, and indirectly by the western Allies, led to the "wild transfer"—months of violence against Germans and Czech collaborators, sometimes aided by Soviet soldiers. Estimates range from tens to hundreds of thousands of Germans killed, and from 600,000 to more than a million forcibly expelled from Czechoslovakia.[162] Beneš arrived in Prague on May 16, 1945, with the country well on its way to becoming, as he had stated during the war, a "Czechoslovak nation-state."

Negotiations through the spring of 1945 had laid the ground for the Košice program, the basis of postwar Czechoslovak politics and society, announced in the easternmost city of Slovakia on April 4, 1945. The program called for thorough political reorganization. It limited the number of parties to four, and banned from public life those parties that had collaborated with the Nazis, including the Agrarians, the largest party in Bohemia and Moravia for a half-century. Banks and insurance companies, energy utilities, and major industries were to be nationalized. The new government parties pledged to control wages and prices on basic goods. Local government was decentralized into committees and granted wide-ranging power. On April 5, 1945, in Košice, in a public address, Beneš drew a direct, if dubious, connection between the interwar Castle's political vision and his postwar plans for change: "To this program—as I already promised in Prague Castle on the day of Masaryk's funeral—I myself remained faithful under all circumstances, and faithful I shall remain."[163]

But the most powerful organization in postwar Czechoslovakia had no intention of remaining faithful to the First Republic or Masarykian ideals. The Czechoslovak Communist Party (KSČ) had been substantially strengthened by the Soviet Union's alliance with Czechoslovakia in 1943 and the Red Army's liberation of East-Central Europe. The KSČ had failed to organize a successful wartime resistance, but it had made the strongest attempt and paid in blood for its efforts. Unlike Beneš, the Communists bore no responsibility for Munich or the other errors of the First Republic. Unsullied by the past, the KSČ was widely viewed as the country's future and attracted members in droves: "the Communist Party of the early postwar years was, and remains, the largest party in Czech history."[164] Beneš, while very popular, was seriously ill when he returned from London. The advantage of strength and dynamism seemed to lie with the Communists, who won 38 percent of the vote in the elections of 1946.[165] In the first postwar cabinet, the KSČ controlled the ministries of agriculture, interior, and information, and both the ministers of education and defense openly sympathized with the Communists. Although historians have argued persuasively that the inevitable rise of the KSČ has been exaggerated, nonetheless the momentum was on its side.

The war had transformed Czech society; the immediate postwar years saw still more radical changes. Fully 25 percent of postwar Czechoslovakia's population was between the ages of fifteen and thirty years old. The Jews and Germans who had once peopled Czechoslovakia's middle class were gone, the former virtually annihilated by the Nazis, the latter forced out by the Czechs. The middle and upper classes remaining in the country were hard hit by postwar anti-inflationary measures that withdrew 85 percent of circulating currency and froze bank accounts, government bonds, and life insurance policies. A 1947 property tax further reduced their standing. Workers, already privileged under Nazism, continued their relative rise; women now joined their ranks.[166] Continued expulsion of Czechoslovakia's German population, as well as postwar trials of Nazis and collaborators, meant that the war's radicalized, reduced notions of identity (Czech or German, guilty or innocent, progressive or reactionary) continued to dominate postwar discourse. The allure of the Soviet Union, and bitterness toward the West for Munich and the war, were unmistakeable.[167]

Thoroughgoing critiques of the First Republic continued, with increased ferocity, in the immediate postwar era; but they now came largely from the Left. In 1938 critics had argued that the First Republic's proliferation of political parties made it unable to act decisively in an authoritarian era. Now, most writers argued that the First Republic's promise had been destroyed by the Czech and German financiers who in fact controlled it, as well as by a problematic Parliament. Daily political life in the First Republic had never realized Masaryk's ideal of de-Austrianization, now redefined as "broad segments of the people ... [participating] in the administration, the economy, and the creation of national history." Instead, democracy had turned to de facto oligarchy. The republic had defended the right of capitalists to exploit workers; "bankers, large-scale capitalists and agrarian magnates" had then sold the country at Munich. Even Castle intellectuals who had survived the war joined in castigating the First Republic for its deficiencies. So loud was the outcry against the past that some writers wondered whether there was a public conspiracy to silence or shame any voices defending the First Republic.[168]

Nevertheless, many postwar Czech writers also lauded the First Republic as a bygone era, a "lost paradise." In this discursive vein, all that was positive about the First Republic was personally identified with Tomáš Masaryk. Even as Karel Hrbas acknowledged that the First Republic was fundamentally flawed, he also noted that "Masarykian democracy was the faith of our lives." Similarly, philosopher J. B. Kozák noted that the First Republic reflected Masaryk's greatness "only sometimes and partially."[169] Every political faction tried to claim Masaryk, however close or distant his ideas might have actually been to their own. Even the Communists tried to bring him into their national pantheon, despite his outspoken opposition to revolutionary socialism and his antipathy to the Bolsheviks, the Soviet Union, and the Czechoslovak Communist Party. Communist Minister of Education and National Enlightenment Zdeněk Nejedlý had written an admiring four-volume biography of Masaryk in the First Republic's last years (1930–1937, published in full in 1938). In 1945, in the government magazine *Československo*, Nejedlý continued praising Masaryk, now from an openly Marxist perspective, arguing that Masaryk was an exemplar of dedication to the people.[170] Party ideologue Václav Kopecký wrote that it would be impossible to construct "the new Czechoslovakia without the foundation of Masaryk." Since Masaryk had himself frequently opposed the Pětka, Kopecký wrote, the bourgeois parties from the First Republic had no right to claim him: rather, Masaryk was socially and intellectually closest to the Communists. He had "heroically struggled for a better tomorrow ... he had a beautiful relationship with the workers."[171] Whether this was a ploy to widen the KSČ's appeal to nationalists or a genuine effort to render Masaryk's life meaningful to the postwar scenario, it succeeded at least partially in linking the KSČ's plans for socioeconomic renewal of Czechoslovak society to those of Masaryk.[172]

Castle intellectuals from the interwar era also sought to claim Masaryk's legacy. Some, in wartime exile, had tried to keep the Masaryk cult alive as part of the Czechoslovak propaganda effort.[173] They continued their efforts between 1945 and 1948. One example is the 1947 volume edited by Josef Hoffman and Oskar Odstrčil, titled *T.G.M. as We Saw Him*. This book represented an obvious attempt to adapt Castle tenets and the Masaryk cult to the postwar era: its essays and selections emphasized "Slavonic" politics, the importance of Slovak culture and values within Czechoslovakia, and Masaryk's dedication to true, "social" democracy rather than nineteenth-century-style oligarchic liberalism. The book's flyleaf holds a pen-and-ink drawing of Masaryk by Communist Adolf Hoffmeister. The next item in the book is a reprint of Masaryk's handwritten thoughts on the term *člověk*, or person. The short piece concludes, "the term 'člověk' [encompasses] various races, nations, and social classes = nationality + social-ness [*sociálnost*] all in one." The book's first long prose piece is a speech excerpt by Milan Štefánik, Masaryk's Slovak colleague abroad during the Great War; its first sentence reads, "I proclaim that Masaryk always was and is a good Slav."[174] Many of the recollections of Masaryk are by Slovaks, in Slovak. Many are by generals. Also, Masaryk as the hero of the prewar myth was now presented as more human, even flawed. In his contribution, painter Max Švabinský recalled asking the president about the worsening international situation in 1933. Masaryk insisted uncategorically that there would be no war: "Who would want a war? Only the Germans, and they are encircled and held in by all of Europe. Not even in twenty years will there be a war. And also, for war there needs to be money, and there isn't any." Švabinský concluded, "This time the great president was wrong."[175]

Among the Castle writers, Ferdinand Peroutka remained one of Czechoslovakia's most important voices in the postwar era. Peroutka had been arrested in the fall of 1939 and sent to Dachau and Buchenwald. He spent twenty-seven months in solitary confinement during his six years in concentration camps. Twice, the Nazis were said to have brought Peroutka back to Prague; they offered him freedom and a lavish lifestyle if he would agree to edit *Přítomnost* in collaboration with the Protectorate authorities. Twice Peroutka refused and was returned to the camps.[176] Following the war, he founded a new magazine, *Dnešek* (*Today*).

Like Beneš, Peroutka represented a connection to the First Republic and the Castle; like Beneš, the experiences of Munich, the Second Republic, and the war had caused Peroutka to reject many of his earlier ideas. Unlike Beneš, Peroutka's postwar work sought a First Republic past worth keeping, a past that might temper the excesses of the present. His skepticism toward power now turned toward the Czechoslovak Communist Party and the Soviet Union. He agreed, for instance, that Masaryk would in principle approve of the radical social and economic changes that accompanied the end of the war. But, Peroutka cautioned, Masaryk would warn the country about the "moral question": "the nation stands at a crossroads and must decide: humanity or something else . . . freedom or bondage? Our own national face or a borrowed mask?" That mask would be borrowed, of course, from the Soviet Union, potentially neglecting Masaryk's humanist legacy. "[M]uch of our fate depends on how much [Communism] is willing to accept from Masaryk's heritage and how much the rest [i.e., non-Communists] succeed in defending it."[177] The First and Third Republics shared many characteristics, Peroutka reminded his readers. For instance, the KSČ's power was not entirely unfamiliar: "compared with it, the Agrarian Party's hegemony during the First Republic was almost imperceptible."[178] This was a deeply provocative statement given Agrarian collaboration with the Nazis. Communist claims that life under the First Republic was more politicized than in the current day were simply untrue, wrote Peroutka bluntly in September 1946. In fact, the Third Republic was palpably more politicized, and public life had suffered as a consequence. "All the great national questions—aside from industrial and social questions—are neglected: population, health, alcoholism, morality in public life, the nature of the national character. In past eras the nation conducted a richer and more subtle dialogue with its fate."[179]

In fact, Peroutka argued, the country now faced a situation similar to the one Masaryk confronted when founding his Realist movement: only politics mattered, and it was politically dangerous to call attention to Czech missteps or errors (*domácí chyby*). A small, but active, movement akin to Masaryk's would be useful, and it ought to adopt at least two of the principles Masaryk cited when he founded the magazine *Čas*. Those were, first, to avoid putting forward a political program in the narrow partisan sense, the better to be able to combat frivolousness in Czech public life and to seek out the bad in the fundamental errors of Czech national conduct; second, to be a constant scourge of public lies.[180] Increasing Communist control over the media made this suggestion highly unrealistic and undeniably courageous, particularly his call to his readers to use Masaryk (even the prewar Masaryk) as a model for contemporary behavior, and his comparison of Communist political dominance to the oppressive rule of Austria-Hungary.

The ironies dominating Peroutka's life were coming full circle. During the interwar era, although the values animating *Přítomnost* seemed similar to the Castle's, his refusal to parrot the Castle's mythic line made him suspect. Throughout the First Republic, Peroutka had entered, left, and reentered Castle circles. *Building the State* was faithful to Castle spirit and ideology, though again not as obedient as the Castle might wish. Munich and the Second Republic had shaken Peroutka's faith in parliamentary democracy and liberalism. Despite all this, between 1945 and 1948, Peroutka became a self-appointed protector of Masaryk's legacy, adapting the best of the Castle vision for a new age. He would not have long to do it.

Conclusion

In 1935, Karel Čapek offered advice to the reader who found the abstract final section of the *Conversations with Masaryk* to be hard going. Those who found "no resonance in Platonic antiquity and Jesus' preaching of love" should contemplate the searching quality of Masaryk's ideas and life, and there find "harmony."[181] Masaryk's thought and life, however harmonious, seemed between 1938 and 1948 to belong to another century. Czechs living through that horrible decade could have found relatively little in Masaryk's life to guide them, aside from moral bromides. Increasingly, they questioned the political and social system Masaryk had helped to build and the postulates on which it was based.

Those ideas and that system were described by the works of prose that cemented the Castle's standing in the eyes of Czechoslovak citizens and the world—the *Conversations* and *Building the State*. Čapek's and Peroutka's books returned their readers to the early days of the republic, an oasis of clarity and hope in contrast to the despair of the late 1930s. The Masaryk and Beneš they portrayed were philosopher-kings and more, men of action as well as thought, leaders within a Europe that supported their ideas, their values, and the state they led. Outside the pages of these texts, the Castle myth had long fallen on deaf ears. Munich and the Second Republic seemingly proved the Castle's fundamental error: democracy and reliance on the West had failed to guarantee Czechoslovakia. Still and all, as Gale Stokes has observed, "Czech democracy failed because Europe failed."[182]

Wartime reinvigorated aspects of the myth in a more complicated form. The interwar Castle myth had talked of liberal parliamentarianism combined with enlightened technocratic rule; a democratized, de-Austrianized society imbued with appropriately egalitarian civic values; reliance on and closeness to the democratic West and the League of Nations; and an inconsistent ethnic tolerance accompanied by Czech dominance. Beneš's wartime myth presented a less sanguine, more conflict-ridden Czech nationalism, with enemies and self-sacrificial heroes similar to the "dark ages" before the First Republic. The Nazis, Czechoslovakia's own German population, and the blind, perfidious West had caused the republic's downfall. Palacký's hopeful assertion that the Czechs constituted a crossroads between German and Slav now seemed impossibly idealistic. Germans had become alien usurpers in the Czech lands, and needed to be expelled from them. The new myth returned the previously European Czechs to Slavdom, proudly allied with their larger Slav brother the Soviets. The great Red Army was Czechoslovakia's heroic ally and liberator, along with (to a lesser extent) the United States, beacon of hope and democracy. Europe would have to work to understand the Soviets rather than fear them; Czechoslovakia would serve as bridge and interpreter. One element of the interwar myth remained unchanged: echoing Masaryk's use of the term *democracy*, Beneš's promises to bring Czechoslovakia "new, fresh" democracy were less than clear about the actual form that democracy would take.

Are Munich and its aftermath proof that Castle propaganda and the Castle myth failed where German propaganda succeeded? Propagandistic failure or success is notoriously difficult to assess. A more relevant question might be how much, or whether, East-Central European propaganda even mattered, when so many other factors mitigated against the West's supporting the Czechs. For example, European international relations were far more important. The Treaty of Versailles aroused traditional British sympathies with Germany, evoking the sense that the French had dishonorably abused a valiant foe. It also created concern that short-sighted French revenge against Germany would hamstring not just the Germans but the postwar recovery of all of Europe, as expressed by British economist John Maynard Keynes in his 1923 *The Economic Consequences of the Peace*. France, and France's allies, were therefore problematic. Moreover, the Foreign Office was tiring of the incestuous disputes among the Habsburg successor states by the mid-1920s, and wistfully recalling the empire, which had contained the nationalities before the war. There was general admiration for the new rightist leaders who "made the trains run on time" and claimed to protect the continent against the Bolsheviks. The cliché about interwar America is that it lapsed into isolationism. In fact, Britain also retreated into concern for its empire, focus on rearmament, and willingness to leave the Continent to the Germans.[183] Other factors were personality and ignorance, particularly the acute, widespread British dislike of and distrust for Edvard Beneš, and growing interest in the affable, "reasonable" Konrad Henlein. Czechoslovakia spent far less on propaganda than its competitors, so perhaps its message reached a more limited audience; but even if disseminated more widely, how could Czechoslovak propaganda have overcome all these other obstacles? Against this backdrop, it would be accurate to say that Sudeten German, Reich German, and Hungarian propaganda received a warmer reception than the Czechoslovak variant; but it is also true that their listeners were predisposed to hear them kindly.[184]

Another response to the question might be to return to Foreign Minister Eden's quotation: good propaganda was ruined by bad policy. Czechoslovakia's German minority had complained to the League of Nations for many years. But after 1932, the obvious contrast between the Czechoslovak myth's insistence on egalitarian tolerance and the disproportionate nationalism and poverty of the Sudeten Germans could no longer be dismissed by Beneš's maneuvering within committees. Meanwhile, the Sudeten German leaders grew more skilled in presenting their views abroad, and in "luxuriously lobbying" foreigners visiting Czechoslovakia's border regions.[185] As more complaints of discrimination reached British ears, Czechoslovak plausibility lessened. Nazi sponsorship of the Sudeten German political leadership raised the stakes. More than loss, Munich simply provided evidence of the limits of myth and propaganda abroad.

Among Czechs, the myth and leader cult fared somewhat better. Certainly between 1945 and 1948 Masaryk and his republic underwent searching scrutiny and reevaluation. Diplomat George Kennan, representing the United States in Prague, wrote in October 1938 that "it is not easy to comfort people for what they regard as twenty years of misplaced endeavor. . . . [I]t is impossible to object when they now turn as bitterly on their erstwhile liberalism as they have on the alliances which supported it."[186] The immediate postwar period saw a similar impulse. Interwar Czechoslovakia was roundly condemned for its imperfections, although Masaryk's reputation and glory survived. His legacy was bent to seemingly odd purposes; he was invoked to defend or criticize almost every aspect of the social and economic restructuring that had altered his country. Despite Soviet pressure and Czechoslovak Communist momentum and popularity, Masaryk continued to symbolize Czechness itself, its noble past, its heroic future. But other elements of the Castle myth were in tatters, particularly its insistence on democracy and tolerance. Edvard Beneš, Ferdinand Peroutka, and other Castle adherents were the last voices speaking for Masaryk's republic. All these were gone soon enough.

Epilogue

The people need a hero, a saint. . . . There must be a "Once upon a time there lived" about it—something of the fairy tale.

—*Maxim Gorky*

In February 1948, Edvard Beneš faced a second historical decision, comparable to his choice not to fight in response to Munich. Once again, he surrendered to a stronger opponent—this time, the Czechoslovak Communist Party, backed by Soviet might. Reports had circulated that non-Communist police officers were being fired, and an unknown troublemaker had mailed bombs to non-Communist cabinet ministers, yet the Communist-controlled Ministry of the Interior refused to begin criminal investigations. In protest, the National Socialist, Populist, and Slovak Democratic ministers resigned from the cabinet, hoping to spur wholesale political change. But they were not numerous enough to destroy the governing coalition or force new elections. Unless President Beneš refused to accept their resignations, their efforts would come to nothing. Beneš, already seriously ill, hesitated. Meanwhile, the Communists took to the streets, organizing large-scale public demonstrations and a nationwide general strike. More ominously, Communist-led police "guarded" the Prague radio station, train stations, and post offices. Conspicuously, the non-Communist parties failed to organize counterdemonstrations urging Beneš to stand firm. The

Communists appeared an unstoppable, vibrant force, and Beneš feared that internal Czechoslovak conflict might tempt the Soviets to intervene. Five days later, Beneš accepted the resignations, allowing Communist leader Klement Gottwald to form a new government. A defeated Beneš resigned after the "February coup," which destroyed even nominal political pluralism in Czechoslovakia; he died soon thereafter.[1]

Gottwald and the Communist Party transformed Czechoslovakia into a Soviet satellite akin to the rest of Eastern Europe, where economies had already been fully nationalized, non-Communist parties made illegal and non-Communist politicians harassed, society reengineered to suppress the bourgeoisie and laud the working class, agriculture collectivized, and Stalinist intellectual and political conformity imposed. Nostalgic reminiscences about Masaryk, Beneš, and the bourgeois First Republic had no place in the minds of the dedicated heroes of labor now devoted to following in Soviet footsteps, creating a worker's state, and filling and overfilling prescribed quotas. But discussion or commemoration of the First Republic and its leaders took on new significance as symbols of political protest. On Masaryk's birthday each year, flowers appeared on his grave; in 1953, more than one hundred policemen were assigned to surround it.[2] When controls on information and public speech were briefly lifted in the spring and summer of 1968, scholars quickly began publishing on previously banned subjects, including Masaryk and Beneš; portraits of Masaryk were sold in newspaper kiosks throughout Prague, briefly reinvigorating the leader cult for a new purpose.[3]

As memories of the First Republic were disparaged or silenced at home, Castle myth was transmuted into fact abroad, particularly in the United States. American professors and diplomats who fondly remembered time spent in interwar Czechoslovakia reacted with horror, first to the Second World War and then to the 1948 Communist coup and its aftermath.[4] Émigrés also helped enshrine Castle myth in Anglo-American historiography. Between 1947 and 1950, roughly 236,000 Czechs and Slovaks left for the West for political reasons.[5] Of those who United States, some found government support or employment, such as Ferdinand Peroutka in the New York office of Radio Free Europe.[6] Many former Castle adherents entered academe, a natural decision given that so many Castle staffers and supporters, especially from Zamini, had come originally from academic life. The result was an American rewriting of the Castle mythology for the Cold War, in a new scholarly guise.

One of the most important American academic practitioners of the Castle myth began writing well before the Cold War. Robert J. Kerner, professor of history at the universities of Missouri and of California at Berkeley, studied with Tomáš Masaryk in Prague in 1912–1913. He later recalled, "I consider as the greatest fortune of my life the spiritual development I received in my youth under the guidance of the great masters of Prague University, among whom President Masaryk occupies a place apart.... [T]o him I am indebted...for my firm orientation in domestic and foreign policy."[7] In 1917, Kerner was appointed to the American official inquiry into setting peace terms in the First World War, and served on the American commission at the Paris peace talks.[8] After Munich, Kerner commissioned an international conference on Czechoslovakia. The result, *Czechoslovakia: Twenty Years of Independence*, was one of relatively few English-language scholarly works on the First Republic available during and after the Second World War. The Castle's myth, now elegiac in tone, dominated the contributions to the landmark volume.[9]

Also significant was the work of S. Harrison Thomson, professor of medieval history at the University of Colorado, founding editor of the *Journal of Central European Affairs* and author of the first synthetic overview of Czechoslovak history written by an American. Thomson had visited Prague between 1924 and 1927, where among other Czech academics he had befriended Karel Čapek's friend and Castle adherent Josef Šusta.[10] Thomson's early work was on Jan Hus and the early modern period. But his 1943 book *Czechoslovakia in European History*, one of the first synthetic overviews of Czechoslovakia in English, took Czech history up to the present day. For centuries, Thomson explained, the Czechs (and Slovaks, who shared with the Czechs "a common destiny") had struggled for freedom and realization of their national aspirations. Masaryk, Beneš, and the interwar republic represented the pinnacle of their "brilliant success": the Nazis, the dream deferred, perhaps destroyed. Thomson's book, he argued, would "lead...to more reliable conclusions than a journalistic essay, written in the heat of battle": in other words, it was clearly written to contradict public voices who warned against intervention on the Continent. Roughly half the sources Thomson cited in the book's bibliography were Orbis texts or Castle memoirs.[11]

Of the Czech émigrés helping to transform the Castle myth, among the most significant were Otakar Odložilík, also a medievalist, who held the Masaryk chair of history at Columbia University and later taught at the University of Pennsylvania; Edvard Taborský, who taught political science at the University of Texas at Austin; and Josef Korbel, a political scientist at the University of Denver. Odložilík was the youngest member of the "Goll school" in Charles University's history department from 1926 to 1938; between 1928 and 1930, he had lectured at the School of Slavonic and East European Studies at the University of London, and Zamini had subsidized the British publication of his research on John Wycliffe and Bohemia.[12] During the Second World War, Odložilík worked with Beneš in London from 1943 to 1945.[13] After the war, he briefly returned to Prague; from 1948 on, he taught at Columbia and at the University of Pennsylvania, mentoring students in East European history and writing on the Czech Reformation and its aftermath, on Prague's Charles University, on František Palacký, and on Masaryk.[14] Taborský, who had received law government degrees from Charles University and done a stint in provincial administration, joined the foreign ministry in 1937 as Beneš's personal secretary. During the Second World War, he served as Beneš's secretary and legal advisor in London, accompanying him on visits to Franklin D. Roosevelt and the Kremlin. In 1945, Taborský was appointed ambassador to Sweden. He resigned from that post in 1948, and after teaching at various universities, accepted an offer from the University of Texas at Austin, where he remained until his retirement in 1990. Taborský wrote roughly 300 articles and 15 books in Czech and English on Eastern Europe, Communism, Czechoslovakia, Beneš and the World War.[15]

The work of Josef Korbel offers an intriguing twist to the Western afterlife of the Castle myth. Korbel was educated at the Sorbonne and at Charles University. In 1934, at the age of twenty-five, he went to work for Zamini, serving as press and cultural attaché in Belgrade from 1937 to 1939. The Nazi invasion directly threatened his family, as Korbel had converted to Catholicism from Judaism. The Korbels fled to London, where Josef served within Beneš's government in exile as Jan Masaryk's personal secretary and as head of broadcasting. After the war, he worked with Masaryk to rebuild Zamini, and was then appointed ambassador to Yugoslavia, the youngest ambassador in the country's history. Korbel fled Czechoslovakia after the February 1948 coup and came to the United States, where the University of Denver hired him to teach international relations.[16] Korbel wrote on Cold War conflicts, including those in East-Central Europe.

Korbel's *Twentieth-Century Czechoslovakia*, published a few months after his death in 1977, presents another form of the Castle myth. Overall, the First Republic is portrayed as Masaryk and Beneš's noble idyll, the embodiment of Hus's, Palacký's, and Havlíček's ideals. Yet he links those achievements with "an equally unique record of defeat and failure."[17] The later part of the book identifies these characteristics particularly with Edvard Beneš, whose capitulation at Munich, Korbel implied, was unforgivably wrong. The Czechs were capable of greatness, as the First Republic demonstrated; they were also capable of cowardice and accommodation. Overall, despite Korbel's frustration with Beneš and the widespread support for Czechoslovak Communism, the book's tone retains the essence of the Castle legacy; it portrays the Czechs romantically, with an idealized Masaryk personifying the Czechoslovak nation. Of all these historians, Korbel's legacy is probably the widest-reaching. Korbel's daughter, Madeleine Albright, was the first female U.S. secretary of state; one of Korbel's doctoral students, Condoleezza

Rice, became the second. Both have said publicly that Korbel inspired them to enter public service and recall his belief in the significance and power of bestowing freedom on the victims of tyranny as deeply influential.[18] As secretaries of state, both portrayed the United States' role in the world as parallel to the depiction of Czechoslovakia in the Castle myth, as a paradigm of democracy and freedom, a model for the rest of the world.

Contemporary historiography of the First Republic and the Castle has moved far from the mythology, both in the United States and in the Czech Republic. But myths, rather than disappearing, evolve. Czechoslovakia's first post-Communist president, Václav Havel, repeatedly invoked Masaryk and the supposedly self-evidently democratic Czech/oslovak past. (The "velvet divorce" of the Czech Republic and Slovakia in 1993 caused Havel for the most part to drop the Slovaks from his reiteration of the myth.) Elements of the Castle's myth still appear in Czech national self-understanding; depictions of Czechs as natural democrats remain part of international discourse. Masaryk and Beneš's national narrative of a martyred nation of democrats remains compelling. Masaryk has transcended the First Republic and become a full-fledged national hero, as the terms of his interwar cult suggested.[19] At no point has the Castle myth gone unchallenged, from its inception in 1915 to the present day. Yet its outlines and influence remain.

The creation, manipulation, and propagation of this set of ideas present a novel way of considering the history of the First Czechoslovak Republic and of interwar Europe. Analysis of myth and propaganda—emphasizing politics as idea and text as well as votes and deeds—offers a necessary complement to more traditional depictions of internal Czechoslovak politics. It allows for the First Republic's political press and personal intervention to be situated at the center of political life rather than ephemeral to it. It also requires the First Republic to be understood within a competitive, tense, text-dependent European political milieu, in which the London *Times* was wooed along with the Foreign Office. This cold war of propaganda helped create a sense of an Eastern Europe as distinct from, dependent on, and culturally and economically behind the prosperous, victorious West. Finally, tracing the shifting myth from the Great War through the Second World War and beyond emphasizes the flexible contours of nationalist narratives and the ways intellectuals wield them at home and abroad in the nation's support and defense. The Castle myth provides an example of simultaneous nation building, aimed both at Czechoslovaks and the European Great Powers, establishing the nation simultaneously at home and abroad.

Twentieth-century Czech political discourse also provides a reminder that the term *democracy* embraces many disparate interpretations. Many historians have castigated the First Republic for its democratic inadequacies, but newer research emphasizes that the insistence on "democracy" in the

Castle myth was usefully ambiguous, a seemingly simplistic moral and political virtue that in fact referred to any number of possible adaptations or developments.[20] European democracies have been populist, technocratic, oligarchic, and authoritarian. Masaryk's and Beneš's written work and political activity invoke, at different points, all of these forms. Both the Castle and the Pětka could safely tout themselves as democratic: both were right, and wrong. Democratic rhetoric and the invocation of a democratic ideal were frequently used to respond to public criticism of the republic's, and the Castle's, democratic deficiencies. "Democracy" was employed both as a transcendent moral claim to virtue and a synonym for the status quo. The relationship between democracy and myth, as well as democracy and propaganda, was closer than observers might assume.

At the same time, the Czechoslovaks are best understood against a European backdrop. During the tumultuous years between 1914 and 1948, national myths were one of the many means by which Europe reinterpreted its past and posited its future. The Czechs participated in this wider trend; the unique element in the Czech myth was its insistence on (vaguely defined) democracy, and to a lesser extent tolerance and nonviolence. In some senses the Czech national narrative as formulated by Masaryk and Beneš resembles civic nationalism, which calls for deriving one's identity from participation in a state, and the virtues that state supposedly embodies.[21] While this book has noted the Castle myth's propagation, limitations, and defects, it might also be argued that Castle myth aided the development of a twentieth-century Czech national consensus—or at least a discourse—about the value of democracy, the legitimate use of power, cultural tolerance, and many other values said to be represented by the West. If this admittedly uneven and contested consensus, bolstered by the international community, dominates Czech or East European politics in the twenty-first century, then it would mark the Castle myth's most important and durable victory.

Abbreviations and Definitions

AHY	*Austrian History Yearbook*
AKPR	Archiv kanceláře presidenta republiky (Archive of the Chancellery of the President of the Republic), Prague, Czech Republic
AMZV	Archiv Ministerstva zahraničních věci (Archive of the Ministry of Foreign Affairs), Prague, Czech Republic
APNP	Archiv pámatník národního písemnictví (National Literary Memorial Archive), Staré Hrady, Czech Republic
AÚTGM	Archiv Ústavu TG Masaryka, Prague, Czech Republic. I used this archive in 1997, before it reorganized its documentary collection.
Boh	*Bohemia: Zeitschrift für Geschichte und Kultur der böhmischen Länder. Jahrbuch des Collegium Carolinum.*
DHČSP	Libuše Otáhalová and Milada Červinková, *Acta Occupationis Bohemiae et Moraviae: Dokumenty z historie československé politiky 1939–1943*, 2 vols. (Prague: Academia, 1966)
EEPS	*East European Politics and Societies*

fond	collection
HRC/PEN	P.E.N. International Archives, Harry Ransom Center, University of Texas, Austin
kar.	karton (box)
MZA	Moravský zemský archiv (Moravian Regional Archive), Brno
NARA	National Archives and Records Administration, College Park, MD
PMV	Presidium ministerstva vnitra
PNP	Památník národního písemnictví (National Literary Memorial), Prague, Czech Republic
sign.	signatura (collection)
sl.	složka (folder)
SÚA	Státní Ústřední Archiv (State Central Archives, now Národní archiv, National Archives), Prague, Czech Republic

Throughout, translations are mine unless otherwise noted.

Notes

Introduction

1. Robert Jackall, ed., *Propaganda* (New York: New York University Press, 1995), 1, 13; Ute Daniel and Wolfram Siemann, "Historische Dimensionen der Propaganda," in Daniel and Siemann, eds., *Propaganda: Meinungskampf, Verführung und politische Sinnstiftung (1789–1989)* (Frankfurt: Fischer Taschenbusch Verlag, 1994), 10.
2. Robert Holtman, *Napoleonic Propaganda* (Baton Rouge: Louisiana State University Press, 1950); Wayne Hanley, *The Genesis of Napoleonic Propaganda 1796–1799* (New York: Columbia University Press, 2003), Gutenberg e-book available at http://www.gutenberg-e.org; Jean Tulard, *Napoleon: The Myth of the Saviour*, trans. T. Waugh (London: Weidenfeld and Nicolson, 1984).
3. Ruth Emily McMurry and Muna Lee, *The Cultural Approach: Another Way in International Relations* (Chapel Hill: University of North Carolina Press, 1947), 19.
4. This literature is vast. I have drawn on: Mark Cornwall, "News, Rumour and the Control of Information in Austria-Hungary, 1914–1918," *History* 77, no. 249 (1992); Mark Cornwall, *The Undermining of Austria-Hungary: The Battle for Hearts and Minds* (New York: St. Martin's Press, 2000); Brett Gary, *The Nervous Liberals: Propaganda Anxieties from WWI to the Cold War* (New York: Columbia University Press, 2000); Victor S. Mamatey, *The United States and East-Central Europe*

1914–1918: A Study in Wilsonian Diplomacy and Propaganda (Princeton, NJ: Princeton University Press, 1957); Aviel Roshwald and Richard Stites, eds., *European Culture in the Great War: The Arts, Entertainment, and Propaganda, 1914–1918* (Cambridge: Cambridge University Press, 1999); David Welch, *Germany, Propaganda, and Total War, 1914–1918: The Sins of Omission* (New Brunswick, NJ: Rutgers University Press, 2000).

5. John M. MacKenzie, *Propaganda and Empire: The Manipulation of British Public Opinion 1880–1960* (Manchester and New York: Manchester University Press and St. Martin's Press, 1986).
6. Philip Taylor, *Munitions of the Mind: A History of Propaganda from the Ancient World to the Present Era* (Manchester: Manchester University Press, 1995), 177–178.
7. East-Central Europe here indicates the states created between Germany and Russia after 1918. Eastern Europe, in chapter 5, denotes the European states between the Iron Curtain and the Soviet border.
8. Margaret MacMillan, *Paris 1919: Six Months That Changed the World* (New York: Random House, 2002), 114.
9. Ibid., 213.
10. Mamatey, *The United States and East Central Europe 1914–1918*, 316–317. Also see Jiří Kovtun, *Masarykův triumf: příběh konce velké války* (Toronto: Sixty-Eight Publishers, 1987).
11. MacMillan, *Paris 1919*, 134, 148.
12. Mamatey, *The United States and East Central Europe 1914–1918*, 299–300.
13. Zbyněk Zeman and Antonín Klímek, *The Life of Edvard Beneš 1884–1948: Czechoslovakia in Peace and War* (Oxford: Clarendon Press, 1997), 21–23.
14. McMurry and Lee, *The Cultural Approach*, 19.
15. Otto Dann, *Nation und Nationalismus in Deutschland, 1770–1990* (Munich: C.H. Beck, 1993); Martin Broszat, "Die völkische Ideologie und der Nationalsozialismus," *Deutsche Rundschau* 84, no. 1 (1958): 59–63; Max Hildebert Boehm, "Die Reorganisation der Deutschtumsarbeit nach dem ersten Weltkrieg," *Ostdeutsche Wissenschaft: Jahrbuch des ostdeutschen Kulturrates* 5 (1959): 12–13, 19.
16. McMurry and Lee, *The Cultural Approach*, 53–54.
17. Ibid., 110–113; Michael David-Fox, "The Fellow Travelers Revisited: The 'Cultured West' Through Soviet Eyes," *Journal of Modern History* 75, no. 2 (2003): 300–336; Peter Kenez, *The Birth of the Propaganda State: Soviet Methods of Mass Mobilization, 1917–1922* (Cambridge: Cambridge University Press, 1985); Nina Tumarkin, *Lenin Lives! The Lenin Cult in Soviet Russia* (Cambridge, MA: Harvard University Press, enlarged edition, 1997); Benno Ennker, *Die Anfänge des Leninkults in der Sowjetunion* (Cologne: Böhlau, 1997).
18. Philip Taylor, *The Projection of Britain: British Overseas Publicity and Propaganda 1919–1939* (Cambridge: Cambridge University Press, 1981), 137; McMurry and Lee, *The Cultural Approach*, 138–144.
19. Taylor, *Munitions of the Mind*, 196–197; Gary, *Nervous Liberals*, 2–3. Ponsonby's inquiry into wartime atrocity propaganda found little or no substantiation, contributing to later Great Power reluctance to believe atrocity stories from Germany and Nazi-occupied Europe. John Horne and Alan Kramer, *German Atrocities, 1914: A History of Denial* (New Haven: Yale University Press, 2002).

20. MacMillan, *Paris 1919*, 229–230.
21. Gabor Batonyi, *Britain and Central Europe 1918–1933* (Oxford: Clarendon Press, 1999); Alena Gajanová, *ČSR a středoevropská politika velmocí (1918–1938)* (Prague, Academia, 1967); Jörg Hoensch, *Der ungarische Revisionismus und die Zerschlagung der Tschechoslowakei* (Tübingen: J.C.B. Mohr/Paul Siebeck, 1976); Aniko Kovacs-Bertrand, *Der ungarische Revisionismus nach dem Ersten Weltkrieg: Der publizistische Kampf gegen den Friedensvertrag von Trianon (1918–1931)* (Munich: R. Oldenbourg Verlag, 1997); Ignác Romsics, ed., *20th Century Hungary and the Great Powers* (Boulder, CO: East European Monographs, distributed by Columbia University Press, 1995); András D. Bán, "Friends of England: Cultural and Political Sympathies on the Eve of the War," *Hungarian Quarterly* 40, no. 153 (1999).
22. Mamatey, *The United States and East-Central Europe 1914–1918*, xiii; Batonyi, *Britain and Central Europe*, 223.
23. Maria Todorova, *Imagining the Balkans* (New York: Oxford University Press, 1997), 119; Milica Bakič-Hayden, "Nesting Orientalisms: The Case of Former Yugoslavia," *Slavic Review* 54, no. 4 (1995): 917–931.
24. Todorova, *Imagining the Balkans*, 122.
25. Batonyi, *Britain and Central Europe*; MacMillan, *Paris 1919*, 211–212, 229.
26. Gary, *Nervous Liberals*, passim. Elizabeth A. Murphy, "Propaganda jako nástroj československé diplomacie za války a po ni," *Dějiny a současnost* 17, no. 5 (1995): 16–20.
27. On the Little Entente, see, *inter alia*, Piotr Wandycz, "Foreign Policy of Eduard Beneš, 1918–1938," in Victor Mamatey and Radomir Luža, eds., *A History of the Czechoslovak Republic 1918–1948* (Princeton, NJ: Princeton University Press, 1973), esp. 220–223, 226–231; on its demise, see Piotr Wandycz, *The Twilight of the French Eastern Alliances, 1926–1936: French-Czechoslovak-Polish Relations from Locarno to the Remilitarization of the Rhineland* (Princeton, NJ: Princeton University Press, 1988).
28. T. Mills Kelly has referred to the myth as "Whig history" in "A Reputation Tarnished: New Perspectives on Interwar Czechoslovakia," Woodrow Wilson International Center, March 26, 2003 (http://www.wilsoncenter.org/topics/pubs/278Kelly.doc, accessed December 15, 2007). Also Vladimír Macura, *Český sen* (Prague: Nakladatelství Lidové noviny, 1998); Vladimír Macura, *Masarykovy boty a jiné semi (o) fejetony* (Prague: Pražská imaginace, 1993); Vladimír Macura, *Znamení zrodu: české národní obrození jako kulturní typ* (Prague: H&H, 1995); Robert Pynsent, *Questions of Identity: Czech and Slovak Ideas of Nationality and Personality* (London: Central European University Press, 1994).
29. Kieran Williams, "National Myths in the New Czech Liberalism," in Geoffrey Hosking and George Schöpflin, eds., *Myths and Nationhood* (New York: Routledge, 1997), 135. The myth could also encompass warlike toughness, embodied by the Hussite leader Jan Žižka. The Right tended to emphasize this element; the Castle occasionally embraced it. On values within myths: Carolyn Humphrey, "Myth-Making, Narratives, and the Dispossessed in Russia," *Cambridge Anthropology* 19, no. 2 (1996–97): 70–93.

30. See the work of Peter Bugge, especially "Czech Democracy 1918–1938: Paragon or Parody?" *Boh* 47, no. 1 (2006–2007): 3–28; many articles by Mark Cornwall and Peter Heumos; Melissa Feinberg, *Elusive Equality: Gender, Citizenship, and the Limits of Democracy in Czechoslovakia, 1918–1950* (Pittsburgh, PA: University of Pittsburgh Press, 2006); Eagle Glassheim, *Noble Nationalists: The Transformation of the Bohemian Aristocracy* (Cambridge, MA: Harvard University Press, 2005); T. Mills Kelly, *Without Remorse: Czech Radical Nationalism in Late-Habsburg Austria* (Boulder, CO: East European Monographs, 2006); Antonín Klímek, *Boj o Hrad I: Hrad a Pětka, 1918–1926* (Prague: Panevropa, 1996), and *Boj o Hrad II: Kdo po Masarykovi? 1926–1935* (Prague: Panevropa, 1998); Daniel Miller, *Forging Political Compromise: Antonín Švehla and the Czechoslovak Republican Party, 1918–1933* (Pittsburgh, PA: University of Pittsburgh Press, 1999); Jan Rataj, *O autoritatívní národní stát* (Prague: Karolinum, 1997); Nancy Meriwether Wingfield, *Flag Wars and Stone Saints: How the Bohemian Lands Became Czech* (Cambridge, MA: Harvard University Press, 2007); Tara Zahra, *Kidnapped Souls: National Indifference and the Battle for Children in the Bohemian Lands, 1900–1948* (Ithaca, NY: Cornell University Press, 2008).
31. Benedict Anderson, *Imagined Communities: Reflections on the Origin and Spread of Nationalism*, rev. ed. (London: Verso, 1991), 205.
32. Vladimír Macura, *Šťastný věk: symboly, emblémy a mýty 1948–1989* (Prague: Pražská imaginace, 1992); Derek Sayer, *The Coasts of Bohemia: A Czech History* (Princeton, NJ: Princeton University Press, 1998), 249–313. Another strand entered the skein of Czech myths in response to 1938 and 1948: that of the Czechs as Eastern Europe's cowards, willing to cooperate with Europe's more powerful states no matter the moral cost, afraid to stand on their own. But this myth is outside the scope of this book and its focus on the Castle's mythic politics.
33. Milan Kundera, "The Tragedy of Central Europe," *New York Review of Books*, April 26, 1984: 33–38; George Schöpflin and Nancy Wood, eds., *In Search of Central Europe* (Totowa, NJ: Barnes and Noble, 1989).
34. Albright made this comment during a talk at Brno's Masaryk University in March 2000. Steve Kettman, "Prague's Native Daughter," March 8, 2000: http://www.salon.com/news/feature/2000/03/08/albright (accessed October 16, 2006).
35. British historian Seton-Watson's journal *The New Europe* began in October 1916. Masaryk titled his wartime treatise "New Europe": see Masaryk, *Nová Evropa, stanovisko slovanské* (Prague: Dubský, 1920). More recent analyses: Tom Lansford and Blagovest Tashev, eds., *Old Europe, New Europe and the US: Renegotiating Transatlantic Security in the Post 9/11 Era* (Burlington, VT: Ashgate, 2005); Daniel Levy, Max Pensky, and John Torpey, eds., *Old Europe, New Europe, Core Europe: Transatlantic Relations after the Iraq War* (London: Verso, 2005).
36. Joanna Overing, "The Role of Myth: An Anthropological Perspective," in Schöpflin and Hosking, eds., *Myths and Nationhood*, 1–3.
37. Pierre Birnbaum, *The Idea of France*, trans. M. B. DeBevoise (New York: Hill and Wang, 2001); Czesław Miłosz, *Native Realm: A Search for Self-Definition* (Garden

City, NY: Doubleday, 1968); Andrzej Walicki, *Philosophy and Romantic Nationalism: The Case of Poland* (Notre Dame: University of Notre Dame Press, 1982); Andrzej Walicki, "The Three Traditions in Polish Patriotism," in Stanisław Gomułka and Antony Polonsky, eds., *Polish Paradoxes* (London: Routledge, 1990).

38. Pynsent, *Questions of Identity*, 43; George Schöpflin, "The Function of Myth and a Taxonomy of Myths," in Schöpflin and Hosking, eds., *Myths and Nationhood*, 20.
39. This point is made by many theorists. See, inter alia, Katherine Verdery, *The Political Lives of Dead Bodies: Reburial and Postsocialist Change* (New York: Columbia University Press, 1999); and E. A. Rees, "Leader Cults: Varieties, Preconditions and Functions," in Balázs Apor et al., eds., *The Leader Cult in Communist Dictatorships: Stalin and the Eastern Bloc* (Houndmills, Basingstoke: Palgrave Macmillan, 2004): 3–26.
40. Christopher Flood, *Political Myth: A Theoretical Introduction* (New York: Routledge, 2002); Yves Bizeul, ed., *Politische Mythen und Rituale in Deutschland, Frankreich, und Polen* (Berlin: Duncker und Humboldt, 2000); Ernst Cassirer, *Der Mythus des Staates* (Frankfurt am Main: Fischer Taschenbusch Verlag, 1988); Heidi Hein-Kircher, *Der Piłsudski-Kult und seine Bedeutung für den polnischen Staat 1926–1939* (Marburg: Herder Institut, 2002); Schöpflin and Hosking, eds., *Myths and Nationhood*; Vladimir Tismaneanu, *Fantasies of Salvation: Democracy, Nationalism, and Myth in Post-Communist Europe* (Princeton, NJ: Princeton University Press, 1998); Tumarkin, *Lenin Lives!*
41. Michael Taussig, *Mimesis and Alterity: A Particular History of the Senses* (London: Routledge, 1993), xv–xix; Macura, *Masarykovy boty*, 5.
42. Overing, "Role of Myth," 7–8, 12.
43. Both men's memoirs invoke this term: Masaryk, *Světová revoluce: za války a ve válce, 1914–1918* (Prague: Orbis and Čin, 1925); Beneš, *Světová válka a naše revoluce* I–III (Prague: Orbis and Čin, 1927–1928).
44. Larry Wolff dates this division to the Enlightenment: *Inventing Eastern Europe: The Map of Civilization on the Mind of the Enlightenment* (Stanford, CA: Stanford University Press, 1996). Ezequiel Adamovsky persuasively questions Wolff's thesis: "Euro-Orientalism and the Making of the Concept of Eastern Europe in France, 1810–1880," *Journal of Modern History* 77, no. 3 (2005): 591–628. Todorova, *Imagining the Balkans*, also emphasizes the nineteenth and twentieth centuries. Peter Bugge accepts Wolff's periodization of intra-European divisions but argues for the interwar period as the origin of the term "Eastern Europe" in "'Shatter Zones': The Creation and Recreation of Europe's East," in Menno Spiering and Michael Wintle, *Ideas of Europe Since 1914: The Legacy of the First World War* (Houndmills, Basingstoke: Palgrave Macmillan, 2002): 47–68; Peter Bugge, "Use of the Middle: *Mitteleuropa* versus *Střední Evropa*," *European Review of History* 6, no. 1 (1999): 15–34.
45. Assessing the myth's reception, both abroad and at home, is far more problematic. International reception of the Czechoslovak myth involves reading between the lines of newspapers and internal diplomatic communiqués, making generalization difficult. Public opinion polling in Czechoslovakia only began in 1946, and was swiftly curtailed thereafter. I thank Brad Abrams for useful discussion on this topic.

46. Jessica C. E. Gienow-Hecht is an important practitioner of the "new diplomatic history" in Central Europe: see her *Transmission Impossible: American Journalism as Cultural Diplomacy in Postwar Germany, 1945–1955* (Baton Rouge: Louisiana State University Press, 1999); Gienow-Hecht and Frank Schumacher, eds., *Culture and International History* (New York: Berghahn Books, 2003).
47. Most recently, Bugge, "Czech Democracy."
48. H. H. Gerth and C. Wright Mills, eds., *From Max Weber: Essays in Sociology* (New York: Oxford University Press, 1958), 176.
49. Katherine Verdery, *National Ideology under Socialism: Identity and Cultural Politics in Ceausescu's Romania* (Berkeley: University of California Press, 1991), 16–18; Zygmunt Baumann, *Legislators and Interpreters: On Modernity, Post-Modernity, and Intellectuals* (Ithaca, NY: Cornell University Press, 1987), 18–19.
50. The quotation is from Philip M. Taylor, "Propaganda in International Politics, 1919–1939," in K. R. M. Short, ed., *Film and Radio Propaganda in World War II* (London: Croom Helm, 1983), 21.
51. George Schöpflin, among others, has noted that myth "has to have some relationship with the memory of the collectivity that has fashioned it." See Schöpflin, "Functions of Myth," 26.
52. Joseph Rothschild, *East-Central Europe between the Two World Wars* (Seattle: University of Washington Press, 1974), 135.
53. Ivan Berend, *Decades of Crisis: Central and Eastern Europe before World War II* (Berkeley: University of California Press, 1998).
54. The actual 1937 quotation: "[G]ood cultural propaganda cannot remedy the damage done by a bad foreign policy, but . . . even the best of diplomatic policies may fail, if it neglects the task of interpretation and persuasion which modern conditions impose." In Reinhold Wagnleitner, *Coca-Colonization and the Cold War: The Cultural Mission of the United States in Austria after the Second World War* (Chapel Hill: University of North Carolina Press, 1994), 50–51.

Chapter 1

1. Margaret MacMillan, *Paris 1919: Six Months That Changed the World* (New York: Random House, 2002), 461. The Czechs were not invited; Beneš used his contacts within the French government to wangle an invitation.
2. Melissa Feinberg, *Elusive Equality: Gender, Citizenship, and the Limits of Democracy in Czechoslovakia, 1918–1950* (Pittsburgh, PA: University of Pittsburgh Press, 2006), 14.
3. Masaryk biographies are legion, though most of them are quite uncritical. The two most recent are the hagiographic Stanislav Polák, *T.G. Masaryk—Za ideálem a pravdou*, 3 vols. (Prague: Masarykův ústav Akademie věd České republiky, 2000–2003); and the more balanced Alain Soubigou, *Tomáš Garrigue Masaryk* (Prague: Paseka, 2004).
4. Zbyněk Zeman, *The Masaryks: The Making of Czechoslovakia* (New York: Barnes and Noble, 1976), 18–19.

5. Soubigou, *Tomáš Garrigue Masaryk*, 21; Derek Sayer, *The Coasts of Bohemia: A Czech History* (Princeton, NJ: Princeton University Press, 1998), 109. Masaryk did not master Czech until he was in his thirties: Sayer, 109.
6. Karel Čapek, *President Masaryk Tells His Story* (New York: Arno Press and the New York Times, 1971), 124–125. Masaryk considered himself a sociologist, but German and Austrian universities were slow to recognize the relatively new discipline.
7. Sayer, *Coasts of Bohemia*, 80, 89; Otto Urban, *České a slovenské dějiny do roku 1918* (Prague: Aleš Skřivan, 2000); in Prague, Gary Cohen, *The Politics of Ethnic Survival: Germans in Prague, 1861–1914* (Princeton, NJ: Princeton University Press, 1986); Nancy Meriwether Wingfield, *Flag Wars and Stone Saints: How the Bohemian Lands became Czech* (Cambridge, MA: Harvard University Press, 2007), chapters 1–4.
8. Sayer, *Coasts of Bohemia*, 76. The best recent discussion of Palacký: Jiří Kořalka, *František Palacký (1798–1876): Der Historiker der Tschechen im österreichischen Vielvölkerstaat* (Vienna: Verlag der Österreichischen Akademie der Wissenschaften, 2006).
9. Sayer, *Coasts of Bohemia*, 128, 129.
10. Vásclav Vlček, "Dějepisecké dílo Frantíška Palackého," *Osvěta* VI (1876), 402, cited in Joseph Zacek, *Palacký: The Historian as Scholar and Nationalist* (The Hague: Mouton, 1970), 61.
11. Jiří Štaif, "The Image of the Other in the Nineteenth Century: Historical Scholarship in the Bohemian Lands," in Nancy Wingfield, ed., *Creating the Other: Ethnic Conflict and Nationalism in Habsburg Central Europe* (New York: Berghahn Books, 2003), 87. Also see Hugh LeCaine Agnew, "Czechs, Germans, Bohemians? Images of Self and Other in Bohemia to 1848," in Wingfield, *Creating the Other*, 56–77.
12. Štaif, "The Image of the Other," 89–91.
13. Zacek, *Palacký*, 62, 106–108.
14. There was room in Palacký's interpretation for belligerence. He celebrated the Hussite general Jan Žižka as the epitome of the godly warrior, even a "fanatic—for godliness . . . for the law of God he styled himself as an avenger." Palacký, *Z dějin národu českého* (Prague: Československý spisovatel, 1976), 209–210.
15. Agnew, *Origins of the Czech National Renascence* (Pittsburgh, PA: University of Pittsburgh Press, 1993), 4.
16. Sayer, *Coasts of Bohemia*, 134–135.
17. Peter Bugge, "The Use of the Middle: *Mitteleuropa* vs. *Střední evropa*," *European Review of History* 6, no. 1 (1999): 20.
18. Sayer, *Coasts of Bohemia*, 137. On Germans in nineteenth-century Czech historiography, see Jiří Rak, "Obraz Němce v české historiografii 19. století," in Jan Křen and Eva Broklová, *Obraz Němců, Rakouska a Německa v české společnosti 19. a 20. století* (Prague: Karolinum, 1998): 49–75.
19. Sayer, *Coasts of Bohemia*, 131.
20. Ibid., 144, 146. The manuscripts were not proved definitively fraudulent until the 1880s. Many patriotic intellectuals across Europe "discovered" similar manuscripts in the latter half of the nineteenth century.
21. Zeman, *The Masaryks*, 48; Štaif, "The Image of the Other," 85, 93.

22. Eva Schmidt-Hartmann, *Thomas G. Masaryk's Realism: Origins of a Political Concept* (Munich: R. Oldenbourg, 1984), 89.
23. Zeman, *The Masaryks*, 47–48.
24. Sayer, *Coasts of Bohemia*, 144–46; Zeman, *The Masaryks*, 51–52. On the Hilsner affair (known in Czech as the Hilsneriada), see Hillel Kieval, *Languages of Community: The Jewish Experience in the Czech Lands* (Berkeley: University of California Press, 2000), 198ff; Jiří Kovtun, *Tajuplná vražda: Případ Leopolda Hilsnera* (Prague: Sefer, 1994); František Červinka, "The Hilsner Affair," in Alan Dundes, ed., *The Blood Libel Legend: A Casebook in Anti-Semitic Folklore* (Madison: University of Wisconsin Press, 1991); Bohumil Černý, *Justičný omyl: Hilsneriada* (Prague: Magnet-Press, 1990).
25. Zeman, *The Masaryks*, 49. On Kramář, the best biography is now Martina Winkler, *Karel Kramář (1860–1937): Selbstbild, Fremdwahrnehmungen und Modernisierungsverständnis eines tschechischen Politikers* (Munich: R. Oldenbourg Verlag, 2002). Also see Bruce Garver, *The Young Czech Party, 1874–1901 and the Emergence of a Multiparty System* (New Haven: Yale University Press, 1978); Vratislav Doubek, *Korespondence T.G. Masaryk–Karel Kramář* (Prague: Masarykův ústav AV ČR, 2005).
26. H. Gordon Skilling, *T.G. Masaryk against the Current, 1882–1914* (University Park, PA: Pennsylvania State University Press, 1994), 63.
27. Zeman, *The Masaryks*, 51.
28. Garver, *The Young Czech Party*, 105.
29. Pieter Judson, *Exclusive Revolutionaries: Liberal Politics, Social Experience, and National Identity in the Austrian Empire, 1848–1914* (Ann Arbor, MI: University of Michigan Press, 1996), 2–3, 262–265. On Austrian liberalism, also see John Boyer, *Political Radicalism in Late-Imperial Vienna: The Origins of the Christian Social Movement 1848–1897* (Chicago: University of Chicago Press, 1981); John Boyer, *Culture and Political Crisis in Vienna: Christian Socialism in Power, 1897–1918* (Chicago: University of Chicago Press, 1995); András Gero, *The Hungarian Parliament (1867–1918): A Mirage of Power* (New York: Columbia University Press, 1997).
30. Marie Neudorflova, *Masaryk's Understanding of Democracy before 1914* (Carl Beck Papers in Russian and East European Studies no. 708, University of Pittsburgh Center for Russian and East European Studies, August 1989), 14, 17, 19, 24. Also, Roman Szporluk, *The Political Thought of Thomas G. Masaryk* (Boulder, CO: East European Monographs, 1981); Eva Schmidt-Hartmann, *Thomas G. Masaryk's Realism: Origins of a Czech Political Concept* (Munich: R. Oldenbourg Verlag, 1984); Peter Bugge, "Czech Nation-Building, National Self-Perception, and Politics, 1780–1914" (PhD dissertation, University of Aarhus, 1994); Zdeněk David, "Thomas G. Masaryk's Ambivalent View of the Enlightenment and Political Liberalism," *Kosmas* 19, no. 2 (2006): 83–85.
31. AÚTGM, MA, 47-III-6, diář V. Kučery. "1925: Středa, 7.X." 25.
32. Schmidt-Hartmann, *Thomas G. Masaryk's Realism*, 56, 74–75, 84, 88, 104–105, 139–140. Also see Stanislaus A. Blejwas, *Realism in Polish Politics: Warsaw Positivism and National Survival in Nineteenth Century Poland* (New Haven: Yale Concilium on International and Area Studies, 1984). Quotation from Jerzy Jedlicki, *A Suburb*

of Europe: Nineteenth-Century Polish Approaches to Western Civilization (Budapest: Central European University Press, 1999), 236. I thank Oxford University Press's anonymous readers for this reference.

33. Many scholars have argued that Masaryk's civic thought was *au fond* religious. See Rene Wellek, "The Philosophical Basis of Masaryk's Political Ideals," *Ethics* 55, no. 4 (1945): 298–304; H. Gordon Skilling, "Masaryk: Religious Heretic," in John Morison, ed., *The Czech and Slovak Experience* (Houndmills, Basingstoke: St. Martin's Press, 1992), 62–88; Jan Zohar, "T. G. Masaryk: From Religion to Democracy," *The New Presence* 3 (2003): 31; Bruce Berglund, "Prague Castle as Sacred Acropolis: Faith, Conviction, and Skepticism in the House of Masaryk," unpublished ms. I thank Bruce Berglund for permission to cite this manuscript.
34. Čapek, *Hovory s T.G. Masarykem* (Prague: Československý spisovatel, 1990), 130.
35. Tomáš Garrigue Masaryk, *Jan Hus: Naše obrození a naše reformace* (Prague: Jan Kanzelsberger, 1990), 105, 166. Emphasis Masaryk's.
36. Skilling, *Masaryk against the Current*, 7.
37. Čapek, *President Masaryk Tells His Story*, 181.
38. T. G. Masaryk, *Světová revoluce: za války a ve válce, 1914–1918* published in English in 1927 as *The Making of a State* (Prague: Orbis and Čin, 1925), 608. A romanticized but perceptive comment: Jaroslav Pelikan, *"Jesus, Not Caesar": The Religious World View of Thomas Garrigue Masaryk and the Spiritual Foundations of Czech and Slovak Culture* (Salt Lake City: The Westminster Tanner-McMurrin Lectures on the History and Philosophy of Religion at Westminster College, 1991).
39. Masaryk, *Světová revoluce*, 550, 552. Masaryk seems to elide liberalism and republicanism.
40. Ibid., 608.
41. T. G. Masaryk, *Česká otázka/Naše nynější krise* (Prague: Svoboda, 1990), 171, 179.
42. Ibid., 94.
43. Ibid., 179–180.
44. Feinberg, *Elusive Equality*, 17. Masaryk's ideas were shared by many interwar leaders. See Daniel Miller, *Forging Political Compromise: Antonín Švehla and the Czechoslovak Republican Party 1918–1933* (Pittsburgh, PA: University of Pittsburgh Press, 1999), 167.
45. His writings on this theme, *The Czech Question* and *Our Current Crisis*, date back to the 1890s: Skilling, *Masaryk against the Current*, 36.
46. On the trope of the peasant and countryside in Czech nationalism, see Jiří Rak, *Bývali čechové: České historické myty a stereotypy* (Praha: H&H, 1994); Andrew Lass, "Romantic Documents and Political Monuments: The Meaning-Fulfillment of History in 19th-Century Czech Nationalism," *American Ethnologist* 15, no. 3 (1988): 456–471.
47. Neudorflova, *Masaryk's Understanding of Democracy*, 5.
48. There is a vast literature on Havlíček Borovský. Inter alia, see Jiří Morava, *C.k. disident Karel Havlíček* (Prague: Panorama, 1991); Barbara K. Reinfeld, *Karel*

Havlíček (1821–1856): A National Liberation Leader of the Czech Renascence (Boulder, CO: East European Monographs, 1982); and Peter Brock and H. Gordon Skilling, eds., *The Czech Renascence of the Nineteenth Century* (Toronto: University of Toronto Press, 1970).

49. Miloš Havelka, "Spor o smysl českých dějin 1895–1938 (Preface)," in Havelka, ed., *Spor o smysl českých dějin 1895–1938* (Prague: Torst, 1995), 8.
50. Ibid., 18–19.
51. Skilling, *Masaryk against the Current*, 7, 47.
52. Alain Soubigou, *Tomáš Garrigue Masaryk* (Prague: Paseka, 2004), 167.
53. Mark Cornwall, "Dr. Edvard Beneš and Czechoslovakia's German Minority, 1918–1943," in John Morison, ed., *The Czech and Slovak Experience* (Houndmills, Basingstoke: St. Martin's Press, 1992), 170–171.
54. Zbyněk Zeman and Antonín Klímek, *The Life of Edvard Beneš 1884–1948: Czechoslovakia in Peace and War* (Oxford: Oxford University Press, 1997), 10, 14–15.
55. Edvard Beneš, *My War Memoirs* (New York: Arno Press and the New York Times, 1971; reprint of 1928 Paul Selver trans.), 15, 17, 21.
56. Ibid., 18, 21.
57. Jiří Kunc, *Stranické systemy v re/konstrukci: Belgie, Itálie, Španělsko, Československo, Česká republika* (Prague: Sociologické nakladatelství, 2000); Jiří Malíř and Pavel Marek, eds., *Politické strany: Vývoj politických stran a hnutí v českých zemích a Československu 1861–2004*, vols. 1–2 (Brno: Doplněk, 2005).
58. See the work of Daniel A. Miller, including *Forging Political Compromise*, and Vladimír V. Dostal, *Agrární strana: Její rozmach a zánik* (Brno: Atlantis, 1998).
59. Miloš Trapl, *Political Catholicism and the Czechoslovak People's Party in Czechoslovakia, 1918–1938* (Boulder, CO: Social Science Monographs, 1995).
60. This party bore no relation to the National Socialist German Workers' Party, or NSDAP/Nazi Party, in neighboring Germany. T. Mills Kelly, *Without Remorse: Czech Radical Nationalism in Late-Habsburg Austria* (Boulder, CO: East European Monographs, 2006).
61. On the Social Democrats: Zdeněk Karník, *Socialisté na rozcestí: Habsburk, Masaryk či Šmeral* (Prague: Universita Karlová, 1996).
62. Derek Sayer, "The Language of Nationality and the Nationality of Language: Prague 1780–1920," *Past and Present* 153 (November 1996): 198.
63. Garver, *The Young Czech Party*, 102.
64. Ibid., 45–46, 103–104, 128–129. During the 1880s, the Taaffe government confiscated the paper 330 times over the course of the decade, roughly once every twelve days. The Young Czech party grew out of the *Národní listy* and other liberal journals (107).
65. T. G. Masaryk, *Česká otázka*, 209. I thank Peter Bugge for insight on this topic.
66. T. G. Masaryk, *Karel Havlíček, Snahy a toužby politického probuzení*, 3rd ed. (Prague: Jan Laichter, 1920), 55.
67. Čapek, *President Masaryk Tells His Story*, 230.
68. Beneš, *My War Memoirs*, 19, 21–23, 25–26.
69. See Robert Seton-Watson, *Racial Problems in Hungary* (London: A. Constable and Co., 1908); Jan Rychlík, Thomas D. Marzik, and Miroslav Bielik, eds.,

R.W. Seton-Watson and His Relations with the Czechs and Slovaks: Documents 1906–1951/R.W. Seton-Watson a jeho vztahy k Čechům a Slovákům: dokumenty 1906–1951, 2 vols. (Prague: Ústav T.G. Masaryka; Martin: Matica slovenská, 1995); and László Péter, "The Political Conflict between R.W. Seton-Watson and C.A. Macartney over Hungary," April 16–17, 2004 (conference paper from British-Hungarian Relations Since 1848, School of Slavonic and East European Studies, University College London, http://www.ssees.ac.uk/confhung/peter.pdf, accessed November 10, 2005).

70. Zeman, *The Masaryks*, 64–65.
71. H. Louis Rees, *The Czechs during World War I: The Path to Independence* (Boulder, CO: East European Monographs, 1992), 8.
72. *Přehled*, May 1, 1914, cited in Zbyněk Zeman, *The Break-Up of the Habsburg Empire, 1914–1918* (London: Oxford University Press, 1961), 20.
73. *Národní listy*, August 4, 1914.
74. Arthur James May, *The Passing of the Habsburg Monarchy 1914–1918*, vol. 1 (Philadelphia: University of Pennsylvania Press, 1966), 353.
75. Rees, *The Czechs during World War I*, 12; Ivan Šedivý, *Češi, české země a velká válka* (Prague: Lidové noviny, 2001).
76. T. G. Masaryk, *The Making of a State: Memories and Observations 1914–1918* (New York: Howard Fertig, 1969), 40–41. On the Družina, see Josef Kalvoda, *The Genesis of Czechoslovakia* (Boulder, CO: East European Monographs, 1986), chapter 3; also see Todd Huebner, "The Multinational 'Nation-State': The Origins and the Paradox of Czechoslovakia, 1914–1920" (PhD dissertation, Columbia University, 1993); and K. Pichlík, B. Klípa, and J. Zabloudilová, eds., *Českoslovenšti legionáři (1914–1920)* (Prague: Mladá fronta, 1996).
77. Mark Cornwall, *The Undermining of Austria-Hungary: The Battle for Hearts and Minds* (New York: St. Martin's Press, 2000), 19; also see Mark Cornwall, "News, Rumour and the Control of Information in Austria-Hungary, 1914–1918," *History* 77, no. 249 (1992): 52; as well as Rees, *The Czechs during World War I*, 15.
78. Cited in Cornwall, *Undermining*, 21; also see Cornwall, "News, Rumour," 56.
79. Zeman and Klímek, *The Life of Edvard Beneš*, 35.
80. Zeman, *The Masaryks*, 67–68; Steven Beller, "The British View of Bohemia before 1914," in Eva Schmidt-Hartmann and Stanley Winters, eds., *Großbritannien, die USA und die böhmischen Länder 1848–1938* (Munich: R. Oldenbourg Verlag, 1991), 75–85; Harry Hanak, *Great Britain and Austria-Hungary during the First World War: A Study in the Formation of Public Opinion* (London: Oxford University Press, 1962), chapter 2.
81. Beller, "The British View of Bohemia," 85.
82. Seton-Watson was also on the Romanian payroll. This insight thanks to Vladimir Solonari and Holly Case: see Case, *Between States: The Transylvanian Question and the European Idea during WWII* (Stanford, CA: Stanford University Press, in press).
83. R. W. Seton-Watson, *Masaryk in England* (Cambridge: The University Press and Macmillan Company, 1943), 125, 128.
84. Beneš, *My War Memoirs*, 27.
85. Ibid., 28–29; Zeman, *The Masaryks*, 68.

86. Čapek, *President Masaryk Tells His Story*, 233.
87. Zeman, *The Masaryks*, 74.
88. Beneš, *My War Memoirs*, 30.
89. Zeman and Klímek, *Life of Edvard Beneš*, 19.
90. Beneš, *My War Memoirs*, 55.
91. Purportedly the words of the Social Democratic leader Bohumir Šmeral: ibid., 32, 35.
92. Zeman, *The Masaryks*, 65; Hugh LeCaine Agnew, *The Czechs and the Lands of the Bohemian Crown* (Stanford, CA: Hoover Institution Press, 2004), 165.
93. Frank Hadler, *Weg von Österreich! Das Weltkriegsexil von Masaryk und Beneš im Spiegel ihrer Briefe und Aufzeichnungen 1914–1918: Eine Quellensammlung* (Berlin: Akademie Verlag, 1995): Dagmar Hájková and Ivan Šedivý, eds., *Korespondence T.G. Masaryk–Edvard Beneš, 1914–1918* (Prague: Ústav T.G. Masaryka, Česká akademie věd, 2004).
94. Beneš, *My War Memoirs*, 68; Zeman, *The Masaryks*, 77.
95. Beneš, *My War Memoirs*, 76–86, 104, 107–108.
96. Masaryk, *Světová revoluce*, 112.
97. Beneš, *My War Memoirs*, 86.
98. Zeman, *The Masaryks*, 78–79.
99. Beneš, *My War Memoirs*, 87.
100. Hanak, *Great Britain and Austria-Hungary*, 103; Čapek, *President Masaryk*, 251–252.
101. Hanak, *Great Britain and Austria-Hungary*, 121–122.
102. Beneš, *My War Memoirs*, 112, 113.
103. Ibid., 93–100.
104. Hanak, *Great Britain and Austria-Hungary*, 122–124.
105. Victor Mamatey, "The Establishment of the Republic," in Mamatey and Radomir Luža, eds., *History of the Czechoslovak Republic* (Princeton, NJ: Princeton University Press), 13.
106. Zeman, *The Masaryks*, 85.
107. Ibid., 77, 82.
108. Hájková and Šedivý, eds., *Korespondence T.G. Masaryk–Edvard Beneš, 1914–1918*; Zdeněk Šolle, ed. *Vzájemná neoficiální korespondence T.G. Masaryka s Eduardem Benešem z doby pařížských mírových jednání (Říjen 1918-prosinec 1919)*, part I (Prague: Archiv Akademie věd ČR, 1993); Šolle, ed., *Vzájemná neoficiální korespondence T.G. Masaryka s Eduardem Benešem z doby pařížských mírových jednání (Říjen 1918-prosinec 1919)*, part II (Prague: Archiv Akademie věd ČR, 1994).
109. Beneš, *My War Memoirs*, 302; Hanak, *Great Britain and Austria-Hungary*, 115–116, chapters 4, 6.
110. One example among many: letter 105 from Beneš to Masaryk in Hájková and Šedivý, eds., *Korespondence T.G. Masaryk–Edvard Beneš, 1914–1918*, 150–152.
111. Ivo Banac, *The National Question in Yugoslavia: Origins, History, Politics* (Ithaca, NY: Cornell University Press, 1984), 96.
112. Seton-Watson, *Masaryk in England*, 129–130.
113. Beneš, *My War Memoirs*, 304, 306; Zeman, *The Masaryks*, 77–78; Milada Paulová, *Tajný výbor (Maffie) a spolupráce s Jihoslovany v letech 1916–1918* (Prague: Academia, 1968).

114. Harry Hanak, "British Views of the Czechoslovaks from 1914–1924," in Schmidt-Hartmann and Winters, *Großbritannien, die USA und die böhmischen Länder 1848–1938*, 89.
115. Zeman, *The Masaryks*, 81–82.
116. Banac, *The National Question in Yugoslavia*, 116–120.
117. Beneš, *My War Memoirs*, 301–304; Masaryk, *Světová revoluce*, 137–139, 282–292.
118. Beneš, *My War Memoirs*, 308–309.
119. Ibid., 311, 313.
120. Margaret MacMillan, *Paris 1919*, 210–211. Masaryk recalls Dmówski's proposal in *Světová revoluce*, 295–297.
121. Beneš, *My War Memoirs*, 313–314.
122. Čapek, *President Masaryk Tells His Story*, 253.
123. Beneš, *My War Memoirs*, 105.
124. Ibid., 108. Masaryk and Miliukov remained in contact through the interwar period: AKPR (Prague), knihy audience.
125. Beneš, *My War Memoirs*, 107–108.
126. Masaryk, *Světová revoluce*, 106.
127. T. G. Masaryk, *The Slavs among the Nations* (pamphlet, reprinted from *La Nation Tchèque*, March 15, 1916; London: The Czech National Alliance in Great Britain and Jas. Truscott and Son, 1916), 2.
128. Beneš, *My War Memoirs*, 107–108.
129. Masaryk, *Světová revoluce*, 100.
130. T. G. Masaryk, "Austria Under Francis Joseph," *The New Europe* 1, no. 7 (1916): 202. See Hugh Seton-Watson and Christopher Seton-Watson, *The Making of a New Europe: R.W. Seton-Watson and the Last Years of Austria-Hungary* (Seattle: University of Washington Press, 1981).
131. T. G. Masaryk, "*Sub specie aeternitatis*," *The New Europe* 1, no. 10 (1916): 300.
132. T. G. Masaryk, "The Future Status of Bohemia," *The New Europe* 2, no. 19 (1917): 173.
133. Masaryk, *Světová revoluce*, 101.
134. Beneš, *My War Memoirs*, 104.
135. Zeman, *The Masaryks*, 81, 100.
136. Ibid., 118; Masaryk, *Světová revoluce*, 101.
137. Beneš, *My War Memoirs*, 88.
138. Čapek, *President Masaryk Tells His Story*, 253.
139. Zeman, *The Masaryks*, 92–93.
140. Agnew, *The Czechs*, 167.
141. Mamatey, "The Establishment of the Republic," 16.
142. Beneš, *My War Memoirs*, 231.
143. Ibid.
144. Ibid., 232–233; Agnew, *The Czechs*, 168.
145. Hanak, *Great Britain and Austria-Hungary*, 253. Czernin accused the French of trying to divide Austria from its ally Germany; the French retaliated by publishing a letter from Emperor Karl to Prince Sixtus in which Karl recognized France's right to Alsace-Lorraine. Karl hastened to Berlin to reassure his ally,

signing a treaty that bound the two states even more tightly, and Czernin resigned.

146. Beneš, *My War Memoirs*, 341–342. Similar demands were made regarding the treaty of Brest-Litovsk.
147. Mamatey, "The Establishment of the Republic," 16–17, 22–23.
148. Masaryk, *Světová revoluce*, 90.
149. Beneš, *My War Memoirs*, 123.
150. Agnew, *The Czechs*, 166.
151. Zeman, *The Masaryks*, 79–80, 83, 94–99. Masaryk devoted almost one-fifth of his war memoirs to his time in Russia: see Masaryk, *Světová revoluce*, 155–237.
152. Betty Miller Unterberger, *The United States, Revolutionary Russia, and the Rise of Czechoslovakia* (Chapel Hill: University of North Carolina Press, 1989).
153. Beneš, *My War Memoirs*, 357.
154. Zdeňek Karník, *České země v eře první republiky (1918–1938): Vzník, budování a zlatá leta republiky (1918–1929)*, vol. 1 (Prague: Libri, 2000), 31.
155. MacMillan, *Paris 1919*, 231.
156. Karník, *České země v eře první republiky*, 31.
157. Beneš, *My War Memoirs*, 359, 369–371; F. Gregory Campbell, *Confrontation in Central Europe: Weimar Germany and Czechoslovakia* (Chicago: University of Chicago Press, 1975), 28–37; Blanka Sevcik Glos and George Ernest Glos, *Czechoslovak Troops in Russia and Siberia during the First World War* (New York: Vantage Press, 2000); Gerhard Thunig-Nittner, *Die tschechoslowakische Legion in Russland: ihre Geschichte und Bedeutung bei der Enstehung der Ersten Republik* (Wiesbaden: Harrassowitz, 1970).
158. Beneš, *My War Memoirs*, 373.
159. Čapek, *President Masaryk*, 281.
160. Beneš, *My War Memoirs*, 139, 186, 276, 368.
161. MacMillan, *Paris 1919*, 233.
162. Gabor Batonyi, *Britain and Central Europe, 1918–1933* (Oxford: Clarendon Press, 1999), 10–11; Hanak, *Great Britain and Austria-Hungary*, 10.
163. Batonyi, *Britain and Central Europe*, 11–12.
164. MacMillan, *Paris 1919*, 233.
165. Beneš, *My War Memoirs*, 234, 442, 445, 452.
166. Mamatey, "The Establishment of the Republic," 22–23, 26.
167. MacMillan, *Paris 1919*, 467, 469, 471.
168. Dagmar Perman, *The Shaping of the Czechoslovak State: Diplomatic History of the Boundaries of Czechoslovakia, 1914–1920* (Leiden: E. J. Brill, 1962).
169. Beneš, *My War Memoirs*, 485–486.
170. Ibid., 497; Masaryk, *Světová revoluce*, 500.
171. Masaryk, *Světová revoluce*, 512.
172. Beneš, *My War Memoirs*, 490.
173. Ibid., 494–495.
174. See Tara Zahra, *Kidnapped Souls: National Indifference and the Battle for Children in the Bohemian Lands, 1900–1948* (Ithaca, NY: Cornell University Press, 2008); Pieter Judson, *Guardians of the Nation: Activists on the Language Frontiers*

of Imperial Austria (Cambridge, MA: Harvard University Press, 2008); Jeremy King, *Budweisers into Czechs and Germans: A Local History of Bohemian Politics, 1848–1948* (Princeton, NJ: Princeton University Press, 2004); Eagle Glassheim, *Noble Nationalists: The Transformation of the Bohemian Aristocracy* (Cambridge, MA: Harvard University Press, 2005); and Wingfield, *Flag Wars and Stone Saints*.

175. Beneš, *My War Memoirs*, 494–495.
176. Masaryk, *Světová revoluce*, 523.
177. Beneš, *My War Memoirs*, 497.
178. Capek, *President Masaryk Tells His Story*, 273.
179. Zeman, *The Masaryks*, 119.
180. Masaryk, "*Sub specie aeternitatis*," 304–305.
181. Robert Kvaček, "The Rise and Fall of Democracy," in Mikulas Teich, ed., *Bohemia in History* (Cambridge: Cambridge University Press, 1998), 252.
182. MacMillan, *Paris 1919*, 316–321, 402–403; Erez Manela, *The Wilsonian Moment: Self-Determination and the International Origins of Anti-Colonial Nationalism* (Oxford: Oxford University Press, 2007); Dermot Keogh, *Twentieth-Century Ireland: Nation and State* (New York: St. Martin's Press, 1994); Marcus Tanner, *Ireland's Holy Wars: The Struggle for a Nation's Soul 1500–2000* (New Haven: Yale University Press, 2001).
183. AÚTGM, MAR, Tisk-propaganda, kar. 1, sl. 13, 1919. Dated July 30, 1919.
184. Peter Bugge, "Czech Democracy: Paragon or Parody?" *Boh* 47, no. 1 (2006–2007): 19, 22.
185. Emanuel Rádl, *Válka Čechů s Němci* (Prague: Melantrich, 1993), 262.

Chapter 2

1. H. Gordon Skilling, *T.G. Masaryk against the Current, 1882–1914* (University Park, PA: Pennsylvania State University Press, 1994), 40–41.
2. Masaryk used the term in his 1919 address to the Czechoslovak Parliament. Josef Korbel, *Twentieth-Century Czechoslovakia: The Meaning of Its History* (New York: Columbia University Press, 1977), 82–83.
3. Václav Beneš, "Czechoslovak Democracy and Its Problems, 1918–1920," in Victor Mamatey and Radomir Luža, eds., *A History of the Czechoslovak Republic 1918–1948* (Princeton, NJ: Princeton University Press, 1973), 93, 96.
4. Peter Bugge, "Czech Democracy: Paragon or Parody?" *Boh* 47, no. 1 (2006–2007): 7–8, fn 17.
5. Karel Čapek, *President Masaryk Tells His Story* (New York: Arno Press and the New York Times, 1971), 289, 291.
6. Bugge, "Paragon or Parody?" 13. Čapek, *President Masaryk Tells His Story*, 292. This proved a common Castle pattern: Masaryk would salt Castle-loyal personnel into legislative or political processes he deemed important, while also bringing external pressure and influence to bear on other staffers working on the same project. On Herben's involvement, see Beneš, "Czechoslovak Democracy and Its Problems," 53.

7. Jiří Kunc, *Stranické systémy v re/konstrukci* (Prague: Sociologické nakladatelství, 1999), 168–171.
8. Skilling, *Masaryk against the Current*, 35–36.
9. Ibid., 50–51.
10. Kunc, *Stranické systémy v re/konstrukci*, 168–170.
11. F. Gregory Campbell, "Central Europe's Bastion of Democracy," *East European Quarterly* 11 (Summer 1977): 155–176.
12. Walter Lippmann, *The Phantom Public* (New York: Harcourt, Brace, Jovanovich, 1925); J. Michael Sproule, *Propaganda and Democracy: The American Experience of Media and Mass Persuasion* (Cambridge: Cambridge University Press, 2005), 94. Giovanni Capoccia has called it a "difficult democracy": "Legislative Responses against Extremism: The 'Protection of Democracy' in the First Czechoslovak Republic (1920–1938)," *EEPS* 16 (2002): 691–738.
13. Karl Bosl, ed., *Die Burg: Einflußreiche politische Kräfte um Masaryk und Beneš*, 2 vols. (Munich: R. Oldenbourg Verlag, 1973–1974); Karl Bosl, ed., *Die demokratisch-parlamentarische Struktur der Ersten Tschechoslowakischen Republik* (Munich: R. Oldenbourg Verlag, 1975); Karl Bosl, *Die Erste Tschechoslowakische Republik als multinationaler Parteienstaat* (Munich: R. Oldenbourg Verlag, 1979); Karl Bosl, *Kultur und Gesellschaft in der Ersten Tchechoslowakischen Republik* (Munich: R. Oldenbourg Verlag, 1982); F. Gregory Campbell, "The Castle, Jaroslav Preiss, and the Živnostenská Bank," *Boh* 15 (1974): 231–253; Zdeněk Kárník, *Česke země v eře první republiky (1918–1938)*, 3 vols. (Prague: Libri, 2000–2003); Antonín Klímek, *Boj o Hrad I: Hrad a Pětka, 1918–1926* (Prague: Panevropa, 1996), and *Boj o Hrad II: Kdo po Masarykovi? 1926–1935* (Prague: Panevropa, 1998), as well as his many articles in *Střední Evropa*; Jaroslav Pecháček, *Masaryk, Beneš, Hrad: Masarykovy dopisy Benešovi* (Prague: Faun, 1996, original publication Munich: České Slovo, 1984).
14. Robert Kvaček, "The Rise and Fall of Democracy," in Mikuláš Teich, ed., *Bohemia in History* (Cambridge: Cambridge University Press, 1998), 251.
15. Just a few examples: within the Castle chancellery, younger staffers frequently chafed against the conservative nationalism of political chief Josef Schieszl. Even Masaryk scolded Schieszl in 1924 when he publicly denigrated the new Castle-sponsored National Labor Party led by Jaroslav Stránský. Josef Schieszl, "Nové strany," *Nová svoboda*, October 1, 1925. Cited in Tomáš Dvořák, "Národní strana práce (1925–1930), II. Část," *Střední evropa* 77 (1998): 123. Also, the holdings for the interwar Czechoslovak Ministry of the Interior, in the Czech National Archives (formerly the State Central Archives, or SÚA), contain a chronological roster of censored publications. On that roster many times, even before the First Republic's 1938 demise, was Ferdinand Peroutka's *Přítomnost*, now regarded as one of the foremost Castle publications. SÚA, fond PMV, Státní zastupitelství v Praze, confiscation of *Přítomnost* (for example), dated April 9, 1924.
16. Ferdinand Peroutka, *Budování státu: Československá politika v letech popřevatových*, vol. 2 (Prague: Nakladatelství Lidové noviny, 1991), 844–845.
17. Klímek, *Boj o Hrad I*, 165–176.

18. Kárník, *Česke země v eře první republiky* I, 50–53.
19. Beneš, "Czechoslovak Democracy and Its Problems," 58; Hugh LeCaine Agnew, *The Czechs and the Lands of the Bohemian Crown* (Stanford, CA: Hoover Institution Press, 2004), 175.
20. Kárník, *Česke země v eře první republiky* I, 60–63.
21. Derek Sayer, *The Coasts of Bohemia: A Czech History* (Princeton, NJ: Princeton University Press, 1998), 164.
22. Agnew, *The Czechs*, 176–177.
23. Bugge, "Paragon or Parody?" 7 n.11.
24. Ibid., 8–9.
25. Nancy Meriwether Wingfield, *Flag Wars and Stone Saints: Making the Bohemian Lands Czech* (Cambridge, MA: Harvard University Press, 2007), 151–156; Nancy Meriwether Wingfield, "Conflicting Constructions of Memory: Attacks on Statues of Joseph II in the Bohemian Lands after the Great War," *AHY* (1997): 147–171.
26. Hillel Kieval, *Languages of Community: The Jewish Experience in the Czech Lands* (Berkeley: University of California Press, 2000), 210; Christoph Stölzl, "Die 'Burg' und die Juden: T.G. Masaryk und sein Kreis im Spannungsfeld der jüdischen Frage," in Bosl, ed., *Die Burg*, 2: 95–98.
27. Agnew, *The Czechs*, 178–180.
28. Klímek, *Boj o Hrad I*, 55–58.
29. William Lee Blackwood, "Czech and Polish National Democracy," *EEPS* 4, no. 3 (1990): 469–488; Stanley Winters, "Passionate Patriots: Czechoslovak National Democracy in the 1920s," *East Central Europe/L'Europe du Centre-Est* 18, no. 1 (1991).
30. Viz. Bugge, "Paragon or Parody?" Also Peter Heumos, "Der Klabautermann und der lydische Hirte: Aus dem Schatzkästlein erbauterlicher Historie," *Boh* 39 (1998): 409–421.
31. Bugge, "Paragon or Parody?" 11–12.
32. Klímek, *Boj o Hrad I*, 44–45.
33. Ibid., 152–154.
34. Zbyněk Zeman, *The Masaryks: The Making of Czechoslovakia* (New York: Harper and Row, 1976), 142.
35. Klímek, *Boj o Hrad I*, 176 ff. On the Pětka, also see Bugge, "Paragon or Parody?"; Klímek, *Velké dějiny zemí Koruny české*, vols. 13–14 (Prague: Paseka, 2000, 2002); Zdeněk Kárník, *České země eře první republiky*, vol. 1 (Prague: Libri, 2000); F. Gregory Campbell, "Central Europe's Bastion of Democracy," *East European Quarterly* 9, no. 2 (1977); Victor Mamatey, "The Development of Czechoslovak Democracy, 1920–1938," in Victor Mamatey and Radomir Luža, eds., *A History of the Czechoslovak Republic 1918–1948* (Princeton, NJ: Princeton University Press, 1973), 105–110; Daniel Miller, *Forging Political Compromise: Antonín Švehla and the Czechoslovak Republican Party, 1918–1933* (Pittsburgh, PA: University of Pittsburgh Press, 1999).
36. Peter Heumos, "Konfliktregelung und soziale Integration: Zur Struktur der Ersten Tschechoslowakischen Republik," *Boh* 30 (1989): 68.

37. Masaryk said as much in his 1922 New Year's address: see Zeman, *The Masaryks*, 143; Klímek, *Boj o Hrad I*, 177.
38. Klímek, *Boj o Hrad I*, 32.
39. Ibid.
40. Bugge, "Paragon or Parody?" 16.
41. Miller, *Forging Political Compromise*, 112–113, 167.
42. T. G. Masaryk, *Světová revoluce: za války a ve válce, 1914–1918* (Prague: Orbis and Čin, 1925), 543.
43. Klímek, *Boj o Hrad I*, 179.
44. Miller, *Forging Political Compromise*, 282.
45. Zeman, *The Masaryks*, 135.
46. Daniel Miller, *Antonín Švehla and the Czechoslovak Republican Party, 1918–1933* (PhD dissertation, University of Pittsburgh, 1989), 253, discusses Beneš's hope in 1923 for another such cabinet.
47. Klímek, *Boj o Hrad I*, 178, 187.
48. Pecháček, *Masaryk, Beneš, Hrad*, 19.
49. Ibid., 16.
50. Beneš, "Czechoslovak Democracy," 141.
51. Klímek, *Boj o Hrad I*, 174–178.
52. Zbyněk Zeman and Antonin Klímek, *The Life of Edvard Beneš 1884–1948: Czechoslovakia in Peace and War* (Oxford: Oxford University Press, 1997), 96.
53. Bugge, "Paragon or Parody?" 21. Józef Pitsudski similarly distrusted democracy, preferring to govern through his "men of trust": see Timothy Snyder, *Sketches from a Secret War: A Polish Artist's Mission to Liberate Soviet Ukraine* (New Haven: Yale University Press, 2005), 24–25.
54. Klímek, *Boj o Hrad I*, 76–77. In Geneva in 1918, Masaryk had suggested Šámal for minister of the interior; Antonín Švehla, determined to control that crucial position, blocked the nomination. Šámal also served briefly as a National Democratic Parliamentary representative and as mayor of Prague.
55. Ibid., 77. Alain Soubigou, *Tomáš Garrigue Masaryk* (Prague: Paseka, 2004), 253.
56. Klímek, *Boj o Hrad I*, 83. Škrach edited the periodical *Masarykův sborník*. After Masaryk's death, it was Škrach who edited the multivolume collection of Masaryk's writings and speeches titled *Cesta demokracie*.
57. There exists a considerable literature on the Masaryk family. A sampling: Zeman, *The Masaryks*; H. Gordon Skilling, *Mother and Daughter: Charlotte Garrigue Masaryk and Alice Garrigue Masaryk* (Prague: Gender Studies, 2001); Jaroslav Soukup and Dagmara Hájková, eds., *Drahá mama/Dear Alice: Korespondence Alice a Charlotty Masarykových* (Prague: Ústav T.G. Masaryka, 2001). A brief summary of the Masaryk children's political work: Klímek, *Boj o Hrad I*, 175–176.
58. Bouček participated in the Hrad's fearsome intelligence network. He helped compile information about Hrad enemy Radola Gajda in the mid-1920s: MZA-Brno, fond G426 (*Lidové noviny*), osobná korespondence, fascikl 87 Václav Bouček, letter from František Šelepa, October 15, 1926.
59. Klímek, *Boj o Hrad I*, 84.
60. Ibid., 77–78.

61. Ibid., 80. KPR personnel often held ministerial offices in Masaryk's "experts' cabinets." General O. Husák, head of the KPR's military section, served as minister of defense from 1920–1921. In 1926, during the second experts' cabinet, Josef Schieszl served both as minister of health and of social welfare. In neither case did they abandon their KPR positions.
62. Ibid., 78.
63. See SÚA, pozůstalost Schieszlova, Schieszl diary. After the Nazis took the Sudetenland and the Second Republic was established in 1939, Schieszl aryanized the Společenský klub, previously a Castle institution. See Julius Firt, *Knihy a osudy* (Brno: Atlantis, 1972), 327–329.
64. Klímek, *Boj o Hrad I*, 79.
65. Soubigou, *Masaryk*, 279–280.
66. Klímek, *Boj o Hrad I*, 74–75, 77, 81. Jaroslav Pecháček described generous financial gifts Masaryk and Beneš made to the Social Democratic Party and press: Pecháček, *Masaryk, Beneš, Hrad*, 91.
67. Klímek, *Boj o Hrad I*, 82; Bugge, "Paragon or Parody?" 19; Soubigou, *Masaryk*, 259–261.
68. There seem to have been many of these discretionary funds. Some were voted to Masaryk and Beneš by Parliament. Others were evidently gifts to Masaryk and Beneš by grateful Czech émigrés in the United States. See Vojtěch Dolejší, *Noviny a novináři: z poznámek a vzpomínek* (Prague: Nakladatelství politické literatury, 1963), 96; Klímek, *Boj o Hrad I*, 71; Pecháček, *Masaryk, Beneš, Hrad*, 88–91.
69. Bugge, "Paragon or Parody?" 19; Klímek, *Boj o Hrad I*, 82–83.
70. Klímek, *Boj o Hrad I*, 319–320.
71. Ibid., 83.
72. On Zamini generally: Zeman and Klímek, *The Life of Edvard Beneš*. On the Third Section: František Ebel, ed., *Deset let československé republiky*, vol. I (Prague: Státní tiskárna v Praze, 1928), 112–114; Rudolf Urban, *Tajné fondy třeti sekce: z archivu ministerstva zahraniči republiky česko-slovenske* (Prague: Orbis, 1943). Information about internal affairs and decision making in Beneš's ministry is difficult to obtain. In addition to Ebel, *Deset let*, see Rudolf Künzl-Jizerský, *V diplomatických službách ČSR* (Prague: Jos. R. Vilímek, 1947); Jindřich Dejmek, *Nenaplněné naděje: Politické a diplomatické vztahy Československa a Velké Británie od zrodu První republiky po konferenci v Mnichově (1918–1938)* (Prague: Karolinum, 2003); Jindřich Dejmek, "Czechoslovak Foreign Policy and the Search for Security in Central Europe between the World Wars (A Survey of Basic Problems), *Historica* 3–4 (1996–1997): 107–145. Paul E. Zinner's essay "Czechoslovakia: The Diplomacy of Eduard Beneš," in Gordon Craig and Felix Gilbert, eds., *The Diplomats 1919–1939, Volume I: The Twenties* (Princeton, NJ: Princeton University Press, 1953) is also useful.
73. Künzl-Jizerský, *V diplomatických službách ČSR*, 22, 34.
74. Klímek, *Boj o Hrad I*, 70.
75. See Zeman and Klímek, *The Life of Edvard Beneš*, 59–60; Ebel, *Deset let československé republiky*, vol. I, 82–84; Frantisek Kubka, *Mezi válkami: Masaryk a Beneš v mých vzpomínek* (Prague: Nakladatelství Svoboda, 1969), 121–122.
76. Zeman and Klímek, *The Life of Edvard Beneš*, 59.

77. AKPR, T 316/21, document T 382/23, from Odbor zpravodajský Ministerstvo zahraničních veci, March 3, 1923. "Propagační činnost ministerstva zahraničních věci," 1–3.
78. AÚTGM, MAR, dokumentace, kar. 7, Nobelová cena, copy of letter from Ministry of Foreign Affairs, Odbor pro politickou a hospodářskou zpravodajstva (Third Section), č.j. 1251/1/32, message dated February 15, 1921, sent to Vasil K. Škrach. On the various newspapers, see Urban, *Tajné fondy třeti sekce*, 206–207.
79. Künzl-Jizersky, *V diplomatických službách ČSR*, 74. He also writes that Hájek frequently participated in the Czechoslovak delegation to the League of Nations, following specifically the question of national minorities. See ibid., 151.
80. AMZV, Third Section, kar. 257, "Zpravodajská společnost 'Radio de l'Europe Centrale,'" March 1, 1924.
81. AMZV, Third Section, kar. 732, "Poznámky k založení akciové společnosti 'ORBIS' a k vydávání německého deníku 'PRAGER PRESSE,'" 1–2.
82. APNP, fond PEN, undated reports from Zamini's *Denní přehled zahraničního tisku* (contents discuss press reports from September 1932), sent as enclosures in a letter to Edmond Konrad from Leo Singer, Budapest correspondent for the *Prager Tagblatt*, postmarked October 12, 1932.
83. AMZV, Third Section, kar. 732, "Poznámky k založení akciové společnosti 'ORBIS' a k vydávání německého deníku 'PRAGER PRESSE,'" 1.
84. AKPR, T 776/21, "Einige gründsätzliche Bemerkungen über die geplannte Neugrundung einer deutschen Zeitung in Prag," February 8, 1921.
85. Ibid., 5.
86. AKPR, T 776/21, undated *Prager Presse* advertising flyer.
87. Milena Beránková, ed., *Dějiny československé žurnalistiky*, vol. 3 (Prague: Novinář, 1981), 152; and Dolejší, *Noviny a novináři*, 63. Dolejší's grudging praise of the *Prager Presse* is striking; his memoirs otherwise malign the Castle.
88. Urban, *Tajné fondy třeti sekce*, 206.
89. AMZV, Third Section, kar. 902, "K namitkám o zbytečnosti zahraniční služby zpravodajské a propagace," September 1, 1925.
90. "Stat zaměstnavatelem," *Rudé právo*, March 11, 1923.
91. Urban, *Tajné fondy třeti sekce*, 205–207.
92. AÚTGM, MAR, Tisk-novináři, kar. 3, sl. 13, "Orbis," document 473/28 (1928).
93. By 1932, the Third Section's propaganda newspapers were losing collectively at least one million crowns yearly. See AMZV, Third Section, FIRMY, Orbis, kar. 263, 28. listopadu 1932, addressed to Pan min rada Ing. Vodsedalek, Zamini.
94. AMZV, Third Section, FIRMY, Orbis, kar. 251, letter 3 února 1931.
95. AMZV, Third Section, kar. 902, "Zpráva o propagáční činnosti ministerstva zahraničních věci," October 22, 1926, 1–2.
96. Ibid.
97. Urban, *Tajné fondy třeti sekce*, 19. Also see AKPR, T 316/21, document T 382/23 (copy of document from Odbor zpravodajský, Ministerstvo zahraničních věci, March 3, 1923), "Propagáční činnosti ministerstva zahraničních věci," 1–3.
98. Künzl-Jizerský, *V diplomatických službách ČSR*, 97.

99. AKPR, T 316/21, document T 382/23 (copy of document from Odbor zpravodajský, Ministerstvo zahraničních věci, March 3, 1923), "Propagáční činnosti ministerstva zahraničních věci," 1–3.
100. AMZV, Third Section, kar. 876 (Společenský klub), doc. 82335, April 11 or 21, 1925 (typography unclear), 2.
101. The best brief overview of the interwar Czechoslovak press (including non-Czech-language outlets) is now Zdeněk Kárník, *České země v eře první republiky*, vol. 1 (Prague: Libri, 2000), 326–341. Also: F. Gregory Campbell, "The Interwar Czech Press," presented at conference, The Role and Functions of the Media in Eastern Europe: Perspectives Over Time, Bloomington, IN, November 9–11, 1983 (I thank Owen Johnson for this source); Dolejší, *Noviny a novináři*; Andrea Orzoff, "'The Literary Organ of Politics': Tomáš Masaryk and Political Journalism, 1925–1929," *Slavic Review* 63, no. 2 (2004): 275–300.
102. On Czechoslovakia's gutter press, see Owen Johnson, "Unbridled Freedom: The Czech Press and Politics, 1918–1938," *Journalism History* 13, no. 3–4: 96–103. On artistic and scholarly journals, see the work of Jindřich Toman, inter alia "Karel Čapek and/vs. the Prague Linguistic Circle," in Mackie, McAuley, and Simmons, eds., *For Henry Kucera: Studies in Slavic Philology and Computational Linguistics* (Ann Arbor, MI: Michigan Slavic Publications, 1992): 365–380.
103. Beránková, *Dějiny československé žurnalistiky*, vol. 3, 58.
104. Jan Nahlovský, "Časopisy v československé republice," *Československý statistický vestník* 4 (Feb. 1932): 4–7, cited in Johnson, "Unbridled Freedom," 98.
105. Firt, "Die 'Burg' und die Zeitschrift *Přítomnost*," in Bosl, ed., *Die Burg*, vol. II, 111. Also see Campbell, "Interwar Czech Press," 6ff.
106. To offer an example, the National Democratic Party published the following papers: the dailies *Národní listy*, *Národ*, and *Role* in Prague; *Český deník* in Plzeň (this paper was associated with the Škoda works); *Moravskoslezský deník* in Ostrava; *Pozor* in Olomouc; *Národní noviny* in Brno; *Obzor* in Přerov; the magazines *Ženský svět, Mladý národ, Národní student, Národní učitel*, and *Česká revue*, among others. On the National Democratic press: Beránková, *Dějiny československé žurnalistiky*, vol. 3, 170ff.
107. Miller, *Forging Political Compromise*, 91–92.
108. František Helešic, "Komunističtí novináři 1921–1938: Příspěvek k formování 'revolučních elit,'" in Ivana Koutská and František Svátek, eds., *Politické elity v Československu 1918–1948* (*Sešity Ústavu pro soudobé dějiny*, vol. 20) (Prague: Ústav pro soudobé dějiny AV ČR, 1994): 194–232.
109. Johnson, "Unbridled Freedom," 98.
110. The Czechoslovak Hungarian press, consisting predominantly of "independent" newspapers, differed from the other ethnic partisan presses. On the German press, see Norbert Linz, "Der Aufbau der deutschen politischen Presse in der Ersten Tschechoslowakischen Republik (1918–1925)," *Boh* 11 (1970): 284–307.
111. Beránková, *Dějiny československé žurnalistiky*, vol. 3, 56 n. 46. The other three important independent newspapers were *Národní osvobození* (Legionary, progressive), *Tribuna* (financial/commercial, centrist), and *Národní politika* (conservative).

112. The memoirs of František Kubka are fascinating sources regarding Prague elite social life, though they should be read carefully: Kubka, *Na vlastní oči: pravdivé malé povídky o mých současnících* (Prague: Československý spisovatel, 1959); Kubka, *Mezi válkami: Masaryk a Beneš v mých vzpomínek* (Prague: Nakladatelství Svoboda, 1969).
113. Beránková, *Dějiny československé žurnalistiky*, vol. 3, 57.
114. Typewritten copy of a letter to Masaryk by the editors of *Tribuna*, August 25, 1926: AKPR, sign. T45/24, document 929/26 (also in AÚTGM, MAR, Tisk-propaganda, kar. 2, sl. 5—Tisk 1923–1932).
115. Kubka, *Na vlastní oči*, 99–101.
116. See MZA, fond G426, (for example) fascikl 40 (K. Z. Klíma) and karton 86 (Eduard Bass). Even such mandarins as Ferdinand Peroutka, Bass, and Klíma were deeply indebted, constantly drawing advances on their pay: Bass was at least once forced to go to trial over unpaid debt.
117. MZA, fond G426, fascikl 39, "Ferdinand Peroutka" contains various bills from van der Rohe's studio sent to Peroutka's office. Also Slávka Peroutková, "Slávka Peroutková," in Ferdinand Peroutka, *Deníky, dopisy, vzpomínky* (Prague: Lidové noviny, 1995), 250.
118. Orzoff, "The Literary Organ of Politics," passim.
119. Campbell, "The Interwar Czech Press," 1–4.
120. Jiří Pernes, *Svět lidových novin 1893–1993: stoletá kapitola z dějin české žurnalistiky, kultury a politiky* (Prague: *Lidové noviny*, 1993), 5.
121. Josef Vyskočil, "Die Tschechische-Juedische Bewegung," *Judaica Bohemiae* 3 (1967): 42; Pernes, *Svět lidových novin*, 7.
122. See Beránková, *Dějiny československé žurnalistiky*, vol. 3, 55, 176.
123. Pernes, *Svět lidových novin*, 27–28, 61. Among the paper's literary luminaries were Stanislav K. Neumann, Viktor Dyk, Antonín Sova, Leoš Janáček, Marie Majerová, the brothers Čapek, Arne Novák, Otokar Fischer, and Bohumil Markalous.
124. Ibid., 56–58.
125. Jiří Opelík, ed., *Karel Čapek ve fotografii* (Prague: Středočeské nakladatelství a knihupectví, 1991), v–xvi; William E. Harkins, "Karel Čapek: From Relativism to Perspectivism," *The History of Ideas Newsletter* 3, no. 3 (1957): 50–53; William E. Harkins, *Pragmatism and the Czech "Pragmatist Generation"* (Gravenhage: self-published, 1958).
126. Miroslav Halík and Jiří Opelík, *Karel Čapek: Život a dílo v datech* (Prague: Academia, 1983), 34.
127. Edmond Konrád, "Karel Čapek novinář," in *Nač vzpomenu* (Prague: Československý spisovatel, 1957), 186–188. Quotation: Kubka, *Na vlastní oči*, 125.
128. Pernes, *Svět lidových novin*, 67. William Harkins considered both novels *romans feuilletons*, a pastiche genre combining various different kinds of writing, such as newspaper articles, memoirs, scholarly works, even manifestoes. "The compositional character is that of journalism; there is no hero, and characters enter or leave the novel in so far as they are 'newsworthy.'" Harkins, *Karel Čapek* (New York: Columbia University Press, 1962), 130.

129. The interwar republic retained a considerable body of Austrian (and in Slovakia, Hungarian) law governing creative production, censorship, and intellectual property until the early 1930s. For more information about the 1924 and 1933 libel and slander laws, see Beránková, *Dějiny československé žurnalistiky*, vol. 3, 79ff.
130. Karel Čapek, "Jak se dělají noviny," in Čapek, *Jak se co dělá* (Prague: Nadas, 1992): 11–12.
131. Ibid., 12–13.
132. Pernes, *Svět lidových novin*, 57.
133. Ibid. But Borový also published the avant-garde as well as literary nationalists: see Zdeněk Kárník, *Česke země v eře první republiky (1918–1938)*, vol. 3 (*O přežití a o život, 1936–1938*) (Prague: Libri, 2003), 288.
134. On the Castle's tendency to meddle in the press, see Orzoff, "The Literary Organ of Politics."
135. F. Gregory Campbell, "The Castle, Jaroslav Preiss, and the Živnostenská Bank," *Boh* 15 (1974): 231–253; Alena Gajanová, *Dvojí tvář: Z historie předmnichovského fašismu* (Prague: Naše vojsko, 1962); David Kelly, *The Czech Fascist Movement, 1922–1942* (Boulder, CO: East European Monographs, 1993); Klímek, *Boj o Hrad I* and *II*; Pavel Kosatík, *Bankér První Republiky: Život Dr. Jaroslav Preisse* (Prague: Motto, 1996). The Castle's dependence on Preiss was long exaggerated by Communist historians trying to dismiss the interwar republic as the plaything of powerful financiers.
136. Igor Lukes describes Preiss as one of Beneš's informants in the 1937 Tukachevsky affair, for example: *Czechoslovakia between Stalin and Hitler: The Diplomacy of Edvard Beneš in the 1930s* (New York: Oxford University Press, 1996), 100.
137. Klímek, *Boj o Hrad I*, 173. The Castle helped found the Anglobánka: see Mark Cornwall, "A Fluctating Barometer: British Diplomatic Views of the Czech-German Relationship in Czechoslovakia, 1918–1938," in Eva Schmidt-Hartmann and Stanley Winters, eds., *Großbritannien, die USA und die böhmischen Länder 1848–1938* (Munich: R. Oldenbourg Verlag, 1991).
138. On Sokol: Mark Dimond, "The Sokol and Czech Nationalism, 1918–1948," in Mark Cornwall and R. J. W. Evans, eds., *Czechoslovakia in a Nationalist and Fascist Europe* (Oxford: Oxford University Press, 2007): 185–205; Claire E. Nolte, *The Sokol in the Czech Lands to 1914: Training for the Nation* (New York: Palgrave Macmillan, 2002).
139. Masaryk's comments on Jews, Judaism, and antisemitism: AÚTGM, MA, kar. 47-III-6, diář V. Kučery. On Czech Jews: Hillel Kieval, *The Making of Czech Jewry: National Conflict and Jewish Society in Bohemia, 1870–1918* (New York: Oxford University Press, 1988); Hillel Kieval, *Languages of Community: The Jewish Experience in the Czech Lands* (Berkeley: University of California Press, 2000), 181–197, 204–205; Roman Szporluk, *The Political Thought of Thomas G. Masaryk* (New York: East European Monographs, 1981), 118–119.
140. Kieval, *Languages of Community*, 213.
141. Ibid., 204–205.
142. See the case of the journal *Tribuna* in Orzoff, "The Literary Organ of Politics."

143. Livia Rothkirchen, "Czechoslovak Jewry: Growth and Decline (1918–1939)," in Natalia Berger, ed., *Where Cultures Meet: The Story of the Jews of Czechoslovakia* (Tel Aviv, 1990), 107, 109; Josef Vyskočil, "Die Tschechisch-Juedische Bewegung," *Judaica Bohemiae* 3 (1967): 36–55. Also see AKPR, Holdy, for example AKPR H 8556/30; Jews wrote in disproportionate numbers to the KPR each year to congratulate the president for his birthday and on October 28.
144. Melissa Feinberg, *Elusive Equality: Gender, Citizenship, and the Limits of Democracy in Czechoslovakia, 1918–1950* (Pittsburgh, PA: University of Pittsburgh Press, 2006), 14.
145. Ibid., 18–20.
146. Ibid., 35.
147. See ibid., passim.
148. Inter alia see Manfred Alexander, "Die Rolle der Legionäre in der Ersten Republik: Ein politischer Verband und sein Geschichtsbild," in Michael Neumüller, *Vereinswesen und Geschichtspflege in den bohmischen Landern* (Munich: R. Oldenbourg Verlag 1986): 265–279; Gerburg Thunig-Nittner, *Die tschechoslowakische Legion in Russland. Ihre Geschichte und ihre Bedeutung bei der Entstehung der ersten Tschechoslowakischen Republik* (Wiesbaden: Harrasowitz, 1970); Karel Pichlík, Bohumír Klípa, and Jitka Zabloudilová, *Českoslovenšti legionáři 1914–1920* (Prague: Mlada Fronta, 1996).
149. Alexander, "Die Rolle der Legionäre in der Ersten Republik," 270.
150. Pichlík et al., *Českoslovenšti legionáři*, 254.
151. Wingfield, *Flag Wars and Stone Saints*, 183–187.
152. Soubigou, *Masaryk*, 293–294.
153. Alexander, "Die Rolle der Legionäre in der Ersten Republik," 273. Borský and Pergler later turned against the Castle: see Petr Pithart, "První republika: jak ji viděla opozice," *Svědectví* 18 (1983): 271–314.
154. Pichlík et al., *Českoslovenšti legionáři*, 254. Not all these newly created small farmers did well; the loan programs ended too early for some of the Legionnaires returning from abroad, who therefore received inadequate land allotments and no loan support. Many of these Legionnaire small farmers went bankrupt. Ibid., 259, 261.
155. Ibid., 263; Katya A.M. Kocourek, "'In the Spirit of Brotherhood, United We Remain!' Czechoslovak Nationalism and Czechoslovak Legionary Traditions in the 1920s," unpublished paper, 2–3. My thanks to Katya Kocourek for permission to cite her work.
156. Alexander, "Die Rolle der Legionäre in der Ersten Republik," 270.
157. Pichlík et al., *Českoslovenšti legionáři*, 262. On Legionnaire literature, see Robert Pynsent, "The Literary Representation of the Czechoslovak 'Legions' in Russia," in Mark Cornwall and R. J. W. Evans, eds., *Czechoslovakia in a Nationalist and Fascist Europe 1918–1948* (Oxford: Oxford University Press, 2007), 63–88.
158. Lev Borský, *Znovudobytí samostatnosti (První diplomatický zástupce čs. v Římě)* (Prague: Otto, 1929), cited in Alexander, "Die Rolle der Legionäre in der Ersten Republik," 273–275.

159. Wingfield, *Flag Wars and Stone Saints*, 186–187; see also Nancy Meriwether Wingfield, "The Battle of Zborov and the Politics of Commemoration in Czechoslovakia," *EEPS* 17, no. 4 (2003): 654–681.
160. Wingfield, *Flag Wars and Stone Saints*, 190–192.
161. Thomas Ort, "Men without Qualities: The Čapek Generation, 1909–1938" (PhD dissertation, New York University, 2005); Petr Pithart, "Čapkovská generace—liberalismus příliš civilní?" in Milan Znoj, Jan Havránek, and Martin Sekera, eds., *Český liberalismus: texty a osobnosti* (Prague: Torst, 1995). Čapek still awaits his biographer. The best in English is Harkins, *Karel Čapek*; in Czech, though somewhat worshipful, Ivan Pfaff, *O perspektivu lidského společenství: politické myšlení Karla Čapka* (Prague: Artforum, 1994); also useful is Ivan Klíma, *Velký věk chce mít též velké mordy: život a dílo Karla Čapka* (Prague: Academia, 2001).
162. František Götz, "Tak zvaná generace Čapkovská," *Přítomnost* (1931): 698–701, 712–715, 726–728 (quotations from 701, 728).
163. Ferdinand Peroutka, "Masaryk a mladší generace," *Přítomnost*, August 14, 1924.
164. Karel Scheinpflug, *Můj švagr Karel Čapek* (Hradec Králové: Kruh, 1991), 58.
165. Kubka, *Na vlastni oči*, 119.
166. Peroutka, *Deníky, dopisy a vzpomínky*, 133–134.
167. Hoffmeister, "Pátečníci," *Přítomnost*, February 24, 1927, cited in Václav Kapoun, *Silvestrovská aféra Karla Čapka* (Prague: Melantrich, 1992), 17–20.
168. Ibid., 51; Peroutka, *Deníky, dopisy a vzpomínky*, 134.
169. Vočadlo, *Anglické listy Karla Čapka*, 15.
170. Ibid., 14.
171. See Klíma, *Karel Čapek*, 80–81. On Friday Men writing for the Prague Linguistic Circle's journal, see, for example, František Travníček, "Slovo a slovesnost," *Lidové noviny*, February 16, 1935, in which the author mentions that the newest Prague Linguistic Circle journal contained contributions by Čapek as well as Vladislav Vančura. They and occasional Friday visitor Vitězslav Nezval also contributed to the 1936 journal.
172. Peroutka, *Deníky, dopisy a vzpomínky*, 134.
173. Klímek, *Boj o Hrad I*, 73–74. It was at this point that the president's political enemies publicized the Fridays, trying to brand them as a Castle cabal. See, for example, Václav Kapoun, *Silvestrovská aféra Karla Čapka* (Prague: Melantrich, 1992).
174. Peroutka, *Deníky, dopisy a vzpomínky*, 134.
175. Anna Horakova-Gasparikova, *Z lánského deníku, 1929–1937* (Prague: Český Rozhlas Radioservis, 1997), 145.
176. Kubka, *Mezi válkami*, 49.
177. Ibid.
178. Kubka, *Mezi válkami*, 52.
179. AÚTGM, MA-KOR, II-56-Čapek, March 23, 1926.
180. Kubka, *Na vlastní oči*, 122.
181. Antonín Klímek, *Velké dějiny zemí koruny České*, vol. XIII (1918–1929) (Prague, Litomyšl: Paseka, 2000), 583–592. For an example of anti-German popular sentiment, see Catherine Albrecht, "Economic Nationalism in the Sudetenland,

1918–1938," in Cornwall and Evans, eds., *Czechoslovakia in a Nationalist and Fascist Europe*, 89–108.

182. Kárník, *České země eře první republiky* vol. 1, 413.
183. See chapter 5; Edmond Konrád, "Politická historie Penklubu," *Přítomnost* (1937): 392–395, mentions that Masaryk founded P.E.N.'s Hungarian subsection; Urban, *Tajné fondy třetí sekce*, 26–27, 30–31, 227–228.
184. Soubigou, *Masaryk*, 262.
185. Kárník, *České země eře první republiky*, vol. 1, 415; on the NLP, see Orzoff, "Battle for the Castle" (PhD dissertation, Stanford University, 2000).
186. James Felak, *"At the Price of the Republic": Hlinka's Slovak People's Party, 1929–1938* (Pittsburgh, PA: University of Pittsburgh Press, 1994), 40–41, 153.
187. On this "Tateleben" controversy, see parliamentary protocols, July 10, 1925, http://www.psp.cz/eknih/1920ns/ps/stenprot/357schuz/s357003.htm, pp. 1–4 (accessed October 7, 2007), as well as *Slovák*, April 2, 1924 and March 9, 1926. I thank James Ward for these references.
188. Mark Cornwall, "'National Reparation'?: The Czech Land Reform and the Sudeten Germans," *Slavonic and East European Review* 75, no. 2 (1997): 259–280; Daniel E. Miller, "Colonizing the Hungarian and German Border Areas during the Czechoslovak Land Reform, 1918–1938," *AHY* 34 (2003): 303–317.
189. Cornwall, "'National Reparation'?" 280.
190. Wingfield, *Flag Wars and Stone Saints*; the work of Mark Cornwall; Marie L. Neudorflová, ed., *Češi a Němci v pojetí a politice T.G. Masaryka: sborník příspěvků z mezinárodní konference* (Prague: Masarykův ústav AV ČR, 2004); Eagle Glassheim, *Noble Nationalists: The Transformation of the Bohemian Aristocracy* (Cambridge, MA: Harvard University Press, 2005).
191. Peroutka, *Deníky, dopisy, vzpomínky*, 149.
192. Bugge, "Paragon or Parody?" 13.

Chapter 3

1. George Kennan, *From Prague after Munich: Diplomatic Papers 1938–1940* (Princeton, NJ: Princeton University Press, 1968), 99.
2. Jaroslav Pecháček, ed., *Masaryk, Beneš, Hrad: Masarykovy dopisy Benešovi* (Prague: Faun, 1996), 41.
3. Peter Bugge, "Czech Democracy 1918–1938: Paragon or Parody?" *Boh* 47, no. 1 (2006–2007): 17.
4. Tomáš Dvořák, "Národní strána práce (1925–1930)/I. část/," *Střední evropa* 76 (1998): 122.
5. Ferdinand Peroutka, *Deníky, dopisy, a vzpomínky* (Prague: Lidové noviny, 1995), 99–100, 142ff.; Julius Firt, *Knihy a osudy* (Brno: Atlantis, 1972), 57–58, 77ff.
6. SÚA PMV (Presidium ministerstva vnitra) 1925–, sign. Xn/5/3, kar. 518, sl. 8. "Leták nové politické strány NSP," August 25, 1925.
7. Cited in Antonín Klímek, *Boj o Hrad I: Hrad a Pětka, 1918–1926* (Prague: Panevropa, 1996), 346. On the NLP's trajectory, see Andrea Orzoff, "Battle for

the Castle: The Friday Men and the Czechoslovak Republic, 1918–1938" (PhD dissertation, Stanford University, 2000), chapter 3.

8. Dvořák, "Národní strána práce (1925–1930)/II. části/" *Střední evropa* 77 (1998): 125.
9. "Programové prohlášení Nár. strany práce," *Přítomnost*, April 17, 1925.
10. Dvořák, "Národní strána práce (1925–1930)/II. části/," 126–127; Martin Čank, "Jaroslav Stránský: právník, žurnalista, politik" (diplomová práce, Filosofická fakulta University Palackého v Olomouci, 1993), 38.
11. Victor Mamatey, "The Development of Czech Democracy, 1920–1938," in Mamatey and Radomir Luža, eds., *A History of the Czechoslovak Republic 1918–1948* (Princeton, NJ: Princeton University Press, 1973), 129.
12. Petr Hofman and Antonín Klímek, *Vitěz, který prohral: generál Radola Gajda* (Prague: Paseka, 1995), 65.
13. Dvořák, "Národní strána práce (1925–1930)/III., zaverečná části/," *Střední evropa* 78 (1998): 119.
14. Hofman and Klímek, *Vitěz, který prohral*, 66–67.
15. Tomáš Pasák, *Český fašismus 1922–1945 a kolaborace 1939–1945* (Prague: Práh, 1999), 62–65.
16. Ibid., 67–68; David Kelly, *The Czech Fascist Movement 1922–1942* (Boulder, CO: East European Monographs, 1995), 53–54.
17. Hofman and Klímek, *Vitěz, který prohral*, 68. Historians have depicted the movement as far weaker. David Kelly has noted that Brno, then a city of 220,000, contained only some 1,200 NOF members. Cited in Kelly, *The Czech Fascist Movement*, 74.
18. Kelly, *The Czech Fascist Movement*, 75–77.
19. On Gajda: Pasák, *Český fašismus*, 75–82; Hofman and Klímek, *Vitěz, který prohral*; Kelly, *The Czech Fascist Movement*; Antonín Klímek, *Velké dějiny zemí koruny České*, vol. 13 (1918–1929) (Prague, Litomyšl: Paseka, 2000), 553–562, 576–580; Ivan Šedivý, "Gajdova aféra 1926–1928," *Český časopis historický* 92 (1994): 732–758; Jonathan Zorach, "The Enigma of the Gajda Affair in Czechoslovak Politics in 1926," *Slavic Review* 35 (December 1976): 683–698.
20. Antonín Klímek, *Boj o Hrad II: Kdo po Masarykovi? 1926–1935* (Prague: Paseka, 1998), 154.
21. Pasák, *Český fašismus, 70.*
22. AKPR, sign. D 15347/47/Db, čislo jednotka D 16267/46, kar. 310, documents D1502/26, also D1671/26. The Friday Men spent May 15–16, 1926, with the president. Dr. Jaroslav Adlof, the Čapek brothers, Kodíček, Kopta, Kubka, Langer, Přikryl, Poláček, Šrámek, and Vančura attended.
23. Frantisek Kubka, *Mezi válkami: Masaryk a Beneš v mých vzpomínek* (Prague: Nakladatelství Svoboda, 1969), 61–62.
24. Dvořák, "Národní strána práce/II. části," 125. Citation from Kopta, *Národní osvobození*, January 13, 1939.
25. Kubka, *Mezi válkami*, 64.
26. Kelly, *The Czech Fascist Movement*, 55.
27. Ibid., 55–56. The historiography suggests that, as a student at the War College, Gajda would hardly have had any access to secret French documents of

any kind and that Gajda, a Pan-Slav with vehement anti-Bolshevik convictions, would have been unwilling to work for the Bolshevik government. Most historians conclude that Gajda was innocent of all the charges against him save consorting with the fascists and breaking military rules against political engagement.

28. Pasák, *Český fašismus*, 78.
29. Kramář, "Moje odpověd," *Národní listy*, September 10, 1926. Cited in Jiří Brabec et al., eds., *T.G. Masaryk, Cesta demokracie III: Projevy, články, rozhovory 1924–1928* (Prague: Ústav T.G. Masaryka, 1994), 162.
30. Dvořák, "Národní strána práce/III. části," 120.
31. SÚA, PMV, 1925–, Xn 5/3, document 518/6.
32. Dvořák, "Národní strána práce/III. části," 121.
33. Hofman and Klímek, *Vitěz, který prohral*, 177.
34. AÚTGM, CD 28, letter to Čapek from Masaryk, August 29, 1926.
35. Klímek, *Boj o Hrad I*, 371.
36. AÚTGM, MA, KOR, II-56-Čapek, August 27, 1926.
37. For example, in late 1926, *Národní listy* referred to the actions of the "levý kartel" in an article defending Gajda: see AKPR, T 31/25, untitled clipping from December 28, 1926.
38. AÚTGM, MA, KOR, II-56-Čapek, letter from Čapek to Masaryk, October 20, 1926.
39. SÚA, PMV, 1925–, Xn 5/3, 518/8. Report from meeting in Bystřice pod Host, May 25, 1927.
40. Vojtech Dolejší, *Noviny a novináři: z poznámek a vzpomínek* (Prague: Nakladatelství politické literatury, 1963).
41. AÚTGM, MA, KOR II, 56- Čapek. September 8, 1926.
42. Jindřiška Smetanová, *TGM: "Proč se neřekne pravda?" Ze vzpomínek dr. Antonína Schenka* (Prague: Primus, 1996), 118ff.
43. Pecháček, *Masaryk, Beneš, Hrad*, 59–62.
44. F. Gregory Campbell, "The Castle, Jaroslav Preiss, and the Živnostenská Bank," *Boh* 15 (1974): 235.
45. For brief statements of Kramář's position, see Stanley Winters, "Passionate Patriots: Czechoslovak National Democracy in the 1920s," *East-Central Europe/L'Europe du Centre-Est* 18, no. 1 (1991): 55–60; Lee Blackwood, "Czech and Polish National Democracy at the Dawn of Independent Statehood, 1918–1919," *EEPS* 4, no. 3 (1990): 477–479, 481–482, 487–488; also see Martina Winkler, *Karel Kramář (1860–1937): Selbstbild, Fremdwahrnehmungen und Modernisierungsverständnis eines tschechischen Politikers* (Munich: R. Oldenbourg Verlag, 2002).
46. Other politicians also made this charge. See Ferdinand Peroutka, *Budování státu: Československá politika v letech popřevatových*, vol. 2 (Prague: *Lidové noviny*, 1991), 843–844.
47. Manfred Alexander, "Die Rolle der Legionäre in der ersten Republik: Ein politischer Verband und sein Geschichtsbild," in Michael Neumüller, ed., *Vereinswesen und Geschichtspflege in den Böhmischen Ländern* (Munich: R. Oldenbourg Verlag,

1986), 276–277. On Fronta, see also Petr Pithart, "První republika: jak ji viděla opozice," *Svědectví* 18 (1983): 271–314.

48. Karel Kramář, *Pět přednášek o zahraniční politika* (Prague: Pražské akciové tiskána, 1922).
49. Dvořák, "Národní strána práce (1925–1930)/I. část/," 126.
50. Kelly, *The Czech Fascist Movement*, 22.
51. AKPR, T 12/24; AÚTGM, MAR, Tisk-propaganda, kar. 2, složky 10, 11, "1927"; AÚTGM, MAR, Dokumentace, kar. 9, sl. 56.
52. AKPR, sign. 12/24, "28. říjen," July 27, 1924.
53. "Protilegionářská zed' národní demokracie zříceninou," *Národní osvobozeni*, July 13, 1924; reprinted in Brabec et al., eds., *T.G. Masaryk, Cesta demokracie III*, 57–62.
54. AKPR, sign. 12/24, "Doslov k diskussi o 28. říjen," November 4, 1924.
55. Kelly, *The Czech Fascist Movement*, 22.
56. AKPR, sign. T 12/24, document T698/25, Lány, May 22, 1925.
57. Ibid.
58. Bruce Garver, *The Young Czech Party, 1874–1901, and the Emergence of a Multi-Party System* (New Haven, CT: Yale University Press, 1978), 213–214.
59. Pecháček, *Masaryk, Beneš, Hrad*, 19.
60. Viktor Dyk, *Ad usum pana presidenta republiky*, 2nd printing (Prague: Zemědelské knihupectví A. Neubert, 1929), 8.
61. Ibid., 97.
62. Pecháček, *Masaryk, Beneš, Hrad*, 29.
63. AKPR, sign. T 804/29, doc. T 804/29 (Záznam, July 5, 1929).
64. AÚTGM, MAR, Kultura, kar. 2, sl. 19. Letter from Čapek to Masaryk, June 17, 1929. Also see Čapek, *Korespondence I* (Prague: Český spisovatel, 1993), 69–70.
65. AÚTGM, MAR, Kultura, kar. 2, sl. 19. Also see Masaryk's letter to Dyk, June 6, 1929, reprinted in Pecháček, *Masaryk, Beneš, Hrad*, 23, 25.
66. Ibid.
67. Ibid., 25.
68. Ibid., 26.
69. Ibid., 27.
70. Ibid., 28.
71. AÚTGM, MAR, Kultura, kar. 2, sl. 19. Copy of letter from Dyk to Masaryk, July 26, 1929.
72. AÚTGM, MA, Dokumentace 7, sv. 9. Masaryk's response to Dyk, August 12, 1929.
73. Ibid.
74. AÚTGM, MAR, Kultura, kar. 2, sl. 19. Copy of letter from Dyk to Masaryk, July 26, 1929.
75. AÚTGM, MA, Dokumentace 7, sv. 9. Masaryk's response to Dyk, August 12, 1929.
76. AÚTGM, MAR, Kultura, kar. 2, sl. 19. Copy of letter from Dyk to Masaryk, July 26, 1929.
77. Alain Soubigou, *Tomáš Garrigue Masaryk* (Prague, Litomyšl: Paseka, 2004), 296.
78. Mamatey, "The Development of Czech Democracy, 1920–1938," 108, 110. The most recent Stříbrný biography: Libor Vykoupil, *Jiří Stříbrný: Portrét politika* (Brno: Masaryková univerzita and Matice moravská, 2003).

79. Kelly, *The Czech Fascist Movement*, 20–21. Zdeňek Kárník argues that Stříbrný's involvement in the Marmaggi Affair, in which the papal nuncio left Prague to protest a state holiday honoring medieval proto-Protestant Jan Hus, forced Stříbrný to resign from government. See Kárník, *České země v eře prnví republiky (1918–1938): Vzník, budování a zlatá leta republiky (1918–1929)*, vol. 1 (Prague: Libri, 2000), 392.
80. Peroutka, in *Budování státu*, argued that Beneš followed the government coalition's instructions to join a major party. Others have claimed that Beneš sought power, and decided on the National Socialists because Klofáč was willing to allow Beneš to enter as a leading member (rather than as a rank-and-file newcomer).
81. Kárník, *České země v eře prnví republiky*, vol. 1, 392.
82. Klímek, *Velké dějiny zemí koruny České*, 562–575.
83. Hofman and Klímek, *Vitěz, který prohral*, 66–67.
84. Klímek, *Boj o Hrad I*, 371.
85. Pasák, *Český fašismus*, 77.
86. Mamatey, "The Development of Czech Democracy, 1920–1938," 132.
87. Pasák, *Český fašismus*, 80.
88. Kelly, *The Czech Fascist Movement*, 25.
89. Bruce Garver, "Václav Klofáč and the Czechoslovak National Socialist Party," in John Morison, ed., *The Czech and Slovak Experience* (Houndmills, Basingstoke: St. Martin's Press, 1992), 106.
90. Klímek, *Boj o Hrad I*, 323.
91. MZA-Brno, fond G426 "Lidové noviny," fascikl 100, Stříbrný contra Stránský. Hlavní přelíčení, January 12, 1927.
92. Ibid.
93. Ibid.
94. Ibid.
95. MZA-Brno, fond G426 "Lidové noviny," fascikl 100, Stříbrný contra Stránský. Document Zm II 162/29, February 8, 1929.
96. Pasák, *Český fašismus*, 81–82.
97. Kelly, *The Czech Fascist Movement*, 72; it was later dubbed the Slav National Socialists, as in Kárník, *České země v eře prnví republiky*, 394.
98. Pasák, *Český fašismus*, 94–95.
99. Mamatey, "The Development of Czech Democracy, 1920–1938," 145.
100. Klímek, *Boj o Hrad II*, 275–285.
101. Stříbrný, *TGM a 28. Říjen* (Prague: Tempo, 1938). Stříbrný abandoned politics after the interwar years, spending the Second World War quietly in his villa in the small Czech town of Káraný. He was caught up in the Communist postwar purge trials and died in jail in 1955.
102. AKPR T 879/27 (27. září 1927).
103. Pecháček, *Masaryk, Beneš, Hrad*, 67.
104. Ibid., 73. Pecháček thinks this point refers to a Brno dermatologist who examined Jiří Stříbrný; I disagree.
105. Vít Vlnas, "Myty a kyče první republiky," *Nová Přítomnost* 8 (1991): 28–29; Robert Pynsent, *Questions of Identity: Czech and Slovak Ideas of Nationality and Personality* (London: Central European University Press, 1994), 193ff.

106. William Bascom, "The Forms of Folklore: Prose Narratives," in Alan Dundes, ed., *Sacred Narrative: Readings in the Theory of Myth* (Berkeley, CA: University of California Press, 1984), 9–10.
107. Joseph Campbell with Bill Moyers, *The Power of Myth* (New York: Doubleday, 1988), 30.
108. On the Lenin cult, see Tumarkin and Benno Ennker, *Die Anfänge des Leninkults in der Sowjetunion* (Cologne: Böhlau, 1997). For some of the most recent work on the Stalin cult, see Bálazs Apor, Jan C. Behrends, Polly Jones, and E. A. Rees, eds., *The Leader Cult in Communist Dictatorships: Stalin and the Eastern Bloc* (Houndmills, Basingstoke: Palgrave Macmillan, 2004).
109. As set out by Heidi Hein-Kircher and Benno Ennker at Der Führer im Europa des. 20. Jahrhunderts, October 2007, Marburg, Germany.
110. E. A. Rees offers a concise presentation of the theory regarding modern leader cults. See Rees, "Leader Cults: Varieties, Preconditions and Functions," in Apor et al., *The Leader Cult in Communist Dictatorships,* 3–26.
111. Zbyněk Zeman, *The Masaryks: The Making of Czechoslovakia* (New York: Barnes and Noble, 1976), 139.
112. On Habsburg imperial myth: Daniel L. Unowsky, *The Pomp and Politics of Patriotism: Imperial Celebrations in Habsburg Austria, 1848–1916* (West Lafayette, IN: Purdue University Press, 2005), 25; Veronika Sušová, "Integrační role rakouského císaře v rakouské státní propagandě 19. století," *Dějiny a současnost* 5 (2004): 15–19; Peter Urbanitsch, "Pluralist Myth and Nationalist Realities: The Dynastic Myth of the Habsburg Monarchy—A Futile Exercise in the Creation of Identity?" *AHY* 35 (2004): 101–152. On Masaryk, see Klímek, *Boj o Hrad I*, 84; also see, for example, Karel Čapek, *President Masaryk Tells His Story* (New York: Arno Press, 1971; reprint of 1935 edition by G.P. Putnam's Sons), 286–289.
113. For examples, see *Kaiser Franz Josef I. und seine Zeit: Porträts und historische Blätter: Kaiser Franz Joseph; Kaiserin Elisabeth; die kais. Familie; Staatsmänner und Feldherren. Zum 60 jähr. Regierungsjubiläum S.M. des Kaisers herausgegeben.* (Vienna: Gilhofer und Ranschburg, 1908) and Karel Čapek, *Masaryk ve fotografii* (Prague: Čin, 1931).
114. Zeman, *The Masaryks*, 121.
115. Peroutka, *Budování státu I (1918–1919)* (Prague: Lidové noviny, 1991), 301.
116. Klímek, *Boj o Hrad I*, 74–75; Soubigou, *Masaryk*, 247–249.
117. "Kronika pestrá," in Karel Čapek, *Hovory s T.G. Masarykem* (Prague: Československý spisovatel, 1990), 369.
118. Jan Rokyta, *President Masaryk. Baseň k jeho sedmdesatým narozeninám* (Prague: Naklad "Kostnických Jisker," 1920), (unnumbered pages: 11th stanza). Like much of this material, this pamphlet was sold very cheaply: the price was 30 halérů, with 100 halérů to the crown.
119. AKPR H 189/26, Václav Němec, "Našemu milému presidentovi," 1926.
120. František Kubka, "Roku 2000 na Hradě pražském," *Národní osvobození.* March 7, 1930, cited in Vlnas, "Myty a kyče," 29.
121. On Kramář, the best source is now Winkler, *Karel Kramář*, although Winkler does not deal much with the creation of a personality cult. Some evidence exists

in the battles between Kramář and the Castle. For example, in late 1926, Karel Scheinpflug, one of the last members of the *Hrad* circle to remain in the National Democratic party, informed the presidential chancellery, "The editors must toss reams of news into the trash, and publish endless boring parliamentary speeches, even the same speech two or three times, as has happened with speeches by Dr. Kramář," AKPR, T 635/21, 1349/26, as reported by Karel Scheinpflug, November 29, 1926.

122. Paces, "'The Czech Nation Must Be Catholic!': An Alternative Version of Czech Nationalism during the First Republic," *Nationalities Papers* 27 (1999): 407.
123. Nancy Meriwether Wingfield, *Flag Wars and Stone Saints: How the Bohemian Lands Became Czech* (Cambridge, MA: Harvard University Press, 2007), 166.
124. Soubigou, *Masaryk* (Prague: Paseka, 2004), 290.
125. Klímek, *Boj o Hrad I*, 85–87.
126. Jaroslav Pelikan, *"Jesus, Not Caesar": The Religious World View of Thomas Garrigue Masaryk and the Spiritual Foundations of Czech and Slovak Culture* (Salt Lake City: Westminster Tanner-McMurrin Lectures on the History and Philosophy of Religion at Westminster College, 1991), 4.
127. Klímek, *Boj o Hrad I*, 88.
128. Bugge, "Czech Democracy," 22–23; and Peter Heumos, "Die Arbeiterschaft in der Ersten Tschechoslowakischen Republik," *Boh* 29 (1988): 69–71.
129. AKPR, inventářní kniha signatury R, žádosti o podporu. 1928 letter from former senator P. Mudroch, from Sotiná pri Senici nad Myjavou: R 7/28. Helena Dědková, Hradec Králove, Husová ul 3. A chancellery staffer marked the letter "Vyšetřeno [Investigated]," and noted the family's verified need for support: R 17273.
130. Arnošt Caha, *Tatíček Masaryk—Osvoboditel* (Brno: Arnošt Caha, 1921). Similarly, for a slightly more sophisticated audience, see Jan Hajšman, *Masaryk—Vůdce, osvoboditel. Jak Masaryk zahajoval odboj za hranicemi* (Prague: Melantrich, 1920).
131. Ivan Herben, "Dáry a lásky," *Lidové noviny* March 8, 1930, reprinted in Vlnas, "Myty a kyče," 29.
132. AÚTGM, Masaryk Archive, photographic archive, VIII/47/2* 411, pictures 4821, 4823. On the Museum of Gifts, see Broklová, Hájková, Tomeš, and Vašek, eds., *Mám jen knihy a skripta, cenná práce životní* (Prague: Masarykův ústav AV CR, 2002), 164–165.
133. Mircea Eliade, *Patterns in Comparative Religion* (New York: New American Library, 1958), 430.
134. Josef Koudelák, *T.G. Masaryk. Dětská hrá o 3 jednáních s dohrou* (Brtnice: Josef Birnbaum, 1930).
135. Among many examples, see R. Eliáš, *T.G. Masaryk* (Prague: Státní školní knihosklad, 1920); and Lída Merlínová, *Tatíček Masaryk* (Prague: Nakadatelství Šolc a Šimáček, 1934). The second piece was edited by Masaryk's secretary, V. K. Škrach.
136. Hans Lemberg, "Ein Gesschichtsbuch unter drei Staatsystemen: Josef Pekařs Oberklassenlehrbuch von 1914–1945," in Hans Lemberg and Ferdinand Seibt, eds., *Deutsch-tschechische Beziehungen in der Schulliteratur und im populären*

Geschichtsbild (Braunschweig: Westermann, Georg-Eckert Institut für internationale Schulbuchforschung, 1980), 85; Josef Pekař, *Dějiny československé: pro nejvyšší třídy škol středních* (Prague: Historický klub, 1921), 45ff.

137. Pekař, *Dějiny československé*, 168.
138. Klímek, *Boj o Hrad I*, 87.
139. *Masaryk ve fotografii* (Prague: Čin, 1931). Many editions of this book were printed between 1931 and 1947, including German- and Hungarian-language versions. Photographs of Masaryk and his daughter Alice walking through Prague to attend the 1929 parliamentary elections are in the Masaryk Archives: AMU/AÚTGM fotografické oddělení, VIII/47/2*389/4–5, 3728, 3730.
140. Masaryk's writing is quoted in Vlnas, "Myty a kyče," 29. On Legionnaire patriotic culture, see Wingfield, *Flag Wars and Stone Saints*, 184–192; and Alexander, "Die Rolle der Legionäre in der Ersten Republik," 270.
141. Robert Pynsent, "The Literary Representation of the Czechoslovak 'Legions' in Russia," in Mark Cornwall and R. J. W. Evans, *Czechoslovakia in a Nationalist and Fascist Europe 1918–1948* (Oxford: Oxford University Press, 2007), 76, 80–87.
142. An example: Jaroslav Papoušek, ed., *Masaryk a revoluční armada: Masarykovy projevy k Legiím a o Legiích v zahraniční revoluci* (Prague: Čin, 1922).
143. Pynsent, "Literary Representation," 65.
144. An example: *Masaryk ve fotografii*, especially the 1922 military maneuvers near Sedlčany. Rudolf Těsnohlídek, ed., *President mezi svými: druhý zájezd na Moravu a navstěva Slezska v roce 1924* (Prague: František Borový, 1924), contains only six pictures; one is Masaryk reviewing a military formation in Znojmo.
145. Christopher Flood, *Political Myth: A Theoretical Introduction* (New York: Routledge, 2002), 35.
146. Rees, "Leader Cults," in Apor, et al., eds., *The Leader Cult in Communist Dictatorships*, 11.
147. Much research indicates a surprising degree of apathy or open resistance to totalitarian leader cults.
148. Bugge, "Czech Democracy"; Melissa Feinberg, *Elusive Equality: Gender, Citizenship, and the Limits of Democracy in Czechoslovakia, 1918–1950* (Pittsburgh, PA: University of Pittsburgh Press, 2006); Jan Rataj, *O autoritativní národní stát: Ideologické proměny české politiky v druhé republice 1938–1939* (Prague: Karolinum, 1997).
149. Pecháček, *Masaryk, Beneš, Hrad*, 56–57.
150. Rees, "Leader Cults," in Apor et al., eds., *The Leader Cult in Communist Dictatorships*, 13.
151. Pecháček, *Masaryk, Beneš, Hrad*, 39.
152. Ibid., 69.
153. Ibid., 72–74.
154. Daniel Miller, *Forging Political Compromise: Antonín Švehla and the Czechoslovak Republican Party, 1918–1933* (Pittsburgh, PA: University of Pittsburgh Press, 1999), 152.
155. F. Gregory Campbell, *Confrontation in Central Europe: Weimar Germany and Czechoslovakia* (Chicago: University of Chicago Press, 1975), 206–208.

Chapter 4

1. Dagmar Perman, *The Shaping of the Czechoslovak State: Diplomatic History of the Boundaries of Czechoslovakia, 1914–1920* (Leiden: E. J. Brill, 1962); Todd Wayne Huebner, "The Multinational 'Nation-State': The Origins and the Paradox of Czechoslovakia, 1914–1920" (PhD dissertation, Columbia University, 1993); Mark Cornwall, "Dr. Edvard Beneš and Czechoslovakia's German Minority, 1918–1943," in John Morison, ed., *The Czech and Slovak Experience* (Houndmills, Basingstoke: St. Martin's Press, 1992), 175–177; Peter Haslinger, "The Nation, the Enemy, and Imagined Territories: Hungarian Elements in the Emergence of a Czechoslovak National Narrative during and after WWI," in Nancy M. Wingfield, ed., *Creating the Other: Ethnic Conflict and Nationalism in Habsburg Central Europe* (New York: Berghahn Books, 2003): 169–182.
2. Carol Skalnik Leff, *National Conflict in Czechoslovakia: The Making and Remaking of a State, 1918–1987* (Princeton, NJ: Princeton University Press, 1988), 135; more generally, Miloslav John, *Čechoslovakismus a ČSR 1914–1938* (Beroun: Baroko & Fox, 1994).
3. Margaret MacMillan, *Paris 1919: Six Months That Changed the World* (New York: Random House, 2002), 113. On the contemporaneous conversations within most of East-Central Europe about each country's putative oriental, occidental, or European characteristics: Richard G. Fox, ed., *Nationalist Ideologies and the Production of National Cultures* (Washington, DC: American Anthropological Association, 1990); Katherine Verdery and Ivo Banac, eds., *National Character and National Ideology in Interwar Europe* (New Haven, CT: Yale University Press, 1995).
4. Maria Todorova, *Imagining the Balkans* (New York: Oxford University Press, 1997), 58.
5. NARA State Central Files 1910–1928, 751.60F/3, January 24, 1923; Piotr Wandycz, "The Foreign Policy of Edvard Beneš, 1918–1938," in Victor S. Mamatey and Radomír Luža, eds., *A History of the Czechoslovak Republic 1918–1948* (Princeton, NJ: Princeton University Press, 1973), 221; F. Gregory Campbell, *Confrontation in Central Europe: Weimar Germany and Czechoslovakia* (Chicago: University of Chicago Press, 1975); Jindřich Dejmek, "Czechoslovak Foreign Policy and the Search for Security in Central Europe between the World Wars (A Survey of Basic Problems), *Historica* 3–4 (1996–1997): 107–145.
6. Campbell, *Confrontation in Central Europe*, 45–46. On the complicated *Begriffsgeschichte* of the term *Mitteleuropa*, see Jacques Le Rider, *Mitteleuropa: Auf dem Spuren eines Begriffes* (Vienna: Deuticke, 1994).
7. Campbell, *Confrontation in Central Europe*, 191, 226.
8. Hugh LeCaine Agnew, *The Czechs and the Lands of the Bohemian Crown* (Stanford, CA: Hoover Institution Press, 2004), 190.
9. Ibid., 179.
10. Mark Cornwall's account of Edvard Beneš's manipulation of German population data at Versailles in 1919 is fascinating. Cornwall, "Dr. Edvard Beneš and Czechoslovakia's German Minority," 175–177.

11. Nancy Meriwether Wingfield, *Flag Wars and Stone Saints: How the Bohemian Lands Became Czech* (Cambridge, MA: Harvard University Press, 2007), 139.
12. Ibid., 151–156.
13. Zdeněk Kárník, *Česke země v eře první republiky (1918–1938)*, vol. 1 (*Vznik, budování a zlatá léta republiky, 1918–1929*) (Prague: Libri, 2000), 94–97.
14. Campbell, *Confrontation in Central Europe*, 48–55, 78–85.
15. Ferdinand Seibt, "T.G. Masaryk und Edvard Beneš: Die 'Burgherren' im politischen Profil," in Karl Bosl, ed. *Die Burg: Einflußreiche politische Kräfte um Masaryk und Beneš*, vol. 1 (Munich: R. Oldenbourg Verlag, 1973–1974), 31. On the comment in the Estates Theater, see E. Rychnovský, *Masaryk* (Prague, 1930), 287, cited in Fred Hahn, "Masaryk and the Germans," in Robert Pynsent, ed., *T.G. Masaryk: Thinker and Critic*, vol. 2 (London: Macmillan and the University of London School of Slavonic Studies, 1989), 108.
16. Jevgenij Firsov, "T.G. Masaryk a význam česko-německého koaličního dorozumění v ČSR," in Marie Neudorflova, ed., *Češi a Němci v pojetí a politice T.G. Masaryka* (Prague: Masarykův ústav AV ČR, 2004), 141–143, although Firsov uses exclusively Castle sources. Also see Antonín Klímek, *Boj o Hrad II: Kdo po Masarykovi? 1926–1935* (Prague: Panevropa, 1998), 13, 29–30, 103.
17. Wingfield, *Flag Wars and Stone Saints*, chapters 5–8.
18. NARA State Central Files 1910–1928, 751.60F11/1, Prague, November 14, 1923.
19. Cornwall, "Dr. Edvard Beneš and Czechoslovakia's German Minority," 173, 176, 184–185.
20. Quotation: Lonnie Johnson, *Central Europe: Enemies, Friends, Neighbors* (Oxford: Oxford University Press, 2002), 193. On Czechoslovak coal: Ferdinand Peroutka, *Budování státu III* (Prague: Lidové noviny, 1991), 915; also Maureen Healy, "Civilizing the Soldier in Postwar Austria," in Nancy Wingfield and Maria Bucur, eds., *Gender and War in Twentieth-Century Europe* (Bloomington, IN: Indiana University Press, 2006), 57, who argues that Czechoslovakia did its best to avoid sending coal.
21. Ivan Berend, *Decades of Crisis: Central and Eastern Europe before World War II* (Berkeley: University of California Press, 1998), 135–138; Barbara Jelavich, *Modern Austria: Empire and Republic, 1815–1986* (Cambridge: Cambridge University Press, 1987).
22. Magda Ádám, "The Legitimists and Central Europe: Habsburg Restoration Attempts and the Successor States of Austria-Hungary," in Ádám, *The Versailles System and Central Europe* (Burlington, VT: Ashgate, 2004), 129–192.
23. Karel Čapek, *President Masaryk Tells His Story* (New York: Arno Press and the New York Times, 1971; reprint of 1935 edition by G.P. Putnam's Sons), 267–268.
24. Zdenek L. Suda, *Zealots and Rebels: A History of the Communist Party of Czechoslovakia* (Stanford, CA: Hoover Institution Press, 1980), 11–13.
25. Igor Lukes, *Czechoslovakia between Stalin and Hitler: The Diplomacy of Edvard Beneš in the 1930s* (New York: Oxford University Press, 1996), 13.
26. Catherine Andreyev and Ivan Savický, *Russia Abroad: Prague and the Russian Diaspora, 1918–1938* (New Haven, CT: Yale University Press, 2004); Elena Chinyaeva, *Russians Outside Russia: The Émigré Community in Czechoslovakia*

1918–1938 (Munich: R. Oldenbourg Verlag, 2001); Svetlana Tejchmanová, *Rusko v Československu: Bílá emigrace v ČSR 1917–1939* (Prague: H&H, 1993); Anastasia Koprivová, *Střediska ruského emigrantského života v Praze, 1921–1952* (Prague: Národní knihovna ČR, 2001); for Zamini's interpretation, Ministerstvo zahraničních věci, *Czechoslovak Help to the Russian and Ukraine [sic] Emigration* (Prague: Ministerstvo zahraničních věci, 1924).

27. Peter Sugar, Péter Hanák, and Tibor Frank, eds., *A History of Hungary* (Bloomington: Indiana University Press, 1990), 319–367; László Kontler, *A History of Hungary: Millennium in Central Europe* (London: Palgrave, 2002), chapter 8; Joseph Rothschild, *East-Central Europe between the Two World Wars* (Seattle: University of Washington Press, 1974), 165.

28. Rothschild, *East-Central Europe*, 100. Rothschild notes that Admiral Horthy, regent of interwar Hungary, offered in 1935 to settle Hungary's political disputes with Czechoslovakia by challenging Masaryk or Beneš to a duel, and drafted a formal challenge, which was never delivered. Ibid., 191.

29. The disparity in numbers here comes from the different sources consulted and the changing number of personal definitions of ethnicity, based on home language, between 1911 (the last Habsburg census) and 1921 (the first census taken in independent Czechoslovakia). On the 1921 census, 745,431 Czechoslovaks listed Magyar as their mother tongue: see Rothschild, *East-Central Europe*, 89.

30. Daniel E. Miller, "Colonizing the Hungarian and German Border Areas during the Czechoslovak Land Reform, 1918–1938," *AHY* 34 (2003): 303–317; Victor Mamatey, "The Establishment of the Republic," and Václav Beneš, "Czechoslovak Democracy and Its Problems, 1918–1920," in Mamatey and Luža, eds., *A History of the Czechoslovak Republic*, 35, 47, 90–91.

31. Rothschild, *East-Central Europe*, 78, 84–85.

32. Wandycz, "Foreign Policy," in Mamatey and Luža, eds., *History of the Czechoslovak Republic*, 221.

33. David Lloyd George was consistently suspicious of Czech territorial claims. See MacMillan, *Paris 1919*, 229.

34. British-French antipathy began during the Paris Peace Conference, where old mutual suspicions flared up. The French determination to punish Germany, an important British trading partner, worsened matters: see MacMillan, *Paris 1919*, 144, 198, 373–375; Jindřich Dejmek, *Nenaplněné naděje: Politické a diplomatické vztahy Československa a Velké Británie od zrodu První republiky po konferenci v Mnichově (1918–1938)* (Prague: Karolinum, 2003), chapter 3.

35. Harry Hanak, "British Views of the Czechoslovaks from 1914–1924," in Eva Schmidt-Hartmann and Stanley Winters, eds., *Großbritannien, die USA und die böhmischen Länder 1848–1938* (Munich: R. Oldenbourg Verlag, 1991), 97.

36. NARA State Central Files 1910–1928, 751.60F11/8, London, January 28, 1924.

37. K.J. Calder, *Britain and the Origins of the New Europe, 1914–1918* (Cambridge: Cambridge University Press, 1976), cited in Gabor Batonyi, *Britain and Central Europe 1918–1933* (Oxford: Clarendon Press, 1999), 11.

38. Copy of memorandum by Jan Hájek, February 12, 1935, "Podle spisu č.1646 kab/35 oznámil p. vysl. Masaryk úmrtí Allana Leepera . . . ," cited in Rudolf Urban, *Tajné*

fondy třetí sekce: z archivu ministerstva zahraniči republiky česko-slovenské (Prague: Orbis, 1943), 105–106. A German translation was also published: *Demokratenpresse im Lichte Prager Geheimeakten* (Prague, 1943).

39. Quotations from Hanak, "British Views of the Czechoslovaks," 99, 101.
40. Batonyi, *Britain and Central Europe*, 223.
41. Headlam-Morley to Seton-Watson, July 11, 1928, cited in ibid., 212.
42. Quoted in Yeshayahu Jelinek, "Thomas G. Masaryk and the British Foreign Office," in Schmidt-Hartmann and Winters, eds., *Großbritannien, die USA und die böhmischen Länder 1848–1938*, 279.
43. John Gunther, *Inside Europe* (New York: Harper and Brothers, 1938), 240.
44. Ibid., 240–241.
45. Alena Gajanová, *ČSR a středoevropská politika velmoci* (Prague: Československá akademie věd, 1967), 219, 222.
46. Mark Cornwall, "A Fluctuating Barometer: British Diplomatic Views of the Czech-German Relationship in Czechoslovakia, 1918–1938," in Eva Schmidt-Hartmann and Stanley Winters, eds., *Großbritannien, die USA und die böhmischen Länder 1848–1938* (Munich: R. Oldenbourg Verlag, 1991), 313–333.
47. Gajanová, *ČSR a středoevropská politika velmoci*, 221, 229.
48. The Little Entente was never significant within European diplomacy, and never reached the status of a regional alliance capable of withstanding pressure from a Great Power. To do so might have aroused concern in Berlin, Rome, or Moscow, and also might have constrained Czechoslovakia's freedom of action in international affairs. See Wandycz, "Foreign Policy," in Mamatey and Luža, eds., *History of the Czechoslovak Republic*, 222–223.
49. Piotr Wandycz, *The Twilight of French Eastern Alliances, 1926–1936: French-Czechoslovak-Polish Relations from Locarno to the Remilitarization of the Rhineland* (Princeton, NJ: Princeton University Press, 1988), 3, 234.
50. See ibid., 5–6, as well as NARA State Central Files 1910–1928. Document 751.60C/10 alleges that a Polish General Zagorski worked with members of the French military mission to embezzle Polish funds, and notes that the French leaked details of Polish proposals. On the Ukraine, see 751.60E2 from Germany (Poole) October 8, 1928, summarizing a press item describing this plan. 751.60E3, a few weeks later, adds the allegation that Masaryk and Beneš worked with Le Rond to craft the plan's details. I have been unable to find corroboration of any such plan, but the allegation is a telling example of the widespread sense that France was eager to meddle in East European affairs.
51. Wandycz, *Twilight of French Eastern Alliances*, 453.
52. Lukes, *Czechoslovakia between Stalin and Hitler*, 25 n. 30.
53. Wandycz, *Twilight of French Eastern Alliances*, 458–459. On the interwar French press, see Marc Martin, *Medias et journalistes de la Republique* (Paris: Editions Odile Jacob, 1997); a more detailed, if dated, portrayal can be found in Claude Bellanger et al., eds., *Histoire generale de la presse francaise vol. 3, de 1871 à 1940* (Paris: Presses Universitaires de France, 1969–1975).
54. AMZV, Third Section, propagace RČS včinné—Francie, kar. 713, "Cizí propaganda ve Francii," December 27, 1933, 1–2.

55. Ibid., 2–3.
56. Ibid., 4.
57. Ibid., 4–5.
58. Ibid., 4, 6.
59. Ibid., 1–2.
60. Ibid., 7. The Russians were in this game, too: Arthur Raffalovich, "*L'abominable vénalité de la presse* . . ." (Paris: Librarie du travail, 1931).
61. Urban, *Tajné fondy třeti sekce*, 14.
62. Ibid., 52.
63. Ibid., 20.
64. Holly Case, *Between States: The Transylvanian Question and the European Idea during World War II* (Palo Alto: Stanford University Press, 2009); Anton Czettler, *Pál Graf Teleki und die Außenpolitik Ungarns, 1939–1941* (Munich: Verlag Ungarisches Institut, 1996), 191.
65. Cited in Wandycz, *Twilight of French Eastern Alliances*, 459 n. 43.
66. Urban, *Tajné fondy třeti sekce*, 68–70. Also Nicolae Dascălu, "Press Co-operation of the Little Entente and Balkan Alliance States (1922–1939)," *Revue Études Sud-est Europeénnes* 20/1 (1982): 25–42.
67. Urban, Tajné fondz třeti sekce, 96ff.
68. Letter from Wickham Steed to Hájek, dated March 27, 1924; cited in ibid., 83.
69. See ibid., 90. On Radio Central, see AMZV, Third Section, kar. 257, "Zpravodajská společnost 'Radio de l'Europe Centrale,'" March 1, 1924.
70. Copy of memorandum from Vasil K. Škrach to the Third Section, April 12, 1930, cited in Urban, *Tajné fondy třeti sekce*, 92.
71. Copy of receipt from Poliakoff to *Lidové noviny*, September 30, 1937, cited in ibid., 99.
72. AMZV, Third Section, osvěta—knihy—propagace, kar. 432, Podpora knih externích nakladatelů, Orbis (vlastní publikace), 1931.
73. C. J. C. Street, *East of Prague* (London: Geoffrey Bles, 1924), 21–22.
74. Ibid., 75–76.
75. Ibid., 94–95.
76. Ibid., 96.
77. C. J. C. Street, *Slovakia Past and Present* (London: Czech Society of Great Britain, 1928).
78. Street, *East of Prague*, 144–145.
79. Ibid., 51.
80. Ibid., 38.
81. Ibid., 42.
82. Ibid., 62–63.
83. Ibid., 70–71.
84. Baerlein began writing about Eastern Europe in the early 1920s. Among his many works on the region: *The Birth of Yugoslavia*, 1922; *Over the Hills of Ruthenia*, 1925; *The March of the Seventy Thousand*, 1926, about the Czechoslovak Legionnaires; *In Search of Slovakia*, 1929; *No Longer Poles Apart*, 1936.
85. Henry Baerlein, *Here Are Dragons* (London: Leonard Parsons, 1925), 31–32.

86. Ibid., 64.
87. Ibid., 84.
88. Ibid., 235.
89. Ibid., 197.
90. AMZV, Third Section, osvěta—knihy—propagace, kar. 432.
91. Urban, *Tajné fondy třetí sekce*, 227–228.
92. Ibid., 26–27, 30–31.
93. Ibid., 23–24.
94. AMZV, Third Section, osvěta—knihy—propagace, kar. 439, December 29, 1931, Vienna.
95. László Péter, "The Political Conflict between R.W. Seton-Watson and C.A. Macartney over Hungary," presented at "British-Hungarian Relations Since 1848," Centre for the Study of Central Europe, School of Slavonic and East European Studies, University College London, April 16–17, 2004, available at http://www.ssees.ac.uk/confhung.html/peter, 9–10. Accessed October 14, 2005.
96. Aniko Kovacs-Bertrand, *Der ungarische Revisionismus nach dem Ersten Weltkrieg: Der publizistische Kampf gegen den Friedensvertrag von Trianon (1918–1931)* (Munich: Oldenbourg Wissenschaftsverlag, 1997), 158.
97. Dudley Heathcote, *My Wanderings in the Balkans* (London, 1925). Heathcote published pro-Hungarian articles in the Sunday *Times* in 1926 and in G. K. Chesterton's *G.K.'s Weekly* in 1927: Otakar Vočadlo, *Anglické listy Karla Čapka* (Prague: Academia, 1975), 133.
98. Kovacs-Bertrand, *Der ungarische Revisionismus*, 255–259.
99. Ibid., 55–57, 65, 67–69. Also important for this period: Peter Haslinger, "Im Schatten von Trianon . . . ungarischen politischen Publicistik 1919–1939," in Gabriella Schubert and Wolfgang Dahmen, eds., *Bilder von Eigenen und Fremden aus den Donau-Balken-Raum: Analysen literarischer und anderer Texte* (Munich: Südosteuropa-Gesellschaft, 2003): 282–302.
100. Kovacs-Bertrand, *Der ungarische Revisionismus*, 99–101, 102 n. 18.
101. Ibid., 103, n. 21, n. 22, n. 26; 104.
102. Ibid., 158; Jörg Hoensch, *Der ungarische Revisionismus und die Zerschlagung der Tschechoslowakei* (Tübingen: Mohr Siebeck, 1976), 11.
103. Kovacs-Bertrand, *Der ungarische Revisionismus*, 178–179.
104. Ibid., 169–170.
105. Ibid., 181.
106. Ibid., 166–167.
107. András D. Bán, "Friends of England: Cultural and Political Sympathies on the Eve of the War," *The Hungarian Quarterly* 40, no. 153 (1999): 37. Teleki, of an august Transylvanian noble family, served as foreign minister from 1919 to 1920, prime minister from 1920 to 1921 and again between 1939 and 1941.
108. Gajanová, *ČSR a středoevropská politika velmocí*, 230 n. 99.
109. Bán, "Friends of England," 37.
110. Ignac Romsics, "Hungary's Place in the Sun: A British Newspaper Article and Its Hungarian Repercussions," presented at "British-Hungarian Relations Since 1848," Centre for the Study of Central Europe, School of Slavonic and

East European Studies, University College London, April 16–17, 2004. Available at http://www.ssees.ac.uk/confhung/romsics.pdf, 1. Accessed November 5, 2005.

111. Viscount Rothermere (Harold Sidney Harmsworth), *Warnings and Predictions* (London: Eyre and Spottiswoode, 1939), 101. The *Daily Mail*'s circulation was 2 million.
112. Romsics, "Hungary's Place in the Sun," 5.
113. Ibid., 1.
114. Rothermere, *Warnings and Predictions*, 104–106.
115. Ibid., 105.
116. Ibid., 106–107.
117. Ibid., 110.
118. Ibid., 110–111.
119. Ibid., 113, 116.
120. Ibid., 114–115.
121. Ibid., 115.
122. Ignac Romsics, "Nation and State in Modern Hungarian History," *Hungarian Quarterly* 164, no. 4 (2001). Available at http://www.hungarianquarterly.com/no164/4.html, 5. Accessed October 14, 2005.
123. Ibid., 5.
124. Romsics, "Hungary's Place in the Sun," 7–8.
125. Cited in ibid., 4.
126. Campbell, *Confrontation in Central Europe*, 196.
127. Romsics, "Hungary's Place in the Sun," 8.
128. Rothermere, *Warnings and Predictions*, 119–120, 123.
129. Ibid., 120.
130. Ibid., 119.
131. Ibid., 13.
132. Ibid., 134–135, 139.
133. Ibid., 92.
134. Board members: AMZV, Third Section, společnosti a spolky, kar. 876, Společenský klub v Praze, "zpráva o činnosti od 15 března do 31. sprna pro valnou hromadu dne 11. října 1927," 15. The club's finances: AMZV, Third Section, společnosti a spolky, kar. 876, Společenský klub v Praze, 30/34 (10 září 1934).
135. Defense of the building's renovation: AMZV, Third Section, společnosti a spolky, kar. 876, Společenský klub v Praze, "Společenský klub v Praze. Motivy pro podporu klubu."
136. AMZV, Third Section, společnosti a spolky, kar. 876, Společenský klub v Praze, memorandum, December 27, 1927; also 148488/29, "1929 Seznam clenů, vyboru Cizineckého odboru Společenského klubu." The chair was Professor Jan Kozák, on the humanities faculty at Charles University; the vice chair was Vladimír Slavík, a Zamini bureaucrat. The members were Václav Posejpal, a dean of the Charles University natural sciences faculty; historian František Dvorník; Professor František Žilka of the Husová fakulta; Josef Macek, a professor at Prague's economic college as well as a National Socialist parliamentarian; Professor J. F. Šimon

of the Academy of Decorative Arts; František Munk, director of the foreign division of the Prague vzork. veletrhu; minister for social welfare Dr. Josef Kotek; *Prager Presse* reporter František Kubka; Emil Walter, a Zamini bureaucrat; and Zdeněk Prager, no affiliation listed.

137. Josef Kroutvor, *Potíže s dějinami: Eseje* (Prague: Prostor, 1990), 23, 25, 34–36.
138. Ibid., 33.
139. AMZV, Third Section, společnosti a spolky, kar. 876, Společenský klub v Praze, "zpráva o činnosti od 15 března do 31. srpna pro valnou hromadu dne 11. října 1927." The list of books from 1927: AMZV, Third Section, společnosti a spolky, kar. 876, Společenský klub v Praze, 2 února 1927.
140. AMZV, Third Section, společnosti a spolky, kar. 876, Společenský klub v Praze, "Zpráva Cizineckého odboru Společenského klubu, Září-listopad 1929."
141. Julius Firt, *Knihy a osudy* (Brno: Atlantis, 1972), 309–331. Karel Steinbach, *Svědek téměř stoletý* (Prague: Státní pedagogické nakladatelství, 1990); and Adina Mandlová, *Dneska už se tomu směju* (Prague: Československý filmový ústav, 1990) also discuss the Táflrunda.
142. AMZV, Third Section, společnosti a spolky, kar. 876, Společenský klub v Praze, letter of invitation, April 1, 1925.
143. By 1928, P.E.N. was affiliated with the League of Nations Sub-Committee on Arts and Letters. HRC/PEN, collection P.E.N. Misc., author John Galsworthy 1867–1933, dated July 23, 1928, Memorandum to League of Nations Sub-Committee on Arts and Letters.
144. Marjorie Watts, *Mrs. Sappho: The Life of C.A. Dawson Scott, Mother of International P.E.N.* (London: Duckworth, 1987), 97.
145. The Czechs' arguments with the Hungarians, as well as the Czechoslovak Germans, were only some of the many battles waged in P.E.N. between 1921 and 1939, most of them dealing with questions of nationalism and language. For example, Yiddish-speaking Jews demanded separate representation in P.E.N., but the New York and Warsaw chapters of P.E.N. resisted affiliation with a Yiddish section. There were also conflicts between French and Flemish speakers in Belgium. See HRC/PEN, collection P.E.N. Misc., International PEN Congress, 4th, Berlin, 1926, May 17–18, 1926, rough notes from Congress, Tms, 3 pp.
146. APNP, PEN, Jiřina Tůmová, "Vznik klubu P.E.N. v Praze: Co vím o založení klubu já," 1.
147. Ibid., 1.
148. Vočadlo, from 1921 to 1928 a professor at the Institute for Slavic Studies at the University of London, had become a member of P.E.N. International's steering committee as early as 1922. Vočadlo's account of Prague P.E.N.'s formation in his *Anglické listy Karla Čapka*, 34ff., differs somewhat from APNP, PEN, Jiřina Tůmová, "Vznik klubu P.E.N. v Praze."
149. Vočadlo, *Anglické listy*, 83.
150. Vočadlo, *Anglické listy*, 52; Karel Čapek, *Korespondence II* (Prague: Český spisovatel, 1993), 176–178 (letter 925, June 9, 1924).

151. APNP, PEN, "Zápisy psané do knihy otnačené na deskách: Protokoly schůzí P.E.N. Klubu od 15.II. 1925 do 7.III.1933," no author (probably written by Jiřina Tůmová), undated.
152. Ibid., meeting 14.IV.1926, 2.
153. APNP, PEN, copy of letter from Tůmová to Ježek, June 2, 1932.
154. APNP, PEN, "Zápisy psane do knihy otnačené na deskách," 10 (meeting 18.II.25) and 14 (meeting 4.IV.25). Krofta was accepted on June 1, 1926. Preiss was accepted as a member on November 4, 1926. APNP, P.E.N., "Protokoly schůzí P.E.N. Klubu," meeting 4.XI.1926, 12–13. Hodža was minister of education and national culture at this time. (The pages of this document are not numbered consecutively: I list both page number and meeting date.)
155. AMZV, Third Section, kar. 870, spolky—P.E.N., sl. 7, March 4, 1925, author P.E.N. (signed by Khol and Čapek), addressee Zamini (Foreign Ministry), sekce zpravodajská.
156. HRC, MS P.E.N. Recip, ALS (autographed letter signed), Otakar Vočadlo to Marjorie Scott, d. 31.XII.1924. Vočadlo utterly mischaracterized Rilke, of course.
157. APNP, PEN, "Protokoly schůzi P.E.N. Klubu," meeting 28.II.1925, "Účast Němců," 6.
158. Ibid.
159. Both Pick and Fuchs were associated with the Prager Kreis, a loose affiliation of Prague German literati most often linked to Max Brod and Franz Kafka. On their prewar work, see Scott Spector, *Prague Territories: National Conflict and Cultural Innovation in Franz Kafka's Fin de Siecle* (Berkeley: University of California Press, 2000).
160. APNP, PEN, "Protokoly schůzi P.E.N. Klubu," meeting 4.IV.1925, "Němci," 14.
161. Ibid., reported by Čapek in meeting 18.V.1926, 4.
162. HRC, MS P.E.N. Letters, author P.E.N., 2 TLS to Čapek, Karel, November 19 and December 16, 1926.
163. HRC, MS P.E.N. Recip, author Čapek, Karel, TLS to P.E.N., November 26, 1926. Original letter is in English.
164. Documents from the P.E.N. international congresses of 1926 and 1927 indicate that London was generally concerned at this time with establishing regional centers for different European linguistic groups, such as Flemish speakers in Belgium and Yiddish speakers in Warsaw and New York. Prague most likely fell naturally into this category. See for HRC, MS P.E.N. Misc, author International P.E.N. Congress, 4th, Berlin, 1926, dated May 17–18, 1926. "Rough notes from Congress," Tms, 3 pp.
165. APNP, PEN-Klub, "Protokoly schůzi P.E.N. Klubu," Second General Assembly meeting, 23.V.1926, 18.
166. Eisner, a prolific translator, also wrote *Chram i tvrz* (*Cathedral and Fortress*), still considered one of the most insightful analyses of the Czech language. Urzidil, a Czech-German-Jewish writer who evidently never took Czechoslovak citizenship, is represented differently on various membership lists in APNP/P.E.N. On a list filed with 1925–1926 papers, Urzidil is listed as "Jan" rather than Johannes, though working at the "Deutsche Gesandschaft." Later (1931, 1934–1935) he is Johannes, or not listed at all; his correspondence with Tůmová was written

in Czech. Urzidil fled Czechoslovakia in 1939 with his wife, the daughter of a Prague rabbi, and lived in England and New York, working as a manual laborer, bookbinder, journalist, and translator. Urzidil briefly reported for the German-language programs on Voice of America, but was fired for his leftist views during the McCarthy era. He returned to Europe and died in Rome in 1970.

167. APNP, PEN-Klub, P.E.N., undated list, no author.
168. Prague repeated this point many times during the period of Prague-Budapest contention. For a decisively Castle analysis of the entire issue, see Edmond Konrád, "Politická historie Penklubu," *Přítomnost* (1937), 392–395.
169. AMZV, Third Section, sig. 12 (PEN Klub), kar. 295, sl. 7, dopis August 19, 1929, od Fr. Kubky, Panu řediteloví J. Hájek, Zamini.
170. APNP, PEN, typed carbon copy of letter by Radó Antal to Prague P.E.N., Budapest, May 18, 1930; enclosed in letter from Prague P.E.N. to Minister J. Slavík, May 23, 1930. Budapest-Prague correspondence was conducted in French or German.
171. APNP, PEN, letter from Jenö Mohacsi to Jiřina Tůmová, December 14, 1930.
172. APNP, PEN, copy of letter from Prague P.E.N. to Minister J. Slávik, May 23, 1930.
173. APNP, PEN, letter from Prague P.E.N. to Edvard Beneš, "Slovutný pane ministře!," May 18, 1931.
174. APNP, PEN, letter from Václav Tille to Jiřina Tůmová, February 22, 1932.
175. APNP, PEN. There are many examples of these reports.
176. AMZV, Third Section, spolky-PEN, kar. 70, April 7, 1932, report from Budapest legation to J. Hájek, head of Third Section. Press reports attached.
177. APNP, PEN, carbon copy of letter from Jiřina Tůmová to Edmond Konrád, "Milý Edmondků," May 6, 1932.
178. APNP, PEN, copies of Edmond Konrád (article signed "kd."), "Spisovatelé v Budapesti," *Národní osvobození*, May 31, 1932, 5; and František Langer (signed F.L.), *Lidové noviny*, May 28, 1932.
179. APNP, PEN, Adolf Hoffmeister, "X. kongres P.E.N. klubů v Budapešti," *Literární noviny*, undated.
180. Ibid.
181. APNP, PEN, letter from Radó Antal to Prague P.E.N., July 20, 1932.
182. APNP, PEN, undated reports from Zamini's *Denní přehled zahraničního tisku* (contents discuss press reports from September 1932), sent as enclosures in a letter to Edmond Konrád from Leo Singer, Budapest correspondent for the *Prager Tagblatt*, postmarked October 12, 1932.
183. APNP, PEN, clipping of "Při otázce přístupu maïarské literatury na Slovensko," *Lidové noviny*, November 4, 1932.
184. APNP, PEN, letter from Radó Antal to Karel Čapek, December 5, 1932.
185. APNP, PEN, letter from Vilém Pospíšil to Karel Čapek, November 24, 1932.
186. APNP, PEN, copy of letter from Zamini to Prague P.E.N., January 23, 1933. "čj 8264/33-III-2. Věc: Devisy pro nákup cizí literatury."
187. On this topic, see APNP, PEN, "La censure en Slovaquie"; APNP, PEN, clipping of "Protest slovenských umělců a spisovatelů proti tiskování Slováků v Mad'arsku," *Národní listy* (undated, March 10 byline); APNP, PEN, letter from

Slovenská odbočka Narodnej Rady československej, Bratislava, to Prague P.E.N., March 6, 1933.

188. APNP, PEN, "The Question of the Entry of Hungarian Publications into Czechoslovakia," anonymous, sent with a letter by J. V. Hyka to Jiřina Tůmová, April 2, 1935, č. 44038/35/III/2.

189. The members of this society petitioned to join the Czechoslovak P.E.N. club's Bratislava section in 1933. Edmond Konrád's history of Prague P.E.N. mentions this group and notes that President Masaryk was its founder. Konrád, "Politická historie Penklubu," *Přítomnost* (1937), 392–395. R. J. W. Evans notes that Masaryk used presidential funds to create a Hungarian academy in Bratislava in 1930: Evans, "Hungarians, Czechs, and Slovaks: Some Mutual Perceptions, 1900–1950," in Mark Cornwall and R. J. W. Evans, eds., *Czechoslovakia in a Nationalist and Fascist Europe 1918–1948* (Oxford: Oxford University Press, 2007), 114, 117–118.

190. APNP, PEN, undated, untitled (first line "C'est avec un attachement presque personnel que je me sense lié a la question de la circulation libre en Slovaquie de la littérature hongroise . . ."), 2–4.

191. APNP, PEN, report to Zamini by Prague P.E.N., June 26, 1935.

192. Karel Čapek, "Pozdravy," *Lidové noviny*, December 25, 1938; reprinted in *Na břehu dnů* (Prague: Československý spisovatel, 1966), 420–424.

193. Gunther, *Inside Europe*, overleaf, 364.

194. Ibid., 370.

195. Peter Bugge, "Longing or Belonging? Czech Perceptions of Europe in the Inter-War Years and Today," *Yearbook of European Studies* (1999): 113.

196. Wandycz, *Twilight of French Eastern Alliances*, 459–460.

197. Gajanová, ČSR a středoevropská politika velmocí, 225.

198. Zbyněk Zeman with Antonín Klímek, *The Life of Edvard Beneš 1884–1948* (Oxford: Clarendon Press, 1997), 93–94.

199. Gunther, *Inside Europe*, 239–241.

200. Storm Jameson, *Journey from the North: Autobiography of Storm Jameson* (London: Collins and Harville Press, 1969), vol. I., p. 376.

201. Rothschild, *East-Central Europe*, 73ff.

Chapter 5

1. Ivan Berend, *Decades of Crisis: Central and Eastern Europe before World War II* (Berkeley: University of California Press, 1998), 300.

2. Mark Cornwall, "'A Leap into Ice-Cold Water': The Manoeuvres of the Henlein Movement in Czechoslovakia, 1933–1938," in Cornwall and R. J. W. Evans, eds., *Czechoslovakia in a Nationalist and Fascist Europe 1918–1948* (Oxford: Oxford University Press, 2007), 134.

3. Hugh LeCaine Agnew, *The Czechs and the Lands of the Bohemian Crown* (Stanford, CA: Hoover Institution Press, 2004), 191.

4. Mark Cornwall, "Dr. Edvard Beneš and Czechoslovakia's German Minority, 1918–1943," in John Morison, ed., *The Czech and Slovak Experience* (Houndmills, Basingstoke: St. Martin's Press, 1992), 178–182.
5. Cornwall, "A Leap into Ice-Cold Water," 125; Michael Walsh Campbell, "A Crisis of Democracy: Czechoslovakia and the Rise of Sudeten German Nationalism, 1918–1938" (PhD dissertation, University of Washington, 2003).
6. Michael Walsh Campbell, "Keepers of Order? Strategic Legality in the 1935 Czechoslovak General Elections," *Nationalities Papers* 31, no. 3 (2003): 298, 302–303.
7. Cornwall, "A Leap into Ice-Cold Water," 136–137; Campbell, "A Crisis of Democracy," 205–206; Eagle Glassheim, "Crafting a Post-Imperial Identity: Nobles and Nationality Politics in Czechoslovakia, 1918–1938" (PhD dissertation, Columbia University, 2000), 224–226; Keith G. Robbins, "Konrad Henlein, the Sudeten Question, and British Foreign Policy," *The Historical Journal* 12, no. 4 (1969): 674–697.
8. Nancy Meriweather Wingfield, *Minority Politics in a Multinational State: The German Social Democrats in Czechoslovakia, 1918–1938* (Boulder, CO: East European Monographs, 1989), 153; Paul Vyšný, *The Runciman Mission to Czechoslovakia, 1938: Prelude to Munich* (Houndmills, Basingstoke: Palgrave Macmillan, 2003), 13.
9. Mark Cornwall, "A Fluctuating Barometer: British Diplomatic Views of the Czech-German Relationship in Czechoslovakia, 1918–1938," in Eva Schmidt-Hartmann and Stanley Winters, eds., *Großbritannien, die USA und die böhmischen Länder 1848–1938* (Munich: R. Oldenbourg Verlag, 1991), 322–326.
10. Igor Lukes, *Czechoslovakia between Stalin and Hitler: The Diplomacy of Eduard Beneš in the 1930s* (Oxford: Oxford University Press, 1996), 38–39, 43.
11. Agnew, *The Czechs*, 193.
12. Lukes, *Czechoslovakia between Stalin and Hitler*, 50, 53, 55–58.
13. Vyšný, *The Runciman Mission to Czechoslovakia*, 8–11, 20 n. 30; Cornwall, "A Fluctuating Barometer," 327; Robbins, "Konrad Henlein, the Sudeten Question, and British Foreign Policy," 686, 691, 695.
14. Peter Bugge, "Czech Democracy: Paragon or Parody?" *Boh* 47, no. 1 (2006–2007): 13.
15. Zbyněk Zeman and Antonin Klímek, *The Life of Edvard Beneš 1884–1948: Czechoslovakia in Peace and War* (Oxford: Oxford University Press, 1997), 100–101.
16. Marta Dandová, "Obraz pátečníků v korespondenci Karla Čapka," in Pavel Janáček and Jan Tydlitát, eds., *Pátečníci a Karel Poláček* (Rychnov nad Kněžnou: Albert, 2001), 46–47.
17. Giovanni Capoccia, "Legislative Responses Against Extremism. The Protection of Democracy in the First Czechoslovak Republic," *EEPS* 16 (2002): 691–738; Karl Loewenstein, "Militant Democracy and Fundamental Rights, II," *American Political Science Review* (1937): 641–644.
18. Bugge, "Paragon or Parody?," 12–13.
19. Antonín Klímek, *Velké dějiny zemí koruny české*, vol. 13, 1918–1929 (Prague: Paseka, 2000), 190–192.

20. Antonín Klímek, *Velké dějiny zemí Koruny české*, vol. 14, 1929–1938 (Prague: Paseka, 2002), 332–384.
21. Rudolf Urban, *Tajné fondy třetí sekce: z archivu ministerstva zahraniči republiky česko-slovenské* (Prague: Orbis, 1943), 213–215, 219, 221–226.
22. AMZV, Third Section, osvěta—knihy—propagace, 432, "Vydávatelské zprava III/5 za rok 1936."
23. AMZV, Third Section, propagace RČS včinné—Francie, 713, "Cizí propaganda ve Francii," December 27, 1933, 7.
24. Karel Čapek, *Korespondence II* (Prague: Český spisovatel, 1993), 220, letter from Čapek to Scheinpflugová, October 6, 1927.
25. The Masaryk archives in Prague contain manuscript sections of the *Conversations*, edited in Masaryk's handwriting. Karel Čapek, *Čtení o T.G. Masarykovi*, ed. Miroslav Halík (Prague: Melantrich, 1969), photograph following 143.
26. Anna Gašparikova-Horakova, *U Masarykovcov: spomienky osobnej archivárky T.G. Masaryka* (Bratislava: Academic Electronic Press, 1995), diary entry for February 14, 1930. Quoted in Bruce Berglund, "Prague Castle as Sacred Acropolis: Faith, Conviction, and Skepticism in the House of Masaryk," unpublished ms., 34.
27. Antonín Klímek, *Boj o Hrad II: Kdo po Masarykovi? 1926–1935* (Prague: Paseka, 1998), 395.
28. Julius Firt, *Knihy a osudy* (Brno: Atlantis, 1972), 263.
29. Cited, without documentary source, in Miloš Pohorský, "Karel Čapek a jeho TGM—Masaryk a jeho K.Č.," in Karel Čapek, *Hovory s T.G. Masarykem* (Prague: Československý spisovatel, 1990), 569.
30. Klímek, *Boj o Hrad II*, 395.
31. Čapek, *Talks with T.G. Masaryk*, trans. Dora Round (North Haven, CT: Catbird Press, 1995), 90, 93.
32. Karel Čapek, *Masaryk on Thought and Life* (London: Allen and Unwin, 1938), 186, 194.
33. Čapek, foreword to *Život a práce* (Prague: F. Borový, 1932); cited in Vydavatelské poznámky Notes," in Čapek, *Hovory s T.G. Masarykem*, 553.
34. Ibid., 175–176, 179.
35. T. G. Masaryk, *Světová revoluce: za války a ve válce, 1914–1918* (Prague: Orbis and Čin, 1925), 100. Čapek was also struck by this story and Masaryk's emphasis on the truth: see the section titled "Nechtěl jsem lhat . . ." in *Mlčení s T.G. Masarykem*, in Čapek, *Hovory s T.G. Masarykem*, 347–351.
36. Čapek, *Hovory s T.G. Masarykem*, 193.
37. Ibid., 317.
38. Ibid., 341.
39. Čapek, foreword to *Život a práce*, in "Publishers' Notes," in ibid., 569–570. Čapek's italics.
40. Ibid., 302–303.
41. Čapek, *Talks with T.G. Masaryk*, 131.
42. A Čapek manuscript from early 1930 for *Lidové noviny* can serve as an example in this case. Its title was "The Presidential Question (Presidentská otázka)"; the manuscript bears penciled-in comments in the president's handwriting. AÚTGM, MAR, Dokumentace, kar. 9, sl. 56.

43. Firt, *Knihy a osudy*, 277; Karel Čapek, ed., *Masaryk ve fotografii* (Prague: Čin, 1931).
44. Karel Čapek, "Váš Masaryk," *Vůdce generace* 1932, reprinted in Čapek, *Hovory s T.G. Masarykem*, 440–441.
45. Karel Čapek, "Dvacáty čtvrty květen," *Lidové noviny*, May 25, 1934, reprinted in Čapek, *Hovory s T.G. Masarykem*, 446–449. Čapek's italics.
46. Quotations from untitled obituary, *Lidové noviny*, September 14, 1937, and "Věčný Masaryk," *Lidové noviny*, September 14, 1937, both reprinted in ibid., 459–461. Čapek's capitalization.
47. Čapek, *Korespondence II*, 245, letter from Čapek to Scheinpflugová, September 1, 1929.
48. Ibid., 217, letter from Čapek to Scheinpflugova, August 1, 1927. The Castle drew close to Švehla during this period. In early 1928, Masaryk offered Topol'čianky, his family villa, to Švehla while he recuperated from heart disease. Jaroslav Pecháček, ed., *Masaryk, Beneš, Hrad: Masarykovy dopisy Benešovi* (Prague: Faun, 1996), 73.
49. Ibid., 34, letter from Čapek to Seton-Watson, July 1928.
50. Karel Čapek, "A Representative Czech: Antonín Švehla," *The Slavonic and East European Review* 7 (January 1929): 268–271.
51. Karel Čapek, *Korespondence II*, 318, letter from Čapek to Švehla, November 9, 1930.
52. There are many observations on this theme from roughly 1928 on. See, for example, Klímek, *Boj o Hrad II*, 247.
53. Ibid., 299.
54. Firt, *Knihy a osudy*, 274.
55. Robert Kvaček, "Co zůstalo utájeno," *Svobodné slovo*, February 13, 1993.
56. Zeman and Klímek, *Edvard Beneš*, 99.
57. Čapek, *Korespondence II*, 256, letter to Scheinpflugová, September 2, 1933.
58. Jindřiška Smetanová, *TGM: "Proč se neřekne pravda?" Ze vzpomínek dr. Antonína Schenka* (Prague: Primus, 1996), 122. The only other witness to Schenk's conversation with the president, presidential archivist Anna Gašpariková, remembered the president's comments as much milder: 145.
59. Daniel Miller, *Forging Political Compromise: Antonín Švehla and the Czechoslovak Republican Party, 1918–1933* (Pittsburgh: University of Pittsburgh Press, 1999), 184.
60. Firt, *Knihy a osudy*, 261ff.
61. Also motivating Zamini's sponsorship of Čapek was the hope that Čapek would be awarded a Nobel Prize for Literature, for which Zamini nominated him four times. On Zamini's Nobel efforts for Čapek, see SÚA, fond Dr. Josef Šusta, korespondence s přáteli a vědci (inv.č. 16), kar. 20 (Návrh na Nobelovou cenu pro Karla Čapka); Andrea Orzoff, "Battle for the Castle: The Friday Men and the Czechoslovak Republic, 1918–1938" (PhD dissertation, Stanford University, 2000), chapter 5.
62. In 1932 Čapek wrote to the secretary of the embassy in the Hague, asking for bulbs: "the Berlin legation sends me seeds, and last year in spring the Paris legation [had to contend with] a packaged glass greenhouse. I fear that at some point I will request a live elephant from the Calcutta consulate: be glad you're not there." Cited in Karel Scheinpflug, *Můj švagr Karel Čapek* (Hradec Králové: Kruh, 1991), 49.

63. SÚA, fond Dr. Josef Šusta, korespondence s přáteli a vědci, kar. 20, "Již po čtvrté přistupují podepsaní profesoři . . .," January 13, 1935.
64. AMZV, Third Section, "Dr. Karel Čapek," kar. 30, č. 80413 1936, odbor III odd.2; č 87250 1936 odbor III odd.2; report from the Stockholm delegation dated July 16, 1936, čj. 307/36; letters to Prague from Stockholm, January 28, 1929.
65. SÚA, fond Dr. Josef Šusta, korespondence s přáteli a vědci, kar. 20, "Seznám prací K. Čapka přeložených do cizích jazyků v roce 1934," undated.
66. Correspondence about *Obrázky z domova* can be found in AMZV, Third Section, 1922–1929, "Dr. Karel Čapek," kar. 30, č.j. 125754, September 13, 1930. Response from November 7, 1930.
67. AÚTGM, Beneš papers, korespondence 1938, "Rozhovor dne 31.III.38" and "Rozhovor dne 3. dubna na Osově." Ferdinand Peroutka, *Deníky, dopisy, a vzpomínky* (Prague: *Lidové noviny*, 1995), 129–130. Firt, *Knihy a osudy*, 279–282. Quotation: Firt, 281–282.
68. AMZV, Third Section, "Dr. Karel Čapek," kar. 30, letters from Bern consulate, July 23, 1938, and August 11, 1938. Čapek sent his refusal to Zamini on July 27, 1938. He received various other offers to help him emigrate before the Second World War: Norma Comrada, "Karel Čapek, Journalist: 1938," *Selecta: Journal of the Pacific Northwest Council on Foreign Languages* 9 (1988): 85.
69. Urban, *Tajné fondy třetí sekce*, 9–10. Hájek was arrested in 1939; he spent the war in Prague's Pankrác prison and in Buchenwald. After 1945, he was barred from working for Zamini. In 1956, he was accused of attempting to subvert the state, and served five years. He died in 1969.
70. AMZV, Third Section, "Dr. Karel Čapek," kar. 30, "Dr. Karel Čapek—nabidka propagační spolupráce," September 14, 1938.
71. Firt, *Knihy a osudy*, 73. Vitězslav Housek, ed., *Polemiky Ferdinanda Peroutky* (Prague: Československý spisovatel, 1995), 103.
72. Housek, *Polemiky Ferdinanda Peroutky*, 103.
73. Peroutka, *Deníky, dopisy, vzpomínky*, 136–137.
74. Ibid., 141.
75. Housek, *Polemiky Ferdinanda Peroutky*, 103–104.
76. Ibid., 136–137, 143.
77. These essays were collected in book form: see Ferdinand Peroutka, *Jáci jsme* (Prague: Nakladatelství "Obelisk," 1924).
78. Peroutka recalled that *Přítomnost* needed only three or four years to become self-supporting; Firt contested that it did not turn a profit until the early 1930s. Only 4,500 people subscribed to *Přítomnost* in 1929. See Firt, *Knihy a osudy*, 58.
79. Peroutka's personnel file in the *Lidové noviny* archives (MZA-Brno, fond G426 *Lidové noviny*, osobná korespondence, sl. 39) dates his arrival at November 1, 1923. Also: Peroutka, *Deníky, dopisy, vzpomínky*, 107ff., 141–142.
80. Inspired by the magazine, the "Klub Přítomnost" discussion club lasted from 1926 to 1938. See Milena Beránková, ed., *Dějiny československé žurnalistiky*, vol. 3 (Prague: Novinář, 1991), 178. Prague archives lack more than a hint of information about this club save its meeting places (usually, after 1930, the Společenský klub).
81. Firt, *Knihy a osudy*, 72–73.

82. Klímek, *Boj o Hrad II*, 249.
83. Peroutka, *Deníky, dopisy, vzpomínky*, 143.
84. Peroutka's own reminiscences of this event are quoted in Julius Firt, "Die 'Burg' und die Zeitschrift *Přítomnost*," in Karl Bosl, ed., *Die Burg: Einflußreiche politische Kräfte um Masaryk und Beneš*, vol. 2 (Munich: R. Oldenbourg Verlag, 1973–1974), 112.
85. Klímek, *Boj o Hrad II*, 284.
86. Peroutka relied particularly on the recollections of Alois Rašín: for example, Ferdinand Peroutka, *Budování státu: Československá politika v letech popřevatových I (1918–1919)* [hereafter BS1] (Prague: *Lidové noviny*, 1991), 294. He also alludes to Karel Kramář's diary entries: Peroutka, *Budování státu II (1919)* [hereafter BS2] (Prague: Lidové noviny, 1991), 723–724.
87. Peroutka, *BS1*, 13.
88. Ibid., 248–249; Peroutka, *BS2*, 486–487.
89. Peroutka, *BS1*, 16.
90. Ibid., 146.
91. Ibid., 365; Peroutka, *BS2*, 722ff.
92. Peroutka, *BS2*, 723.
93. Peroutka, *BS1*, 297, 299.
94. Ibid., 296.
95. Peroutka, *BS1*, 72.
96. Peroutka, *BS2*, 772–773.
97. Ibid., 838.
98. Peroutka, *BS1*, 299.
99. Peroutka, *BS2*, 724.
100. Ibid., 842, 843.
101. Ibid., 765–766.
102. Ibid., 737–738.
103. Ferdinand Peroutka, *Budování státu III (1920)* [hereafter BS3] (Prague: Lidové noviny, 1991), 927.
104. Ibid., 929.
105. Peroutka, *BS1*, 15.
106. Peroutka, *BS3*, 918.
107. Comrada, "Karel Čapek, Journalist: 1938," 85.
108. Dagmara Švihlová and Jaroslav Soukup, "Dopis Edvarda Beneše Karlu Čapkovi z podzimu 1938," *Střední Evropa* 72–73 (1997): 177–189. Letter cited on 187.
109. Ibid. Čapek's wife, Olga Scheinpflugová, also discussed the letter in her autobiographical *Český roman* (Prague: František Borový, 1946), 530. The "Beneš letter" had a long afterlife: the Nazis became interested in its possible propaganda usage in 1943, interested enough to interrogate and briefly imprison Scheinpflugová. Between 1945 and 1948, the letter continued to circulate, and it appeared again after 1989. Švihlová and Soukup conclude that the letter contains many phrases and terms that Beneš did not use; if not entirely false, it was edited and rewritten by someone else.

110. Edvard Beneš, *Memoirs of Dr. Eduard Beneš: From Munich to New War and New Victory* (New York: Arno Press and the New York Times, 1972: reprint of 1954 ed. by Houghton Mifflin, Boston), 55.
111. Dr. Edvard Beneš, *Šest let exilu a druhé světové války: Řeči, projevy a dokumenty z r. 1938–1945* (Prague: Orbis, 1946), 39–41, 43.
112. On this period of Beneš's exile: Milan Hauner et al., eds., *Formování čsl. zahraničního odboje 1938–39. Svědectví Jana Opočenského "Presidentův pobyt ve Spojených státech amerických"* (Prague: Akademie česká věd, 2000); Jan Křen, *Do emigrace. Západní zahraniční odboj 1938–1945*, 2nd ed. (Prague: Naše vojsko, 1963), 449–470. The official perspective: Bohuš Beneš, *Amerika jde s námi: Reportáž z přednáškového turné Edvarda Beneše po amerických univerzitách v roce 1939* (Prague: Společnost Edvarda Beneše, 1998).
113. Edward Taborsky, "Politics in Exile, 1939–1945," in Victor Mamatey and Radomir Luža, eds., *A History of the Czechoslovak Republic 1918–1948* (Princeton, NJ: Princeton University Press, 1973), 323–328.
114. For examples of Osuský's dissension, see Jaromír Smutný, February 10, 1940, and April 3, 1941, London, in Libuše Otáhalová and Milada Červinková, *DHČSP*, vol. 1 (Prague: Academia, 1966), 76, 197.
115. Inter alia: Beneš's messages home February 8, 1940, and March 14, 1940, London, as well as his conversation with Jaromír Smutný, November 2, 1940, in ibid., 72–74, 89–90, 137–138.
116. Jaromír Smutný, April 3, 1941, London, in ibid., 196.
117. Jaromír Smutný, October 22, 1940, London, in ibid., 135–136.
118. Bruce Berglund, "'We Wish We Were Home': The Czechoslovak Émigré Community in Britain 1940–1945" (PhD dissertation, University of Kansas, 1999), 7. Jan Kuklík and Jan Němeček, in *Proti Benešovi! Česká a slovenská protibenešovská opozice v Londýně 1939–1945* (Prague: Karolinum, 2004), caution that too much is often made of these disputes. Many supposed opponents of Beneš still considered him suprapartisan, similar to Masaryk, and retained prominent positions in the exile government while criticizing him. Kuklík and Němeček, 8.
119. Jindřich Dejmek, "Milan Hodža a československá zahraniční politika v třícatych letech (1935–1938)," *Moderní dějiny* 7 (1999): 65–84.
120. Edvard Beneš, *Demokracie dnes a zitra*, vol. II (London: Unwin Brothers for Kruh přátel československé knihy, péčí týdeníku "Čechoslovák," 1941–1942), 172–173.
121. Milan Hodža, *Federation in Central Europe: Reflections and Reminiscences* (London: Jarrolds, 1942).
122. Firt, *Knihy a osudy*, 277. See *Dr. Edvard Beneš ve fotografii: historie velkého života* (Prague: Orbis, 1936). F. X. Šalda wrote the foreword, and the book came out in German, Hungarian, and Russian as well as in Czech.
123. Jaromír Smutný, March 22, 1940, London, in Otáhalová and Červinková, *DHČSP*, vol. 1, 91–92. Smutný's coworkers questioned his loyalty to Beneš, for obvious reasons.
124. Bruce Berglund, "We Wish We Were Home," 30, 407–452.

125. See, for example, Beneš's July 1940 letter to Msgr. Jan Šramek, in which he says, "We are continuing in the tradition of the First Republic, the Republic of Masaryk . . ." He uses the same phrase in his first address to Czechoslovakia on July 24, 1940. Quoted in *Memoirs of Dr. Eduard Beneš*, 113, 114.
126. Conversation between Beneš and Jaromír Smutný, January 15, 1943, London, in Otáhalová and Červinková, *DHČSP*, vol. 1, 306.
127. Berglund, "We Wish We Were Home," 213–217.
128. *Memoirs of Dr. Eduard Beneš*, 57.
129. Ibid., 104–105; Agnew, *The Czechs*, 219–220.
130. Bugge, "Paragon or Parody?," 19. Castle intellectuals, such as Ferdinand Peroutka, had been using terms like these since the 1920s; see Orzoff, "Battle for the Castle" (PhD dissertation), chapter 2.
131. *Memoirs of Dr. Eduard Beneš*, 106.
132. Ibid., 107. Beneš's italics.
133. Conversation between Beneš and Jaromír Smutný, July 20, 1943, London, in Otáhalová and Červinková, *DHČSP*, vol. 2, 718–719.
134. See Osuský's letter to Beneš of October 29, 1939, in Otáhalová and Červinková, *DHČSP*, vol. 1, 53.
135. *Memoirs of Dr. Eduard Beneš*, 219.
136. Ibid., 102.
137. Detlef Brandes, "Benešova politika v letech 1939–1945," *Dějiny a současnost* 1 (2003): 37.
138. *Memoirs of Dr. Eduard Beneš*, 222, Beneš's italics.
139. Ibid., 137ff., 192, 230, 235, 240, 262. Beneš's enthusiasm about the Soviets once again cost him Western support: the United States informed Jan Masaryk that Czechoslovakia would receive only "moral" assistance in a crisis. The Americans considered Czechoslovakia less reliably anti-Soviet and democratic than occupied Germany; this inflamed Czech public opinion. John D. Crane and Sylvia Crane, *Czechoslovakia: Anvil of the Cold War* (New York: Praeger, 1991), 297, 310.
140. For example, Beneš, *Demokracie dnes a zitra*, vol. II, 204–220.
141. Ibid., 203–204.
142. Beneš, *Šest let exilu*, 251–252, 257–258.
143. Ibid., 254, 257.
144. Throughout the rest of this chapter, my debt to Chad Bryant's work will be clear. Bryant, "The Language of Resistance? Czech Jokes and Joke-Telling under Nazi Occupation, 1939–1945," *Journal of Contemporary History* 41, no. 1 (2006): 137 n. 20, 138. Also: Tomáš Pasák, *Pod ochranou Říše* (Prague: Práh, 1998); Vojtěch Mastný, *The Czechs under Nazi Rule: The Failure of National Resistance* (New York: Columbia University Press, 1971); Detlef Brandes, *Die Tschechen unter deutschem Protektorat* (Munich: R. Oldenbourg, 1969–1975).
145. Chad Bryant, *Prague in Black: Nazi Rule and Czech Nationalism* (Cambridge, MA: Harvard University Press, 2007), 36–41.

146. Ferdinand Peroutka, "Úvaha o stranach," *Přítomnost*, November 9, 1938, in Peroutka, *O věcech obecných II: Výbor z politické publicistiky* (Prague: Státní pedagogické nakladatelství, 1991), 435–438.
147. Ferdinand Peroutka, "Tvrdé slovo,"*Přítomnost*, November 16, 1938, in ibid., 442.
148. Ferdinand Peroutka, "Co by dělal dnes Masaryk?" *Přítomnost*, March 8, 1939, in ibid., 452–455.
149. Bryant, *Prague in Black*, 60, 65.
150. Anonymous informant, "Přehledu politické situace v Čechach a na Moravě v letních měsicích 1940," in Otáhalová and Červinková, *DHČSP*, vol. 2, 576–577.
151. Luža, "The Czech Resistance Movement," in Mamatey and Luža, eds., *A History of the Czechoslovak Republic*, 348, 359. Also see Bryant, *Prague in Black*, 218.
152. Bryant, *Prague in Black*, 97–98.
153. Jan Šach, "Poválečný stranicko-politický system v představách domácího odboje v roce 1939," *Historie a vojenství* 6 (1997): 35–56. Also see Luža, "The Czech Resistance Movement," 345–346, and Luža's memoir of his participation in the resistance: *The Hitler Kiss: A Memoir of the Czech Resistance* (Baton Rouge: Louisiana State University Press, 2002).
154. Luža, "The Czech Resistance Movement," 345–346; Bryant, *Prague in Black*, 215; Zdeňek Suda, *Zealots and Rebels: A History of the Ruling Party of Czechoslovakia* (Stanford, CA: Stanford University Press, 1981); Paul Zinner, *Communist Strategy and Tactics in Czechoslovakia, 1918–1948* (New York: Frederick A. Praeger, 1963).
155. On Vlajka, see Milan Nakonečný, *Vlajka: K historii a ideologii českého fašismu* (Prague: Chvojkovo nakladatelství, 2001).
156. Bryant, *Prague in Black*, passim.
157. Bryant, "The Language of Resistance?," 133–134.
158. Ibid., 137–138; Bryant, *Prague in Black*, 130, 183–184.
159. Bryant, *Prague in Black*, 188.
160. Ibid., 227–230.
161. Stanislav Kokoška, *Praha v květnu 1945. Historie jednoho povstání* (Prague: *Lidové noviny*, 2005).
162. Bryant, *Prague in Black*, 239, 250. These numbers are controversial. See, inter alia Tomáš Staněk, *Verfolgung 1945: Die Stellung des Deutschen in Böhmen, Mähren, und Schlesien (außerhalb der Lager und Gefängnisse)*, trans. Otfrid Pustějovský (Vienna: Böhlau, 2002); Benjamin Frommer, *National Cleansing: Retribution against Nazi Collaborators in Postwar Czechoslovakia* (Cambridge: Cambridge University Press, 2005); Eagle Glassheim, "The Mechanics of Ethnic Cleansing: The Expulsion of the Germans from Czechoslovakia, 1945–1947," in Philip Ther and Ana Siljak, eds., *Redrawing Nations: Ethnic Cleansing in East-Central Europe, 1944–1948* (Lanham, MD: Rowman and Littlefield, 2001).
163. V. Žižka, *Bojující Československo 1938–1945* (Košice: Žikeš, 1945), 230.
164. Bradley F. Abrams, *The Struggle for the Soul of the Nation: Czech Culture and the Rise of Communism* (New York: Rowman and Littlefield, 2004), 57.
165. On the coup, see inter alia Zdeněk Karník and Michal Kopeček, *Bolševismus, komunismus a radikální socialismus v Československu* (Prague: Ústav pro soudobé dějiny/Dokorán, 2003–); Karel Kaplan, *The Short March: The Communist Takeover*

in Czechoslovakia 1945–1948 (London: C. Hurst, 1987); Martin Myant, *Socialism and Democracy in Czechoslovakia 1945–1948* (Cambridge: Cambridge University Press, 1981); Jon Bloomfield, *Passive Revolution: Politics and the Czechoslovak Working Class, 1945–1948* (New York: St. Martin's Press, 1979).

166. Alice Teichova, *The Czechoslovak Economy 1918–1980* (London: Routledge, 1988), 99, 109.
167. Abrams, *Struggle for the Soul of the Nation*, 104ff. See also Crane and Crane, *Czechoslovakia*, 297.
168. Abrams, *Struggle for the Soul of the Nation*, 120–122. Also see Josef Harna, "Nad reflexí první republiky v české společnosti po druhé světové válce 1945–1948," in Lubomír Slezák and Radomír Vlček, eds., *K poctě Jaroslava Marka. Sborník prací k 70. narozeninám prof. dr. Jaroslava Marka* (Prague: Historický ústav AV ČR, 1996), 215–226.
169. Abrams, *Struggle for the Soul of the Nation*, 123, 127–128.
170. Nejedlý, "Za novou kulturu," *Československo* 1 (1945): 36, cited in Derek Sayer, *The Coasts of Bohemia: A Czech History* (Princeton, NJ: Princeton University Press, 1998), 238.
171. Cited in Abrams, *Struggle for the Soul of the Nation*, 127, 129.
172. On the remaking of the Czech myth by the Czechoslovak Communists, see inter alia Peter Bugge, "Václav Černý, 1945–1948," in Robert Pynsent, ed., *The Phoney Peace: Power and Culture in Central Europe 1945–1949* (London: School of Slavonic and East European Studies, University College London, 2000): 230–240; Milan Drápala, *Na ztracené vartě západu: Antologie české nesocialistické publicistiky z let 1945–1948* (Prague: Prostor, 2000); Abrams, *Struggle for the Soul of the Nation*, especially 89–103, 118–138; Martina Winkler, "'In unteilbarere Einheit mit unserer Geschichte': Die Geschichte der KSČ als neue Meistererzählung," *Comparativ. Leipziger Beiträge zur Universalgeschichte und vergleichenden Gesellschaftsforschung* 10, no. 2 (2000): 61–80.
173. For example: Ivan Herben and Josef Mach, eds., *T.G.M. Malé historky o velkém muži* (London, undated manuscript [roughly 1941]).
174. Josef Hofmann, ed., *T.G.M. jak jsme ho viděli* (Prague: Ing. Mikuta, 1947), 8–9.
175. Max Švabinský, "Potretoval jsem Masaryka," in ibid., 309.
176. Pavel Kosatík, *Ferdinand Peroutka: pozdější život, 1938–1978* (Prague: Paseka, 2000), 26–32; Lev Braun, "Peroutka v otázkach a odpovědich," in Jaroslav Strnad, ed., *Muz Přítomnosti* (Zurich: Konfrontace, 1985), 60.
177. Ferdinand Peroutka, "Dědictví," *Svobodné noviny*, September 14, 1945. Cited in Abrams, *Struggle for the Soul of the Nation*, 134.
178. Ferdinand Peroutka, "Odpověd levici," in Daniel Bohdan, ed., *Ferdinand Peroutka: O věcech obecných II: Výbor z politické publicistiky* (Prague: Státní pedagogické nakladatelství, 1991), 490.
179. Ferdinand Peroutka, "Druhá výstavba," in Bohdan, *Ferdinand Peroutka*, 551–552.
180. Ibid., 553.
181. Čapek, *Mlčení s T.G. Masarykem* in *Hovory s T.G. Masarykem*, 362.
182. Gale Stokes, "Czech National Democracy: A First Approximation," *Slavic Review* 44, no. 1 (1985): 19.

183. Jindřich Dejmek, *Nenaplněné naděje: Politické a diplomatické vztahy Československa a Velké Británie od zrodu První republiky po konferenci v Mnichově (1918–1938)* (Prague: Karolinum, 2003); Harry Hanak, "British Views of the Czechoslovaks from 1914–1924," and Cornwall, "A Fluctuating Barometer," in Schmidt-Hartmann and Winters, *Großbritannien, die USA und die böhmischen Länder 1848–1938*; Gabor Batonyi, *Britain and Central Europe 1918–1933* (Oxford: Clarendon Press, 1999); Thomas Wittek, *Das Deutschlandbild in den Massenmedien nach dem Ersten Weltkrieg* (Munich: R. Oldenbourg Verlag, 2005); John Gunther, *Inside Europe* (New York: Harper and Brothers, 1938).

184. On the competition for British support: Dejmek, *Nenaplněné naděje*; Eagle Glassheim, *Noble Nationalists: The Transformation of the Bohemian Aristocracy* (Cambridge, MA: Harvard University Press, 2005); Paul Vysný, *The Runciman Mission to Czechoslovakia, 1938*; Robbins, "Konrad Henlein, the Sudeten Question and British Foreign Policy." G. T. Waddington, in "'An Idyllic and Unruffled Atmosphere of Complete Anglo-German Misunderstanding': Aspects of the Operations of the Dienststelle Ribbentrop in Great Britain, 1934–1938," *History* 82, no. 265 (1997): 44–72, argues that the Nazis also overestimated the importance of propaganda and cultural relations in wooing British aristocratic opinion, and that the Foreign Office resented the "ambulant amateurs" visiting Berlin and then excitedly demanding an audience with the Foreign Minister.

185. The phrase is Michael Walsh Campbell's: "A Crisis of Democracy," 206 n. 556.

186. George Kennan, *From Prague after Munich: Diplomatic Papers 1938–1940* (Princeton, NJ: Princeton University Press, 1968), 4.

Epilogue

1. Hugh LeCaine Agnew, *The Czechs and the Lands of the Bohemian Crown* (Stanford, CA: Hoover Institution Press, 2004), 230–232.

2. Mark Mazower, *Dark Continent: Europe's Twentieth Century* (New York: Vintage Books, 1998), 283.

3. F. Gregory Campbell, "Empty Pedestals?" *Slavic Review* 44, no. 1 (1985): 1.

4. On American historiography of the Czech lands and Slovakia, see Stanley B. Winters, "Introductory Essay: The Beginnings of American Scholarship on Czech and Slovak History," in George J. Kovtun, ed., Czech and Slovak History: An American Bibliography (Washington, DC: Library of Congress, 1996), available at: http://www.loc.gov/rr/european/cash/cash2.html, accessed December 10, 2006.

5. Igor Lukes, "Czechoslovak Political Exile in the Cold War: The Early Years," *The Polish Review* 47, no. 3 (2002): 332–343, quote from 333.

6. Ibid., 335–336. Peroutka's cold war essays and journalism have been collected in Milan Drápala, *Na ztracené vartě západu: Antologie české nesocialistické publicistiky z let 1945–1948* (Prague: Prostor, 2000); and Pavel Kosatík, *Ferdinand Peroutka: pozdější život, 1938–1978* (Prague: Paseka, 2000). His only work translated into

English is *Demokratický manifest/Democratic Manifesto* (New York: Universum/ Voyages Press, both 1959).

7. George Svoboda, "Robert J. Kerner and the U.S. Conception of Czechoslovak Independence," in Harry Hanak, ed., *T.G. Masaryk 1850–1937, Vol. 3: Statesman and Cultural Force* (London: Macmillan in association with the School of Slavonic and East European Studies, 1990): 45. Kerner's dissertation became *Bohemia in the Eighteenth Century: A Study in Political, Economic, and Social History, with Special Reference to the Reign of Leopold II, 1790–1792* (New York: Macmillan, 1932).
8. On Kerner and the peace talks: Lawrence Gelfand, *The Inquiry: American Preparations for Peace, 1917–1919* (New Haven, CT: Yale University Press, 1963). On Kerner's relationship to Masaryk and importance for Czechoslovak studies in the United States, see George Svoboda, "Robert Kerner and the US Conception of Czechoslovak Independence," in Hanak, *T.G. Masaryk 1850–1937, Vol. 3: Statesman and Cultural Force*, 43–56.
9. Robert Kerner, ed., *Czechoslovakia: Twenty Years of Independence* (Berkeley: University of California Press, 1940).
10. R. John Roth, "S. Harrison Thomson," *AHY* 11 (1975): 382–383; Joseph F. Zacek, "S. Harrison Thomson, 1895–1975," *Slavic Review* 36, no. 1 (1977): 174.
11. S. Harrison Thomson, *Czechoslovakia in European History* (Princeton, NJ: Princeton University Press, 1943), vi, 4, 6, 284.
12. Rudolf Urban, *Demokratenpresse im Lichte Prager Geheimeakten* (Prague: Orbis, 1943), 152.
13. Francis Dvorník, "Otakar Odložilik, 1899–1973," *Slavic Review* 33, no. 1 (1974): 204–205; Stanley B. Winters, "Otakar Odložilik's American Career: The Uneasy Self-Exile of a Czech Historian, 1948–1973," in Eva Schmidt-Hartmann and Stanley Winters, eds., *Großbritannien, die USA und die böhmischen Länder 1848–1938* (Munich: R. Oldenbourg Verlag, 1991), 153–169; Joseph F. Zacek, "Otakar Odložilik, 1899–1973," *Canadian-American Slavic Studies* 8, no. 4 (1974): 618–620.
14. Dvorník, "Otakar Odložilík," 204–205.
15. "Edward J. Taborsky," obituary found at http://www.utexas.edu/faculty/council/pages/colleges_depts/liberal_arts.html (accessed December 23, 2008).
16. Hans Brisch and Iván Völgyes, eds., *Czechoslovakia: The Heritage of Ages Past. Essays in Memory of Josef Korbel* (Boulder, CO: East European Monographs, 1979), 3–24; Victor S. Mamatey, "Josef Korbel, 1909–1977," *Slavic Review* 36, no. 4 (1977): 731–732.
17. Josef Korbel, *Twentieth-Century Czechoslovakia: The Meaning of Its History* (New York: Columbia University Press, 1977), vii.
18. Guy Raz, "A Tale of Two Korbels," National Public Radio, *All Things Considered*, June 28, 2006, available at: http://www.npr.org/templates/story/story.php?storyId=5516648, accessed December 14, 2006.
19. The Masaryk Institute of the Czech Academy of Sciences has published new editions of Masaryk's work, including his speeches, correspondence, and journalism, as well as many important recent biographies of Masaryk. The institute has also published many volumes concerning Beneš. The Edvard Beneš Society has worked to publicize Beneš's works and ideas.

20. Melissa Feinberg, *Elusive Equality: Gender, Citizenship, and the Limits of Democracy in Czechoslovakia, 1918–1950* (Pittsburgh, PA: University of Pittsburgh Press, 2006); Peter Bugge, especially "Czech Democracy 1918–1938: Paragon or Parody?" *Boh* 47, no. 1 (2006–2007): 3–28.
21. The concept of civic nationalism is said to have originated with Jean-Jacques Rousseau's 1762 *The Social Contract*, in which he argued that the state's political legitimacy depended on the extent to which it embodied the will of its citizens. Most recently the term has been identified with the work of German sociologist and public intellectual Jürgen Habermas, although he uses the term *constitutional patriotism*, arguing that patriots can and should identify with the achievements of a state, inasmuch as that state succeeds in institutionalizing values such as tolerance, democracy, and egalitarianism.

Index